Virtual lesions

Virtual Lesions

examining cortical function with reversible
deactivation

Edited by

Stephen G. Lomber

Assistant Professor of Neuroscience, School of Human Development,
University of Texas at Dallas, USA

Ralf A. W. Galuske

Team Leader, Department of Neurophysiology, Max-Planck-Institute
for Brain Research in Frankfurt, Germany

OXFORD
UNIVERSITY PRESS

OXFORD
UNIVERSITY PRESS

Great Clarendon Street, Oxford OX2 6DP

Oxford University Press is a department of the University of Oxford. It furthers the University's objective of excellence in research, scholarship, and education by publishing worldwide in

Oxford New York

Auckland   Bangkok   Buenos Aires   Cape Town   Chennai   Dar es Salaam   Delhi   Hong Kong   Istanbul   Karachi   Kolkata   Kuala Lumpur   Madrid   Melbourne   Mexico City   Mumbai   Nairobi   São Paulo   Shanghai   Taipei   Tokyo   Toronto

and an associated company in Berlin

Oxford is a registered trade mark of Oxford University Press in the UK and in certain other countries

Published in the United States by Oxford University Press Inc., New York

A catalogue record for this title is available from the British Library.

Library of Congress Cataloging in Publication Data

(Data available)

ISBN 0 19 850893 X

10 9 8 7 6 5 4 3 2 1

Typeset by Cepha Imaging Pvt. Ltd.

Printed in Great Britain

on acid-free paper by T.J. International Ltd., Padstow, Cornwall

Preface

Over the past thirty years, we have experienced an unprecedented rise in our understanding of brain function. This increase in our knowledge of neural function can be directly attributed to the rapid development and implementation of many technologies, including anatomical methods that have permitted us to reveal the fine structure of neural circuits, electrophysiologic recording procedures in awake animals, high-speed data analysis on powerful computers, and sophisticated structural and functional imaging procedures. Prior to the utilization of these techniques, the history of neurobiologic research describes that the most valuable functional tool, or method, available was the examination of brain lesions and their correlation with neuropsychologic deficits. Despite its many shortcomings, the analysis of brain lesions has provided important insights into our understanding of brain function and organization. Even today, many experimental questions are difficult, if not impossible, to address in any way other than with the lesion technique. However, it has long been recognized that many pitfalls of the lesion method can be avoided with reversible deactivation procedures, while at the same time retaining most of its advantages.

Over the past two decades, many new methods have emerged that use reversible deactivation techniques to probe the function of the brain. These methods permit individual structures in the nervous system to be selectively turned "off" and "on" depending on the question or condition being examined. These reversible deactivation procedures create "virtual lesions," as the underlying neural circuitry is not structurally disrupted and a particular site is only temporarily deactivated. The use of "virtual lesion" techniques, such as chemicals (anesthetics or pharmacologic agents), cold, or magnetism, have provided many emerging neurobiologic disciplines such as neural modeling, computational neuroscience, cognitive neuroscience, and artificial intelligence with much more accurate information about the intact system, upon which they may base their more theoretical work. However, these recent technical advances in reversible deactivation methods, which further our understanding of the neural basis of perception and behaviour, do not undermine previous work utilizing permanent deactivations. In fact, comparisons between permanent and reversible deactivation studies can provide more information than either technique could ever reveal by itself.

Reversible deactivation techniques are a very efficient and economical approach to isolate and characterize the functional contributions of individual brain regions, and even subdomains within regions, to global representations, perception and behavior. These methods have many advantages over traditional permanent lesion techniques. In all likelihood, the most significant reason to use reversible deactivations is that each subject serves as its own control. Other benefits are that a brain region can be reversibly deactivated and control and experimental measurements can be made within minutes. The techniques permit reversible deactivation during different phases of behavioral or learning processes and allow for a more detailed analysis of the contribution of the examined area. Neither widespread degenerative nor compensatory structural and functional changes are induced, which could otherwise compromise conclusions. This is even the case with repetitive deactivations. Furthermore, since a subject participating in a virtual lesion study is unable to practice outside of the testing session with the region deactivated, there is little opportunity for alternative circuits to develop in order to solve the tasks. As a result, reversible deactivation-induced deficits tend to be more profound than those induced by ablations, because there is no deficit attenuation. Since a structure is never removed, the subjects can be trained on modified or new tasks as the investigations proceed and the experiments are afforded a greater flexibility. The sum of these benefits results in fewer subjects being needed for a study that eventually produces results on a more reliable ground.

In this special compendium on reversible deactivation, we have assembled articles that use chemical, cooling and transcranial magnetic stimulation (TMS) approaches to interfere with neural functions in different brain regions and on different scales of deactivation. Our intent is to provide the reader with a solid overview of the potential impact of applying different individual deactivation techniques, and their combination, to different available approaches to monitor brain function, ranging from single neuron recording in animals to behavioral testing in humans. Therefore, the aim of the book is a combined description of the current state of methodology, by giving examples for the applications of "virtual lesions," and a practical guide for future experiments by discussion of the advantages and pitfalls of the respective method under the particular experimental conditions.

As outlined above, reversible deactivation techniques are uniquely suited for studies of functional interactions in the central nervous system that underlie brain functions at the level of individual neurons, as well as on the level of neuronal populations such as cortical areas or subcortical nuclei. Likewise, the scientific questions addressed in studies using "virtual lesions" range from the impact of the respective interactions on the properties of individuals neurons to the emergence of complex behaviors produced by the human brain. In order to reflect the full range of these investigations, the volume is divided into three sections, in which the advantages and disadvantages of reversible deactivation techniques are presented in the context of actual experimental work.

The first section, Exploring Neural Circuits, examines the use of reversible deactivation techniques on questions that concern the basis of neuronal interactions behind the emergence of neuronal response properties and representations underlying perception. This section begins with two contributions, one by Crook, Kisvárday and Eysel and the other by Dragoi, Rivadulla and Sur, which both provide insights into the local circuits underlying the response properties of neurons in primary visual cortex.

These chapters offer an overview of the diverse types of pharmacologic deactivation techniques available to study interactions on a restricted spatial scale and provide advice as to how these techniques can be combined with electrophysiologic, anatomic, and optical recording techniques. The subsequent chapters concentrate on the contributions of long-range interactions to the formation of neuronal response characteristics and representations. The contributions by Villa and by Casanova exemplify the use of reversible deactivation techniques in the study of interactions between cortical and subcortical sites in both the visual and the auditory systems, respectively. The contribution by Villa presents a comprehensive overview of the different functional aspects of neuronal properties that may depend on the interaction of individual neurons in distributed circuits. Casanova provides a summary and a comparison of pharmacologic and thermal reversible deactivation techniques and shows how these can also be applied to the study of thalamic structures and their interactions. The chapter by Girard and Bullier reveals how deactivation techniques can be used to study impact on corticocortical connection systems. Girard and Bullier demonstrate and discuss the use of reversible pharmacologic and thermal techniques in the process of separating the contributions of different visual cortical areas of the primate visual system to perceptual performance and neuronal responses. Finally, Galuske and Schmidt describe the use of long term pharmacologic manipulations in combination optical imaging for the study of the neural basis of developmental plasticity.

The second section, Investigating Behavior in Animals, considers how different deactivations can be used to localize cognitive and motor functions within the brain and examine neural plasticity in mature and immature behaving animals. The contribution by Payne and Lomber provides insight into the capacity of the developing and mature visual system to reorganize after permanent lesions, and how "virtual lesions" can be used to localize the neural substrate responsible for behavioral sparing and recovery of visual function after cerebral damage. Martin and Ghez consider the developing and mature cortical and subcortical motor system and the contributions its individual components make to the initiation, control and learning of skilled limb movements. Their chapter provides a broad overview of the available pharmacologic inactivation techniques to interfere with activity in superficial and deep brain structures and, in addition, reviews how these pharmacologic agents can be used on different time scales ranging from minutes to weeks. Segraves illustrates the application of reversible thermal and pharmacologic intervention for the study of the neural basis of eye movements in different cortical areas and points out how the results from reversible studies relate to data obtained with permanent lesion techniques. Finally, Sierra-Paredes and Fuster demonstrate how thermal deactivation can be used to study the functional substrate of cross-modal integration in working memory processes and discuss the limitations of reversible techniques in this context.

The third section, Probing the Human Brain, examines how the techniques of transcranial magnetic stimulation (TMS) can be used effectively to interfere with neural processing in the human cerebrum, thus providing a better understanding of its function. The first chapter, by Walsh and Pascual-Leone, describes a series of neuro-psychologic issues that have been addressed using TMS, including visual attention and neglect, consciousness, and the phenomenon of behavioral improvements as a consequence of a secondary deactivation. The second part of their chapter provides a thorough description of the TMS apparatus, the use of repetitive transcranial magnetic stimulation (rTMS), known mechanisms of action, functional localization issues, and safety considerations. Pascual-Leone and Hamilton describe TMS studies they have performed to examine processing in occipital cortex by blind Braille-readers versus normally-sighted subjects. Boroojerdi and Cohen specifically discuss the perceptions that may be induced by TMS application to the visual cortex, including phosphenes, motion deficits, target unmasking and the perception of target disappearance. They also consider the functional and clinical significance of phosphenes induced by migraine headaches, visual imagery and experience, and the role of occipital cortex in blind individuals. In the final chapter, Ziemann focuses on the application of TMS to human motor cortex. He describes how TMS can be used to reveal the physiology of motor cortex which, in turn, leads to a better understanding of motor cortex output, its involvement in the processing and control of complex finger movements, and in motor learning.

The editors wish to express their appreciation to all those that contributed to this volume and thank them for the manuscripts which they prepared. We appreciate the support of Drs. Vincent Walsh and Alvaro Pascual-Leone who encouraged us to initiate this book. We are grateful to Professors Wolf Singer, Bert Payne, Alan Peters, and Bert Moore for their support and encouragement during this project. The editors acknowledge the financial support of the National Science Foundation, Max-Planck Gesellschaft, and the Deutsche Akademische Austauschdienst. We are also grateful to Dagmar and Albert Galuske for providing us with a peaceful and well-fed environment while we edited this volume and to Sandra Schwegmann for her help with the preparation of the figures. Finally, special thanks are due to Martin Baum at Oxford University Press for his interest in the work described herein and the care that he devoted to our efforts.

Texas, USA   S.G.L.
Frankfurt, Germany   R.A.W.G.
March 2002

Contents

Part III: **Probing the Human Brain**

Contributors

Babak Boroojerdi
Neurologische Klinik
Universitätsklinikum
Pauwelstrasse 30
52074 Aachen
Germany
boroojeb@ninds.nih.gov

Jean Bullier
Centre de Recherche Cerveau et
Cognition
CNRS-UPS UMR 5549
133, route de Narbonne
31062 Toulouse Cedex
France
bullier@cerco.ups-tlse.fr

Christian Casanova
Laboratoire des Neurosciences de la
Vision
École d'Optometrie
Université de Montréal
C.P. 6128, Succ. Centre-Ville
Montréal, Québec, H3C 3J7
Canada
Christian.Casanova@umontreal.ca

Leonardo G. Cohen
National Institutes of Health, NINDS
Building 10, Room 5N234
Bethesda, Maryland 20892-1430
USA
cohenl@ninds.nih.gov

John M. Crook
Leibniz-Institut für Neurobiologie
Brenneckestrasse 6
39118 Magdeburg

Germany
crook@ifn-magdeburg.de

Valentin Dragoi
Department of Brain and Cognitive
Sciences
Massachusetts Institute of Technology
E25-235
45 Carleton Street
Cambridge, Massachusetts 02139
USA
vdragoi@ai.mit.edu

Ulf T. Eysel
Department of Neurophysiology
Ruhr-Universität Bochum
Medizinische Fakultät
Universitätstrasse 150
44780 Bochum
Germany
eysel@neurop-uni-bochum.de

Joaquín M. Fuster
Neuropsychiatric Institute
School of Medicine
University of California, Los Angeles
760 Westwood Plaza
Los Angeles, California 90095
USA
joaquinf@ucla.edu

Ralf A.W. Galuske
Department of Neurophysiology
Max-Planck-Institute for Brain Research
Deutschordenstrasse 46
60528 Frankfurt
Germany
galuske@mpih-frankfurt.mpg.de

Claude Ghez
Center of Neurobiology and Behavior
Research Foundation for Mental Hygiene
New York State Psychiatric Institute
1051, Riverside Drive
New York, New York 10032
USA
cpg1@columbia.edu

Pascal Girard
Centre de Recherche Cerveau et
Cognition
CNRS-UPS UMR 5549
133, route de Narbonne
31062 Toulouse Cedex
France
girard@cerco.ups-tlse.fr

Roy H. Hamilton
Laboratory for Magnetic Brain
Stimulation
Beth Israel Deaconess Medical Center
Harvard Medical School
330 Brookline Avenue
Kirsten Hall KS454
Boston, Massachusetts 02115
USA

Dae-Shik Kim
Centre for Magnetic Resonance Research
University of Minnesota Medical School
2021 6th St SE
Minneapolis, MN 55455
USA
dskimecmrr.umn.edu

Zoltan F. Kisvárday
Abteilung für Neurophysiologie
Ruhr-Universität Bochum
Medizinische Fakultät
Universitätstrasse 150
44801 Bochum
Germany
kisva@neurop.ruhr-uni-bochum.de

Stephen G. Lomber
Cerebral Systems Laboratory
School of Human Development
University of Texas at Dallas
P.O. Box 830688, GR41
Richardson, Texas 75083-0688
USA
lomber@utdallas.edu

John H. Martin
Center for Neurobiology and Behavior
Columbia University
1051 Riverside Drive
New York, New York 10032
USA
Jm17@columbia.edu

Alvaro Pascual-Leone
Laboratory for Magnetic Brain
Stimulation
Beth Israel Deaconess Medical Center
Harvard Medical School
330 Brookline Avenue
Kirsten Hall KS454
Boston, Massachusetts 02115
USA
apleone@caregroup.harzard.edu

Bertram R. Payne
Laboratory for Visual Perception and
Cognition
Department of Anatomy and
Neurobiology
Boston University School of Medicine
700 Albany Street
Boston, Massachusetts 02118
USA
bpayne@bu.edu

Casto Rivadulla
Departmento de Medicina
EU de Fisioterapia
Centro Universitario de Oza
15006 A. Coruha

Spain
casto@udc.es

Kerstin E. Schmidt
Department of Neurophysiology
Max-Planck-Institute for Brain Research
Deutschordenstrasse 46
60528 Frankfurt
Germany
schmidt@mpih-frankfurt.mpg.de

Mark A. Segraves
Department of Neurobiology and
Physiology
Northwestern University
2153 North Campus Drive
Evanston, Illinois 60208-3520
USA
m-segraves@northwestern.edu

Germán Sierra-Paredes
Neuroscience Division
Department of Biochemistry and
Molecular Biology
School of Medicine
University of Santiago
San Francisco 1
15705 Santiago de Compostela
Spain
bngersp@usc.es

Mriganka Sur
Department of Brain and Cognitive
Sciences
Massachusetts Institute of Technology

E25-235
45 Carleton Street
Cambridge, Massachusetts 02139
USA
msur@ai.mit.edu

Alessandro E. P. Villa
Laboratoire de Neurobiophysique
Université Joseph Fourier, Grenoble 1
INSERM U 318 – Pavillon B
CHU de Grenoble BP 217
38043 Grenoble Cedex 9
France
avilla@neuroheuristic.org

Vincent Walsh
Department of Experimental Psychology
University of Oxford
South Parks Road
Oxford OX1 3UD
United Kingdom
vin@psy.ox.ac.uk

Ulf Ziemann
Neurologische Klinik
Johann Wolfgang Goethe-Universität
Theodor-Stern-Kai 7
60590 Frankfurt am Main
Germany
u.ziemann@em.uni-frankfurt.de

Part I

Exploring neural circuits

Chapter I

Intracortical Mechanisms Underlying Orientation and Direction Selectivity Studied with the GABA-Inactivation Technique

John M. Crook, Zoltan F. Kisvárday, Ulf T. Eysel[1]

Introduction

It is 40 years since Hubel and Wiesel (1962) showed that cells in primary visual cortex (area 17) respond selectively to contours of a certain orientation and that most of these cells also show a preference for the direction of motion of optimally oriented contours. However, the mechanisms underlying both orientation and direction selectivity are still the subject of intense debate. Hubel and Wiesel (1962) proposed that orientation and direction selectivity in cat area 17 are established by the spatial organization of the excitatory input from the lateral geniculate nucleus (LGN) to simple cells in layer IV (the main geniculocortical recipient zone). These cells are characterized by the presence of elongated ON- and OFF-subregions in their receptive fields, which are arranged side-by-side with their long axes parallel to the axis of preferred orientation. Each of these subregions was thought to arise as a result of excitatory convergence from either ON- or OFF-center geniculate cells whose receptive fields are aligned in a row in visual space, with the axis of alignment determining the orientation preference of the postsynaptic cell. A light bar with the orientation of an ON-subregion that is moved or flashed within the subregion would simultaneously excite all the presynaptic geniculate ON-center cells and evoke the best response. In contrast, a bar moved or flashed at right angles to the ON-subregion would excite a small subset of the underlying ON-center geniculate cells and simultaneously cause a withdrawal of excitation from OFF-center cells, with the consequence that the response remains below threshold. Direction selectivity was thought to originate in simple cells via synergistic and/or antagonistic interactions between their receptive field subregions. For example, according to Hubel and Wiesel, a cell with two parallel, adjacent ON- and OFF-subregions would respond preferentially to an optimally oriented light bar moving in the direction in which it first encounters the OFF-subregion, due to the synergistic effect that would be elicited by the light bar leaving the OFF-subregion and simultaneously entering the ON-subregion. The orientation and direction selectivity of complex cells, which are found predominantly outside layer IV and whose receptive fields do not possess spatially discrete subregions, was thought to derive from an excitatory convergence of simple cells within the same column with similar orientation and direction preferences. This concept was consistent with results of classical Golgi-impregnation studies that revealed intracortical connections predominantly in the columnar dimension (across cortical layers) with little connectivity between different orientation columns. Orientation and direction selectivity in area 18 was proposed to reflect that present in the dominant excitatory input from area 17 complex cells (Hubel and Wiesel 1965).

Hubel and Wiesel's hypothesis, which was based primarily on excitatory convergence, was first challenged by the results of intracellular studies (Creutzfeldt *et al.* 1974; Innocenti and Fiore 1974) which demonstrated that the receptive fields of some area 17 cells were virtually circular despite their orientation tuning, and that stimuli presented at nonoptimal orientations or moving in the nonpreferred direction could evoke hyperpolarizing potentials traditionally associated with inhibition. More direct evidence for a major contribution of intracortical inhibition to cortical orientation and direction selectivity derived from experiments in which gamma-aminobutyric acid (GABA) the antagonist, bicuculline, was iontophoretically applied in the vicinity of extracellularly recorded single cells in area 17 to produce a localized block of GABA-mediated inhibitory processes (Sillito 1975, 1977, 1979; Tsumoto *et al.* 1979; Sillito *et al.* 1980). This inhibitory blockade led to a reduction or elimination of orientation/direction selectivity in virtually all cells. These effects were commensurate with the loss of an inhibitory input that normally suppresses responses to nonoptimal orientations and directions. Independent evidence for this notion accumulated from a number of studies employing multiple visual stimuli (Emerson and Gerstein 1977; Morrone *et al.* 1982; Ganz and Felder 1984; Emerson *et al.* 1987) that demonstrated suppressive effects in area 17 cells at nonoptimal orientations and directions of motion. Based largely on the results of bicuculline experiments, Sillito (1979) suggested that orientation selectivity is sharpened via inhibition between cells located in different orientation columns with overlapping receptive fields but radically different orientation preferences (cross-orientation inhibition). Support for this hypothesis derived from studies in which the use of modern neuroanatomical tracing techniques revealed the presence of inhibitory neurones with long-range projections extending laterally for up to ~1 mm, thus providing an anatomical substrate for inhibition between columns of dissimilar orientation preference (Martin *et al.* 1983; Somogyi *et al.* 1983; Kisvárday *et al.* 1985, 1987; Matsubara *et al.* 1987).

The next major contribution to the debate came from the work of Ferster (1986, 1987) who extended the intracellular recording techniques of Creutzfeldt *et al.* (1974) and determined the orientation selectivity of the excitatory and inhibitory postsynaptic potentials (EPSPs and IPSPs) in cells of area 17. Intuitively, one would expect the EPSPs and IPSPs in a single cell to be tuned to radically different orientations were cross-orientation inhibition to make a major contribution to orientation selectivity. Ferster (1986) found that this was not the case. EPSPs and IPSPs showed similar orientation preferences and selectivity, and the postulated inhibition at orientations orthogonal to the optimum was not detected. This and other results of intracellular studies (Ferster 1987) were consistent with Hubel and Wiesel's (1962) model.

At this stage, studies of the mechanisms underlying cortical orientation/direction selectivity generated a paradox. On the one hand, they provided strong evidence that intracortical inhibition makes a major contribution to both properties. On the other hand, at least in the case of orientation selectivity, intracellular recordings did not detect strong inhibition during nonoptimal stimulation. It was this paradox that prompted us to reinvestigate the mechanisms underlying cortical orientation and direction selectivity. In this chapter we describe experiments carried out over the last 15 years, in which we have used local inactivation techniques, partly in combination with neuroanatomical tracing methods, to study the contribution of horizontal intrinsic connections to orientation and direction selectivity in cat areas 17 and 18. Our results provide strong evidence that in each area, intracortical excitatory and inhibitory interactions play a crucial role in the generation of both properties.

Logic of the GABA-inactivation method

The bicuculline experiments described above provided valuable information concerning the contribution of inhibitory mechanisms to a number of response properties, including orientation and direction selectivity. However, with this method it is not possible to study directly the topographic and functional interactions underlying the generation of a particular response property. This can be achieved by making simultaneous double recordings (T'so et al. 1986; Hata et al. 1988) or by simultaneously recording and pharmacologically manipulating cortical cells at different locations (Hess et al. 1975; Bolz et al. 1989). Our approach consisted of using microiontophoresis of the inhibitory neurotransmitter GABA to locally inactivate small cortical sites while continuously monitoring the orientation/direction selectivity of laterally remote extracellularly recorded single cells. The use of GABA-iontophoresis for inactivation has several advantages. First, the inactivation is reversible, and recovery upon termination of GABA application is rapid. This allows one to test the effect of inactivating the same site on the response properties of a large number of cells and to verify that the elicited effects are actually due to the experimental manipulation. In contrast, the use of the potent GABA-agonist muscimol (Grieve and Sillito 1991, 1995) results in long-lasting inactivation (several hours) during which time a recorded cell may be lost. Second, GABA inactivates cells via the activation of $GABA_A$ and $GABA_B$ receptors, but it does not affect axons of passage (Curtis and Crawford 1969; Hess and Murata 1974), as is the case with the local anaesthetic lidocaine. Thus, the inactivated area is approximately equal to the radius of diffusion of GABA. Third, the diffusion of GABA is locally restricted by the high metabolic turnover of the compound and the powerful, high-affinity uptake mechanism for GABA in the brain (Curtis and Johnston 1974). Using relatively small ejecting currents (20–100 nA), it is possible to restrict inactivation to a region of ~300–400 µm in diameter (Crook et al. 1998; Hupé et al. 1999). In both areas 17 and 18 of cat visual cortex, orientation and direction preference show a modular organization (Hubel and Wiesel 1962, 1965; Berman *et al.* 1987; Swindale *et al.* 1987; Bonhoeffer and Grinvald 1993; Bonhoeffer *et al.* 1995; Shumuel and Grinvald 1996). Cells with similar orientation preferences are organized in iso-orientation domains, which are typically subdivided into regions preferring opposite directions of motion extending a few hundred microns in the laminar and columnar dimensions. Using iontophoresis of GABA, it is therefore possible, in principle, to simultaneously inactivate large populations of cells with similar orientation/direction preferences and thereby block orientationally and directionally congruent signals projecting to laterally remote recording sites. The effects that are elicited in a recorded cell provide important insights into the normal function of horizontal connections in the generation of orientation and direction selectivity.

Influence of GABA-inactivation on cortical orientation and direction selectivity

Effects on direction selectivity

There is now a general consensus that Hubel and Wiesel's (1962) hypothesis concerning the generation of cortical direction selectivity is no longer tenable. Simple-cell direction selectivity is not generally predictable on the basis of the disposition and relative strength of ON- and OFF-subregions within the receptive field (Bishop *et al.* 1971; Goodwin *et al.* 1975; Heggelund 1984; Peterhans *et al.* 1985). Moreover, most simple cells show direction selectivity for stimulus motion within a single receptive field subregion (Goodwin *et al.* 1975; Crook *et al.* 1996; and see Fig. 1.9). Intracellular recordings (Creutzfeldt *et al.* 1974; Innocenti and Fiore 1974) and results of experiments employing localized blockade of $GABA_A$-mediated inhibition (Sillito 1975, 1977; Tsumoto *et al.* 1979) established the importance of postsynaptic inhibitory processes for direction selectivity of cells in area 17. In the same area, quantitative analyses of receptive fields with flash sequences (Emerson and Gerstein 1977; Movshon *et al.* 1978; Ganz and Felder 1984; Baker and Cynader 1986; Emerson *et al.* 1987) demonstrated nonlinear suppression of responses in the nonpreferred direction and facilitation in the preferred direction. Finally, in both areas 17 and 18, linear predictions of direction selectivity in simple cells based on spatiotemporal receptive field profiles overestimate responses in the nonpreferred direction (Reid *et al.* 1991; Tolhurst and Dean 1991; McLean *et al.* 1994), implying that a nonlinear suppressive mechanism sharpens direction selectivity.

Taken together, the results of the above studies suggest strongly that intracortical laterally directed excitatory and inhibitory projections play an important role in the generation of direction selectivity. Eysel *et al.* (1987, 1988) used local inactivation techniques to gain insight into the topographic and functional specificity of lateral connections underlying direction selectivity. In these experiments, the orientation/ direction selectivity of single cells in area 17 was continuously monitored during local inactivation of a cortical site 0.5–2.5 mm anterior or posterior to the recording site (see Fig. 1.1). Initially, inactivation was achieved by localized cooling or by heat lesions. In subsequent experiments, microiontophoresis of GABA was used extensively as the method of choice, since it combines local restriction with reversibility. Remote inactivation elicited two fundamentally different types of effect on directionality: a decrease in response to the preferred direction and an increase in response to either the preferred or nonpreferred direction. These effects were attributed, respectively, to the loss of lateral excitation and inhibition. Increases in response were observed only when the stimulus-evoked response wave moved across the cortex in a direction from the inactivation site to the recording site; that is, when the inactivation site was posterior to the recording site for downward motion and anterior to the recording site for upward motion. An example of this type of effect is shown in Fig. 1.2 for a layer-IV simple cell which was direction-selective for a bar stimulus moving obliquely upwards (Fig. 1.2A). As illustrated schematically in Fig. 1.1, GABA was applied posterior to the recording site, thus influencing cells that were activated before the recorded cell during stimulus motion in the nonpreferred direction. GABA-inactivation caused a substantial and reversible increase in response to the nonpreferred direction that resulted in a loss of direction selectivity (Fig. 1.2B, C). The topographical specificity of the disinhibitory effects that were elicited on directionality suggested that stimulus motion in both the

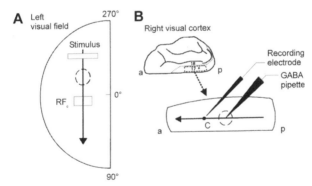

Fig. 1.1 Topographical transformation of a visual stimulus by area 17 and juxtaposition of recording and inactivation sites. (A) A bar stimulus moves downwards in the visual field (see arrow) across the retinotopic site of inactivation by GABA-iontophoresis (broken circle) and subsequently across the receptive field (RFc) of the recorded cell (open rectangle). (B) Dorsal view of the right hemisphere of the cat cortex. The border between areas 17 and 18 is indicated by the dotted line. a, anterior; p, posterior. The cortical area within the broken rectangle was exposed during the experiment (asterisk=area centralis representation). The enlarged view of this area below shows schematically the recording electrode at cell C and the GABA pipette located posterior to it. The arrow indicates that the stimulus trajectory in A elicits a response wave travelling from posterior to anterior in the cortex, that is, in a direction from the inactivation site (broken circle) to the recording site. Modified from Eysel *et al.* (1988), with permission of The Physiological Society.

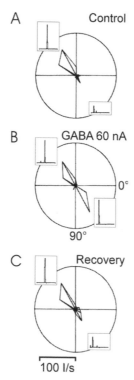

Fig. 1.2 Disinhibitory effect on direction selectivity elicited in a layer-IV simple cell in area 17 by GABA-inactivation. The inactivation site was located in layer II/III, 700 μm posterior to the recording site. Prior to GABA-inactivation (A), the cell showed a strong direction preference for a bar stimulus moving obliquely upwards. In the polar diagrams, direction of motion, which was orthogonal to bar orientation, is plotted as vector angle and response as vector length. Orientation of polar diagrams: vertical bar moving to the right at 0°; horizontal bar moving downwards at 90°. Insets to polar diagrams show PSTHs in response to the preferred and opposite directions of motion. GABA-iontophoresis (60 nA ejecting current, 12 min) caused a marked increase in response to the nonpreferred direction, resulting in a loss of direction selectivity (B). Motion in the nonpreferred direction elicited a response wave traveling from posterior to anterior in the cortex, that is, in a direction from the inactivation site to the recording site (see Fig. 1.1). The effect on directionality occurred in the absence of a significant change in orientation tuning or in the response to the preferred direction of motion. (C) Recovery 8 min after termination of GABA-iontophoresis. PSTH binwidth 20 ms; 5 sweeps. The scale bar applies to both polar diagrams and PSTHs. Modified from Eysel et al. (1988), with permission of The Physiological Society.

preferred and nonpreferred directions across a cell's receptive field activates a wave of laterally directed feedforward inhibition which suppresses the response to its excitatory input. Both the suppressive and disinhibitory effects were most readily elicited by inactivation at a lateral distance of ~1 mm (Wörgötter and Eysel 1991), where the receptive fields would have overlapped with those at the recording site and where the statistical probability of encountering cells with similar orientation preferences to that of a recorded cell is high. The results of these inactivation studies suggested that a cortical cell receives intracortical excitatory inputs during stimulus motion in the preferred direction and inhibitory inputs during stimulus motion in the preferred and nonpreferred directions that derive from laterally remote cells with similar orientation preference, with an interplay of all three influences determining direction selectivity. Interestingly, the effects that were elicited on direction selectivity occurred in the absence of a significant change in orientation tuning (Fig. 1.2), pointing to a high degree of independence of the intracortical mechanisms underlying each property.

Effects on orientation tuning

While it is highly plausible that intracortical connections between cells with similar orientation preferences contribute to direction selectivity for optimally oriented stimuli, sharpening of orientation tuning might be expected to occur intracortically via inhibition between cells with dissimilar orientation preferences. Evidence for this type of cross-orientation inhibition derived not only from the bicuculline experiments described in the introduction (Sillito 1975, 1979; Tsumoto *et al.* 1979; Sillito *et al.* 1980), but also from studies which demonstrated that the presentation of a nonoptimally oriented stimulus can suppress both the spontaneous activity and the response to a simultaneously presented optimally oriented stimulus in area 17 cells (Morrone *et al.* 1982; Crook 1990). However, cross-oriented IPSPs were not detected in intracellular studies (Ferster 1986, 1987). It was this paradox that prompted us to reinvestigate the intracortical mechanisms underlying orientation selectivity with an independent method—that of GABA-inactivation (Eysel *et al.* 1990; Crook *et al.* 1991).

The experimental approach is illustrated schematically in Fig. 1.3. Single units were recorded extracellularly during penetrations through the center of a fixed array of four GABA-containing pipettes each located at a horizontal distance of ~500 µm (in area 17) or ~600 µm (in area 18). The logic of this approach is that given the layout of orientation in each area (Hubel and Wiesel 1962, 1965; Albus 1975; Berman *et al.* 1987; Swindale *et al.* 1987), the predicted effect of GABA application at a horizontal distance of 500–600 µm is the inactivation of cells whose receptive fields overlap extensively with that of a recorded cell, but whose preferred orientations are radically different. These cells would be ideal candidates for providing cross-orientation inhibition to a cell under study, and broadening of orientation tuning during GABA application might reasonably be assumed to reflect the inactivation of such an inhibitory input. A specific reason for studying the effect of GABA-inactivation in area 18 stemmed from the report that iontophoretic application of bicuculline in the vicinity of cells recorded in this area had a relatively weak effect on their orientation tuning (Vidyasagar and Heide 1986). These results seemed to suggest that intracortical inhibition does not make a major contribution to orientation tuning in area 18, and they were consistent with Hubel and Wiesel's (1965) hypothesis that orientation selectivity in this area derives from a convergent excitatory input from area 17 cells.

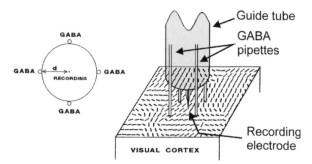

Fig. 1.3 Schematic representation of the configuration of electrodes for recording and GABA-iontophoresis used for studying effects on orientation tuning. On the left is a view of the configuration from below showing the tip positions of the four GABA-containing pipettes (tip diameter 5–10 μm) and the electrode for single-unit recording. d denotes the average horizontal distance of 500–600 μm between recording and inactivation sites. On the right, the array of inactivation pipettes and the recording electrode are superimposed on a cortical map of orientation preference (modified from Swindale *et al.* 1987). Each pipette was contiguous with and ran parallel to a guide tube with an outer diameter of 1–1.2 mm. The array of inactivation pipettes was first lowered to a cortical depth of 500–800 μm and a tungsten-in-glass microelectrode was then driven independently through the center of the guide tube to record single cells. Modified from Eysel, *Progress in Brain Research*, 1992;**90**:407–22 with permission of Elsevier Science.

As illustrated in Fig. 1.4, we found that GABA-inactivation could have dramatic deleterious effects on the orientation tuning of cells in both areas 17 and 18. Figure 1.4A–C documents the effect of GABA-inactivation on the orientation tuning for a moving bar in a simple cell from area 17. The cell responded to only a narrow range of orientations prior to GABA application (Fig. 1.4A). Iontophoresis of GABA with a low ejecting current (20 nA) simultaneously via all four inactivation pipettes (Fig. 1.4B) caused substantial broadening of orientation tuning which was due to an increase in response to nonoptimal orientations. Indeed, responses to some nonoptimal orientations now exceeded the response to the optimum, and the cell retained only a weak orientation bias. In this cell, broadening of orientation tuning was accompanied by an increase in response to the nonpreferred direction, resulting in a slight reduction in direction selectivity. The GABA-induced effects were reversible following termination of GABA application (Fig. 1.4C).

As was the case in Fig. 1.4A–C, orientation tuning was usually derived using a bar that was moved in opposite directions along the axis orthogonal to its orientation. However, with this stimulus it is impossible to dissociate orientation from direction of motion, and there was already substantial indirect evidence that, at least in complex cells, orientation tuning for a moving bar does not merely reflect that for a stationary bar (Hammond 1978; Crook 1990). In a direct test of this hypothesis, 16/21 complex cells recorded in areas 17 and 18 were found to have much sharper orientation tuning for a

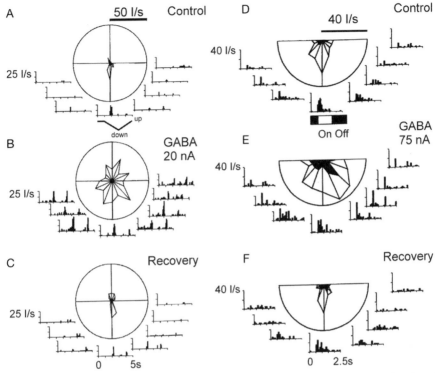

Fig. 1.4 Broadening of orientation tuning for a moving bar in an area 17 simple cell (A–C) and for a stationary bar in an area 18 simple cell (D–F) during iontophoresis of GABA simultaneously via four inactivation pipettes, as illustrated in Fig. 1.3. (A) Prior to GABA-iontophoresis, the area 17 simple cell was sharply tuned for downward motion of a horizontal bar. (B) During GABA-iontophoresis (20 nA, 12 min), the cell showed an increase in response to nonoptimal orientations and directions, resulting in substantial broadening of orientation tuning, together with a slight reduction in direction selectivity. (C) Recovery of orientation tuning and direction selectivity 12 min following termination of GABA application. The time course of stimulus motion is indicated by the lowermost trace in A. (D) Orientation tuning of an area 18 simple cell for a stationary flash-presented bar rotated symmetrically about the ON-subregion of the receptive field. The lowermost trace indicates the duration of periods of light ON and OFF. The tuning curve for responses to stimulus OFF is indicated by the dark area within the tuning curve for responses to stimulus ON. (E) During GABA-iontophoresis (75 nA; 14 min), both the ON- and OFF-responses to some nonoptimal orientations increased, resulting in substantial broadening of orientation tuning. (F) Recovery within 8 min of termination of GABA application. For each testing orientation, the peri-stimulus-time histograms (A–C) and poststimulus-time histograms (D–F) are placed at the appropriate vector angle around the perimeter of each polar diagram. Binwidths: A–C: 80 ms; D–F: 100 ms; 5 stimulus presentations per orientation in each case. Modified from Figure 2, Eysel et al., GABA-induced remote inactivation reveals cross-orientation inhibition in the cat striate cortex, *Experimental Brain Research* 1990;**80**:626–30 with permission of Springer-Verlag, and from Figure 2, Crook et al., Influence of GABA-induced remote inactivation on the orientation tuning of cells in area 18 of feline visual cortex: a comparison with area 17, *Neuroscience* 1991;**40**:1–12 with permission of Elsevier Science.

stationary flash-presented bar than for a moving bar (Crook 1991). It was therefore important to establish whether the GABA-induced effects on orientation tuning were dependent on stimulus motion. We found that this was not the case, as is documented in Fig. 1.4D–F, which illustrates substantial broadening of orientation tuning for a stationary flash-presented bar in a simple cell from area 18. Its receptive field consisted of a dominant ON-subregion and an adjacent, parallel OFF-subregion. For the derivation of orientation tuning, the bar was rotated symmetrically about the ON-subregion. The tuning curve for responses to stimulus OFF is indicated by the dark area within the tuning curve for responses to stimulus ON. Tuning broadened substantially during GABA application (compare Fig. 1.4D with Fig. 1.4E), with the ON-responses to some nonoptimal orientations now exceeding the response to the original optimum orientation. However, broadening of tuning was not specific to ON-responses, the appearance of a transient OFF-response to an orientation 45° from the optimum being particularly striking. The GABA-induced effects were reversible (Fig. 1.4F) and they occurred in the absence of a change in the response to the optimum orientation.

To quantify the effects on orientation selectivity, orientationtuning width at half the maximum response was compared before and during GABA-iontophoresis. An increase in tuning width of >25% (twice the standard deviation of spontaneously occurring changes observed in 50 cells; Wörgötter and Eysel 1991) was considered to represent a significant effect of GABA-inactivation. In area 17, 66% of 54 recorded cells showed significant broadening of orientation tuning, with a mean increase in tuning width of 90%. There was no significant difference between these results and those from area 18, in which 61% of 74 cells showed significant broadening of tuning with a mean increase in tuning width of 79% (Crook et al. 1991). The orientation tuning of a few cells in each area was eliminated during GABA-inactivation. In 11 cells from area 18, the influence of GABA-inactivation on orientation tuning was investigated using a stationary flash-presented bar either instead of (n=8) or in addition to (n=3) a moving bar (Crook et al. 1991). Seven of these cells showed significant broadening of orientation tuning for a stationary bar, with a mean increase in tuning width of 132%. In the three cells in which direct comparisons were made, the mean increase in tuning width was greater for stationary (147%) than for moving bars (55%). These results demonstrate that GABA-inactivation could have a powerful influence on genuine orientation tuning, which can be tested only with a flash-presented elongated stimulus. Moreover, it is likely that the results from these experiments underestimated the influence of GABA-inactivation on orientation tuning, because greater effects were elicited with stationary bars than with moving bars and most cells were tested only with moving bars.

In all cases, broadening of orientation tuning reflected an increase in response to nonoptimal orientations, and there was essentially no correlation between GABA-induced changes in orientation tuning and in the response to the preferred orientation. These results strongly suggested that GABA application inactivated cross-orientation inhibitory inputs that normally sharpen orientation tuning by suppressing responses to nonoptimal orientations. They implied that inhibition between columns of radically different orientation preference plays an equally important role in the generation of orientation selectivity in areas 17 and 18.

New insights provided by recordings at inactivation sites

Methodology

The interpretation of the effects on orientation and direction selectivity described in the previous section was based primarily on the horizontal distance between the recording and inactivation sites in relation to the layout of orientation preference in areas 17 and 18. However, in these experiments, the crucial information regarding the actual orientation and direction preference at the inactivation sites was lacking. We therefore specifically addressed this issue in a second series of experiments in which we used double-barrel pipettes (tip diameter 10–20 μm) for GABA-inactivation and made multi-unit recordings via one of the barrels (Crook and Eysel 1992; Crook *et al.* 1996, 1997). This enabled us to determine the local orientation/direction preference in the vicinity of the inactivation sites and to verify that the cells recorded there were reversibly inactivated by GABA-iontophoresis. The locations of the recording and inactivation sites were labeled via iontophoresis of biocytin, which was added to the electrolyte, and subsequently identified histologically. The aim of these experiments was to compare the effect of inactivating sites where the orientation preference was either the same as (±22.5°; iso-orientation sites) or radically different from (±45–90°; cross-orientation sites) that of a recorded cell. In the initial experiments of this series, we used the fixed array of four inactivation pipettes described in the previous section (see Fig. 1.3) and tested the effect of applying GABA simultaneously at either iso-orientation sites or cross-orientation sites on the orientation tuning of single cells. Later, we used a single pipette or two independently moveable pipettes for GABA-iontophoresis at a horizontal distance of 350–700 μm. In these cases, we used a plastic recording chamber for cortical stability whose base was covered with transparent elastic foil that could be readily penetrated by the recording and inactivation pipettes. The use of the recording chamber allowed us to make multiple penetrations with a recording pipette while the inactivation pipette(s) remained *in situ*. In this way, we were able to compare the effect of inactivating a single site on the orientation and direction selectivity of cells recorded at different iso-orientation and cross-orientation sites. In all cases, the experimental procedure was the same. First, multiunit activity was recorded at the inactivation site(s) and, for each monocular input, the receptive field was mapped, orientation/direction selectivity determined quantitatively over a range of velocities, and it was verified that iontophoresis of GABA (50–100 nA; 3–5 min) reversibly abolished the response to an optimally oriented moving bar. Thereafter, a single unit was recorded extracellularly, its receptive field mapped and classified, and orientation/direction selectivity for the dominant eye was determined quantitatively before, during and after iontophoresis of GABA (50–100 nA) at the inactivation site(s).

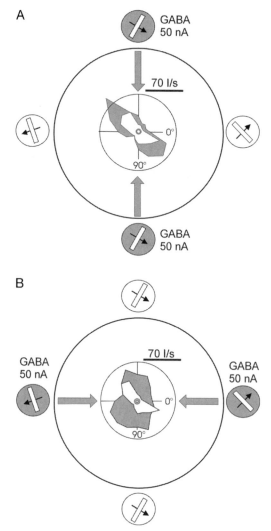

Fig. 1.5 Differential effects on the orientation tuning of a complex cell in area 18 elicited by alternate inactivation of iso-orientation and cross-orientation sites. The cell was recorded during a penetration through the center of the fixed array of four GABA-containing pipettes, as illustrated in Fig. 1.3. Recording and inactivation sites located in layer II/III. The location, orientation and direction preference of each inactivation site is indicated by the schematics around the perimeter of the outer circle whose radius represents a horizontal distance of ~600 μm from the recording site. Shaded schematics indicate sites where GABA was applied. (A) Simultaneous application of GABA at two sites with similar preferred orientations to that of the recorded cell (iso-orientation sites). (B) Simultaneous application of GABA at two different sites where the orientation preference was approximately orthogonal to that of the recorded cell (cross-orientation sites); GABA-iontophoresis began 5 min after the termination of GABA application at the iso-orientation sites. In A and B, the polar plot derived prior to inactivation (unshaded area) is superimposed on that obtained during inactivation (shaded area).

Velocity of motion approximated the preferred velocity of each recorded cell and it matched one of the velocities used for quantitative testing at the inactivation site(s). This was essential to allow reliable comparisons to be made between the orientation/direction selectivity of cells at the recording and inactivation sites, for both of these properties may vary with velocity in both areas 17 and 18 (Orban *et al.* 1981; Crook 1990).

Differential effects of iso-orientation and cross-orientation inactivation on orientation tuning and direction selectivity

This series of experiments yielded three important results that provided new insights into the intracortical mechanisms underlying orientation and direction selectivity:

1. Cross-orientation and iso-orientation inactivation had their major impact, respectively, on orientation tuning and direction selectivity;

2. Iso-orientation inactivation elicited multiple effects on directionality which were broadly predictable on the basis of the relative direction preference at the recording and inactivation sites; and

3. Differential effects on orientation tuning and direction selectivity could be elicited both in single cells from iso-orientation and cross-orientation inactivation sites (Fig. 1.5) and from a single inactivation site in cells recorded at iso-orientation and cross-orientation sites (Figs. 1.6 and 1.7).

Figure 1.5 shows an example of a dramatic effect on orientation tuning that occurred only during the inactivation of cross-orientation sites. Results are for a complex cell in area 18 which was recorded in layer II/III during a penetration through the center of the array of four GABA-inactivation pipettes, each located at a horizontal distance of ~600 μm in the superficial layers. The polar plots show the cell's orientation tuning for a moving bar prior to inactivation (unshaded) and during inactivation (shaded) of iso-orientation sites (Fig. 1.5A) and cross-orientation sites (Fig. 1.5B). Inactivation by iontophoresis of GABA (50 nA) of two iso-orientation sites anterior and posterior to the recorded cell (see shaded schematics in Fig. 1.5A) had a negligible influence on orientation tuning (tuning widths before and during inactivation 60° and 56°). In contrast, iontophoresis of GABA with the same ejecting current as in A simultaneously at two cross-orientation sites medial and lateral to the recorded cell (Fig. 1.5B) caused an increase in response to nonoptimal orientations and an elimination of orientation tuning. This effect is commensurate with a loss of cross-orientation inhibition that normally suppresses responses to nonoptimal orientations. An important point to note

---

Fig. 1.5 (continued)
GABA-inactivation of cross-orientation sites caused an increase in response to nonoptimal orientations, resulting in an elimination of orientation tuning, whereas inactivation of iso-orientation sites had no influence on orientation selectivity. Modified from Crook and Eysel, *Journal of Neuroscience* 1992;**12**:1816–25, with permission of The Society for Neuroscience, copyright 1992 by the Society for Neuroscience.

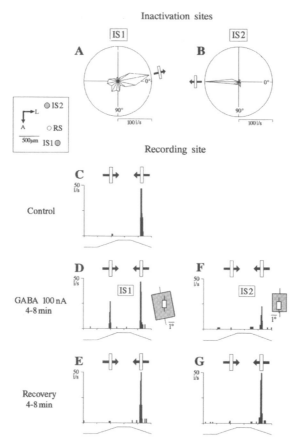

Fig. 1.6 Differential effects on directionality elicited in an area 17 simple cell by alternate inactivation of two iso-orientation sites with opposite direction preference (IS1 and IS2). The cell was recorded at the layer III/IV border region at a horizontal distance of ~400 μm from IS1 (located in upper layer IV) and ~550 μm from IS2 (located in layer II). Inset (in this and subsequent figures) shows the topographical location of the recording site (RS; open circle) and the inactivation sites (shaded circles); A, anterior; L, lateral. (A, B) Polar diagrams derived for multiunit activity at IS1 (A) and IS2 (B), with orientation and direction preference at each site indicated schematically for direct comparison with C–G. (C, D) PSTHs for the recorded cell in response to opposite directions of motion of an optimally oriented bar, prior to (C) and during (D) inactivation by GABA-iontophoresis at IS1. The recorded cell and IS1 showed virtually opposite direction preferences. GABA-inactivation caused an increase in the cell's response to the nonpreferred direction, but did not influence the response to the preferred direction. (F) Iontophoresis of GABA at IS2, where the direction preference matched that of the recorded cell, caused a marked decrease in response to the preferred direction (compare with C), but did not influence the response to the nonpreferred direction. (E, G) Following termination of GABA-iontophoresis at each site, the cell's directionality returned to control levels. Data in (D and F) and (E and G) obtained 4–8 min after onset and offset of GABA iontophoresis, respectively. Spatial relationship between the recorded cell's receptive field (white rectangle) and that for multiunit activity at IS1 and IS2 (shaded rectangles) shown to the right of (D) and (F); axis orientation

about the result in Fig. 1.5A is that, although iso-orientation inactivation did not significantly influence orientation tuning, it caused a marked increase in the response to motion of an optimally oriented bar. Similar effects were observed in many other cells, and they introduced the possibility that iso-orientation inactivation could release inhibitory inputs which contribute to direction selectivity along the preferred axis of motion. In subsequent experiments, we therefore made detailed comparisons of the effect of inactivating single iso-orientation sites on the direction selectivity of recorded cells with approximately the same or opposite direction preference. To quantify directionality, we calculated a direction selectivity index (DI): [1-(response to nonpreferred direction/response to preferred direction)] ranging from 0 (non-biased) to 1 (totally directional), with a change of >0.2 representing a significant effect of inactivation. Additionally, strongly direction-selective cells could show a significant (>25%) change in the response to the preferred direction that did not result in a significant change in DI, and this was also considered to represent an effect on directionality.

The two major types of effect on directionality that were elicited by iso-orientation inactivation are documented in Fig. 1.6. This figure additionally illustrates that differential effects on directionality could be elicited in the same cell by alternate inactivation of two iso-orientation sites with opposite direction preference. The orientation/direction selectivity at each site is indicated in Fig. 1.6A (IS1) and Fig. 1.6B (IS2). The illustrated results are for a direction-selective simple cell recorded in area 17 at the layer III/IV border region. Its direction preference was virtually opposite that at IS1 (compare Fig. 1.6A with C) which was located in upper layer IV at a horizontal distance of ~400 μm (see inset). Inactivation of this site by GABA-iontophoresis caused an increase in the cell's response to the nonpreferred direction (Fig. 1.6D), which resulted in a marked reduction in direction selectivity (decrease in DI from 0.95 to 0.42). Once directionality had recovered following termination of GABA-iontophoresis at IS1 (Fig. 1.6E), GABA was applied at a different iso-orientation site (IS2), which was located in layer II at a horizontal distance of ~550 μm from the recording site. The direction preference at this site matched that of the recorded cell (compare Fig. 1.6B with C), and GABA-inactivation caused a pronounced (55%) and reversible decrease in response to the preferred direction (Fig. 1.6E–G). Although not shown, both types of effect on directionality occurred in the absence of a significant change in orientation tuning.

Figure 1.7 illustrates results of a different experiment in area 17, in which we compared the effect of inactivating a single site on the orientation tuning and direction

---

Fig. 1.6 (continued)
indicated by short lines adjoining each rectangle. Each PSTH taken from a complete set of histograms used to derive polar diagrams (5 stimulus presentations); bin-width: 40 msec. Stimulus waveform indicated below each PSTH; cycle duration: 5 sec. Throughout, stimulus velocity: 6.7°/sec. Reprinted from Crook *et al.* GABA-induced inactivation of functionally characterized sites in cat striate cortex: effects on orientation tuning and direction selectivity, *Visual Neuroscience* 1997;**14**:141–58 with permission of Cambridge University Press.

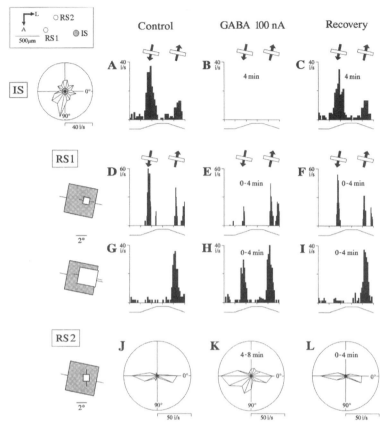

Fig. 1.7 Inactivation of a single site (IS) in area 17 elicited effects on directionality at an iso-orientation recording site (RS1) and caused broadening of orientation tuning at a cross-orientation site (RS2). Polar diagram on left of top row derived for multiunit activity at IS which was located in upper layer IV; horizontal distance from RS1: ~650μm, from RS2: ~520μm. (A–I) PSTHs in response to opposite directions of motion of an optimally oriented bar, for multiunit activity at IS (A–C), and for a simple cell (D–F) and a complex cell (G–I) recorded respectively in upper and lower layer IV at RS1, before, during and after inactivation by GABA-iontophoresis (left to right columns) GABA-inactivation caused a decrease in response to the preferred direction in the simple cell whose direction preference matched that at IS, but an increase in response to the nonpreferred direction in the complex cell whose direction preference was opposite that at IS. (J–L) Polar diagrams derived for a simple cell recorded in layer IV at RS2, before (J), during (K) and after (L) iontophoresis of GABA at IS. The cell's orientation preference was approximately orthogonal to that at IS and GABA-inactivation caused an increase in response to nonoptimal orientations and broadening of orientation tuning. Spatial relationship between each cell's receptive field and that for multiunit activity at IS shown to left of appropriate row of PSTHs or polar diagrams. Derivation of PSTHs: A–C: 5 stimulus repetitions; D–I: as in Fig. 1.6. Bin-widths: A–C: 120ms; D–F: 40ms; G–I: 100ms. Stimulus velocity 6.7°/s, throughout. Reprinted from Crook *et al.* GABA-induced inactivation of functionally characterized sites in cat striate cortex: effects on orientation tuning and direction selectivity, *Visual Neuroscience* 1997;**14**:141–58 with permission of Cambridge University Press.

selectivity of cells recorded at iso-orientation and cross-orientation sites. The inactivation site (IS) was located in upper layer IV. Its orientation preference (see polar diagram) matched that of a simple cell (Fig. 1.7D–F) and a complex cell (Fig. 1.7G–I) recorded respectively in upper and lower layer IV at RS1, but was almost orthogonal to that of a simple cell recorded in layer IV at RS2. The simple cell at RS1 showed a moderate bias for the direction of motion preferred at IS, whereas the complex cell showed the opposite direction preference and was virtually direction-selective (compare Fig. 1.7A with D and G). GABA-inactivation (B) caused a 68% decrease in response to the preferred direction in Fig. 1.7D and 1.7E, resulting in a reversal of direction preference (change in DI from 0.33 to −0.57), but it produced a vigorous response to the nonpreferred direction in Fig. 1.7G and 1.7H, resulting in a substantial reduction in direction bias (decrease in DI from 0.97 to 0.26). These effects on directionality occurred in the absence of a significant change in orientation tuning (data not shown). By contrast, in the simple cell recorded at RS2, inactivation of the same site caused an increase in response to nonoptimal orientations and substantial broadening of orientation tuning (105% increase in tuning width from 42° to 86°), without significantly influencing directionality (DI in Fig. 1.7J and 1.7K: 0.19 and 0.30). As was typically the case, the effects on the recorded cells had a short time course that closely paralleled that for the abolition of multiunit activity at IS (compare Figs 1.7E, H, and K with B).

Summary of the effects of iso-orientation and cross-orientation inactivation

The following comparisons are based on the inactivation of over a hundred iso-orientation sites and cross-orientation sites in areas 17 and 18. In view of the short time course of the effects elicited in recorded cells, the differential effects of iso-orientation and cross-orientation inactivation and the sphere of influence of GABA-iontophoresis in relation to the size of iso-orientation/direction domains, the orientation/direction preferences determined at these sites can be considered to reflect the combined preference of all inactivated cells. Since the results derived from the two areas were qualitatively and quantitatively similar, they will be described together.

About two-thirds of cells showed significant broadening of orientation tuning during the inactivation of cross-orientation sites, with a mean increase in tuning width (at half the maximum response) of more than 100%. These effects always reflected an increase in response to nonoptimal orientations. In contrast, only ~20% of cells showed a significant change in directionality during cross-orientation inactivation. These effects were also due to increases in response (to preferred or nonpreferred directions) and they were always accompanied by broadening of orientation tuning. Thus, the effects of cross-orientation inactivation could be attributed to a loss of inhibition between cells with radically different orientation preferences that contributes primarily to orientation tuning by suppressing responses to nonoptimal orientations. During the inactivation of iso-orientation sites, about two-thirds of cells showed a significant effect on directionality, with a mean change in DI of ~0.6. With few exceptions,

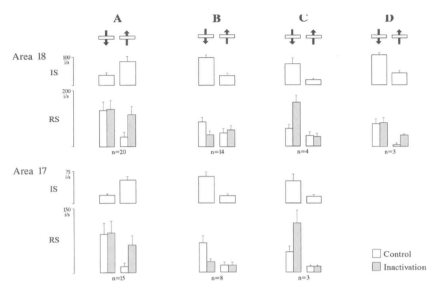

Fig. 1.8 Predictability of the effects of iso-orientation inactivation on directionality. The top two and bottom two rows of histograms illustrate data for area 18 and area 17, respectively. IS=inactivation site; RS=recording site. Cells showing significant effects were subdivided into four groups (A–D) according to (1) their direction preference relative to that at the related inactivation site; (2) whether GABA-inactivation predominantly affected the response to the preferred or nonpreferred direction; and (3) whether this response increased or decreased. The lower rows of histograms compare the mean evoked responses (after subtraction of spontaneous activity) of all cells within each group, to preferred and opposite directions of motion (left and right pairs of histograms), in the control situation (open histograms) and during iso-orientation inactivation (shaded histograms) Histograms directly above each pair in the lower rows show mean evoked responses to the same relative directions of motion at corresponding inactivation sites. Vertical lines: standard deviations of these mean responses (drawn in one direction only) Direction of motion indicated schematically at the top of each column, with preferred orientation arbitrarily set to 90°. A recorded cell and an iso-orientation site were considered to have matching preferred orientations, although their orientation preferences could differ by up to 22.5°. The number of cells in each group (n) is indicated below each set of histograms in the lower rows. Note that in most cases (groups A–C) the results were predictable in the sense that GABA-inactivation predominantly affected a cell's response to the direction of motion preferred at the inactivation site. Adapted from Crook *et al.* GABA-induced inactivation of functionally characterized sites in cat striate cortex: effects on orientation tuning and direction selectivity, *Visual Neuroscience* 1997;**14**: 141-58 with permission of Cambridge University Press, and from Crook *et al. Journal of Neurophysiology* 1996;**75**:2071–88 with permission of The American Physiological Society.

these effects occurred in the absence of a significant change in orientation tuning. In contrast to the uniform influence of cross-orientation inactivation, iso-orientation inactivation elicited multiple effects on directionality, as shown in Fig. 1.8. In most cases (Fig. 1.8A, B, and C), these effects were broadly predictable in the sense that iso-orientation inactivation predominantly affected a cell's response to the direction of motion of an optimally oriented bar which was closest to the preferred direction at the inactivation site. The sign of the effects was also predictable when the recording and inactivation sites showed opposite direction preferences (Fig. 1.8A), for in these cases GABA-inactivation always caused an increase in response to the nonpreferred direction without significantly influencing the response to the preferred direction. By analogy with the effects of cross-orientation inactivation on orientation tuning, these effects can be attributed to the loss of inhibition between cells with opposite direction preferences that contributes to direction selectivity by suppressing responses to the nonpreferred direction. When the recording and inactivation sites had the same direction preference, a recorded cell could show a decrease (Fig. 1.8B) or, less frequently, an increase (Fig. 1.8C) in the response to the preferred direction in the absence of a change in response to the nonpreferred direction. These effects presumably reflected the loss of iso-orientation excitatory and inhibitory influences, which play a major role in determining the magnitude of the response to the preferred direction.

It is important to emphasize that the suppressive effects on directionality could not be attributed to a direct inhibitory action of GABA on a recorded cell, or to a GABA-induced reduction in the strength of the thalamocortical input because such effects were observed only when the recording and inactivation sites showed the same orientation and direction preference and because GABA affects cells but not afferents. The suppression must have been due to the loss of excitatory interactions within the cortex. Therefore it is significant that some of the most potent suppressive effects were observed in cells recorded at the layer III/IV border region or in layer IV (Fig. 1.6F and Fig. 1.7E) which almost certainly received a monosynaptic excitatory input from the thalamus (Harvey 1980; Ferster and Lindström 1983; Martin and Whitteridge 1984). Intuitively, one might not expect the responses of these cells to be heavily dependent on an intracortical excitatory input. However, it is already known from anatomical studies that even in layer IV the intracortical excitatory input is numerically dominant relative to the geniculate input (Garey and Powell 1971; LeVay and Gilbert 1976; Peters and Payne 1993; Ahmed *et al.* 1994). Our results suggest that the intracortical input is also functionally dominant. Because a single pyramidal or spiny stellate cell provides only a small fraction of the excitatory input to its target cells (Kisvárday *et al.* 1986; Anderson *et al.* 1994), it is improbable that the more pronounced decreases in response were due solely to the loss of a monosynaptic excitatory input from an inactivation site to a recorded cell. The most plausible explanation for these effects is that GABA-inactivation initiated a loss of mutual excitation among highly interconnected populations of cells in the vicinity of an inactivation site that had iso-orientation connections with each other and a recorded cell. The GABA-induced suppressive effects thus provide experimental support for the notion that responses to optimal orientations and directions are amplified intracortically via local recurrent excitatory connections (Douglas and Martin 1991; Douglas *et al.* 1995; Somers *et al.* 1995; Suarez *et al.* 1995).

GABA-inactivation combined with a "masking" paradigm

In cases where iso-orientation inactivation caused a marked increase in the response to the nonpreferred direction, we found that the effects could be essentially replicated when a mask was left exposed only the ON-subregion in simple cells and the most responsive part of the excitatory discharge region in complex cells. This is documented in Fig. 1.9, which compares the effect of inactivating the same iso-orientation site (Figs 1.9A–C) on the directionality of a layer-III complex cell (Fig. 1.9D–I) and a layer-IV simple cell (Fig. 1.9J–O) from area 18, with and without a mask. The cells were recorded during the same penetration at a horizontal distance of ~ 500 μm from the inactivation site that was located in layer III. The inactivation site and the recorded cells had matching orientation preferences, but opposite direction preferences. The complex cell was direction-selective in the no mask condition, prior to inactivation (Fig. 1.9D). During iso-orientation inactivation (Fig. 1.9E) the cell showed a vigorous response to the nonpreferred direction, resulting in a reversal of direction preference (change in DI from 1.0 to –0.26). A comparable effect on directionality (decrease in DI from 0.84 to 0) was elicited from the same inactivation site in the presence of a mask (Fig. 1.9G, H) which, along the width axis through the receptive field, left exposed only the central 2° of the excitatory discharge region (see schematic to the left of Fig. 1.9G). Similar results were obtained in the simple cell. Its receptive field consisted of two adjacent ON- and OFF-subregions (see schematic to the left of Fig. 1.9J). For motion of a light bar, it was essentially direction-selective prior to inactivation (Fig. 1.9J, M). Iso-orientation inactivation caused a marked increase in the response to the light bar moving in the nonpreferred direction, resulting in a reduction in direction bias, both in the no mask condition (Fig. 1.9J–K; decrease in DI from 0.95 to 0.33) and in the presence of a mask which left exposed only the ON-subregion of the receptive field (Fig. 1.9M–N; decrease in DI from 0.85 to 0.23).

The results of these "masking experiments" imply (1) that in simple cells the inhibitory input that contributed to direction selectivity for responses elicited in the ON-subregion was normally activated from within the ON-subregion itself; and (2) that in complex cells the inhibition was maximally effective at or close to the location across the width of the receptive field where the excitatory response it normally suppressed was maximal. These results are consistent with those of two-bar interaction experiments in cat areas 17 and 18 (Emerson and Gerstein 1977; Ganz and Felder 1984; Baker and Cynader 1986; Emerson *et al.* 1987) that demonstrated short-range, suppressive influences in a cell's nonpreferred direction that were restricted to the excitatory discharge region. Moreover, our results demonstrate that short-range lateral inhibitory interactions actually contribute to direction selectivity and that the inhibitory input which suppresses responses to the nonpreferred direction derives from cells with the opposite direction preference. The subdivision of iso-orientation domains into regions selective for opposite directions of motion (Shumuel and Grinvald 1996) provides an ideal substrate for short-range inhibitory interactions between populations of neurons with opposite direction preferences. Indeed, this type

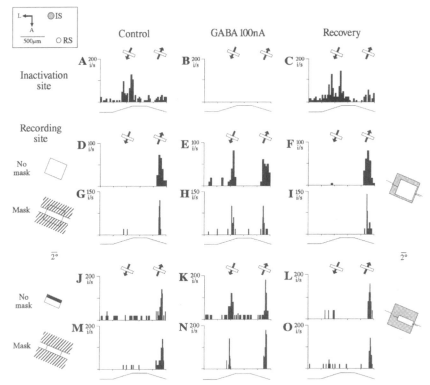

Fig. 1.9 Effect of iso-orientation inactivation on directionalities and the influence of masking in a simple cell and a complex cell from area 18. (A–C) GABA-induced reversible abolition of multiunit activity recorded at an inactivation site located in layer III; horizontal distance from recording sites: ~500 μm. (D–F) response of a complex cell recorded in lower layer III to opposite directions of motion of an optimally oriented light bar, before (D), during (E) and after (F) iontophoresis of GABA at the inactivation site. The inactivation site and the recorded cell had matching orientation preferences, but opposite direction preferences. The receptive field of the recorded cell is represented by the open rectangle to the left of D. The spatial relationship between this receptive field and that for multiunit activity at the inactivation site is indicated on the extreme right. (G–I) repeat of D–F, but with an opaque mask (hatched areas in schematic on left) covering the entire visual display, except for a 2°-wide window whose long axis was parallel with the cell's preferred orientation and which was centered on the most responsive part of the excitatory discharge region (note the narrower response profiles compared with D–F). (J–O) comparable data for a simple cell recorded in layer IV during the same penetration. Schematic to the left of J shows the disposition of the cell's ON and OFF receptive field subregions (indicated by light and dark areas), mapped with a stationary flashed bar. The mask left exposed only the ON-subregion of the receptive field (see schematic to the left of M). Note that GABA-inactivation induced a strong response to motion in the nonpreferred direction in both cells; also that the GABA-induced effects were of comparable magnitude in the mask and no mask conditions. Time following onset and offset of GABA-iontophoresis ranged from 3 to 5 min. All PSTHs derived from 5 stimulus repetitions. Bin-widths: A–C: 25 ms; D–F: 30 ms; G–O: 10 ms. Stimulus velocity 53°/s, amplitude 20°, cycle duration 1.25 s. Modified from Crook *et al. Journal of Neurophysiology* 1996; **75**:2071–88 with permission of The American Physiological Society.

of inhibition has recently been demonstrated in ferret visual cortex by combining *in vivo* optical imaging with *in vitro* photostimulation (Roerig and Kao 1999).

GABA-inactivation combined with neuroanatomical tracing techniques

Rationale and experimental procedure

The most direct explanation for the disinhibitory effects on orientation/direction selectivity which occurred when the recording and inactivation sites showed radically different orientation preferences or opposite direction preferences is that GABA application blocked inhibitory projections originating at the inactivation site which normally suppressed the responses of a recorded cell to nonoptimal stimuli. To test for the presence of direct inhibitory projections from an inactivation site to recording sites where such disinhibitory effects were elicited, we combined GABA-inactivation with neuroanatomical tracing techniques (Crook *et al.* 1998; and see Kisvárday *et al.* 2000). The experimental approach is illustrated schematically in Fig. 1.10. An inactivation experiment was performed in area 17 or area 18 as described in the previous section, with a single pipette being used for GABA-iontophoresis. The inactivation site and recording sites where disinhibitory effects were elicited were marked by iontophoresis of biocytin (diameter of label 30–60 μm). We sometimes made larger injections of biocytin at the inactivation site (~200 μm diameter) in an attempt to anterogradely label the projections of nearby inhibitory neurons and to test for the presence of labeled terminal boutons in the vicinity of the recording site (Fig. 1.10A). At the end of an experiment, the recording and inactivation pipettes were withdrawn, and a pressure injection of [³H]-nipecotic acid (45–320 nl; diameter of injection site 170–250 μm) was targeted at a group of closely spaced recording sites where disinhibitory effects had been elicited (Fig. 1.10B). The stereotaxic coordinates of the recording penetrations and their recorded location relative to the superficial vasculature were used to guide placement of the nipecotic acid containing pipette. Nipecotic acid competes with the high-affinity uptake system for endogenous GABA at the presynaptic site (e.g., Johnston *et al.* 1976a,b), and once it is taken up, it travels retrogradely towards the soma of the cell via fast transport mechanisms and accumulates in the soma region. Experiments in monkey visual cortex had already demonstrated that injections of [³H]-nipecotic acid can produce selective retrograde labeling of GABAergic neurons (Kritzer *et al.* 1992) and we verified that this was also the case with our injections. This approach thus allowed us to visualize the distribution of GABAergic inhibitory neurons with projections that terminated close to recording sites where disinhibitory effects had been elicited and to test for their presence in the vicinity of the inactivation site.

Retrograde tracing with [³H]-nipecotic acid

Of 11 injections of [³H]-nipecotic acid, seven (2 in area 17 and 5 in area 18) were successfully placed <100 μm from one or two recording sites where cells had shown either

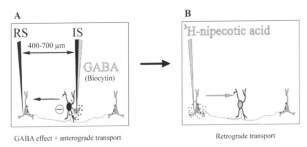

Fig. 1.10 GABA-inactivation combined with neuroanatomical tracing techniques to study the contribution of lateral inhibition to orientation and direction selectivity. (A) The basic inactivation paradigm combined with iontophoresis of biocytin. For functional characterization of the inactivation site (IS), multiunit recordings are made via one barrel of a double-barrel inactivation pipette (in black) containing 5% biocytin in 0.5 M sodium acetate. Via the second barrel of the same pipette (in grey), GABA is applied iontophoretically (small circles) to inactivate multiunits, including inhibitory cells with lateral projections (black cell-icon), while a remotely placed pipette (in black), which also contains biocytin (5% in 0.5 M sodium acetate), is used to monitor changes in the orientation/direction selectivity of extracellularly recorded single cells (grey cell-icons; RS=recording site). The locations of the inactivation site and of recording sites where disinhibitory effects on orientation/direction selectivity are elicited are marked by iontophoresis of biocytin (0.5–0.7 μA injection current for 5–10 min; diameter of label 30–60 μm). By making larger injections of biocytin at the inactivation site (large grey circle; 1 μA injection current for 20 min; diameter of label ~200 μm), it is possible, in principle, to anterogradely label the axonal projections of neighboring inhibitory neurones and to test for the presence of labeled axon terminals (black dots) in the vicinity of the recording site. (B) At the end of an experiment, the recording and inactivation pipettes are withdrawn and, using the branching pattern of blood vessels as landmarks, a pressure injection of [³H]-nipecotic acid (small grey circles), which produces selective retrograde labelling of GABAergic neurones, is made close to recording sites where disinhibitory effects on orientation/direction selectivity had been elicited. Retrogradely labeled GABAergic cell somata are identified autoradiographically and their distribution is reconstructed from series of horizontal sections. This approach allowed us to test for the presence of inhibitory neurones in the vicinity of the inactivation site (black cell-icon; labeled soma in grey) with projections that terminate close to the recording site (black dots).

an increase in response to nonoptimal orientations during cross-orientation inactivation ($n=2$) or an increase in response to the nonpreferred direction during inactivation of an iso-orientation site with opposite direction preference ($n=5$). The recording and inactivation sites were located in layers II/III-IV and their horizontal separation ranged from 400 to 560 μm. In every case, we detected radiolabeled cells in the vicinity of the inactivation site (three to six within 150 μm). These cells would have been inactivated by our GABA applications which influence a cortical region ~300–400 μm in diameter (Crook *et al.* 1998; Hupé *et al.* 1999).

A representative example of results from this type of experiment is shown in Fig. 1.11. The injection of [³H]-nipecotic acid (see asterisk in G) was made <100 μm

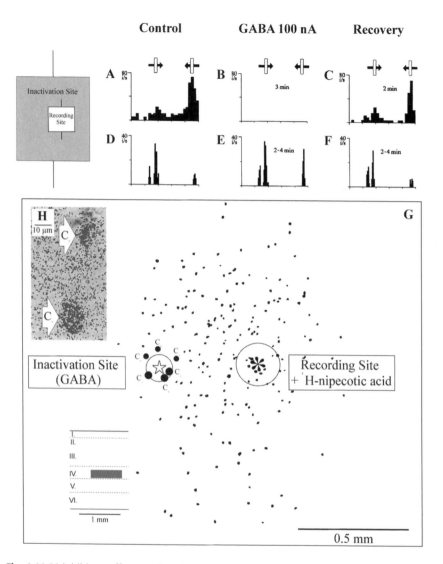

Fig. 1.11 Disinhibitory effect on directionality elicited in a simple cell recorded in layer IV (area 18) by iso-orientation inactivation in the same layer, and evidence for inhibitory projections from the inactivation site to the recording site. A–C: as in Fig. 1.9A–C. D–F: Response of the recorded simple cell to opposite directions of motion of an optimally oriented bar before (D), during (E) and after (F) iontophoresis of GABA at the inactivation site. The direction preference at the inactivation site was opposite that of the recorded cell which showed a marked increase in response to the nonpreferred direction during GABA-inactivation, resulting in a reduction of direction bias (decrease in DI from 0.71 to 0.15). PSTH bin-widths: A–C: 90 ms; D–F: 30 ms; cycle duration 2.5 s; stimulus velocity 27°/s. All data derived for ipsilateral eye. (G) Horizontal distribution of retrogradely labelled GABAergic cells in layer IV (dots) following an injection of [3H]-nipecotic acid (320 nl; diameter ~200 μm) <100 μm from the recording site. The asterisk and concentric circle indicate, respectively, the

from two recording sites in lower layer IV of area 18 at each of which a simple cell had shown a marked increase in response to the nonpreferred direction during inactivation of a site with opposite direction preference in the same layer. Data for one of these cells are shown in Fig. 1.11D–F. Figure 1.11G shows the horizontal distribution of retrogradely labeled GABAergic cells (dots) in layer IV (see Fig. 1.11, inset, bottom left). Three radiolabeled cells were located within 100 μm (C_1-C_3) and three within 150 μm (C_4-C_6) of the inactivation site (star). As illustrated in Fig. 1.11H, most radiolabeled cells in the vicinity of inactivation sites showed high grain densities, suggesting that they had high terminal densities and contacted a large number of cells at the injection sites. Moreover, the actual number of GABAergic cells within 150 μm of the inactivation sites would have been much larger than the three to six cells that were radiolabeled, because radiolabeling was confined to the upper surface of each (50–80 μm) autoradiographic section and, in order to facilitate the reconstruction of electrode tracks, every third section was osmium-treated and hence could not be processed for autoradiography.

In view of the lateral distance between the inactivation and recording sites, the only realistic candidates for radiolabeled cells in the vicinity of inactivation sites are basket cells, which project laterally for 0.3–1.5 mm within layers II/III-IV (Martin *et al.* 1983; Somogyi *et al.* 1983; Fairen *et al.* 1984; Kisvárday *et al.* 1985, 1994; Naegele and Katz 1990; Kisvárday and Eysel 1993), and so-called dendrite-targeting cells whose axonal arborizations extend for up to 300 μm in layer IV and 800 μm in layer II/III (Tamás *et al.* 1997a,b). Both cell types make synaptic contact primarily with the proximal processes of their target neurons. Since the injections of [^{3}H]-nipecotic acid were placed < 100 μm from the recording sites, and since the injection sites were only 170–250 μm in diameter, radiolabeled cells in the vicinity of the inactivation sites must have made contact with recorded cells or with cells in their vicinity, most of which will have had similar orientation/direction preferences to those of recorded cells. These experiments thus provided strong evidence for the presence of direct inhibitory connections between cells in the vicinity of the inactivation and recording sites with radically different orientation preferences or opposite direction preferences in cases where GABA-inactivation elicited disinhibitory effects on orientation/direction selectivity.

Fig. 1.11 (continued)
topographical location and the approximate lateral extent of the [^{3}H]-nipecotic acid injection. Large and small filled circles highlight radiolabeled cells located within 100 μm (C_1–C_3) and 150 μm (C_4–C_6) of the inactivation site (star) Shading in inset to G indicates the laminar location of all radiolabelled cells shown. (H) Cells C_2 and C_3 are shown on photomicrographs of autoradiographic sections. Modified from Crook *et al.*, Evidence for a contribution of lateral inhibition to orientation tuning and direction selectivity in cat visual cortex: reversible inactivation of functionally characterized sites combining with neuroanatomical tracing techniques, *European Journal of Neuroscience* 1998;**10**:2056–75, with permission of Blackwell Science.

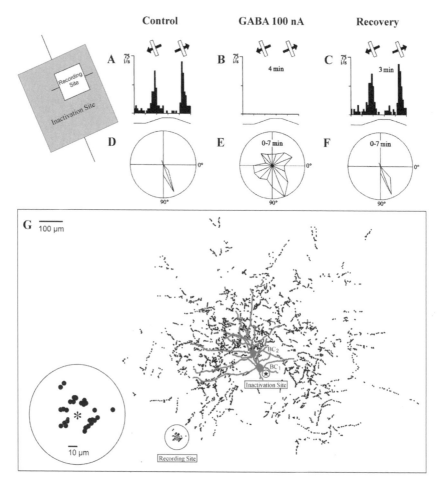

Fig. 1.12 Disinhibitory effect on orientation tuning elicited in a simple cell recorded in layer II/III (area 17) during cross-orientation inactivation in the same layer, and evidence for inhibitory projections from the inactivation site to the recording site. (A–C) as in Fig. 1.9A–C. (D–F) Orientation tuning of the recorded simple cell for a moving bar before (D), during (E) and after (F) iontophoresis of GABA at the inactivation site. The orientation preference at the inactivation site was orthogonal to that of the recorded cell which showed an increase in response to nonoptimal orientations and broadening of tuning during GABA-inactivation (227% increase in tuning width from 36° to 118°). (G) Surface view of the somata and dendritic fields (shaded) and the axonal boutons (dots) of two large basket cells (BC_1 and BC_2) labeled by iontophoresis of biocytin at the inactivation site (star) that was located in layer III. Reconstruction from horizontal sections through layer II/III. Both basket cells emitted axonal boutons (ringed) in close proximity to the recording site (asterisk) and they made contact with the somata and proximal dendrites of their target neurones. An enlarged view of these boutons is shown on the extreme left. Modified from Crook et al., Evidence for a contribution of lateral inhibition to orientation tuning and direction selectivity in cat visual cortex: reversible inactivation of functionally characterized sites combining with neuroanatomical tracing techniques, European Journal of Neuroscience 1998;**10**:2056–75, with permission of Blackwell Science.

Anterograde tracing with biocytin

In some of the experiments in which we combined GABA-inactivation with injections of [^{3}H]-nipecotic acid, we made large injections of biocytin at the inactivation site in an attempt to anterogradely label the projections of neighboring inhibitory neurons. Figure 1.12 illustrates a fortuitous case in which iontophoresis of biocytin at an inactivation site in layer III of area 17 labeled two large basket cells. These basket cells were located within ~100 μm of the inactivation site and they had projections which terminated in the vicinity of two closely spaced cross-orientation recording sites in layer II/III where cells had shown an increase in response to nonoptimal orientations and broadening of orientation tuning during GABA-inactivation. Data for one of these cells are shown in Fig. 1.12D–F. Figure 1.12G shows a reconstruction of the soma and dendrites (shaded) of each labeled basket cell (BC$_1$ and BC$_2$) and the pooled distribution of axonal boutons (dots) of both cells in layer II/III. Labeled boutons of both basket cells were detected in close proximity to the recording sites (ringed). Since the terminals of large basket cells contain GABA (Somogyi and Soltész 1986; Kisvárday *et al.* 1987), this is strong evidence for an inhibitory projection from the inactivation site to recording sites where disinhibitory effects on orientation selectivity had been elicited. It should also be pointed out that the ringed boutons in Fig. 1.12G represent a minimal estimate of the total number of boutons supplied by each basket cell in proximity to the recording sites. This is because it was difficult to trace fine axon collaterals in the core region of dense biocytin labeling at the recording sites. Since the majority of synapses made by large basket cells are on the somata and proximal dendrites of their target cells (Somogyi *et al.* 1983; Kisvárday *et al.* 1987), the labeled basket cells must have made synaptic contact either with the recorded cells or with cells in close proximity with similar orientation preference. Thus, in this case we able to demonstrate the presence of direct inhibitory projections from cells at the inactivation site to cells with radically different orientation preferences at recording sites where disinhibitory effects on orientation selectivity had been elicited.

Advantages and disadvantages of [^{3}H]-nipecotic acid and biocytin as neuroanatomical tracers for use in combination with GABA-inactivation

Injections of [^{3}H]-nipecotic acid are well-suited for use with the GABA-inactivation technique, because they potentially produce retrograde labeling of all GABAergic neurons with projections from inactivation to recording sites. In addition, injections of nipecotic acid provide highly efficient labeling of GABAergic neurons, because this substance competes selectively with GABA for uptake with an apparent affinity greater than that of GABA itself (Johnston *et al.* 1976a,b). One obvious drawback with the use of nipecotic acid is that the injections have to be aimed at recording sites at the end of an inactivation experiment. Inevitably, some injections are placed too remote from targeted recording sites for meaningful conclusions to be drawn. Additionally, injections of nipecotic acid yield no direct information on the morphological type of cell being labeled. In contrast, injections of biocytin can be made directly at an inactivation site (with the inactivation pipette *in situ*), and they reveal the entire dendritic and axonal fields of labeled neurons, including all types of inhibitory basket cell, in a Golgi-like manner. However, biocytin injections label only a small proportion of cells within the injection site, making this approach quite capricious. An additional drawback with the use of biocytin is that the dark deposit of the reaction end-product at the core of the injection site potentially obscures labeled cells at the inactivation site and labeled fine axon collaterals and terminal boutons at the recording sites. These two neuroanatomical tracing techniques should thus be regarded as complementary for use in combination with the GABA-inactivation paradigm.

Discussion

Contribution of lateral excitatory and inhibitory connections to cortical orientation tuning and direction selectivity

In discussing the implications of our inactivation studies for the generation of cortical orientation and direction selectivity, it is important to consider results from intracellular studies that have cast light on the ways in which excitatory and inhibitory influences interact to produce response selectivity (Creutzfeldt *et al.* 1974; Innocenti and Fiore 1974; Ferster 1986; Douglas *et al.* 1991; Sato *et al.* 1991; Berman *et al.* 1992; Volgushev *et al.* 1993; Nelson *et al.* 1994; Pei *et al.* 1994). Taken together, these studies can be considered to have demonstrated the following major points:

1. In most cases, the excitatory and inhibitory inputs to a cortical cell are tuned to the optimal orientation and direction of motion;

2. IPSPs can be evoked in response to stimuli presented at extreme nonoptimal orientations and nonpreferred directions of motion; and

3. The magnitude of inhibition during nonoptimal stimulation is insufficient to suppress strong excitation comparable to that evoked by optimal stimuli.

These findings led several authors to propose that intracortical inhibition contributes to orientation/direction selectivity primarily via the rapid suppression of the thalamic excitatory input during nonoptimal stimulation, and that remaining excitation is amplified via recurrent excitatory connections among cortical cells with similar orientation/ direction preferences (Douglas and Martin 1991; Douglas *et al.* 1995; Somers *et al.* 1995; Suarez *et al.* 1995; Vidyasagar *et al.* 1996). In this case, the excitatory load that needs to be opposed during nonoptimal stimulation would be small, because the thalamic input, which provides only 5–10% of the excitatory synapses in layer IV (Garey and Powell 1971; LeVay and Gilbert 1976; Peters and Payne 1993; Ahmed *et al.* 1994), is relatively weak and the intracortical excitatory input would be biased for orientation and direction. The substantial decreases in response to optimal orientations/directions, and the increases in response to nonoptimal stimuli that we observed in cells which almost certainly received a monosynaptic input from the thalamus (Figs. 1.6, 1.7, 1.9, and 1.11), together with the demonstration of both types of effect in the same cell (Fig. 1.6) provide experimental support for this hypothesis. Additionally, intracellular studies using stationary stimuli (Volgushev *et al.* 1993; Pei *et al.* 1994) have demonstrated that in most area 17 cells which are driven monosynaptically from the LGN, the excitatory input is initially weakly biased for orientation and that sharp orientation tuning develops as a result of inhibition at cross-orientations and facilitation around the optimum orientation. Therefore, the most plausible explanation for the GABA-induced disinhibitory effects on orientation/direction selectivity is that they were due to the loss of an inhibitory input from cells at the inactivation site to excitatory neurons in the vicinity of the recording sites with radically different orientation preferences (for cross-orientation inactivation) or opposite direction preferences (for iso-orientation inactivation) which, in turn, had recurrent excitatory connections with each other and a recorded cell. This would have allowed intracortical amplification of responses to optimal and nonoptimal stimuli, leading to a degradation of response selectivity in a recorded cell. We demonstrated the presence of direct inhibitory projections from inactivation sites to recording sites where disinhibitory effects on orientation/direction selectivity were elicited (Figs. 1.11, 1.12) and, for a number of reasons, the inactivation of these projections would have had a major impact on the response selectivity of recurrently connected excitatory neurons in the vicinity of a recorded cell. The cells supplying these projections (basket cells and dendrite-targeting cells) make synaptic contact primarily with spiny (excitatory) neurons (pyramidal and spiny stellate cells: DeFelipe and Fairen 1982; Somogyi *et al.* 1983; Kisvárday *et al.* 1985). Together, basket cells and dendrite-targeting cells provide a rich synaptic innervation of the somata and proximal dendritic shafts of spiny neurons (DeFelipe and Fairen 1982; Somogyi *et al.* 1983; Kisvárday *et al.* 1985; Tamás *et al.* 1997a). These are very effective locations for inhibiting the excitatory input to spiny cells that arrives on dendritic spines and distal dendritic shafts (LeVay 1973; Ahmed *et al.* 1994). Finally, single basket or dendrite-targeting cells elicit in spiny neurons fast IPSPs similar to those mediated by $GABA_A$-receptors (Tamás *et al.* 1997b), and blockade of $GABA_A$-receptors has deleterious effects on cortical orientation/direction selectivity (Sillito 1977, 1979; Tsumoto *et al.* 1979; Sillito *et al.* 1980).

If intracortical inhibition contributes to response selectivity primarily via the rapid suppression of thalamic excitation, this raises the question of how the selectivity of the inhibitory input is established. An orientation bias could be conferred on excitatory and inhibitory neurons via an oriented convergence of thalamocortical afferents (Hubel and Wiesel 1962; Chapman *et al.* 1991; Reid and Alonso 1995). An alternative possibility takes into account the orientation and direction biases shown by a substantial proportion of cells in the LGN (Vidyasagar and Urbas 1982; Jones and Sillito 1994; Thompson *et al.* 1994a,b). If these biases were present in the thalamic input to cortical inhibitory neurons, this would allow for rapid (disynaptic) inhibition that is already tuned for orientation and direction. Ferster *et al.* (1996) claimed that the thalamic input is sufficient to establish cortical orientation selectivity, because they found that inactivating intracortical interactions via cortical cooling left intact the orientation selectivity of postsynaptic potentials to moving sine-wave gratings in layer-IV simple cells of area 17. However, their results are not inconsistent with a contribution of intracortical circuitry to orientation selectivity. For sine-wave gratings close to or higher than the optimum for cortical cells, individual geniculate cells show orientation sensitivities not much lower than those of striate cells (Vidyasagar and Heide 1984; Thompson *et al.* 1994a). This would explain why in area 17 complex cells, local application of bicuculline has a much weaker effect on the orientation selectivity for gratings than for bar stimuli (Pfleger and Bonds 1995). Additionally there must be some doubt as to whether the cooling procedure employed by Ferster *et al.* (1996) was adequate to silence inhibitory neurons, for in no case did they observe a significant decrease in direction selectivity, a property which is readily disrupted by intracellular blockade of inhibition in single cells (Nelson *et al.* 1994).

What of the increases in response to optimal orientations/directions that were attributed to the loss of iso-orientation inhibition (Fig. 1.8C)? Intracortical amplification of responses to optimal stimuli via recurrent excitatory connections is presumably under the control of feedback inhibition, which prevents "runaway" excitation (Douglas and Martin 1991; Berman *et al.* 1992). The neurons providing the inhibitory input would have the same orientation/direction preference as the excitatory neurons that activate them, explaining why the inhibitory input to a cortical cell is tuned to the optimal orientation and direction of motion. Thus, increases in response to optimal stimuli during inactivation of iso-orientation sites probably reflected the release of this type of feedback inhibition.

Orientation and direction selectivity in area 18: Contribution of intrinsic connections and the projection from area 17

The results from our local inactivation studies have an important bearing on the long-standing issue of whether orientation and direction selectivity in area 18 is generated by intrinsic circuitry or derives from the associational input from area 17. Hubel and Wiesel (1962, 1965) regarded area 18 as a secondary area that derives its response selectivity from the dominant excitatory input from area 17. This hypothesis was challenged by the results of studies which showed that areas 17 and 18 contain a similar proportion of cells receiving a monosynaptic input from the thalamus (Singer *et al.* 1975; Tretter *et al.* 1975) and that orientation and direction selectivity in area 18 do not depend on the functional integrity of area 17 (Dreher and Cottee 1975; Sherk 1978). More recently, strong reciprocal connections have been demonstrated between areas 17 and 18 (Bullier *et al.* 1984; Symonds and Rosenquist 1984), suggesting that both areas operate in parallel on the same hierarchical level. Dreher *et al.* (1992) reported that removal of the predominant thalamic input to area 18 by selective pressure block of

Y-type optic nerve fibers produces only modest changes to the orientation/direction selectivity of cells in that area. They concluded that area 18 contains mechanisms responsible for the generation of orientation/direction selectivity which can be accessed either by the thalamic Y input or by the non-Y input, most of which is relayed via area 17. Our demonstration that the orientation tuning and directionality of cells in area 18 can be substantially modified via local inactivation of visuotopically corresponding sites in the same area provides the most direct evidence to date for a major role of intrinsic connections in the generation of orientation and direction selectivity in area 18. Our results, which have emphasized the importance of intracortical inhibition in the generation of both properties, seem at variance with those of Vidyasagar and Heide (1986), who reported that iontophoresis of bicuculline in the vicinity of cells recorded in area 18 had little influence overall on their orientation/direction selectivity. This apparent discrepancy reflects primarily Vidyasagar and Heide's use of grating stimuli (see above). Additionally, it is likely that intracortical inhibition has its major influence on the orientation/direction selectivity of cells that receive a monosynaptic input from the thalamus. Two-thirds of cells recorded by Vidyasagar and Heide (1986) were complex cells and most complex cells in area 18 are indirectly driven by thalamic afferents (Harvey 1980).

Conclusions

Hubel and Wiesel's pioneering and seminal studies initiated an extensive and highly successful program of research in laboratories throughout the world. Today, it is fair to say that their hypotheses concerning the generation of orientation and direction selectivity are almost certainly incorrect. It is highly unlikely that cortical orientation selectivity in area 17 derives solely from an oriented excitatory convergence of thalamocortical afferents, although this may well confer an orientation bias on cortical cells that is then sharpened via intracortical excitatory and inhibitory interactions. Cortical direction selectivity is largely independent of interactions between receptive field subregions, but it depends crucially on short-range, lateral excitatory and inhibitory interactions that can occur within a single subregion. Finally, orientation and direction selectivity in area 18 does not merely reflect that presence in the excitatory input from area 17, but is generated by intrinsic circuitry. The results from our local inactivation studies provide strong evidence for the involvement of three different intracortical processes in the generation of orientation and direction selectivity in cat areas 17 and 18:

1. Suppression of responses to nonoptimal orientations and directions as a result of cross-orientation inhibition and iso-orientation inhibition;

2. Amplification of responses to optimal stimuli via iso-orientation excitatory connections; and

3. Regulation of cortical amplification via iso-orientation inhibition.

Outlook

To date, we have used the GABA-inactivation technique to investigate the topographic and functional specificity of horizontal excitatory and inhibitory connections underlying orientation and direction selectivity for simple bar stimuli in cat areas 17 and 18. In principle, the technique may be applied in any cortical area which lies on the surface of the brain and in cases where the response property to be studied shows a modular organization such that cells with similar response characteristics occupy a sufficiently large cortical volume to allow them to be isolated and inactivated en masse by GABA-iontophoresis. The technique is of limited use in cases where the response property to be studied is randomly organized. Additionally, it may not always be appropriate for the study of intracortical connections underlying more complex response properties such as modulatory effects that can be elicited by stimuli falling outside a cell's classical receptive field. Responses to certain contextual stimuli may depend on the integration of input from large regions of cortex, and it may not be possible to inactivate a sufficiently large cortical area for effects on a recorded cell to be elicited. However, in cases where contextual effects originate from topographically restricted regions in the visual field, the GABA-inactivation technique potentially provides a powerful tool for investigating the underlying intracortical connections. Work in this direction has already begun (Crook et al. 2000), and it is to be expected that over the next few years the use of the GABA inactivation technique will provide important insights into the intracortical circuitry underlying a number of contextual effects at the single-cell level and ultimately contribute to our understanding of the mechanisms underlying complex visual perceptions.

References

Ahmed, B., Anderson, J. C., Douglas, R. J. et al. (1994) Polyneuronal innervation of spiny stellate neurons in cat visual cortex. Journal of Comparative Neurology, 341:39–49.

Albus, K. (1975) A quantitative study of the projection area of the central and the paracentral visual field in area 17 of the cat. II. The spatial organization of the orientation domain. Experimental Brain Research, 24:181–202.

Anderson, J. C., Douglas, R. J., Martin, K. A. C. et al. (1994) Synaptic output of physiologically identified spiny stellate neurons in cat visual cortex. Journal of Comparative Neurology, 341:16–24.

Baker, C. L. and Cynader, M. S. (1986) Spatial receptive-field properties of direction-selective neurons in cat striate cortex. Journal of Neurophysiology, 55:1136–52.

Berman, N. E. J., Wilkes, N. E. and Payne, B. R. (1987) Organisation of orientation and direction selectivity in areas 17 and 18 of cat cerebral cortex. Journal of Neurophysiology, 58:676–99.

Berman, N. J., Douglas, R. J. and Martin, K. A. C. (1992) GABA-mediated inhibition in the neural networks of visual cortex. Progress in Brain Research, 90:443–76.

Bishop, P. O., Coombs, J. S. and Henry, G. H. (1971) Responses to visual contours: spatiotemporal aspects of excitation in the receptive fields of simple striate neurons. Journal of Physiology (London), 219:625–57.

Bolz, J., Gilbert, C. D. and Wiesel, T. N. (1989) Pharmacological analysis of cortical circuitry. *Trends in Neuroscience*, 12:292–6.

Bonhoeffer, T. and Grinvald, A. (1993) The layout of iso-orientation domains in area 18 of cat visual cortex: optical imaging reveals a pinwheel-like organization. *Journal of Neuroscience*, 13:4157–80.

Bonhoeffer, T., Kim, D.-S., Malonek, D. *et al.* (1995) Optical imaging of the layout of functional domains in area 17 and across the area 17/18 border in cat visual cortex. *European Journal of Neuroscience*, 7:1973–88.

Bullier, J., Kennedy, H. and Salinger, W. (1984) Branching and laminar origin of projections between visual cortical areas in the cat. *Journal of Comparative Neurology*, 228:329–41.

Chapman, B., Zahs, K. R. and Stryker, M. P. (1991) Relation of cortical cell orientation selectivity to alignment of receptive fields of the geniculocortical afferents that arborize within a single orientation column in ferret visual cortex. *Journal of Neuroscience*, 11:1347–58.

Creutzfeldt, O. D., Kuhnt, U. and Benevento, L. A. (1974) An intracellular analysis of visual cortical neurones to moving stimuli: responses in a co-operative neuronal network. *Experimental Brain Research*, 21:251–74.

Crook, J. M. (1990) Directional tuning of cells in area 18 of feline visual cortex for visual noise, bar and spot stimuli: a comparison with area 17. *Experimental Brain Research*, 80:545–61.

Crook, J. M. (1991) Dissimilar orientation tuning for moving and stationary bar stimuli in cat visual cortex: association with velocity dependent directional tuning for single spot stimuli. *European Journal of Neuroscience Supplement*, 4:P51.

Crook, J. M. and Eysel, U. T. (1992) GABA-induced inactivation of functionally characterized sites in cat visual cortex (area 18): Effects on orientation tuning. *Journal of Neuroscience*, 12:1816–25.

Crook, J. M., Eysel, U. T. and Machemer, H. F. (1991) Influence of GABA-induced remote inactivation on the orientation tuning of cells in area 18 of feline visual cortex: a comparison with area 17. *Neuroscience*, 40:1–12.

Crook, J. M., Kisvárday, Z. F. and Eysel, U. T. (1996) GABA-induced inactivation of functionally characterized sites in cat visual cortex (area 18): Effects on direction selectivity. *Journal of Neurophysiology*, 75:2071–88.

Crook, J. M., Kisvárday, Z. F. and Eysel, U. T. (1997) GABA-induced inactivation of functionally characterized sites in cat striate cortex: Effects on orientation tuning and direction selectivity. *Visual Neuroscience*, 14:141–58.

Crook, J. M., Kisvárday, Z. F. and Eysel, U. T. (1998) Evidence for a contribution of lateral inhibitory connections to orientation tuning and direction selectivity in cat visual cortex: reversible inactivation of functionally characterized sites combined with neuroanatomical tracing techniques. *European Journal of Neuroscience*, 10:2056–75.

Crook, J. M., Engelmann, R. and Löwel, S. (2000) GABA-inactivation modulates context-dependent processing in cat primary visual cortex. *Society for Neuroscience Abstracts*, 26:P131.

Curtis, D. R. and Crawford, J. M. (1969) Central synaptic transmission: microelectrophoretic studies. *Annual Review of Pharmacology*, 9:209–40.

Curtis, D. R. and Johnston, G. A. R. (1974) Amino acid transmitters in the mammalian central nervous system. *Review of Physiology*, 69:98–188.

DeFelipe, J. and Fairen, A. (1982) A type of basket cell in superficial layers of the cat visual cortex. A Golgi-electron microscope study. *Brain Research*, 244:9–16.

Douglas, R. J. and Martin, K. A. C. (1991) A functional microcircuit for cat visual cortex. *Journal of Physiology (London)*, 440:735–69.

Douglas, R. J., Martin, K. A. C. and Whitteridge, D. (1991) An intracellular analysis of the visual response of neurones in cat visual cortex. *Journal of Physiology (London)*, 440:659–96.

Douglas, R. J., Koch, C., Mahowald, M., Martin, K. A. C. and Suarez, H. H. (1995) Recurrent excitation in neocortical circuits. *Science*, **269**:981–5.

Dreher, B. and Cottee, L. J. (1975) Visual receptive field properties of cells in area 18 of cat's cerebral cortex before and after lesions in area 17. *Journal of Neurophysiology*, **38**:735–50.

Dreher, B., Michalski, A., Cleland, B. G. *et al.* (1992) Effects of selective pressure block of Y-type optic nerve fibers on the receptive-field properties of neurons in area 18 of the visual cortex of the cat. *Visual Neuroscience*, **9**:65–78.

Emerson, R. C. and Gerstein, G. L. (1977) Simple striate neurons in the cat. II. Mechanisms underlying directional asymmetry and directional selectivity. *Journal of Neurophysiology*, **40**:136–55.

Emerson, R. C., Citron, M. C., Vaughn, W. J. *et al.* (1987) Nonlinear directionally selective subunits in complex cells of cat striate cortex. *Journal of Neurophysiology*, **58**:33–65.

Eysel, U. T. (1992) Lateral inhibitory interactions in areas 17 and 18 of the cat visual cortex. *Progress in Brain Research*, **90**:407–22.

Eysel, U. T., Wörgötter, F. and Pape, H. C. (1987) Local cortical lesions abolish lateral inhibition at direction selective cells in cat visual cortex. *Experimental Brain Research*, **68**:606–12.

Eysel, U. T., Muche, T. and Wörgötter, F. (1988) Lateral interactions at direction-selective striate neurones in the cat demonstrated by local cortical inactivation. *Journal of Physiology (London)*, **399**:657–75.

Eysel, U. T., Crook, J. M. and Machemer, H. F. (1990) GABA-induced remote inactivation reveals cross-orientation inhibition in the cat striate cortex. *Experimental Brain Research*, **80**:626–30.

Fairen, A., DeFelipe, J. and Regidor, J. (1984) Nonpyramidal cells: General account. In A. Peters and E. G. Jones (eds) *Cerebral Cortex, Vol. 1, Cellular Components of the Cerebral Cortex*, pp. 201–53. Plenum Press, New York.

Ferster, D. (1986) Orientation selectivity of synaptic potentials in neurons of cat primary visual cortex. *Journal of Neuroscience*, **6**:1284–301.

Ferster, D. (1987) Origin of orientation selective EPSPs in simple cells of cat visual cortex. *Journal of Neuroscience*, **7**:1780–91.

Ferster, D. and Lindström, S. (1983) An intracellular analysis of geniculo-cortical connectivity in area 17 of the cat. *Journal of Physiology (London)*, **342**:181–215.

Ferster, D., Chung, S. and Wheat, H. (1996) Orientation selectivity of thalamic input to simple cells of cat visual cortex. *Nature*, **380**:249–52.

Ganz, L. and Felder, R. (1984) Mechanism of directional selectivity in simple neurons of the cat's visual cortex analyzed with stationary flash sequences. *Journal of Neurophysiology*, **51**:294–323.

Garey, L. J. and Powell, T. P. S. (1971) An experimental study of the termination of the lateral geniculo-cortical pathway in the cat and monkey. *Proceedings of the Royal Society of London*, **B179**:41–63.

Goodwin, A. W., Henry, G. H. and Bishop, P. O. (1975) Direction selectivity of simple striate cells: properties and mechanism. *Journal of Neurophysiology*, **38**:1500–23.

Grieve, K. L. and Sillito, A. M. (1991) A re-appraisal of the role of layer VI of the visual cortex in the generation of cortical end inhibition. *Experimental Brain Research*, **87**:521–529.

Grieve, K. L. and Sillito, A. M. (1995) Non-length-tuned cells in layers II/III and IV of the visual cortex: the effect of blockade of layer VI on responses to stimuli of different lengths. *Experimental Brain Research*, **104**:12–20.

Hammond, P. (1978) Direction tuning of complex cells in area 17 of the feline visual cortex. *Journal of Physiology (London)*, **285**:479–91.

Harvey, A. R. (1980) The afferent connections and laminar distribution of cells in area 18 of the cat. *Journal of Physiology (London)*, **302**:483–505.

Hata, Y., Tsumoto, T., Sato, H. *et al.* (1988) Inhibition contributes to orientation selectivity in visual cortex of cat. *Nature*, **335**:815–17.

Heggelund, P. (1984) Direction asymmetry by moving stimuli and static receptive field plots for simple cells in cat striate cortex. *Vision Research*, **24**:13–16.

Hess R. and Murata, K. (1974) Effects of glutamate and GABA on specific responses properties of neurones in the visual cortex. *Experimental Brain Research*, **21**:285–97.

Hess R., Negishi K. and Creutzfeldt O. D. (1975) The horizontal spread of intracortical inhibition in the visual cortex. *Experimental Brain Research*, **22**:415–9.

Hubel, D. H. and Wiesel, T. N. (1962) Receptive fields, binocular interaction and functional architecture in the cat's visual cortex. *Journal of Physiology (London)*, **160**:106–54.

Hubel, D. H. and Wiesel, T. N. (1965) Receptive fields and functional architecture in two nonstriate visual areas (18 and 19) of the cat. *Journal of Neurophysiology*, **28**:229–89.

Hupé, J. M., Chouvet, G. and Bullier, J. (1999) Spatial and temporal parameters of cortical inactivation by GABA. *Journal of Neuroscience Methods*, **86**:129–43.

Innocenti, G. M. and Fiore, L. (1974) Post-synaptic inhibitory components of the responses to moving stimuli in area 17. *Brain Research*, **80**:122–6.

Johnston, G. A. R., Krogsgaard-Larsen, P., Stephanson, A. L. *et al.* (1976a) Inhibition of the uptake of GABA and related amino acids in rat brain slices by the optical isomers of nipecotic acid. *Journal of Neurochemistry*, **26**:1029–32.

Johnston, G. A. R., Stephanson, A. L. and Twitchin, B. (1976b) Uptake and release of nipecotic acid by rat brain slices. *Journal of Neurochemistry*, **26**:83–7.

Jones, H. E. and Sillito, A. M. (1994) Directional asymmetries in the length-response profiles of cells in the feline dorsal lateral geniculate nucleus. *Journal of Physiology (London)*, **479**:475–86.

Kisvárday, Z. F. and Eysel, U. T. (1993) Functional and structural topography of horizontal inhibitory connections in cat visual cortex. *European Journal of Neuroscience*, **5**:1558–72.

Kisvárday, Z. F., Kim, D.-S., Eysel, U. T. *et al.* (1994) Relationship between lateral inhibitory connections and the topography of the orientation map in cat visual cortex. *European Journal of Neuroscience*, **6**:1619–32.

Kisvárday, Z. F., Martin, K. A. C., Whitteridge, D. *et al.* (1985) Synaptic connections of intracellularly filled clutch cells: a type of small basket cell in the visual cortex. *Journal of Comparative Neurology*, **241**:111–37.

Kisvárday, Z. F., Martin, K. A. C., Freund, T. F. *et al.* (1986) Synaptic targets of HRP-filled layer III pyramidal cells in the cat striate cortex. *Experimental Brain Research*, **64**:541–52.

Kisvárday, Z. F., Martin, K. A. C., Friedlander, M. J. *et al.* (1987) Evidence for interlaminar inhibitory circuits in the striate cortex of the cat. *Journal of Comparative Neurology*, **260**:1–19.

Kisvárday, Z. F., Crook, J. M., Buzás, P. and Eysel, U. T. (2000) Combined physiological-anatomical approaches to study lateral inhibition. *Journal of Neuroscience Methods*, **103**:91–106.

Kritzer, M. F., Cowey, A. and Somogyi, P. (1992) Patterns of inter- and intralaminar GABAergic connections distinguish striate (V1) and extrastriate (V2, V4) visual cortices and their functionally specialized subdivisions in the rhesus monkey. *Journal of Neuroscience*, **12**:4545–64.

LeVay, S. (1973) Synaptic patterns in the visual cortex of the cat and monkey. Electron microscopy of Golgi preparations. *Journal of Comparative Neurology*, **150**:53–86.

LeVay, S. and Gilbert, C. D. (1976) Laminar patterns of geniculocortical projection in the cat. *Brain Research*, **113**:1–19.

Martin, K. A. C. and Whitteridge, D. (1984) Form, function and intracortical projections of spiny neurones in the striate visual cortex of the cat. *Journal of Physiology (London)*, **353**:463–504.

Martin, K. A. C., Somogyi, P. and Whitteridge, D. (1983) Physiological and morphological properties of identified basket cells in the cat's visual cortex. *Experimental Brain Research*, **50**:193–200.

Matsubara, J. A., Nance, D. M. and Cynader, M. (1987) Laminar distribution of GABA-immunoreactive neurons and processes in area 18 of the cat. *Brain Research Bulletin*, **18**:121–6.

McLean, J., Raab, S. and Palmer, L. A. (1994) Contribution of linear mechanisms to the specification of local motion by simple cells in areas 17 and 18. *Visual Neuroscience*, **11**:271–4.

Morrone, M. C., Burr, D. C. and Maffei, L. (1982) Functional implications of cross-orientation inhibition of cortical visual cells. I. Neurophysiological evidence. *Proceedings of the Royal Society of London*, **B216**:335–54.

Movshon, J. A., Thompson, I. D. and Tolhurst, D. J. (1978) Receptive field organisation of complex cells in the cat's striate cortex. *Journal of Physiology (London)*, **283**:79–99.

Naegele, J. R. and Katz, L. C. (1990) Cell surface molecules containing N-acetylgalactosamine are associated with basket cells and neurogliaform cells in cat visual cortex. *Journal of Neuroscience*, **10**:540–57.

Nelson, S., Toth, L., Sheth, B. and Sur, M. (1994) Orientation selectivity of cortical neurons during intracellular blockade of inhibition. *Science*, **265**:774–7.

Orban, G. A., Kennedy, H. and Maes, H. (1981) Response to movement of neurons in areas 17 and 18 of the cat: directional selectivity. *Journal of Neurophysiology*, **45**:1059–73.

Pei, X., Vidyasagar, T. R., Volgushev, M. *et al.* (1994) Receptive field analysis and orientation selectivity of postsynaptic potentials of simple cells in cat visual cortex. *Journal of Neuroscience*, **14**:7130–40.

Peterhans, E., Bishop, P. O. and Camarda, R .M. (1985) Direction selectivity of simple cells in cat striate cortex to moving light bars. I. Relation to stationary flashing bar and moving edge responses. *Experimental Brain Research*, **57**:512–22.

Peters, A. and Payne, B. R. (1993) Numerical relationships between geniculocortical afferents and pyramidal cell modules in cat primary visual cortex. *Cerebral Cortex*, **3**:69–78.

Pfleger, B. and Bonds, A. B. (1995) Dynamic differentiation of GABA$_A$-sensitive influences on orientation selectivity of complex cells in the cat striate cortex. *Experimental Brain Research*, **104**:81–8.

Reid, R. C. and Alonso, J. M. (1995) Specificity of monosynaptic connections from thalamus to visual cortex. *Nature*, **378**:281–4.

Reid, R. C., Soodak, R. E. and Shapley, R. M. (1991) Directional selectivity and spatiotemporal structure of receptive fields of simple cells in cat striate cortex. *Journal of Neurophysiology*, **66**:505–29.

Roerig, B. and Kao, J. P. Y. (1999) Organization of intracortical circuits in relation to direction preference maps in ferret visual cortex. *Journal of Neuroscience*, **19**:1–5.

Sato, H., Daw, N. W. and Fox, K. (1991) An intracellular recording study of stimulus specific response properties in cat area 17. *Brain Research*, **544**:156–61.

Sherk, H. (1978) Area 18 cell responses in the cat during reversible inactivation of area 17. *Journal of Neurophysiology*, **41**:204–15.

Shumuel, A. and Grinvald, A. (1996) Functional organization for direction of motion and its relationship to orientation maps in cat area 18. *Journal of Neuroscience*, **16**:6945–64.

Sillito, A. M. (1975) The effectiveness of bicuculline as an antagonist of GABA and visually evoked inhibition in the cat's striate cortex. *Journal of Physiology (London)*, **250**:287–304.

Sillito, A. M. (1977) Inhibitory processes underlying the directional specificity of simple, complex and hypercomplex cells in the cat's visual cortex. *Journal of Physiology (London)*, **271**:699–720.

Sillito, A. M. (1979) Inhibitory mechanisms influencing complex cell orientation selectivity and their modification at high resting discharge levels. *Journal of Physiology (London)*, **289**:33–53.

Sillito, A. M., Kemp, J. A., Milson, J. A. *et al.* (1980) A re-evaluation of the mechanisms underlying simple cell orientation selectivity. *Brain Research*, **19**:517–20.

Singer, W., Tretter, F. and Cynader, M. (1975) Organization of cat striate cortex: a correlation of receptive-field properties with afferent and efferent connections. *Journal of Neurophysiology*, **38**:1080–98.

Somers, D. C., Nelson, S. B. and Sur, M. (1995) An emergent model of orientation selectivity in cat visual cortical simple cells. *Journal of Neuroscience*, **15**:5448–65.

Somogyi, P. and Soltész, I. (1986) Immunogold demonstration of GABA in synaptic terminals of intracellularly recorded, horseradish peroxidase-filled basket cells and clutch cells in the cat's visual cortex. *Neuroscience*, **19**:1051–65.

Somogyi, P., Kisvárday, Z. F., Martin, K. A. C. *et al.* (1983) Synaptic connections of morphologically identified and physiologically characterized large basket cells in the striate cortex of cat. *Neuroscience*, **10**:261–94.

Suarez, H., Koch, C. and Douglas, R. (1995) Modeling direction selectivity of simple cells in striate visual cortex within the framework of the canonical microcircuit. *Journal of Neuroscience*, **15**:6700–19.

Swindale, N. V., Matsubara, J. A. and Cynader, M. S. (1987) Surface organization of orientation and direction selectivity in cat area 18. *Journal of Neuroscience*, **7**:1414–27.

Symonds, L. L. and Rosenquist, A. C. (1984) Corticocortical connections among visual areas in the cat. *Journal of Comparative Neurology*, **229**:1–38.

Tamás, G., Buhl, E. H. and Somogyi, P. (1997a) Fast IPSPs elicited via multiple synaptic release sites by different types of GABAergic neurone in the cat visual cortex. *Journal of Physiology (London)*, **500**:715–38.

Tamás, G., Buhl, E. H. and Somogyi, P. (1997b) Massive autaptic self-innervation of GABAergic neurons in cat visual cortex. *Journal of Neuroscience*, **17**:6352–64.

Thompson, K. G., Leventhal, A. G., Zhou, Y. *et al.* (1994a) Stimulus dependence of orientation and direction sensitivity of cat LGNd relay cells without cortical inputs: A comparison with area 17 cells. *Visual Neuroscience*, **11**:939–51.

Thompson, K. G., Zhou, Y. and Leventhal, A. G. (1994b) Direction-sensitive X and Y cells within the A laminae of the cat's LGNd. *Visual Neuroscience*, **11**:927–38.

Tolhurst, D. J. and Dean, A. F. (1991) Evaluation of a linear model of directional selectivity in simple cells of the cat's striate cortex. *Visual Neuroscience*, **6**:421–8.

Tretter, F., Cynader, M. and Singer, W. (1975) Cat parastriate cortex: a primary or secondary visual area? *Journal of Neurophysiology*, **38**:1099–1113.

Ts'o, D. Y., Gilbert, C. D. and Wiesel, T. N. (1986) Relationships between horizontal interactions and functional architecture in cat striate cortex as revealed by cross-correlation analysis. *Journal of Neuroscience*, **6**:1160–70.

Tsumoto, T., Eckart, W. and Creutzfeldt, O. D. (1979) Modification of orientation sensitivity of cat visual cortex neurones by removal of GABA-mediated inhibition. *Experimental Brain Research*, **34**:351–63.

Vidyasagar, T. R. and Heide, W. (1984) Geniculate biases seen with moving sine wave gratings: implications for a model of simple cell afferent connectivity. *Experimental Brain Research*, **57**:196–200.

Vidyasagar, T. R. and Heide, W. (1986) The role of GABAergic inhibition in the response properties of neurones in cat visual area 18. *Neuroscience*, **17**:49–55.

Vidyasagar, T. R. and Urbas, J. V. (1982) Orientation sensitivity of cat LGN neurones with and without inputs from visual cortical areas 17 and 18. *Experimental Brain Research*, **46**:157–69.

Vidyasagar, T. R., Pei, X. and Volgushev, M. (1996) Multiple mechanisms underlying the orientation selectivity of visual cortical neurones. *Trends in Neuroscience*, **19**:272–7.

Volgushev, M., Pei, X., Vidyasagar, T. R. and Creutzfeldt, O. D. (1993) Excitation and inhibition in orientation selectivity of cat visual cortex neurons revealed by whole-cell recordings *in vivo*. *Visual Neuroscience*, **10:**1151–5.

Wörgötter, F. and Eysel, U. T. (1991) Topographical aspects of intracortical excitation and inhibition contributing to orientation specificity in area 17 of the cat visual cortex. *European Journal of Neuroscience*, **3:**1232–44.

Chapter 2

Contributions of Ascending Thalamic and Local Intracortical Connections to Visual Cortical Function

Valentin Dragoi, Casto Rivadulla, Mriganka Sur

The emergent properties of visual cortical networks arise from specific features of the cortical circuitry. A mechanistic description of how response properties arise in networks of cortical neurons is central to understanding information processing by the visual cortex. Primary visual cortical (V1) neurons receive their major input through thalamocortical or feedforward excitatory connections, with a role for local recurrent networks and of long-range connections in modulating neuronal responses in different layers of the cortex. We have examined mechanisms underlying three types of emergent responses that are created in V1 of cats—orientation selectivity, direction selectivity and spatial phase invariance—using selective blockade of neurotransmitter systems and selective inactivation of neurons by stimulus-induced adaptation.

Orientation selectivity

Orientation selectivity of neurons in the primary visual cortex (V1) is one of the most thoroughly investigated receptive field properties in the neocortex, and yet its underlying neural mechanisms are still debated (Sompolinsky and Shapley 1997; Ferster and Miller 2000). One prominent model of orientation selectivity is the "feedforward model," which proposes that a cortical simple cell receives input from a row of neurons in the lateral geniculate nucleus (LGN) whose receptive fields are aligned along the axis of orientation of the cortical receptive field (Hubel and Wiesel 1962). However, although it is true that weakly biased feedforward inputs can be sharpened by using high firing thresholds (the "iceberg" effect, Creutzfeldt *et al.* 1974a), the feedforward model incorrectly predicts broadening of orientation tuning with increasing stimulus contrast (Sclar and Freeman 1982; Wehmeier *et al.* 1989). Pure feedforward models also cannot account for the loss of orientation selectivity under iontophoresis of bicculine, a $GABA_A$ antagonist, which reduces inhibition over a localized population of cortical neurons (Sillito 1975; Tsumoto *et al.* 1979; Sillito *et al.* 1980). For this reason, it has been proposed that mechanisms utilizing shunting ("divisive") inhibition (e.g. Koch and Poggio 1985; Carandini and Heeger 1994), or hyperpolarizing ("subtractive") inhibition at nonpreferred orientations (e.g. Wehmeier *et al.* 1989; Wörgötter and Koch 1991), can sharpen tuning in cells which have mildly oriented thalamocortical inputs; such models can also produce contrast-invariant orientation tuning, and can account for bicuculline-induced tuning loss. However, these inhibitory models are inconsistent with other experimental data. Although shunting inhibition has recently been rediscovered in cortex (Borg-Graham *et al.* 1998; Hirsch *et al.* 1998), it occurs only very transiently and appears insufficient to account for orientation selectivity (Douglas *et al.* 1988; Berman *et al.* 1991; Dehay *et al.* 1991; Ferster and Jagadeesh 1992; Anderson *et al.* 2000).

Moreover, results from our laboratory (Nelson *et al.* 1994) conflict with all orientation models that rely on inhibitory mechanisms to create orientation selectivity. In one set of experiments, intracellular blockade of inhibition in single cells of cat V1 was used to show that the sharpness of orientation tuning of blocked cells remains intact. In these experiments, whole-cell pipettes were used to deliver CsF-DIDS (cesium fluoride—4,4'-diisothiocyanatostilbene-2,2'-disulfonic acid) solution intracellularly to silence inhibitory voltage conductances (Cl−, K+). A mild, fixed hyperpolarizing current was injected to compensate for the increase in spontaneous firing rate. These results appear to conflict with reports that orientation tuning can be abolished by bicuculline-induced extracellular inhibitory blockade (Sillito *et al.* 1980; Nelson 1991). The critical difference between this type of inhibitory blockade and previous reports (e.g., Sillito *et al.* 1980) is the number of cells that lose inhibitory inputs. Disruption of orientation selectivity requires long bicuculline ejection times (Sillito *et al.* 1980; Nelson 1991), suggesting that the drug effects spread across a local population of neurons. In contrast, intracellular blockade (Nelson *et al.* 1994) affects only the recorded neuron. Thus, we infer that inhibition cannot play a major role in the generation of orientation selectivity.

Computer simulations in our laboratory have complemented the physiologic experiments, demonstrating that local, recurrent, cortical excitation can generate sharp, contrast-invariant orientation tuning in circuits that have strong iso-orientation inhibition and weakly oriented thalamocortical excitation (Somers *et al.* 1995). This model primarily addresses the circuitry within a single cortical "hypercolumn" and relies on only three assumptions. First, converging LGN inputs must provide some orientation bias at the columnar population level. Consistent with previous studies (Creutzfeldt *et al.* 1974b; Watkins and Berkley 1974; Jones and Palmer 1987; Chapman *et al.* 1991), this bias may be weak and distributed across a population with many cells that receive unoriented input. The second assumption of the model, that local (<1 mm horizontal distance) intracortical inhibitory connections must arise from cells with an effective broader distribution of orientation preferences than do intracortical excitatory connections, differs from prior inhibitory models in that it is consistent with experimental evidence for strong iso-orientation inhibition (Ferster 1986; Douglas *et al.* 1991a; Anderson *et al.* 2000). Narrowly tuned iso-orientation excitation and more broadly tuned iso-orientation inhibition can be realized by a simple difference-of-gaussian-like structure in the orientation domain. This idea is supported by cross-correlation data (Michalski *et al.* 1983; Hata *et al.* 1988) and is consistent with a key hypothesis of many models of orientation selectivity development (e.g. Rojer and Schwartz 1990; Miller 1992; Swindale 1992). However, more recent simulations (Somers *et al.* 2001) show that inhibitory inputs can in fact be much narrower than originally thought (Somers *et al.* 1995); inhibitory inputs need only be slightly broader than excitatory cortical inputs. This seems consistent with recent experimental reports (Anderson *et al.* 2000). The final assumption is that cortical inhibition must approximately balance cortical excitation. Too much inhibition produced low response rates, and too little inhibition permitted nonselective amplification of all stimulus responses. However, many sets of parameters satisfied the "balance" requirement. This hypothesis is consistent with reports that EPSP and IPSP strengths roughly covary across orientations (Ferster 1986; Douglas *et al.* 1991; see Pei *et al.* 1994 for a differing view).

Integration of local inputs

Modulation of excitation and inhibition level using focal iontophoresis

Research in our laboratory (Toth *et al.* 1997) has investigated the role of local excitation and inhibition in modulating visual cortical responses. Using a combination of intrinsic signal imaging, single-unit recording, and focal iontophoresis of the $GABA_A$ antagonist bicuculline, as well as focal iontophoresis of GABA, Toth and colleagues have demonstrated that local connections provide strong excitatory inputs that are integrated nonlinearly by postsynaptic neurons. A micropipette was introduced in layer II/III of cat area 18, and intrinsic signal maps were recorded for several millimeters around the pipette (Fig. 2.1A). A critical issue in optical imaging is to avoid artifacts due to heart beat and respiratory movement. The traditional approach in intrinsic imaging experiments is to use a chamber filled with mineral oil and sealed with a glass cover in order to minimize brain movement. However, since perfect sealing cannot be achieved as iontophoresis requires the insertion of a glass micropipette, we had to use an additional method to reduce brain movement. We thus performed a bilateral pneumotorax to eliminate respiratory movements (occasionally, we had to drain the CSF by penetrating foramen magnum). Subsequently, warm agarose (1.5% in distilled water) was poured on the exposed cortex to avoid desiccation, and, finally, we added mineral oil on top of the agarose cushion. The pipette was moved with a mechanical microdrive until the desired position and depth were reached.

As Fig. 2.1B indicates, focal disinhibition causes the region around the pipette to become dominated by nearby orientations. Within this region, orientation singularities (or pinwheel centers) disappear and the normal structure of orientation domains is profoundly altered. Figure 2.1D shows that during bicuculline iontophoresis neurons of all orientations within the iontophoresis region shift toward the disinhibited

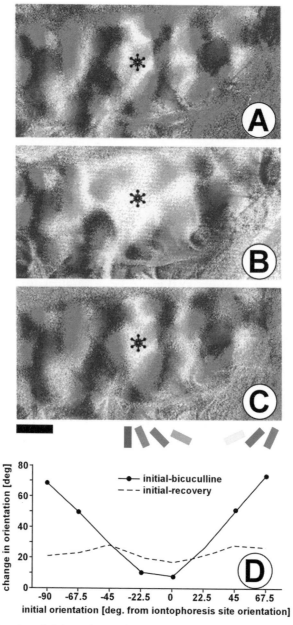

Fig. 2.1 (and color plate 1) Orientation angle maps in cat V2 and the effect of disinhibition with focal iontophoresis of bicuculline. Maps shown are: (A) prior to focal disinhibition, (B) during focal disinhibition and (C) after recovery. The map in (A) is obtained with the pipette in position (asterisk) and retention current applied. During bicuculline iontophoresis (B), the normal orientation map in the region around the pipette is altered, such that the initial orientation at the pipette location is drastically overrepresented. Recovery of the normal map upon cessation of iontophoresis is shown in (C). Scale bar: 1 mm. To produce the vector angle

orientation, and they revert toward control levels after cessation of iontophoresis (Fig. 2.1C). If bicuculline is indeed acting focally and specifically to disinhibit a cortical column, one prediction is that increasing the inhibition to a column, for example by iontophoresis of the inhibitory transmitter GABA, would lead to a reduction of the area preferring the inhibited orientation over a local region; this is found to be the case (Toth *et al.* 1997). These experiments suggest that local connections distribute information to columns of widely varying orientation preference, and that these connections are predominantly excitatory, since an increase in their activity leads to an overrepresentation of the tuning orientation at the iontophoresis location and a decrease to an underrepresentation of the iontophoresis orientation. These results, i.e., altering the balance of excitation and inhibition in cortical columns to affect the orientation tuning of adjacent columns, are well explained by local networks influencing orientation tuning (e.g. Somers *et al.* 1995).

Perturbation of orientation-specific responses induced by adaptation

In the previous section we have shown that changing the efficacy of local inputs by focal iontophoresis affects the orientation tuning of visual cortical neurons. To verify these results, we have subsequently used pattern adaptation (Movshon and Lennie 1979; Saul and Cynader 1989; Carandini *et al.* 1998) to examine how changes in the strength of local intracortical inputs affect orientation selectivity. It is known that adapting neurons to a potent stimulus can reduce responses to subsequent similar stimuli. In a recent study (Dragoi *et al.* 2000), we examined how far the entire profile of the orientation tuning curve changes after short and long-term adaptation to a particular stimulus orientation.

Figure 2.2A shows how the preferred orientation of a representative cell changes after 2 minutes of exposure to one orientation located on one flank of the cell's tuning curve, followed by a period of recovery, subsequent adaptation to a different orientation located on the opposite flank with respect to the preferred orientation, and a final

---

Fig. 2.1 (continued)
map, imaging data was treated vectorially by assigning each pixel of the 16 single-condition maps a magnitude representing the strength of the signal, and an angle representing 2× the orientation of the inducing stimulus. The 16 vectors at each pixel were added, and the resulting vector angle color coded according to the scheme at the bottom of the figure. (D) shows that the shift in orientation occurs in columns spanning all possible initial orientations. (The x-axis represents the difference in vector angles taken pixel-by-pixel in the original images, and binned for clarity.) The solid curve shows the orientation shift within the affected region [map (B) minus map (A)], and dashed line shows the recovery of the same region [map (C) minus map (A)]. The analyzed region includes 30,793 pixels (18% of image). A strong shift to the bicuculline orientation is seen across all initial values of orientation, nearby orientations changing relatively little, and orthogonal orientations changing nearly 90°, suggesting that areas of all orientation preference receive input from the manipulated orientation column.

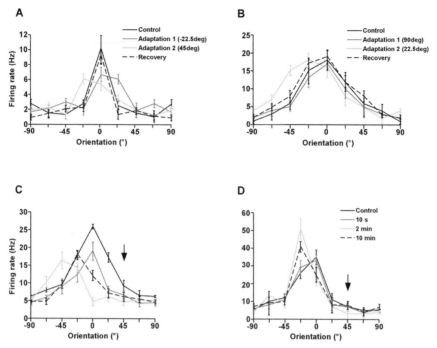

Fig. 2.2 Plasticity of orientation tuning in cat V1 cells. (A, B) Orientation tuning curves of two representative cells that were successively adapted to two different orientations. Each graph represents orientation tuning during four conditions: control (solid black), adaptation to the first orientation (medium grey), adaptation to the second orientation (light grey), and recovery (dashed black). In our tuning curve display convention, the control optimal orientation is represented as 0°, and all subsequent tuning curves (during adaptation and recovery) are represented relative to the control condition. (C, D) Tuning curves of cells that show adaptation-induced response suppression on the near flank and response facilitation on the far flank. Each cell was serially exposed to different adaptation periods: 10 s, 2 mins, and 10 mins. Tuning curves were calculated in each of the four conditions: control, 10 s adaptation, 2 min adaptation, and 10 min adaptation. The adapting orientation is marked by the arrow.

period of recovery. When the difference between the cell's preferred orientation and that of the adapting stimulus ($\Delta\theta$) is $-22.5°$, there is a shift in preferred orientation to the right, away from the adapting stimulus. In contrast, when the adapting stimulus is presented on the right flank of the tuning curve ($\Delta\theta=45°$), the preferred orientation shifts to the left and then returns to the original value after 10 mins of recovery. However, adaptation to stimuli orthogonal to the cell's preferred orientation ($\Delta\theta$ between approximately 60° and 90°) does not induce any change in preferred orientation. Figure 2.2B illustrates the behavior of one representative cell that exhibits a stimulus-dependent shift after 2 mins of adaptation to a 22.5° stimulus, but the orientation preference remains unchanged when $\Delta\theta$ is 90°.

Interestingly, the shape of the orientation tuning curve undergoes pronounced reversible changes when neurons are serially exposed to different adaptation periods. Figures 2.2C and 2.2D show one cell that exhibits significant shifts in orientation following adaptation for 10 s, 2 mins, and 10 mins to a stimulus oriented 45° away from the cell's peak orientation. Both the response reduction on the near flank (toward the adapting orientation) and facilitation on the far flank of the tuning curve (away from the adapting orientation) build up gradually in time: increasing the adaptation time from 10 s to 10 mins shows a progressive depression of responses on the near flank and a progressive facilitation of responses on the far flank. For the largest adaptation period (10 mins) we found that many cells increase their response at the new preferred orientation by a factor of 2 or more (Fig. 2.2D).

We argue that this type of orientation plasticity involves an active process of network synaptic changes that lead to a new preferred orientation rather than simply a passive reduction of orientation selective responses around the adapting orientation. The shifts in orientation preference by depression of responses on the near flank and facilitation of responses on the far flank imply a network mechanism that reorganizes responses across a broad range of orientations, possibly through changes in the gain of local cortical circuits that mediate recurrent excitation and inhibition (Douglas *et al.* 1995; Somers *et al.* 1995, 2001) and include disinhibitory mechanisms (Dragoi and Sur 2000). For example, if the local cortical circuit includes broadly tuned orientation inhibition, hyperpolarization of neurons representing the adapting orientation could cause disinhibition of responses on the far flank of the tuning curve in the recorded neuron, an effect that could be further amplified via local excitatory interactions.

Altering the efficacy of cortical networks at specific map locations

We subsequently investigated the relationship between orientation plasticity and a neuron's location in the orientation preference map in V1 of adult cats (Dragoi *et al.* 2001). Optical imaging of intrinsic signals was used to obtain the orientation map in a patch of V1 (Fig. 2.3A). We used the vascular pattern of the cortical surface in relation to the orientation map (Fig. 2.3B) to guide electrode penetrations aimed at iso-orientation domains or pinwheel centers. Since pinwheel centers are locations where the preferred orientation of neurons changes rapidly, we determined an orientation gradient map as the two-dimensional spatial derivative at each pixel to identify these foci. The gradient map (Fig. 2.3C) shows that pinwheel centers are included in regions with the highest rate of orientation change, whereas the gradient is low in iso-orientation domains. Figure 2.3D–F illustrates the relationship between location within the orientation map and adaptation-induced plasticity of orientation tuning for representative neurons. Adaptation to a given orientation induces a repulsive shift in orientation preference away from the adapting stimulus. Interestingly, the higher the value of the orientation gradient at the recording site, the larger is the magnitude of the shift in preferred orientation.

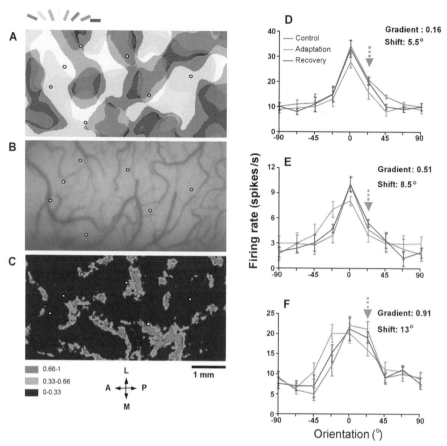

Fig. 2.3 (and color plate 2) Adaptation-induced plasticity of orientation tuning and the orientation architecture of V1. (A) Composite orientation map obtained by intrinsic signal imaging. The angle of preferred orientation of each pixel is shown in pseudo-color according to the key at top. The map was smoothed using a low-pass filter (5×5 pixels) The circles show the location of 7 representative neurons (of 40 that were recorded in this animal) to illustrate the range of orientation and gradient distributions. (B) Vascular pattern of the cortical surface for the region shown in (A) (C) Orientation gradient map, in which gradient was discretized as follows: red (range: 0.66–1), green (range: 0.33–0.66), and blue (range: <0.33). (D–F) Orientation tuning curves of three representative cells during control, adaptation, and recovery conditions. In our tuning curve display convention, the control optimal orientation is represented as 0°, and all subsequent tuning curves (during adaptation and recovery) are represented relative to the control condition. The adapting orientation is marked by the green arrow. Each point in panels (D), (E), and (F) represents mean value +/–S.E.M.

These results could be explained by the nature of inputs to neurons at different locations in the orientation map: Neurons in iso-orientation domains would be only weakly activated by intracortical inputs with orientations that differ from the domain's preferred orientation, while neurons located at or near pinwheel centers would receive strong local inputs from neurons of all orientations (Dragoi et al. 2001). Therefore, altering the efficacy of these inputs through adaptation is likely to induce more profound changes in the orientation preference of neurons at or near pinwheel centers (Fig. 2.3). This suggests that adaptation-induced orientation plasticity in V1 is an emergent property of a local cortical network embedded in a non-uniform orientation map. Indeed, these data indicate the existence of a map of orientation plasticity, closely related to the map of orientation preference, in which pinwheel centers constitute foci of maximal plasticity and the orientation gradient is a measure of the degree of plasticity across V1.

Generation of direction selectivity in superficial layers

Another major emergent response property of V1 neurons is their selectivity for direction of motion. Despite over 30 years of research on the genesis of direction selectivity in V1, the mechanism by which direction selectivity arises in different cortical layers is still imperfectly understood. Most theories rely either on inhibitory mechanisms acting at the nonpreferred direction (Barlow and Levick 1965; Goodwin and Henry 1975; Sillito 1975, 1977; Tsumoto et al. 1979; Bishop et al. 1980; Ganz and Felder 1984; Nelson et al. 1994; Sato et al. 1995; Crook et al. 1997, 1998), or on recurrent excitation as a mechanism to increase the responses in the preferred direction in a nonlinear fashion (Douglas et al. 1995; Suarez et al. 1995). Studies on direction selectivity in layer 4 simple cells (Reid et al. 1987, 1991; McLean and Palmer 1989; Jagadeesh et al. 1993, 1997; Livingstone 1998; Murthy et al. 1998) have shown that the receptive fields of these cells have an asymmetric time course of the evoked response, and that a linear summation of these asymmetries could allow us to predict direction preference. However, this procedure overestimates the response in the nonpreferred direction. Most of these considerations apply to the situation in superficial layers. Information about direction selectivity in other cortical layers is limited. An important difference between layer 4 and superficial layers is the presence of NMDA receptors in layer 2/3 (Fox et al. 1989, 1990) and the particular properties of these receptors provide new insights into their role in generating direction selectivity.

We have used pharmacological blockade of AMPA and NMDA receptors (Rivadulla et al. 2001), and the blockade of inhibition to assign specific roles to these receptors in the generation of direction selectivity in the superficial layers. This section presents results obtained in cells recorded extracellularly in V1 of anesthetized cats using multi-barrel pipettes to eject blockers into cortex and to record responses (Rivadulla et al. 2001). As expected from their different properties, our experiments show that AMPA and NMDA receptors play different and specific roles in direction selectivity.

Figures 2.4A and 2.4B show the effect of blocking AMPA and NMDA receptors in two visual cortical cells. Five or seven barrel pipettes were hand-made in our laboratory from individual glass capillaries. We used barrels of 1.5 mm outer diameter (OD) and 0.75 mm inner diameter (ID) with inner filament (note that slight changes in the OD/ID ratio provokes considerable changes in the final properties of the pipette that

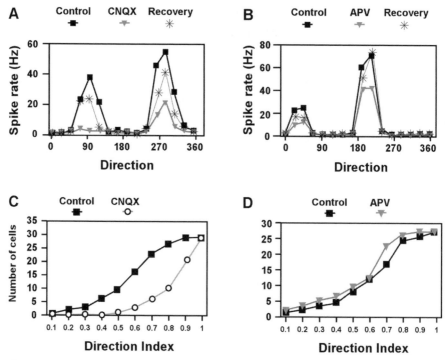

Fig. 2.4 CNQX and APV have different effects on direction selective visual responses of layer 2/3 cells in cat V1. (A) Direction tuning curves of a complex cell in the control condition, during CNQX iontophoresis, and after recovery. (B) Direction tuning curves from another complex cell in the control condition, during APV iontophoresis, and after recovery. (C, D) Effect of CNQX and APV on the direction index of layer 2/3 cells. (C) Cumulative histogram showing the effect of CNQX (n=30 cells) (D) Cumulative histogram showing the effect of APV (n=27 cells) The x-axis represents the direction index (DI). The y-axis represents the number of cells in each bin.

affect the quality of both recording and ejection). The barrels were attached using heat shrink cable and twisted around by hand approximately 270° using a burner (pipettes were pulled with a vertical puller). In order to avoid the mixing of drugs during the filling process and to eliminate possible artifacts during recording, we ensured that the top of each barrel was slightly separated from all others. The barrel tip was broken under the microscope to achieve the desired diameter (3–8 M, corresponding to a resistance around 8–12 MΩ). One of the barrels was used for recording, and thus filled with a solution of NaCl 3 M, whereas the others were filled with a combination of D-2-amino-5-phosphonovaleric acid (APV; 50 mM, pH 8), a selective NMDA receptor antagonist, 6-cyano-7-nitroquinoxaline-2,3-dione (CNQX; 1 mM, pH 8), a selective AMPA receptor antagonist and bicuculline methiodide (20 mM, pH 4), a potent and selective antagonist of the GABA$_A$ receptor. Using this technique, we were able to eject together or individually all the drugs inside the pipette (ejection currents were in the range of 10–40 nA). Unlike using pressure ejection, our method affects only a small area of tissue (less than 150 µm radius), and ensures stability of drug concentration during a continuous ejection. In order to reach a stable drug concentration, we started the ejection and waited until the visual response of the cell was diminished with respect to the control condition, usually after 2–3 minutes of continuous ejection of CNQX or APV. Stability was evaluated by comparing responses collected during the first and the last set of trials and calculating whether the observed differences were significant.

During CNQX ejection (1 mM pH 8) there is a decrease in the response of the cell, with the reduction being clearly more prominent in the nonpreferred direction (Fig. 2.4A). The effect of APV (50 mM, pH 8), shown in Fig. 2.4B, is similar in the preferred and nonpreferred direction. During CNQX blockade, since the residual response is mediated by NMDA receptors, and because of the pronounced effect on the non-optimal response, neurons exhibit significant changes in direction selectivity (Fig. 2.4C). Direction index [DI=maximum response—opposite response/maximum response] is represented for the whole population (n=29) and compared to control values in Fig. 2.4C. Note that during CNQX ejection there is a displacement of the curve to the right, showing that DI values are increased relative to control. Blockade of NMDA receptors does not change the DI for the population (Fig. 2.4D). These results show that responses during CNQX ejection (i.e. NMDA mediated responses) are highly direction selective, postulating a prominent role for NMDA receptors in mediating direction selectivity.

One advantage of using iontophoresis is the possibility to study the effects of several compounds independently or in combination on the same cell, and thus we studied the effect of APV and CNQX on direction selectivity in the absence of inhibition achieved by ejection of Bicuculline (20 mM, pH 4). Application of bicuculline causes a larger increase in the response in the nonpreferred direction as compared to the increase in the preferred direction, leading to a decrease in the direction selectivity index (Fig. 2.5A, 2.5C, 2.5D). As in Fig. 2.4, application of CNQX alone increases the direction index by causing a larger reduction in the nonpreferred response. Surprisingly, ejection of CNQX in the presence of bicuculline caused a similar reduction in the preferred and nonpreferred directions, when compared with bicuculline alone, leading to a similar DI in both conditions (Fig. 2.5C). This result indicates that the response in the nonoptimal direction contains an NMDA mediated component that, in normal conditions, is removed by GABAergic inhibition. This effect is detailed in Fig. 2.5B where peristimulus time histograms are shown for preferred and nonpreferred conditions. During bicuculline ejection (notice the different scale on the y-axis), the responses increase preferentially in the nonpreferred direction and the neuron becomes less directional. This is the opposite of the effects observed with CNQX application. Removing inhibition during AMPA blockade increases the response in both directions but, again, the effect is preferentially on the nonoptimal response, causing the DI to be similar to that obtained with bicuculline alone (Fig. 2.5C). These results

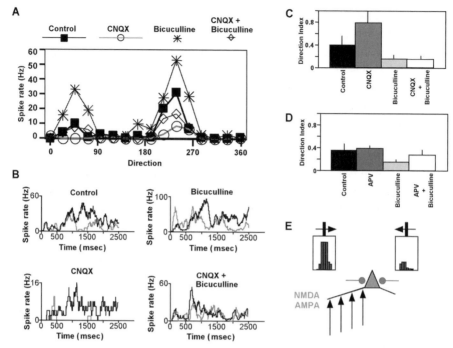

Fig. 2.5 Interactions between AMPA and GABA receptors during direction-selective responses. (A) Direction tuning curves of a complex cell in the control condition and during ejection of CNQX, bicuculline, and both simultaneously. (B) Peri-stimulus time histograms of responses from another complex cell showing the control response and the effect of the drugs on the preferred (shown in black) and nonpreferred (gray) directions. Each histogram is the average response to seven stimulus presentations and shows the entire 2.5 sec of stimulus duration: the grating was stationary for the first 500 msec and drifted for the next 2 sec. (C) Bar histogram showing the mean value (standard deviation [SD]) of the direction index for the population of cells in the different conditions (*n* = 4 cells). (D) Modulation of NMDA activity by GABA during generation of direction selective responses. Bar histogram showing the mean (+/– SD) of the direction index for the population of cells in the different conditions (*n* = 4 cells). (E) Schematic showing that NMDA and AMPA receptors together provide direction selective feedforward input to layer 2/3 cells. NMDA receptors contribute prominently to responses in the preferred direction (left response histogram), while their contribution to responses in the nonpreferred direction (right response histogram) is reduced substantially by GABAergic inhibition (circles). Such inhibition may be greater in the nonpreferred direction (right to left).

indicate the presence of an excitatory NMDA-mediated component in the nonpreferred direction that is absent during the control condition because of GABAergic inhibition. We have seen consistently during our experiments that the DI varies from trial to trial. This variability could be due to a continuous modulation of the NMDA mediated response through GABAergic inhibition. This idea is supported by data obtained while simultaneously ejecting APV and bicuculline (Fig. 2.5D). The effect of bicuculline on the DI is reversed by simultaneous ejection of APV, showing that bicuculline acts mainly on the NMDA-mediated component of the response.

Taken together, our results demonstrate that both AMPA and NMDA receptors contribute to the generation of direction selectivity in the superficial layers of V1. However, their effects can be delimited (Fig. 2.5E). During control conditions, AMPA receptors are sufficient for generating direction selectivity, but NMDA receptors are needed to increase the response in the preferred direction in a nonlinear fashion. In the nonpreferred direction, the NMDA mediated component of the response is suppressed by inhibition (Artola and Singer 1987; Shirokawa *et al.* 1989; Schroeder *et al.* 1997). A possible interpretation of these results is that NMDA mediated responses are only effective during stimulation in the preferred direction because a sufficient amount of excitation is provided in this condition. However, a comparison of CNQX effect on nonpreferred responses (when CNQX causes an average reduction of 90%) and spontaneous activity (when CNQX causes an average reduction of 28%, and there is less excitation) supports the presence of an active inhibitory component in the response to the nonpreferred direction. This modulatory action of inhibition provides a rich substrate for a dynamic control of neuron responses based on stimulus configuration or spatial and temporal history and context.

Phase invariance in visual cortex

It is known that most cells in layer 4 are simple cells, while those in layers 2/3 are predominantly complex (Hubel and Wiesel 1962). How simple cell responses are converted to complex cell responses is still an open question. The main excitatory and inhibitory input to the superficial layers of the cortex is provided by feedforward connections from layer 4 and by intracortical connections within layer 2/3. Experiments blocking the inhibitory inputs have reported a widening of ON and OFF subregions of simple cells and an increase in the overlap between ON and OFF subfields, suggesting that under these conditions simple cells responses can become similar to those of complex cells (Pernberg *et al.* 1998; Sillito 1975). These data suggest a combination of feedforward and intracortical inputs as generating complex cell properties. Indeed, Chance *et al.* (1999) have proposed a model in which complex cells properties arise as a consequence of decreasing the phase selectivity of simple cell responses by recurrent intracortical connections. A key test for this model is whether blockade of intracortical excitation causes complex cells to respond like simple cells.

An important difference between simple and complex cells is their temporal pattern of response when they are stimulated with drifting gratings (Movshon *et al.* 1978a,b; Skottun *et al.* 1991). We used this difference to classify simple and complex cells based on the ratio between the first two Fourier harmonics of the response (F1/F0 ratio). We studied the effect of blocking AMPA and NMDA receptors on the F1/F0 ratio in layer 2/3 cells. Figure 2.6A shows two subpopulations in our sample: cells with a F1/F0 ratio less than 1 were classified as complex cells and those with a F1/F0 ratio greater than 1

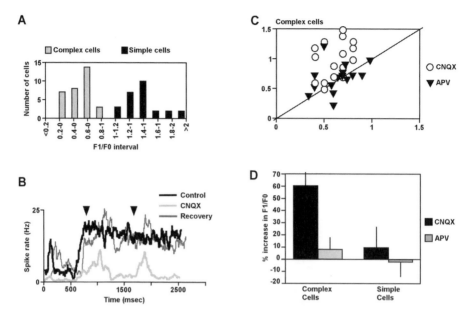

Fig. 2.6 Effect of CNQX and APV on responses of simple and complex cells. (A) Histogram of F1/F0 values of simple and complex cells in the control condition. F1: amplitude of the first Fourier component of response, showing modulation at the grating temporal frequency. F0: the dc or mean response level. (B) Peri-stimulus time histograms showing the response of one complex cell to a drifting grating moving in the preferred direction during the control condition, ejection of CNQX, and after recovery. (C) Scatter plot showing the change in F1/F0 for each complex cell ($n=16$ cells) during CNQX and AMPA ejection. (D) Histogram showing the variation in the F1/F0 ratio under CNQX and APV for simple and complex cells. The F1/F0 ratio increases significantly for complex cells under CNQX, denoting an increase in the temporal modulation of responses by the grating.

were classified as simple cells. The most important result (Fig. 2.6B) is that AMPA blockade makes complex cells behave like simple cells. The visual stimulus is a drifting grating at the optimal orientation presented for 500 ms. During the control condition, the response of the cell shows an absence of modulation characteristic of complex cells, while during AMPA blockade the response decreases and changes the temporal pattern of response to exhibit a modulation by the grating cycle, in a manner that is typical for simple cells. Figure 2.6C shows a scatter plot representing the change in the F1/F0 ratios during CNQX and APV ejection on all the complex cells recorded. APV decreases the response of the cell but does not change the temporal structure of the response, while CNQX increases the F1/F0 ratio of complex cells and alters the temporal pattern of responses.

In simple cells neither APV nor CNQX affects the temporal response pattern. Figure 2.6D shows population data for simple and complex cells during APV and CNQX ejection and it is clear that only CNQX applied to complex cells modifies the temporal structure of the visual response. We also tested the effect of bicuculline on simple and complex cell properties and the interactions with AMPA and NMDA receptors. Intracortical inhibition has been related to the generation of simple cell subfields. However, in our experiments (Fig. 2.7) we do not find any effect of bicuculline on the temporal modulation of the responses in simple and complex cells. Figure 2.7A shows a PSTH from a simple cell responding to a grating drifting in the preferred direction. During bicuculline ejection a clear increase in the response is achieved, but no change in the modulation of the response (F1/F0=1.59 in the control condition and 1.34 during bicuculline application; this result holds for the population). Our data apparently disagree with previous experiments (Pernberg *et al.* 1998) showing that in absence of inhibition different subregions of simple cells overlap, a typical complex cell property. However, several methodological differences could explain this discrepancy. For example, Pernberg *et al.* (1998) used the reverse correlation method with flashed bar stimuli to study the spatial separation of On and Off subfields of cells in area 18. We studied changes in the temporal modulation of responses in area 17 using drifting gratings. Of course, a relationship between receptive field structure and temporal properties of responses must exist, but it may not relate in a simple way to the temporal structure of

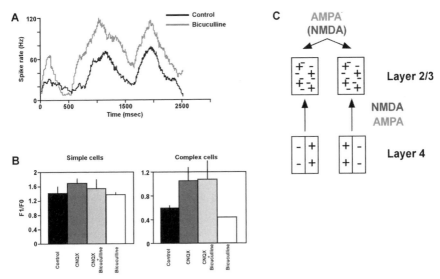

Fig. 2.7 (and color plate 3) Blockade of inhibition does not affect the temporal modulation of simple or complex cell responses. (A) Peristimulus histogram of the response of a simple cell to a grating drifting in the preferred direction, in the control condition and during bicuculline application. (B) The effect of bicuculline, CNQX and bicuculline+CNQX on F1/F0 values of simple cells (left) and complex cells (right) Bars show mean (+/–SD). (C) Cartoon showing that simple cells in layer 4 provide feedforward input to cells in layer 2/3 via NMDA and AMPA receptors. Our data suggest that short-range recurrent excitatory connections in layer 2/3 via AMPA receptors are responsible for reducing the spatial phase-selectivity of simple cells and creating phase-invariant complex cell responses.

the grating response, during which orientation selectivity, stimulus motion and full field stimulation are all involved. In our experiments we also analyzed the effect of removing inhibition on complex cells. In this case, there was a possible decrease in the F1/F0 ratio during bicuculline application ($p=0.2$). Importantly, bicuculline did not modify the change in F1/F0 produced by AMPA blockade. Figure 2.7B represents the average values obtained for the F1/F0 in the different experimental conditions. Thus, blockade of inhibition does not affect temporal response modulation in simple or complex cells, and the effect of blocking AMPA receptors is to increase phase-selective modulation even when inhibition is removed.

In summary, CNQX ejection (i.e. AMPA receptor blockade) increases the modulation of complex cell responses by a drifting grating stimulus. Thus, AMPA receptors decrease the selectivity of complex cells for spatial phase or the spatial location of visual stimuli. Blocking NMDA receptors or inhibition has little effect on the temporal modulation of simple or complex cell responses.

Our results provide a new view on cortical networks by proposing specific roles for different subtypes of glutamate receptors in the generation of phase selectivity in visual cortical cells. Our data suggest that a specific input to a cortical cell primarily uses one type of receptor. We propose that AMPA and NMDA receptors in layer 2/3 have different spatial distributions on cells, with both present on the same cell but in different proportions at different inputs. In this model (Fig. 2.7C) feedforward connections are mediated through both AMPA and NMDA receptors while local recurrent connections are mainly mediated through AMPA receptors only. These latter connections are responsible for smearing the phase-selectivity of simple cells to create phase-invariant complex cell responses.

Conclusions

We have used orientation selectivity, direction selectivity, and modulation of phase selectivity in V1 neurons as experimental models that could help understanding the role of excitatory and inhibitory cortical networks and the action of specific receptor types in visual information processing. By combining extracellular recording, iontophoresis of receptor blockers, and optical imaging of intrinsic signals, we demonstrate the following results:

First, blockade of local inhibition and excitation causes profound changes in the layout of orientation maps. Specifically, blockade of inhibition by bicuculline iontophoresis (Toth *et al.* 1997) causes a shift in the orientation preference of neurons toward the preferred orientation at the ejection location, whereas blockade of excitation through GABA iontophoresis (Toth *et al.* 1997) or visual adaptation (Dragoi *et al.* 2000) causes a shift in the orientation preference of neurons away from the iontophoresis or adapting orientation. These results argue strongly that local excitation balances the effect of inhibition to maintain stable orientation preference during vision. These changes in orientation selectivity imply a network mechanism that reorganizes responses across a broad range of orientations, possibly through changes in the gain of local cortical circuits that mediate recurrent excitation and inhibition (Ben-Yishai *et al.* 1995; Douglas *et al.* 1995; Somers *et al.* 1995) and include disinhibitory mechanisms (Dragoi and Sur 2000).

Second, disruption of excitation and inhibition in local cortical networks depends on cortical location. The structure of the orientation map in V1 implies that the orientation distribution of local connections would vary with a neuron's position within the map: neurons in pinwheel centers are likely to be connected to neurons of a broader range of orientations than neurons in iso-orientation domains. Thus, altering the efficacy of intracortical orientation-specific inputs to neurons in different locations of the orientation map through adaptation induces changes in the tuning properties of neurons in a manner that depends on cortical location, i.e., more pronounced changes in the orientation preference of neurons at or near pinwheel centers (Dragoi *et al.* 2001).

Third, blocking AMPA receptors reduces responses to nonpreferred directions stronger than to preferred directions and, consequently, increases direction selectivity, while blocking NMDA receptors removes proportional components from preferred and nonpreferred responses which eventually preserves direction selectivity at the same level (Rivadulla *et al.* 2001). On the other hand, blocking inhibition enhances the contribution of NMDA receptors to nonpreferred responses to reduce direction selectivity.

Finally, blocking AMPA receptors increases the modulation of complex cell responses by drifting gratings; thus there is an increase in the selectivity for spatial phase or the spatial location of visual stimuli. Blocking NMDA receptors or inhibition has little effect on the temporal modulation of simple and complex cell responses (Rivadulla *et al.* 2001). Thus, AMPA receptors have a major role in creating phase-insensitive complex cell responses in the superficial layers of V1.

Acknowledgments

We thank Jitendra Sharma for participating in experiments. Supported by McDonnell-Pew and Merck fellowships (V. D.), by a Fulbright fellowship (C. R.), and by grants from NIH (M. S.).

References

Abbott, L. F., Varela, J. A., Sen, K. *et al.* (1997) Synaptic depression and cortical gain control. *Science,* **275**:220–4.

Anderson, J. S., Carandini, M. and Ferster, D. (2000) Orientation tuning of input conductance, excitation, and inhibition in cat primary visual cortex. *Journal of Neurophysiology,* **84**:909–26.

Artola, A. and Singer, W. (1987) Long-term potentiation and NMDA receptors in rat visual cortex. *Nature,* **330**:649–52.

Barlow, H. B. and Levick, W. R. (1965) The mechanism of directionally selective units in rabbit's retina. *Journal of Physiology (London),* **178**:477–504.

Ben-Yishai, R., Bar-Or, R.L., Sompolinsky, H. (1995) Theory of orientation tuning in visual cortex. *Proceedings of the National Academy of Sciences of the United States of America,* **92**:3844–3848.

Berman, N. J., Douglas, R. J., Martin, K. A. C. *et al.* (1991) Mechanisms of inhibition in cat visual cortex. *Journal of Physiology,* **440**:697–722.

Bishop, P. O., Kato, H. and Orban, G. A. (1980) Direction-selective cells in complex family in cat striate cortex. *Journal of Neurophysiology*, **43**:1266–83.

Borg-Graham, L. J., Monier, C. and Fregnac, Y. (1998) Visual input evokes transient and strong shunting inhibition in visual cortical neurons. *Nature*, **393**:369–73.

Carandini, M. and Heeger, D. J. (1994) Summation and division by neurons in primate visual cortex. *Science*, **264**:1333–6.

Carandini, M., Movshon, J. A. and Ferster, D. (1998) Pattern adaptation and cross-orientation interactions in the primary visual cortex. *Neuropharmacology*, **37**:501–11.

Chance, F. S., Nelson, S. B. and Abbott, L. F. (1999) Complex cells as cortically amplified simple cells. *Nature Neuroscience*, **2**:277–82.

Chapman, B., Zahs, K. R. and Stryker, M. P. (1991) Relation of cortical cell orientation selectivity to alignment of receptive fields of the geniculocortical afferents that arborize within a single orientation column in ferret visual cortex. *Journal of Neuroscience*, **11**:1347–58.

Creutzfeldt, O. D., Innocenti, G. and Brooks, D. (1974a) Vertical organization in the visual cortex (area 17). *Experimental Brain Research*, **21**:315–36.

Creutzfeldt, O. D., Kuhnt, U. and Benevento, L. A. (1974b) An intracellular analysis of visual cortical neurons to moving stimuli: Responses in a cooperative neuronal network. *Experimental Brain Research*, **21**:251–74.

Crook, J. M., Kisvarday, Z. F. and Eysel, U. T. (1997) GABA-induced inactivation of functionally characterized sites in cat striate cortex: effects on orientation tuning and direction selectivity. *Visual Neuroscience*, **14**:141–58.

Crook, J. M., Kisvarday, Z. F., Eysel, U. T. (1998) Evidence for a contribution of lateral inhibition to orientation tuning and direction selectivity in cat visual cortex: reversible inactivation of functionally characterized sites combined with neuroanatomical tracing techniques. *European Journal of Neuroscience*, **10**:2056–2075.

Dehay, C., Douglas, R. J., Martin, K. A. C. *et al.* (1991) Excitation by geniculocortical synapses is not "vetoed" at the level of dendritic spines in cat visual cortex. *Journal of Physiology*, **440**:723–34.

Douglas, R. J., Martin, K. A. C. and Whitteridge, D. (1988) Selective responses of visual cortical neurones do not depend on shunting inhibition. *Nature*, **332**:642–4.

Douglas, R. J., Koch, C., Mahowald, M. *et al.* (1995) Recurrent excitation in neocortical circuits. *Science*, **269**:981–5.

Douglas, R. J., Martin, K. A. C. and Whitteridge, D. (1991) An intracellular analysis of the visual responses of neurones in cat visual cortex. *Journal of Physiology*, **44**:659–96.

Dragoi, V. and Sur, M. (2000) Dynamic properties of recurrent inhibition in primary visual cortex: contrast and orientation dependence of contextual effects. *Journal of Neurophysiology*, **83**:1019–30.

Dragoi, V., Sharma, J. and Sur, M. (2000) Adaptation-induced plasticity of orientation tuning in adult visual cortex. *Neuron*, **28**:287–98.

Dragoi, V., Rivadulla, C. and Sur M. (2001) Foci of orientation plasticity in visual cortex. *Nature*, **411**:80–6.

Ferster, D. (1986) Orientation selectivity of synaptic potentials in neurons of cat primary visual cortex. *Journal of Neuroscience*, **6**:1284–301.

Ferster, D. and Jagadeesh, B. (1992) EPSP-IPSP interactions in cat visual cortex studied with *in vivo* whole-cell patch recording. *Journal of Neuroscience*, **12**:1262–74.

Ferster, D. and Miller, K. D. (2000) Neural mechanisms of orientation selectivity in the visual cortex. *Annual Reviews of Neuroscience*, **23**:441–71.

Fox, K., Sato, H. and Daw, N. (1989) The location and function of NMDA receptors in cat and kitten visual cortex. *Journal of Neuroscience*, **9**:2443–54.

Fox, K., Sato, H. and Daw, N. (1990) The effect of varying stimulus intensity on NMDA-receptor activity in cat visual cortex. *Journal of Neurophysiology*, **64**:1413–28.

Ganz, L. and Felder, R. (1984) Mechanism of directional selectivity in simple neurons of the cat's visual cortex analyzed with stationary flash sequences. *Journal of Neurophysiology*, **51**:294–324.

Goodwin, A. W. and Henry, G. H. (1975) Direction selectivity of complex cells in cats: a comparison with simple cells. *Journal of Neurophysiology*, **38**:1524–40.

Hata, Y., Tsumoto, T., Sato, H. *et al.* (1988) Inhibition contributes to orientation selectivity in visual cortex of cat. *Nature*, **335**:815–17.

Hirsch, J. A., Alonso, J. M., Reid, R. C. *et al.* (1998) Synaptic integration in striate cortical simple cells. *Journal of Neuroscience*, **18**:9517–28.

Hubel, D. H. and Wiesel, T. N. (1962) Receptive fields, binocular interaction and functional architecture in the cat's visual cortex. *Journal of Physiology*, **165**:559–68.

Jagadeesh, B., Wheat, H. S. and Ferster, D. (1993) Linearity of summation of synaptic potentials underlying direction selectivity in simple cells of the cat visual cortex. *Science*, **262**:1901–4.

Jagadeesh, B., Wheat, H. S., Kontsevich, L. L. *et al.* (1997) Direction selectivity of synaptic potentials in simple cells of the cat visual cortex. *Journal of Neurophysiology*, **78**:2772–89.

Jones, J. P. and Palmer, L. A. (1987) The two-dimensional spatial structure of simple receptive fields in cat striate cortex. *Journal of Neurophysiology*, **58**:1187–211.

Koch, C. and Poggio, T. (1985) The synaptic veto mechanism: does it underlie direction and orientation selectivity in the visual cortex? In D. R. Rose, and V. G. Dobson (eds) *Models of the Visual Cortex*, pp. 408–19. Wiley, New York.

Livingstone, M. S. (1998) Mechanisms of direction selectivity in macaque V1. *Neuron*, **20**:509–26.

McLean, J. and Palmer, L. A. (1989) Contribution of linear spatiotemporal receptive field structure to velocity selectivity of simple cells in area 17 of cat. *Vision Research*, **29**:675–9.

Michalski, A., Gerstein, G. I., Czarkowska, J. *et al.* (1983) Interactions between cat striate cortex neurons. *Experimental Brain Research*, **51**:97–107.

Miller, K. D. (1992) Development of orientation columns via competition between on- and off-center inputs. *NeuroReport*, **3**:73–6.

Movshon, A. and Lennie, P. (1979) Pattern-selective adaptation in visual cortical neurones. *Nature*, **278**:850–2.

Movshon, J. A., Thompson, I. D. and Tolhurst, D. J. (1978a) Spatial summation in the receptive fields of simple cells in the cat's striate cortex. *Journal of Physiology (London)*, **283**:53–77.

Movshon, J. A., Thompson, I. D. and Tolhurst, D. J. (1978b) Receptive field organization of complex cells in the cat's striate cortex. *Journal of Physiology (London)*, **283**:79–99.

Murthy, A., Humphrey, A. L., Saul, A. B. *et al.* (1998) Laminar differences in the spatiotemporal structure of simple cell receptive fields in cat area 17. *Visual Neuroscience*, **15**:239–56.

Nelson, S. B. (1991) Temporal interactions in the cat visual system. III. Pharmacological studies of cortical suppression suggest a presynaptic mechanism. *Journal of Neuroscience*, **11**:369–80.

Nelson, S., Toth, L., Sheth, B. *et al.* (1994) Orientation selectivity of cortical neurons during intracellular blockade of inhibition. *Science*, **265**:774–7.

Pei, X., Vidyasagar, T. R., Volgushev, M., Creutzfeldt, O. D. (1994) Receptive field analysis and orientation selectivity of postsynaptic potentials of simple cells in cat visual cortex. *Journal of Neuroscience*, **14(2)**:7130–7140.

Pernberg, J., Jirmann, K. U. and Eysel, U. T. (1998) Structure and dynamics of receptive fields in the visual cortex of the cat (area 18) and the influence of GABAergic inhibition. *European Journal of Neuroscience*, **10**:3596–606.

Reid, R. C., Soodak, R. E. and Shapley, R. M. (1987) Linear mechanisms of directional selectivity in simple cells of cat striate cortex. *Proceedings of the National Academy of Science USA*, **84**:8740–4.

Reid, R. C., Soodak, R. E. and Shapley, R. M. (1991) Directional selectivity and spatiotemporal structure of receptive fields of simple cells in cat striate cortex. *Journal of Neurophysiology*, **66**:505–29.

Rivadulla, C., Sharma, J. and Sur, M. (2001) Specific roles of NMDA and AMPA receptors in direction-selective and spatial phase-selective responses in visual cortex. *Journal of Neuroscience*, 21:1710–19.

Rojer, A. and Schwartz, E. L. (1990) Cat and monkey cortical columnar patterns modeled by band-pass-filtered 2d white noise. *Biological Cybernetics*, 62:381–91.

Sanchez-Vives, M. V., Nowak, L. G. and McCormick, D. A. (2000) Membrane mechanisms underlying contrast adaptation in cat area 17 *in vivo*. *Journal of Neuroscience*, 20:4267–85.

Sato, H., Katsuyama, N., Tamura, H. *et al.* (1995) Mechanisms underlying direction selectivity of neurons in the primary visual cortex of the macaque. *Journal of Neurophysiology*, 74:1382–94.

Saul, A. B. and Cynader, M. S. (1989) Adaptation in single units in visual cortex: the tuning of after-effects in the spatial domain. *Visual Neuroscience*, 2:593–607.

Schroeder, C. E., Javitt, D. C., Steinschneider, M. *et al.* (1997) N-methyl-D-aspartate enhancement of phasic responses in primate neocortex. *Experimental Brain Research*, 114:271–8.

Sclar, G. and Freeman, R. D. (1982) Orientation selectivity in the cat's striate cortex is invariant with stimulus contrast. *Experimental Brain Research*, 46:457–61.

Shirokawa, T., Nishigori, A., Kimura, F. *et al.* (1989) Actions of excitatory amino acid antagonists on synaptic potentials of layer II/III neurons of the cat's visual cortex. *Experimental Brain Research*, 78:489–500.

Sillito, A. M. (1975) The contribution of inhibitory mechanisms to the receptive field properties of neurones in the striate cortex of the cat. *Journal of Physiology (London)*, 250:305–29.

Sillito, A. M. (1977) Inhibitory processes underlying the directional specificity of simple, complex and hypercomplex cells in the cat's visual cortex. *Journal of Physiology (London)*, 271:699–720.

Sillito, A. M., Kemp, J. A., Milson, J. A. *et al.* (1980) A re-evaluation of the mechanisms underlying simple cell orientation selectivity. *Brain Research*, 194:517–20.

Skottun, B. C., De Valois, R. L., Grosof, D. H., *et al.* (1991) Classifying simple and complex cells on the basis of response modulation. *Vision Research*, 31:1079–86.

Somers, D. C., Nelson, S. B. and Sur, M. (1995) An emergent model of orientation selectivity in cat visual cortical simple cells. *Journal of Neuroscience*, 15:5448–65.

Somers, D. C., Dragoi, V. and Sur, M. (2001) Orientation selectivity and its modulation by local and long-range connections in visual cortex. In A. Peters and B. Payne (eds) *Cat Primary Visual Cortex*, pp. 471–510. Academic Press, San Diego.

Sompolinsky, H. and Shapley, R. (1997) New perspectives on the mechanisms for orientation tuning. *Current Opinions in Neurobiology*, 7:514–22.

Suarez, H., Koch, C. and Douglas, R. (1995) Modeling direction selectivity of simple cells in striate visual cortex within the framework of the canonical microcircuit. *Journal of Neuroscience*, 15:6700–19.

Swindale, N. V. (1992) A model for the coordinated development of columnar systems in primate striate cortex. *Biological Cybernetics*, 66:217–30.

Toth, L. J., Kim, D.-S., Rao, S. C. *et al.* (1997) Integration of local inputs in visual cortex. *Cerebral Cortex*, 7:703–10.

Tsumoto, T., Eckart, W. and Creutzfeldt, O. D. (1979) Modification of orientation sensitivity of cat visual cortex neurons by removal of GABA-mediated inhibition. *Experimental Brain Research*, 34:351–63.

Watkins, D. W. and Berkley, M. A. (1974) The orientation selectivity of single neurons in cat striate cortex. *Experimental Brain Research*, 19:433–46.

Wehmeier, U., Dong, D., Koch, C. *et al.* (1989) Modeling the visual system. In C. Koch and I. Segev (eds) *Methods in Neuronal Modeling*, pp. 335–59. MIT Press, Cambridge, MA.

Wörgötter, F. and Koch, C. (1991) A detailed model of the primary visual pathway in the cat: Comparison of afferent excitatory and intracortical inhibitory connection schemes for orientation selectivity. *Journal of Neuroscience*, 11:1959–79.

Chapter 3

In Search of the Role of Extrageniculate Corticothalamic Loops in Visual Processing using Reversible Deactivation Techniques

Christian Casanova

Introduction

The importance of visual extrageniculate nuclei, such as the pulvinar complex, became apparent when Diamond and colleagues (Diamond and Hall 1969; Killackey and Diamond 1971), Schneider (1967, 1969) and Trevarthen (1968) demonstrated the involvement of a second retinofugal visual system, the retino-collicular pathway, in orienting behavior (the Where pathway as opposed to the What or retino-geniculocortical pathway). Indeed, in order to reach the visual cortex, signals from the superior colliculus and the pretectum must be relayed by thalamic nuclei, and in particular, the pulvinar complex. Since this pioneering work, there have been a number of investigations that revealed the complex organization and connectivity of pulvinar nuclei in cats and monkeys (Vidnyánszky et al. 1996; Rockland 1996, 1998; Rockland et al. 1999). In the former group, the lateral posterior–pulvinar (LP–pulvinar) can be subdivided into at least three sections, each containing a representation of the contralateral visual field (Hutchins and Updyke 1989; Chalupa 1991): the lateral and medial part of the LP nucleus (LPl and LPm) and the pulvinar (Graybiel and Berson 1980; Updyke 1983; Chalupa and Abramson 1988). Remarkably, every one of these subdivisions is reciprocally connected with virtually all visual cortical areas (Fig. 3.1; Graybiel and Berson 1980; Raczkowski and Rosenquist 1983; Garey et al. 1991).

When compared to other subcortical areas such as the lateral geniculate nucleus or the superior colliculus, few studies have investigated the response properties of neurons in the pulvinar complex of either cats or monkeys. This could be due in part to the difficulty in characterizing these neurons' receptive field properties. It is also possible that some researchers were discouraged by the findings from some behavioral studies (e.g., Nagel-Leiby et al. 1984; Bender and Butter 1987) which revealed no strong impairments of visual capacities after destruction of the pulvinar (for a comprehensive discussion on this subject, see the review by Chalupa 1991). Fortunately, a number of investigators

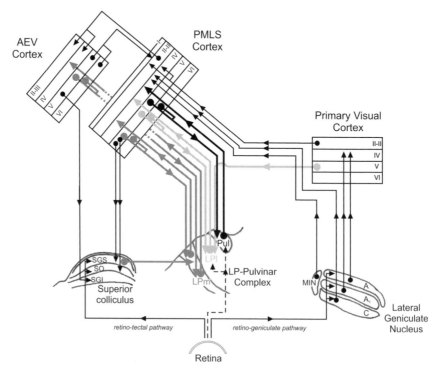

Fig. 3.1 Illustration representing major visual pathways implicating subcortical–cortical inter-relationships in the cat. The connections involving the LP–pulvinar complex are represented by thick lines of different gray levels. Note that some projections are not shown in order to clarify the diagram (e.g., area 17 to LGN).

(see reviews of Casanova *et al.* 1991; Chalupa 1991) were not deterred by these obstacles and their studies provided information for contemporary researchers about the functional organization of the pulvinar complex. On the basis of these studies, this thalamic region has often been associated with various functions such as visual attention (Petersen *et al.* 1987; Robinson and Petersen 1992), and visually guided movement (Fabre-Thorpe *et al.* 1986; Grieve *et al.* 2000), but for the most part its function in normal vision has remained speculative (Casanova *et al.* 1991; Chalupa 1991).[1]

The pulvinar complex: an active partner of cortical areas

As stated above, the LP–pulvinar receives prominent signals from the mesencephalon and the primary visual cortex, and establishes reciprocal connections with practically all visual cortical areas. The LP–pulvinar thus represents a strategic thalamic structure

---

[1] The pulvinar complex is also associated with residual visual capacities observed in animals and humans that have sustained early or late visual cortex damage (Payne *et al.* 1996; Ptito *et al.* 1999).

and a unique platform, because it receives and may even integrate neural signals from the two main retinofugal pathways: retino–tectal and retino–geniculo–striate (Benedek *et al.* 1983; Casanova *et al.* 1991). It is in an exceptional position to either influence or inform multiple cortical areas about processing occurring in lower- or higher-level areas, or to increase the effectiveness (e.g., stimulus salience) of the processing taking place in a given cortical area. Another approach is to consider the pulvinar complex as the base for multiple extrageniculate cortico–thalamo–cortical loops that may be implicated in higher-order visual processing.[2] In support of this last assumption, we discovered that a subset of cells in the LPm respond to moving plaids with pattern-motion responses (Merabet *et al.* 1998) indicating that these thalamic cells can integrate separate motion signals into a coherent moving percept. Recently, we further reported that another subset of neurons, located in the LPl, can code the displacement of complex random dot kinematograms (RDKs) whose constituting elements per se cannot provide information about the direction of motion (Dumbrava *et al.* 2001). These two findings are important because they indicate that (1) LP–pulvinar neurons can perform complex neuronal operations, (2) that pattern-motion and global RDK selective neurons appear to be distinct; and (3) that two extrageniculate pathways or cortico–thalamo–cortical loops may be involved in specific aspects of motion processing, because the LPl and LPm are preferentially connected to the suprasylvian cortex (containing complex RDK-selective units; [unpublished observation]) and the ectosylvian cortex (containing PM-selective cells).

Paraphrasing Sillito and Jones (1997), I believe that pulvinar and cortical levels of visual processing cannot be separated easily: they form a circuit, not a sequence. As such, the understanding of pulvinar function largely depends on our ability to clearly establish the functional significance of the bidirectional connections between this large extrageniculate nucleus and the visual cortex. In recent years, numerous attempts have been made to understand the role of corticocortical pathways in the computation of specific aspects of an image (Bullier *et al.* 1984; Kreiter and Singer 1996; Spillmann and Werner 1996). By contrast, little effort has been directed towards the role of extrageniculate thalamic visual nuclei that provide substantial inputs to the visual cortex (Crick and Koch 1998). This chapter will concentrate on the first efforts of my laboratory to determine the functional relationship between neurons in the two main subdivisions of the LP nucleus and those in the primary visual and higher-order cortical areas. Two reversible deactivation techniques will be described: the cooling of large portions of

---

[2] Despite the original statement by Le Gros Clark (1932) on the possible associative function of the pulvinar, thalamic nuclei have been generally regarded as stations passively relaying sensory information to the cortex, in relation with the state of arousal. In recent years, the role of the thalamus has been reassessed and it has been proposed that thalamic nuclei may actively participate in the processing of specific information in conjunction with cortical areas, through cortico-thalamo-cortical loops (Mumford 1991; Macchi *et al.* 1996; Miller 1996; Sherman and Guillery 1996, 1998, 2001; Grieve *et al.* 2000).

the visual cortex and the pharmacological deactivation of restricted thalamic and cortical regions. It will be shown that these techniques represent promising avenues in our aim to determine the contribution of ascending and descending extrageniculate pathways in the functioning of their target areas.

Experimental procedures

Reversible deactivation by cooling

Despite the fact that the cooling technique is not a new one, it remains the most efficient way by which one can investigate the impact of a large portion of the cortex upon other cortical areas or subcortical structures (e.g., Baker and Malpeli 1977; Sherk 1978; Girard and Bullier 1989; Clemo and Stein 1986; Michalski *et al.* 1993; Jiang *et al.* 2001). Many devices used in recent years were laboratory made, and are consequently inexpensive. The cooling probe that we used represents a modified version of the cooling apparatus described by Skinner and Lindsley (1968) and Molotchnikoff *et al.* (1986). The method is relatively simple; the cooling device consists of a custom-made glass cryoprobe through which cooled ethanol runs. The cryoprobe consists of a horse-shoe shaped glass micropipette (of an external diameter varying according to the region and extent to be inactivated) fashioned by heat to fit the cortical curvature (Fig. 3.2A). A varnished tungsten microelectrode and a thermocouple (e.g., flexible and implantable Physitemp type T probes, connected to a Barnant thermistor thermometer) are inserted in the middle of the probe to monitor changes in neuronal activity and cortical temperature, respectively, during cooling. The inflow opening of the glass cryoprobe is connected through a series of tubing to a tank filled with ethanol, placed two meters from the ground (panel B of Fig. 3.2). Pushed by gravity, the liquid from the tank travels down a line of decreasing diameter to a relay container filled with ethanol, which is cooled with dry ice and maintained at a temperature of $-20\,°C$. Two adjustable valves are used to control the flow rate. The temperature of the probe is set to, and maintained at, a specific value by adjusting the flow rate. The cooled ethanol reaches the cryoprobe via short-length, thermally isolated tubing. The outflow opening is also connected to a waste recipient with isolated tubing. A second thermocouple is used to measure the temperature of the ethanol collected from the probe.

Several control experiments were conducted to measure the efficacy and reversibility of cooling. One advantage of this technique is that lowering the temperature of the cortex can be achieved very rapidly, and the temperature necessary to block synaptic activity can be maintained throughout a testing period with very little variation (less than $1\,°C$). As shown in Fig. 3.2 (panel C), when cold ethanol was allowed to flow within the cryoprobe, the temperature at the cortical surface (about $100–200\,\mu m$ below the surface) could be lowered to values between 5 and $10\,°C$ within two to three minutes. Rewarming is also accomplished rapidly. A disadvantage of this method is that cooling varies as a function of cortical depth. For example, panel D of Fig. 3.2 shows that

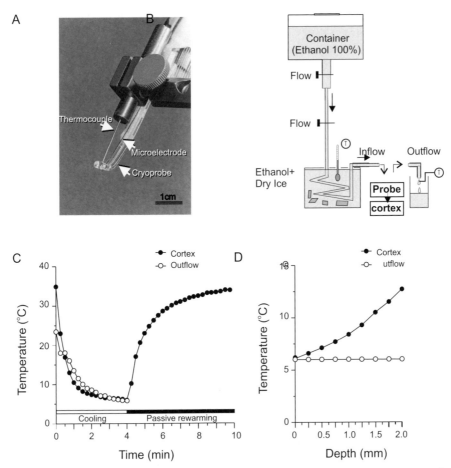

Fig. 3.2 (A) Photograph of one of the cryoprobes used to deactivate the central representation of the visual field in area 17. Under microscope viewing, the microelectrode is placed so that its tip is positioned 1.2–1.5 mm from the ventral surface of the cryoprobe, allowing recordings in the vicinity of layer V. Activity of the deep layers of area 17 was monitored throughout all experiments (and for each LPl cell tested) to verify the success of the inactivation. The thermocouple shown (Physitemp type IT-23) was later changed to a smaller device (Physitemp flexible implantable probe, type T18 or T23). (B) Apparatus used to cool the ethanol flowing through the cryoprobe. Two adjustable valves (Δ) were used to control the flow rate which could attain a maximum value of 7.5 ml/min. (C) Temperature measurements (cortex and ethanol out-flowing) during cooling and subsequent re-warming. (D) Change in cortical temperature as a function of cortical depth.

temperature increases along the dorsoventral axis, reaching a maximum in the deep cortical layers (the temperature in the cooling apparatus was constant as shown by the measure at the cryoprobe outflow opening). Temperature measurements at various cortical depths showed that, for a surface temperature of 6 °C, gradients were generally

2–4 °C/mm. In others words, during cooling of the upper layers at 6°, the temperature of deep cortical layers is always less than 10–12 °C, a value well below the temperature generally considered to block synaptic activity in the central nervous system (Brooks 1983, Lomber *et al.* 1999). Therefore, despite the disadvantage of not having a constant temperature across cortical depth, the cryoprobe successfully blocks all layers. This is especially important to study the impact of cortico-LPl neurons because they are mainly located in layer V (Abramson and Chalupa 1985). We have however found, as other investigators did (e.g., Michalski *et al.* 1993), that the effective temperature may vary from cell to cell. For instance, Fig. 3.3A shows that while most units (panel 1) were silenced at a temperature of 9 °C (at the cortical surface), and sometimes higher (panel 2), some cells (panel 3) still responded to the stimulus at a temperature near 5 °C. Despite the fact that a temperature of 8–10 °C would normally block the activity

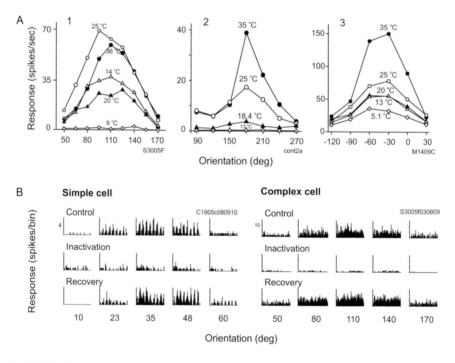

Fig. 3.3 (A) Orientation tuning curves of neurons in the deep layers of area 17 as a function of the temperature monitored at the cortical surface. Responses of the cells shown in panel 1 was abolished at a temperature of 9 °C. In panel 2, the cell stopped firing at 13 °C. The neuron shown in panel 3 was still responsive near 5 °C and a tuning curve could still be distinguished. (B) Effect of cooling on the response of a simple and a complex cell recorded in layers VI and V of area 17, as a function of the orientation of a drifting grating. For each cell, cooling reduced neuronal activity at each orientation tested. After cortical recovery, the profile and strength of the cells' discharges were similar to that observed prior to cooling. PSTHs duration is 4 sec (Modified from Casanova *et al.* 1997).

of most cells, it is thus possible for a few neurons to somehow remain active. In Casanova *et al.* (1997), the extent of the cooling process was also estimated by monitoring the temperature at different mediolateral and rostro–caudal positions. On the mediolateral axis, temperatures below 20 °C were observed at the surface of the cortex, up to 1.5 mm from the cooling probe. The spread of cold in the rostro-caudal axis was less pronounced. As the thermocouple was moved away from the cryoprobe, surface temperature increased rapidly and reached a value equal to, or greater than 20 °C, at a distance of 500 μm. The difference in cooling-extent between the two axes is most likely due to the shape of the probe itself i.e., elongated in the rostro-caudal axis (increased contact surface at the medial and lateral sides of the probe). Despite the difficulty in evaluating the extent of the cooling with great accuracy, our control experiments suggest therefore that the inactivation is not restricted to the cortical region beneath the probe but may extend for at least 1 mm laterally.

A major concern when using this cooling technique relates to the integrity of the cortex. One wants to ascertain that cooling does not damage the cells beneath the cryoprobe or modify their properties. While recording multiunit activity, we monitored the discharges of single simple and complex cells to determine if cooling had any deleterious effects. Panel B in Fig. 3.3 illustrates the responses of a simple cell and a complex cell in layers VI and V, respectively, as a function of the orientation of a drifting grating. In both cases, the discharge rate was almost completely or totally abolished by cooling. Three observations can be made. First, cellular activity in deep cortical layers could be successfully blocked. Second, cell properties were not altered by the cooling procedure as the strength and pattern of neuronal discharges (modulated versus unmodulated) were similar prior to, and after the cooling procedure. Third, the preferred orientations as well as the bandwidth of the tuning functions did not change. It is thus clear that the cooling procedure is effective because cortical neurons could be shut down without damaging their physiology. The only case in which cortical activity became uncharacteristic during the recovery period (e.g., increased spontaneous discharge level, a burst pattern) was after repeated cooling. When this happens, the experiment should be terminated since the damage is not reversible.

Studying the pathway from the primary visual cortex to the LPl nucleus

The lateral part of the LP or LPl nucleus is also often referred to as the striato-recipient zone of the pulvinar complex because it is the only subregion that receives direct projections from the primary visual cortex. We investigated the possibility that the input from area 17 is necessary for maintaining visual responsiveness of cells in the LPl and to some extent, its visuotopic map. We used a cryoprobe that was generally 8 and 6 mm in length (rostro–caudal axis) and width (mediolateral axis), respectively. The cooling device was placed so as to inactivate area 17 central representation of the visual field, which is over-represented in LPl. It covered the posterior region of the marginal gyrus and parts of the posterolateral gyrus. Therefore, a small region of area 18, in the lateral part of the marginal gyrus, was also inactivated.

Deactivating area 17 provoked an overall decrease of visual responsiveness for about one third of LPl neurons tested. An example is shown in Fig. 3.4. Very rarely did we observe specific effects such as a change of spatial frequency tuning (Figure 6D in Casanova *et al.* 1997). The persistence of visual responses during cortical deactivation was confirmed by subsequent experiments in which area 17 was destroyed by aspiration (Casanova *et al.* 1997). In these brain-damaged animals, a few LPl receptive fields within the cortical scotoma were still sensitive to the orientation and/or direction of a moving stimulus. Altogether, these data suggest that striate cortex input may be less critical than that in primates, because removing the primary visual cortex in the latter yielded virtually a total loss of visual responses in the pulvinar (Bender 1983). It is likely that in cats, both striate and extrastriate cortical areas are necessary to establish the retinotopic

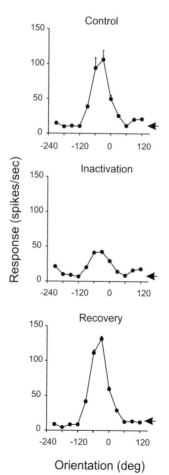

Fig. 3.4 Representative effect of cooling area 17 on the orientation tuning function of a LPl cell. Cortical deactivation reduced the overall responsiveness of the thalamic unit. The arrows represent spontaneous discharge levels. (Modified from Casanova *et al.* 1997).

map found in the LP–pulvinar. No definite answer can be given until the exact contribution of each extrastriate area is determined by deactivation techniques.

Reversible deactivation by pharmacological means

Deactivating restricted pools of neurons by local injection of a blocking agent is one of the more elegant techniques used to investigate connectivity between brain structures. It has been successfully used in cats and monkeys, in studies aimed at understanding the function of corticocortical and geniculocortical connections (e.g., Malpeli *et al.* 1986; Bolz *et al.* 1989; Mignard and Malpeli 1991; Nealey and Maunsell 1994; Grieve and Sillito 1995 Crook *et al.* 1996). One of the advantages of this technique is that one is able to deactivate very restricted parts of a brain structure, such as specific cortical and geniculate layers

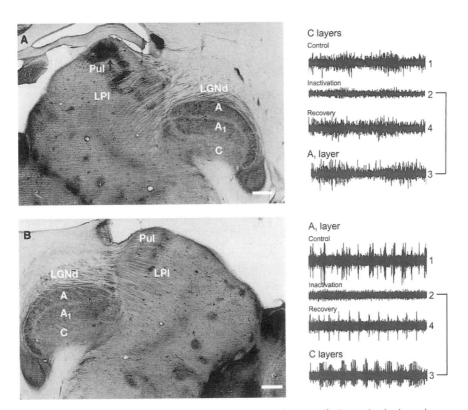

Fig. 3.5 (and color plate 4) Deactivation can be restricted to specific layers in the lateral geniculate nucleus. Top of figure: Visual activity was abolished in the C layers without blocking the visual activity in layer A1. Bottom of figure: Injection of GABA in layer A1 abolished the visually evoked multiunit responses without affecting activity in the neighbouring C layers. Injection volumes in A and B: ~100 nl. Scales: 500 μm.

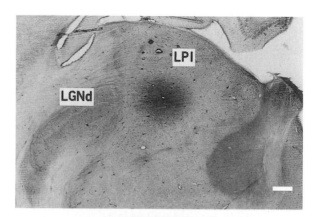

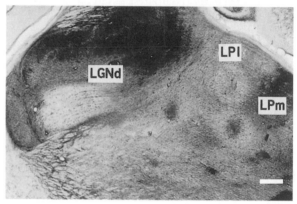

Fig. 3.6 (and color plate 5) Injection of the deactivating drug can be made to shut down large regions in the LP-pulvinar complex. Top of figure: a large injection was made in the LPl ~2 μl. Bottom of figure: multiple injections can be made during a single experiment. In this case, two injections were located in the LPl while a third one targeted the LPm. Injection volumes: 800 nl Scales: 500 μm.

(Fig. 3.5). It also allows for the activity of a larger group of neurons to be blocked, when necessary, as is the case when studying the extrageniculate pathways originating from the pulvinar complex (Fig. 3.6).

Different kinds of devices are used, but in most cases, they allow the experimenter to monitor simultaneously the neuronal activity at the injection and recording sites. This is essential to determine with exactitude the final placement of the injection electrode (generally in a region displaying visuotopic correspondence with the target site) and the amplitude and time course of the blocking agent effects. The placement of the electrodes can be verified post-mortem by injecting a stained solution. In my laboratory, an inactivating solution colored with agents such as Chicago Sky Blue (CSB, 1%; see Figs. 3.5 and 3.6) or neutral red is used. This method has proven to be useful in locating the center of the injection and to some degree, its extent. In the latter case, caution is required because the diffusion of the pharmacological agent does not necessarily correspond to that of the staining agent. Consequently, one should monitor activity near the injection site with a remote electrode to estimate with exactitude the dimension of the deactivated area (see Hupé *et al.* 1999 for a thorough discussion). While control experiments have clearly indicated that the use of a colored agent in adult animal models (cats and rats) does not alter the physiology of the cells beneath the electrode, this was not the case when administered in immature animals. For rats aged between 15 and 25 postnatal days, CSB was detrimental to cell physiology, the damaging effect being stronger for younger animals (Marois 1997; Coudé *et al.* 2000) (Fig. 3.7). I am not aware of similar immature cell sensitivity in kittens, but one should be careful and make appropriate control injections (e.g., colored vehicle) before using dye agent such as CSB in young animals.

The system we used over the last ten years consisted of the following: first, glass microelectrodes are made from borosilicate capillaries (OD: 1 mm) pulled by a vertical pipette puller (David Kopf Inc.). The extremity of the pipette is manually broken to obtain a sharp tip with an opening of ~ 15–30 μm, the best experimental results being often obtained for an opening of ~ 24 μm. The pipette is then filled with the inactivating solution and is inserted into the electrode holder of a WPI 1400 nanopump (World Precision Instruments Inc.). The holder was slightly modified in order to introduce a silver wire for the simultaneous recording of multiunit activity. The 1400 nanopump is unfortunately discontinued. A comparable device is offered by WPI (Nanoliter injector 2000), but the electrode holder would also have to be modified for concomitant recordings. Nevertheless, as previously stated, many laboratory-made injecting systems based on either pressure or iontophoresis are described in the literature (see for example, Lomber and Payne 1999) and can be used to perform deactivation experiments.

The electrode is advanced and positioned within the zone to be inactivated (based on stereotaxic and visual response cues): when the target is located deeply in the brain,

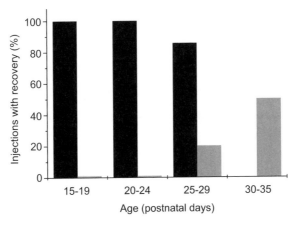

Fig. 3.7 The use of CSB can be damaging in juvenile animals. In a project aimed at determining the effect of Angiotensin II (Ang II) on visual evoked potentials in the superior colliculus, it was observed that the recovery that normally follows the Ang II effect was absent or strongly reduced in animals younger than 30 days of age when the solution was stained with CSB. Filled bars represent the percentage of experiments in which the potential recovered after injection of noncolored (black bars) and CSB (0.5%) colored (gray bars) solutions.

a minimum injection (5 nl/min) is made throughout the descent to prevent clogging. The inactivation is carried out through an initial solution injection at a rate dependent on the extent of the zone to be silenced. For example, in order to deactivate a large cellular pool, initial injections in the LP–pulvinar complex vary between 60–80 nl/min. Once the measured neural activity is diminished (generally after two minutes), the rate is reduced between 20–30 nl/min to maintain the effect of the drug during testing and to avoid any premature recovery in the deactivated area. In almost all cases, these volumes did not provoke any lesions of the tissues and a complete recovery was obtained (Figs. 3.5 and 3.6). The activity of the inactivated zone is continuously monitored, which allows us to adjust the rate of injection accordingly.

When deactivating a new thalamic region, for the initial experiments we typically used a solution of lidocaine chlorohydrate (2%) that is known to block sodium channels (Sandkühler and Gerbhart 1991). The use of lidocaine is motivated by the fact that the distribution of GABA receptors in the thalamus is heterogeneous (Palacios *et al.* 1981; Richards *et al.* 1987). The advantages of using lidocaine are: (i) it is a non viscous solution that can be easily colored and injected; (ii) it has no toxic effects; (iii) its effect is of sufficient duration to allow a series of tests; (iv) it allows a complete recovery of neuronal activity; and (v) it is effective on all cellular types (Malpeli and Schiller 1979; Martin 1991; Tehovnik and Sommer 1997). Therefore, the use of lidocaine assures that all components of a given cellular pool are silenced and allows one to rapidly evaluate whether the block has any physiologic effect on targeted neurons. The great disadvantage of lidocaine is that it also blocks fibers of passage; a drawback that is definitely not appropriate in LP–pulvinar complex deactivation, as many fibers pass through this region. For this reason, subsequent experiments should rely on the use of γ-aminobutyric acid (GABA, 0.01–0.2 M) or its potent $GABA_A$ receptor agonist, muscimol (as in Grieve and Sillito 1995), to rule out any possible contribution of fibers of passage as these drugs block synaptic activity without affecting the conduction in passing fibers.

Studying the thalamic projections to the PMLS cortex

The apparatus and methods described above were used to study the projections from the cat's LP–pulvinar to the posteromedial part of the lateral suprasylvian (PMLS) cortex. In normal cats, the main afferent of the PMLS cortex comes from other visual cortical areas (e.g., areas 17, 18 and 19 (Swadlow 1983; Sherk and Ombrellaro 1988; Shipp and Grant 1991); and from several thalamic nuclei, such as the lateral geniculate nucleus (C layers), the medial interlaminar nucleus (MIN), the geniculate wing (GW) (or retino-recipient zone of the pulvinar; see Updyke [1983]), the LPm, the LPl and the pulvinar (Updyke 1977, 1981; Garey *et al.* 1991; Spear 1991; Norita *et al.* 1996). Spear and colleagues reported that removing areas 17, 18 and 19 had little effect, if any, on the spatial and temporal contrast sensitivity of PMLS cells (Guido *et al.* 1990). These results suggest that some properties of PMLS cells, including spatiotemporal characteristics, are generated by signals arising from thalamic nuclei. Among the latter, the

LPl may play a prominent role in establishing the properties of PMLS: projections from the LPl represent the most dense thalamic projections to PMLS (Grant and Shipp 1991; Norita *et al.* 1996), and PMLS and LPl neurons share many properties (Casanova *et al.* 1989; Chalupa and Abramson 1989; Danilov *et al.* 1995; Guido *et al.* 1990; Morrone *et al.* 1986; Savard *et al.* 1995; Zumbroich *et al.* 1988). Given these last observations, we hypothesized that signals from the striate-recipient zone of the LP–pulvinar complex were necessary for spatial (and temporal) frequency processing in the PMLS cortex of normal cats. The outcome of this study was surprising and disappointing at first. Despite numerous large injections of lidocaine or GABA, deactivation of the LPl had little effect on the spatial and temporal frequency tuning of neurons in the PMLS cortex, and on their direction selectivity (for details, see Minville and Casanova 1998). Less than 20% of PMLS cells were affected by the deactivation, and the observed effect consisted of a strong decrease in the cells' overall responsiveness

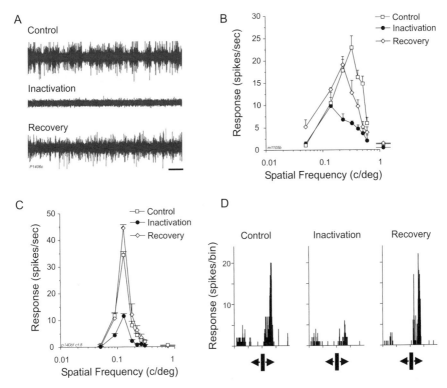

Fig. 3.8 (A) Inhibitory effect of the injection of GABA (200 µM) on multiunit activity in LPl (scale = 500 msec). (B) When deactivation of the LPl affected PMLS cells, the effect almost always consisted of an overall reduction of the responses (here, as a function of the grating spatial frequency). (C, D) Preliminary data showing that deactivating the C layers of the L6N provoked a robust decrease of the spatial frequency tuning function and of the discharges evoked by a bar moving in the preferred direction of a PMLS neuron. PSTHs duration is 4 sec.

(Fig. 3.8B). The conclusions of this investigation were that a small proportion of the projections from LPl to PMLS are excitatory in nature and necessary to drive cortical neurons and that the signals from the remaining projection cells may be used for more subtle function (e.g., response modulation). This last assumption was confirmed by some data obtained subsequently, and an example is presented in Fig. 3.9. Responses of PMLS and LPl neurons to a visual target (whether bars or gratings) can be modified by the presence of a moving texture pattern presented as background (Von Grünau and Frost 1983; Casanova and Savard 1996). Preliminary data suggest that the stimulus–background interactions observed in PMLS cortex may depend on the integrity of the LPl (Fig. 3.9). It is therefore possible that the LPl-PMLS loop may be involved in other functions such as the analysis of complex motion, as is the case for the reciprocal link between the LPm and the anterior ectosylvian visual (AEV) cortex (see next section).

Since the spatiotemporal properties of most PMLS cells are not derived from cortical and LPl inputs, they must be built from the projections of other thalamic nuclei. Guido *et al.* (1990) proposed the C layers as a likely candidate. This may well be the case, given preliminary data that we obtained a few years ago in a study that it might be worth pursuing (Fig. 3.8C, D).

Studying the reciprocal connections between the LP–pulvinar complex and the ectosylvian cortex

As mentioned earlier, cells in the LPm exhibit higher-order properties because they can code the veridical direction of plaid patterns (pattern motion selectivity; Merabet *et al.*

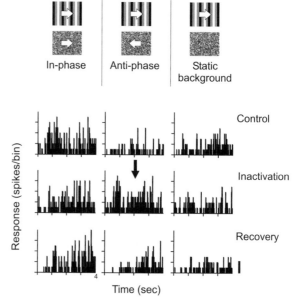

Fig. 3.9 Preliminary data showing that deactivating the LPl can modify stimulus-background interactions in PMLS cortex (see Casanova and Savard [1996] for details on the stimulus). The first PSTHs row shows that the cell's discharges were reduced when the superimposed grating and the textured pattern moved in opposite directions (anti-phase condition). This inhibition was not present during LPl deactivation (filled arrow).

In-phase   Anti-phase   Static background

Control

Inactivation

Recovery

Response (spikes/bin)

Time (sec)

1998). The LPm establishes reciprocal connections with the AEV cortex (Mucke *et al.* 1982) which is the only region described so far, in the cat visual cortex, that possesses a population of pattern-motion selective cells (Scannell *et al.* 1996). The presence of pattern-motion cells at both ends of the AEV-LPm loop raised the possibility that this corticothalamic network represents a module specifically involved in the processing of complex motion information. In order to demonstrate a physiological link between these two regions, we measured the responses of LPm neurons to plaids before and after pharmacological deactivation of visuotopically corresponding regions of the AEV

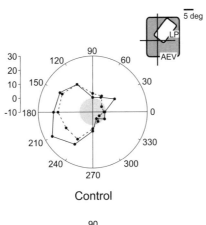

Control

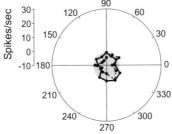

AEV Deactivation

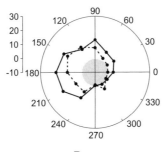

Recovery

Fig. 3.10 Effect of deactivating the AEV cortex on a LP-pulvinar pattern-motion selective neuron. During deactivation, a suppression of the cell's response and a concomitant loss of its ability to signal the direction of the drifting grating (solid line) and plaid pattern (dashed line) were observed. In each polar graph, data points within the shaded region represent cellular discharges below spontaneous activity levels. The inset shows the location of the thalamic neuron's receptive field in reference to the AEV scotoma. Reproduced with permission from *Nature*, **396**:265-8, copyright 1998 Macmillan Magazines Ltd.

cortex. Half of the pattern-motion selective LPm units tested were affected by the cortical deactivation (Fig. 3.10) indicating that the LP and AEV cortex are functionally linked, and further, that this loop is likely to be involved in the processing of higher-order motion information. The remaining pattern-motion selective units were not affected by the deactivation of the AEV cortex. This could have been due to our failure to deactivate the neurons projecting to the LPm. The AEV cortex is difficult to reach and its visuotopic organization is rather loose (Mucke *et al.* 1982; Scannell *et al.* 1996). Thus despite careful placement of the electrode and careful analysis of the visual field represented, we did not know if the lack of effect was factual, or if it resulted from the deactivation of AEV cells projecting to LPm neurons other that those we recorded from. To answer this, it was necessary to ensure that the whole AEV cortex was "put to sleep." This was not possible with the pharmacological technique used, given the limited extent of the deactivated region. We considered that the cryogenic blockade of the whole AEV was not an option given the great difficulty in placing a cryoprobe at that level, although some have been recently successful (Jiang *et al.* 2001). We thus complemented the reversible deactivation study by investigating pattern motion selectivity in LPm after acute AEV lesions. Destroying the AEV cortex by aspiration confirmed the deactivating experiments: pattern-motion selective cells could still be found in the LPm of AEV lesioned animals. This suggested that pattern motion selectivity either exists in cortical areas other than the AEV cortex (preliminary unpublished data indicate that it may well be the AMLS cortex) or, that LP-pulvinar receptive fields can integrate local motion signals into a global percept (intrinsic computation) Nevertheless, we have here an example in which the reversible deactivation procedure alone was not sufficient to draw firm conclusions.

We then turned our attention to the reciprocal projections: those from the LPm to the AEV cortex. These experiments were also difficult, if not more so, than the ones described above. Both regions have a complex visuotopic organization and reaching the correct part of the LPm with the injection electrode, in most cases without clear visual cues, is easier said than done. It is perhaps for these reasons that the results acquired so far are not conclusive: Out of 21 cells, only 6 AEV neurons were successfully tested: in all cases except for one, deactivation failed to modify the pattern-motion selectivity in the AEV cortex. In order to reach a definite answer, the next obvious step is for these experiments to be carried through; a task that may require several attempts before a reasonable sample we can rely on is obtained.

Conclusion

As stated throughout the text, the advantages of reversible deactivation techniques clearly outnumber the disadvantages. Since the deactivation devices can be laboratory made, they do not necessitate major and expensive apparatuses, but rather some patience and imagination. Also, in contrast to lesion studies, a large population of cells is not needed because each neuron serves as its own control. The success of the deactivation experiments depends, in part, on the researcher's ability to place electrodes in visuo-topically corresponding regions, which can prove to be difficult when studying thalamic extrageniculate pathways. Uncovering the nature and function of the signals transferred along the cortico–thalamocortical loops represents a challenge given the number of connections between the neocortex and the thalamus. Results coming from deactivation techniques will provide essential cues as to the function of these extra-geniculate pathways. Ideally, the nature of the signals traveling from cortex to thalamus (or vice-versa) should be determined by antidromic techniques, prior to the deactivation experiments. This is a logical prerequisite for studying cortico–thalamocortical loops and for unveiling their function in visual processing.

Acknowledgments

I am grateful to all members of my laboratory who worked day in and day out on the projects described in this chapter and helped develop and refine the deactivation techniques: my research assistant, Karine Minville, and graduate students Lotfi Merabet, Alex Desautels, Annecy Marois, and Tony Savard. The work presented here was supported by CIHR, FRSQ and FCAR.

References

Abramson, B. P. and Chalupa, L. M. (1985) The laminar distribution of cortical connections with the tecto- and cortico-recipient zones in the cat's lateral posterior nucleus. *Neuroscience*, **15**:81–95.

Baker, F. H. and Malpeli, J. G. (1977) Effects of cryogenic blockade of visual cortex on the responses of lateral geniculate neurons in the monkey. *Experimental Brain Research*, **29**:433–44.

Benedek, G., Norita, M. and Creutzfeldt, O. D. (1983) Electrophysiological and anatomical demonstration of an overlapping striate and tectal projection to the lateral posterior-pulvinar complex of the cat. *Experimental Brain Research*, **52**:157–69.

Bender, D. B. (1983) Visual activation of neurons in the primate pulvinar depends on cortex but not colliculus. *Brain Research*, **279**:258–61.

Bender, D. B. and Butter, C. M. (1987) Comparison of the effects of superior colliculus and pulvinar lesions on visual search and tachistoscopic pattern discrimination in monkeys. *Experimental Brain Research*, **69**:140–54.

Bolz, J., Gilbert, C. D. and Wiesel, T. N. (1989) Pharmacological analysis of cortical circuitry. *Trends in Neuroscience*, **12**:292–296.

Brooks, V. B. (1983) Study of brain function by local, reversible cooling. *Reviews in Physiology, Biochemistry and Pharmacology*, **95**:1–92.

Bullier, J., Kennedy, H. and Salinger, W. (1984) Branching and laminar origin of projections between visual cortical areas in the cat. *Journal of Comparative Neurology*, **228**:329–41.

Casanova, C., Freeman, R. D. and Nordmann, J. P. (1989) Monocular and binocular response properties of cells in the striate-recipient zone of the cat's lateral posterior-pulvinar complex. *Journal of Neurophysiology*, **62**:544–57.

Casanova, C., Nordmann, J. P. and Molotchnikoff, S. (1991) Pulvinar-lateralis posterior nucleus complex of mammals and the visual function. *Journal of Physiology*, **85**:44–57.

Casanova, C. and Savard, T. (1996) Motion sensitivity and stimulus interactions in the striate-recipient zone of the lateral posterior-pulvinar complex. *Progress in Brain Research*, **112**:277–87.

Casanova, C., Savard, T. and Darveau, S. (1997) Contribution of area 17 to cell responses in the striate-recipient zone of the cat's lateral posterior-pulvinar complex. *European Journal of Neuroscience*, **9:**1026–36.

Chalupa, L. M. and Abramson, B. P. (1988) Receptive-field properties in the tecto- and striate-recipient zones of the cat's lateral posterior nucleus. *Progress in Brain Research*, **75:**85–94.

Chalupa, L. M. and Abramson, B. P. (1989) Visual receptive fields in the striate-recipient zone of the lateral posterior-pulvinar complex. *Journal of Neuroscience*, **9:**347–57.

Chalupa, L. M. (1991) Vision function of the pulvinar. In A. G. Leventhal (ed.) *The Neural Basis of Visual Function*, pp.140–59. CRC Press, Boca Raton, FL.

Clemo, H. R. and Stein, B. E. (1986) Effects of cooling somatosensory cortex on response properties of tactile cells in the superior colliculus. *Journal of Neurophysiology*, **55:**1352–68.

Coudé, G., Marois, A. and Casanova, C. (2000) Effects of angiotensin II on visual evoked potentials in the superior colliculus of juvenile rats. *Neuropeptides*, **34:**203–10.

Crick, F. and Koch, C. (1998) Constraints on cortical and thalamic projections: the no-strong-loops hypothesis. *Nature*, **391:**245–50.

Crook, J. M., Kisvarday, Z. F. and Eysel, U. T. (1996) GABA-induced inactivation of functionally characterized sites in cat visual cortex (area 18): effects on direction selectivity. *Journal of Neurophysiology*, **75:**2071–88.

Danilov, Y., Moore, R. J., King, V. R. *et al.* (1995) Are neurons in cat posteromedial lateral suprasylvian visual cortex orientation selective? Tests with bars and gratings. *Visual Neuroscience*, **12:**141–51.

Diamond, I. T. and Hall, W. C. (1969) Evolution of neocortex. *Science*, **164:**251–62.

Dumbrava, D., Faubert, J. and Casanova, C. (2001) Global motion integration in the cat's lateral posterior-pulvinar complex. *European Journal of Neuroscience* **13:**2218–26.

Fabre-Thorpe, M., Vievard, A. and Buser, P. (1986) Role of the extra-geniculate pathway in visual guidance. II. Effects of lesioning the pulvinar-lateral posterior thalamic complex in the cat. *Experimental Brain Research*, **62:**596–606.

Garey, L. J., Dreher, B. and Robinson, S. R. (1991) The organization of the visual thalamus. In B. Dreher and S. R. Robinson (eds) *Neuroanatomy of the Visual Pathways and their Development*, pp. 176–201. CRC Press, Boca Raton, FL.

Girard, P. and Bullier, J. (1989) Visual activity in area V2 during reversible inactivation of area 17 in the macaque monkey. *Journal of Neurophysiology*, **62:**1287–302.

Grant, S. and Shipp, S. (1991) Visuotopic organization of the lateral suprasylvian area and of an adjacent area of the ectosylvian gyrus of cat cortex: A physiological and connectional study. *Visual Neuroscience*, **6:**315–18.

Graybiel, A. M. and Berson, D. M. (1980) Histochemical identification and afferent connections of subdivisions in the lateralis posterior-pulvinar complex and related thalamic nuclei in the cat. *Neuroscience*, **5:**1175–238.

Grieve, K. L. and Sillito, A. M. (1995) Non-length-tuned cells in layers II/III and IV of the visual cortex: the effect of blockade of layer VI on responses to stimuli of different lengths. *Experimental Brain Research*, **104:**12–20.

Grieve, K. L., Acuna, C. and Cudeiro, J. (2000) The primate pulvinar nuclei: vision and action. *Trends in Neuroscience*, **23:**35–9.

Guido, W., Tong, L. and Spear, P. D. (1990) Afferent bases of spatial- and temporal-frequency processing by neurons in the cat's posteromedial lateral suprasylvian cortex: effects of removing areas 17,18, and 19. *Journal of Neurophysiology*, **64:**1636–51.

Hupé, J. M., Chouvet, G. and Bullier, J. (1999) Spatial and temporal parameters of cortical inactivation by GABA. *Journal of Neuroscience Methods*, **86:**129–43.

Hutchins, B. and Updyke, B. V. (1989) Retinotopic organization within the lateral posterior complex of the cat. *Journal of Comparative Neurology*, **285**:350–98.

Jiang, W., Wallace, M. T., Jiang, H. *et al.* (2001) Two cortical areas mediate multisensory integration in superior colliculus neurons. *Journal of Neurophysiology*, **85**:506–22.

Killackey, H. and Diamond, I. T. (1971) Visual attention in the tree shrew: an ablation study of the striate and extrastriate visual cortex. *Science*, **171**:696–9.

Kreiter, A. K. and Singer, W. (1996) Stimulus-dependent synchronization of neuronal responses in the visual cortex of the awake macaque monkey. *Journal of Neuroscience*, **16**:2381–96.

Le Gros Clark, W. E. (1932) The structure and connections of the thalamus. *Brain*, **55**:406–70.

Macchi, G., Bentivoglio, M., Minciacchi, D. *et al.* (1996) Trends in the anatomical organization and functional significance of the mammalian thalamus. *Italian Journal of Neurological Science*, **17**:105–29.

Lomber, S. G. and Payne, B. R. (1999) Assessment of neural function with reversible deactivation methods. *Journal of Neuroscience Methods*, **86**.

Lomber, S. G., Payne, B. R. and Horel, J. A. (1999) The cryoloop: An adaptable reversible cooling deactivation method for behavioral and electrophysiological assessment of neural function. *Journal of Neuroscience Methods*, **86**:179–94.

Malpeli, J. G. and Schiller, P. H. (1979) A method of reversible inactivation of small regions of brain tissue. *Journal of Neuroscience Methods*, **1**:143–51.

Malpeli, J. G., Lee, C., Schwark, H. D. *et al.* (1986) Cat area 17. I. Pattern of thalamic control of cortical layers. *Journal of Neurophysiology*, **56**:1062–73.

Martin, J. H. (1991) Autoradiographic estimation of the extent of reversible inactivation produced by microinjection of lidocaine and muscimol in the rat. *Neuroscience Letters*, **127**:160–4.

Marois, A. (1997) Effets de l'angiotensine II sur les réponses visuelles du colliculus supérieur au cours du développement post-natal chez le rat. PhD thesis, Université de Montréal.

Merabet, L., Desautels, A., Minville, K. *et al.* (1998) Motion integration in a thalamic visual nucleus. *Nature*, **396**:265–8.

Michalski, A., Wimborne, B. M. and Henry, G. H. (1993) The effect of reversible cooling of cat's primary visual cortex on the responses of area 21a neurons. *Journal of Physiology (London)*, **446**:133–56.

Mignard, M. and Malpeli, J. G. (1991) Paths of information flow through visual cortex. *Science*, **251**:1249–51.

Miller, R. (1996) Cortico-thalamic interplay and the security of operation of neural assemblies and temporal chains in the cerebral cortex. *Biological Cybernetics*, **75**:263–75.

Minville, K. and Casanova, C. (1998) Spatial frequency processing in posteromedial lateral suprasylvian cortex does not depend on the projections from the striate-recipient zone of the cat's lateral posterior-pulvinar complex. *Neuroscience*, **84**:699–711.

Molotchnikoff, S., Morin, C., Cerat, A. *et al.* (1986) An efficient cryoprobe to inactivate cortical surfaces. *Brain Research Bulletin*, **16**:557–9.

Morrone, M. C., Di Stephano, M. and Burr, D. C. (1986) Spatial and temporal properties of neurons of the lateral suprasylvian cortex of the cat. *Journal of Neurophysiology*, **56**:969–86.

Mucke, L., Norita, M., Benedek, G. *et al.* (1982) Physiologic and anatomic investigation of a visual cortical area situated in the ventral bank of the anterior ectosylvian sulcus of the cat. *Experimental Brain Research*, **46**:1–11.

Mumford, D. (1991) On the computational architecture of the neocortex. I. The role of the thalamo-cortical loop. *Biological Cybernetics*, **65**:135–45.

Nagel-Leiby, S., Bender, D. B. and Butter, C. M. (1984) Effects of kainic acid and radiofrequency lesions of the pulvinar on visual discrimination in the monkey. *Brain Research*, **300:**295–303.

Nealey, T. A. and Maunsell, J. H. (1994) Magnocellular and parvocellular contributions to the responses of neurons in macaque striate cortex. *Journal of Neuroscience*, **14:**2069–79.

Norita, M., Kase, M., Hoshino, K. *et al.* (1996) Extrinsic and intrinsic connections of the cat's lateral suprasylvian visual area. *Progress in Brain Research*, **112:**231–50.

Palacios, J. M., Wamsley, J. K. and Kuhar, M. J. (1981) High affinity GABA receptors-autoradiographic localization. *Brain Research*, **222:**285–307.

Payne, B. R., Lomber, S. G., MacNeil, M. A. *et al.* (1996) Evidence for greater sight in blindsight following damage of primary visual cortex early in life. *Neuropsychologia*, **34:**741–74.

Petersen, S. E., Robinson, D. L. and Morris, J. D. (1987) Contributions of the pulvinar to visual spatial attention. *Neuropsychologia*, **25:**97–105.

Ptito, M., Johannsen, P., Faubert, J. *et al.* (1999) Activation of human extrageniculostriate pathways after damage to area V1. *Neuroimage*, **9:**97–107.

Raczkowski, D. and Rosenquist, A. C. (1983) Connections of the multiple visual cortical areas with the lateral posterior-pulvinar complex and adjacent thalamic nuclei in the cat. *Journal of Neuroscience*, **3:**1912–42.

Richards, J. G., Schoch, P., Haring, P. *et al.* (1987) Resolving $GABA_A$/benzodiazepine receptors: cellular and subcellular localization in the CNS with monoclonal antibodies. *Journal of Neuroscience*, **7:**1866–86.

Robinson, D. L. and Peterson, S. E. (1992) The pulvinar and visual salience. *Trends in Neuroscience*, **15:**127–32.

Rockland, K. S. (1996) Two types of corticopulvinar terminations: round (type 2) and elongate (type 1). *Journal of Comparative Neurology*, **368:**57–87.

Rockland, K. S. (1998) Convergence and branching patterns of round, type 2 corticopulvinar axons. *Journal of Comparative Neurology*, **390:**515–36.

Rockland, K. S. Andresen, J., Cowie, R. J. *et al.* (1999) Single axon analysis of pulvinocortical connections to several visual areas in the macaque. *Journal of Comparative Neurology*, **406:**221–50.

Sandkühler, J. and Gebhart, G. F. (1991) Production of reversible local blockage of neural function. *Methods in Neuroscience*, **7:**122–38.

Savard, T., Minville, K., Merabet, L. *et al.* (1995) Properties of cells in the striate-recipient zone of the cat's LP: Length summation, contrast, and phase sensitivity. *Society for Neuroscience Abstracts*, **21:**133.

Scannell, J. W., Sengpiel, F., Tovee, M. J. *et al.* (1996) Visual motion processing in the anterior ectosylvian sulcus of the cat. *Journal of Neurophysiology*, **76:**895–907.

Schneider, G. E. (1967) Contrasting visuomotor functions of tectum and cortex in the golden hamster. *Psychologische Forschung*, **31:**52–62.

Schneider, G. E. (1969) Two visual systems: brain mechanisms for localization and discrimination are dissociated by tectal and cortical lesions. *Science*, **163:**895–902.

Sherk, H. (1978) Area 18 cell responses in cat during reversible inactivation of area 17. *Journal of Neurophysiology*, **41:**204–15.

Sherk, H. and Ombrellaro, M. (1988) The retinotopic match between area 17 and its targets in visual suprasylvian cortex. *Experimental Brain Research*, **72:**225–36.

Sherman, S. M. and Guillery, R. W. (1996) Functional organization of thalamocortical relays. *Journal of Neurophysiology*, **76:**1367–95.

Sherman, S. M. and Guillery, R. W. (1998) On the actions that one nerve cell can have on another: distinguishing "drivers" from "modulators." *Proceeding of the National Academy of Sciences (USA),* **95:**7121–6.

Sherman, S. M. and Guillery, R. W. (2001) *Exploring the thalamus.* Academic Press, San Diego.

Sillito, A. and Jones, H. E. (1997) Functional organization influencing neurotransmission in the lateral geniculate nucleus. In M. Steriade, E. G. Jones, and D. A. McCormick (eds) *Thalamus: Experimental and Clinical Aspects,* pp. 1–52. Elsevier Science, Oxford.

Skinner, J. E. and Lindsley, D. B. (1968) Reversible cryogenic blockade of neural function in the brain of unrestrained animals. *Science,* **161:**595–7.

Shipp, S. and Grant, S. (1991) Organization of reciprocal connections between area 17 and the lateral suprasylvian area of cat visual cortex. *Visual Neuroscience,* **6:**339–55.

Spear, P. D. (1991) Functions of extrastriate visual cortex in non-primate species. In A. G. Leventhal (ed.) *The Neural Basis of Visual Function,* pp. 339–70. CRC Press, Boca Raton, FL.

Spillmann, L. and Werner, J. S. (1996) Long-range interactions in visual perception. *Trends in Neuroscience,* **19:**428–34.

Swadlow, H. A. (1983) Efferent systems of primary visual cortex: A review of structure and function. *Brain Research Review,* **6:**1–24.

Tehovnik, E. J. and Sommer, M. A. (1997) Effective spread and timecourse of neural inactivation caused by lidocaine injection in monkey cerebral cortex. *Journal of Neuroscience Methods,* **74:**17–26.

Trevarthen, C. B. (1968) Two mechanisms of vision in primates. *Psychologische Forschung,* **31:**299–348.

Updyke, B. V. (1977) Topographic organization of the projections from cortical areas 17:18 and 19 onto the thalamus, pretectum and superior colliculus in the cat. *Journal of Comparative Neurology,* **173:**81–122.

Updyke, B. V. (1981) Projection from visual areas of the middle suprasylvian sulcus onto the lateral posterior complex and adjacent thalamic nuclei in cat. *Journal of Comparative Neurology,* **201:**477–506.

Updyke, B. V. (1983) A re-evaluation of the functional organization and cytoarchitecture of the feline lateral posterior complex, with observations of adjoining cell groups. *Journal of Comparative Neurology,* **219:**143–81.

Vidnyánszky, Z., Borostyankoi, Z., Gorcs, T. J. *et al.* (1996) Light and electron microscopic analysis of synaptic input from cortical area 17 to the lateral posterior nucleus in cats. *Experimental Brain Research,* **109:**63–70.

Von Grünau, M. and Frost, B. J. (1983) Double-opponent-process mechanisms underlying Rf structure of directionally specific cells of cat lateral suprasylvian visual area. *Experimental Brain Research,* **49:**84–92.

Zumbroich, T. J., Blakemore, C. and Price, D. J. (1988) Stimulus selectivity and its postnatal development in the cats suprasylvian visual cortex. *Progress in Brain Research,* **75:**95–107.

Chapter 4

Cortical Modulation of Auditory Processing in the Thalamus

Alessandro E.P. Villa

Introduction

The thalamus is the main source of input to the sensory areas of the cerebral cortex of mammals. Reciprocal connections exist between these structures and sensory information is processed in a complex way in the thalamus, so it cannot be regarded as a mere relay station conveying peripheral inputs to the cortex (Jones 1985; Steriade and Llinas 1988; Murray and Guillery 1996). Furthermore, there is now convincing evidence that the different states of consciousness (*a fortiori* wakefulness vs. sleep) are correlated with a modified output of the thalamus to the cortex, and that alterations of information processing by thalamic circuits may play a role in certain forms of epilepsy (Steriade *et al.* 1990, 1993). Intracellular recordings and models of the electrophysiologic properties of thalamocortical relay cells have demonstrated that these cells may discharge either in a "tonic" or a "bursting" mode (Jahnsen and Llinas 1984a,b; McCormick and Huguenard 1992). The "tonic" mode is presumed to be associated with a nearly linear, unmodified, transfer of information to the cortex, whereas the "burst" mode, often observed during sleep or epileptic discharges, is considered to be a mechanism to prevent the transfer of information to the cortex. The switch between these two states is presumably controlled by a variety of subcortical modulatory systems as well as by descending projections from the cerebral cortex (Llinas *et al.* 1999).

In all sensory modalities multiple modules characterized by the same basic connectivity are assumed to work in parallel and include three main components:

1. Dorsal thalamic neurons which receive the sensory input from the periphery, e.g. in the medial geniculate body, mgB, for the auditory pathway (Rose and Galambos 1952);

2. Cells of the thalamic reticular nucleus (RE) almost exclusively formed by GABAergic inhibitory neurons (Jones 1975; Villa, 1990); and

3. The cortical area receiving the corresponding thalamic input (Andersen *et al.* 1980).

Based on cytoarchitectonics and thalamocortical pattern of projections, the mgB of the rat (Winer and Larue 1987; Clerici and Coleman 1990), guinea pig (Redies *et al.* 1989a,b; Kvasnak *et al.* 2000), cat (Morest 1964; Winer 1985) and primates (Jordan 1973;

Allon and Yeshurun 1985; Pandya *et al.* 1994; Hackett *et al.* 1998) has been subdivided into dorsal, ventral, and medial divisions. These subdivisions correspond in some degree to ascending parallel auditory pathways (Calford and Aitkin 1983). The dorsal division sends its projections mainly to the secondary auditory cortex, whereas the ventral division of the mgB is known to be tonotopically organized and its cortical targets are the tonotopically primary (AI) auditory fields. The medial division of mgB is characterized by a widespread pattern of projection to all the auditory cortical fields. Global corticothalamic–thalamocortical reciprocity appears to be a general rule, although significant instances of nonreciprocal projections have been described, with the corticothalamic input often more extensive (Winer *et al.* 2001).

It is worth reporting that significant species-specific differences exist at the level of thalamic organization (Winer and Larue 1996). In rodents and bats the pattern of connection is characterized by thalamocortical cells and cortical cells interconnected by excitatory projections and with both types of cells sending excitatory collaterals to RE. In turn, RE sends an inhibitory axon to the mgB thalamocortical cell (Fig. 4.1a). In carnivores and in primates inhibitory local circuit cells (Golgi Type II, inhibitory interneurons) have been described within mgB and corticothalamic fibers make excitatory synaptic contacts on the distal dendrites of thalamic principal cells, as well as on inhibitory local circuit cells. In addition, it is important to note that RE sends

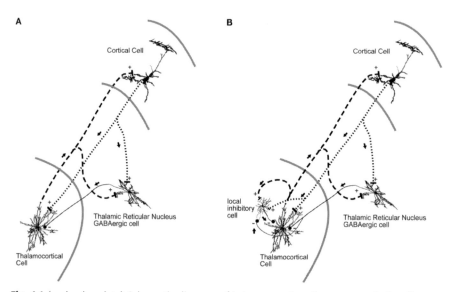

Fig. 4.1 (and color plate) Schematic diagram of interconnections in a prototypical auditory thalamocortical circuit. (A) Rodent mgB is characterized by virtually exclusive inhibitory activity driven by the GABAergic cells of the thalamic reticular nucleus. (B) Feline and primate mgB are characterized by a large proportion (in rage 25–30%) of local inhibitory cells that receive convergent input from thalamocortical and corticothalamic collaterals and from the thalamic reticular neurons as well.

inhibitory projections back to both thalamocortical cells and local circuit cells in the main thalamic nuclei (Fig. 4.1b). Two types of corticothalamic terminals have been described morphologically (Rouiller and Welker 2000; Bajo *et al.* 1995; Rockland 1996). The main corticothalamic pathway is characterized by small spherical endings whereas giant, finger-like endings characterize part of the cortical projection to the dorsal division of mgB and to the posterior nucleus of the thalamus (Fig. 4.2). The functional difference between these pathways is not clear although recent evidence suggest that giant corticothalamic endings could be counterbalanced by a GABAergic system and play an important role in descending control affecting thalamic oscillations implicated in shifts in vigilance and attention (Winer *et al.* 1999).

The role and nature of corticofugal projections have been investigated by electro-physiologic means in an extensive way, but controversial data have been reported in the literature on the auditory pathway. Initially, several authors suggested an inhibitory role of the corticofugal projections (Desmedt and Mechelse 1958; Watanabe *et al.* 1966; Amato *et al.* 1969), whereas others did not report any corticofugal effect on the thalamus (Aitkin and Dunlop 1969). Complex effects, mixing excitations, and inhibitions were reported (Ryugo and Weinberger 1976) but the most recent findings provide increasing evidence that corticothalamic projections exert an excitatory and/or facilitatory role

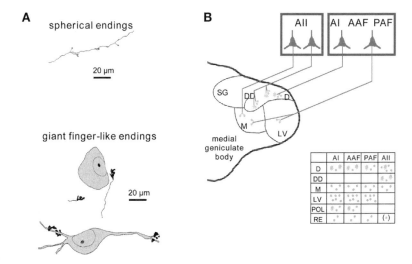

Fig. 4.2 (and color plate) Two types of corticothalamic endings. (A) Diagram of camera lucida drawings of small spherical endings (upper panel) and giant, finger-like endings lower panel) in mgB. (B) Cartoon and table summarizing the origins and targets of the two morphologically distinct corticothalamic projections in the cat. AI: primary auditory cortex; AII: secondary auditory cortex AAF: anterior auditory field; PAF: posterior auditory field; D: dorsal division of mgB; DD: deep dorsal subdivision; M: medial division of mgB; LV: ventral division of mgB; POL: lateral part of the posterior nucleus of the thalamus; RE: thalamic reticular nucleus; SG: suprageniculate nucleus. Modified from Bajo *et al.* (1995).

(Singer 1977; Orman and Humphrey 1981; Villa 1988; Villa *et al.* 1991; Zhang *et al.* 1997). Acoustically evoked activity in thalamic single units is often characterized by a complex response pattern which can be modified in its time course and in its components by cooling of the auditory cortex (Villa *et al.* 1991). Corticofugal modulation could regulate the response properties of thalamic units by modifying their firing rate and bandwidth responsiveness to pure tones. This processing (called "functional selectivity– adaptive filtering" theory) would allow to selectively extract information from the incoming signals according to the cortical activity (Villa 1988; Villa *et al.* 1991; Tetko and Villa 1997).

The technique of reversible deactivation of the cerebral cortex (Payne *et al.* 1996) is a tool of importance to study the cortical influence on thalamic activity. Of the available deactivation techniques, reversible cooling offers several advantages, in particular because steady state deactivated conditions can be maintained over a period of time long enough to allow the recording of spike trains during several conditions of stimulation. This article will illustrate some techniques and findings that support the "functional selectivity–adaptive filtering" theory. Simultaneous recordings of cell discharges in the auditory thalamus prior to, during, and after cooling deactivation allow to estimate the extent of corticofugal modulation of auditory signals in the time and frequency domain (Villa 2000). The study of interactions between two thalamic cells estimated by cross-correlations and bicoherence analysis sheds new light on the control exerted by the auditory cortex on thalamic functional connectivity.

Surgical and experimental procedures

The experiments were carried out in compliance with Swiss guidelines for the care and use of laboratory animals and after receiving governmental veterinary approval. The animals were placed in a sound-attenuating room. All animals were given atropine sulfate (i.p. 0.08 mg/kg) immediately before surgery as a prophylaxis against respiratory distress. All surgical wounds were infiltrated with local anesthetic. In cats (weighing 1.5–2.9 kg) surgery was performed under deep anesthesia (sodium pentobarbital, 40 mg/kg). After surgery the cats were muscle relaxed (gallamine triethiodide, 10 mg/kg per hour) and artificially ventilated with a mixture of 80% N_2O and 20% O_2. The arterial pulse, rectal temperature, and concentrations of CO_2 and O_2 in the expired air were continuously monitored and the pupil size periodically checked. The guinea pigs (*Cavia porcellus* GOHI strain, weighing 310–370 g) were injected i.p. with diazepam (8 mg/kg) followed 20 minutes later by sodium pentobarbital (20 mg/kg). In rats (Long-Evans hooded rats, weighing 235 and 250 g) anesthesia was induced by an i.m. injection (1.0 ml/kg body weight) of a 4:3 mixture of ketamine and xylazine hydrochloride. This dose corresponded to 57 mg/kg of ketamine and 8 mg/kg of xylazine. In guinea pigs and rats anesthesia was maintained during the whole recording session by supplementary intramuscular injections of approximately 0.3 ml/kg of the 4:3 mixture of ketamine and xylazine, nearly every 90 minutes. The limb withdrawal reflex was checked regularly in order to monitor the depth of anesthesia. All animals were mounted in a stereotaxic apparatus without ear bars. Body temperature was maintained between 37–39 °C, by means of a heating pad. Openings for the thalamic microelectrodes and for the cortical cooling probe were drilled through the skull. The dura mater was removed from the cortical area corresponding to the penetration of the thalamic electrodes. Upon completion of the recording session (lasting approximately 60 hours in cats and 12 hours in rats and guinea pigs), an electrolytic lesion was placed at a specific depth for each track, by passing a current of about 8 μA for 10 s. The animals then received a sublethal dose of sodium pentobarbital i.p. (180 mg/kg body weight) and were perfused transcardially with 0.9% NaCl immediately followed fixative solution (4% paraformaldehyde in phosphate buffer 0.1 M, pH 7.3). The brains were removed after the perfusion, postfixed and prepared for standard histological procedures. The surgical procedures are described in more detail elsewhere (Villa *et al.* 1991, 1996).

Multisite electrophysiologic recordings

Extracellular single unit recordings in the auditory thalamus were made with glass-coated platinum-plated tungsten microelectrodes having an impedance in the range 0.5–2 MΩ measured at a frequency of 1 kHz (Frederick Haer & Co., Brunswick, Maine, USA). The experiments were performed with multielectrode devices constructed at the Institute of Physiology of the University of Lausanne (more details are described elsewhere, cf. Figure 1 in Villa *et al.* 1999a) and now commercially available (Alpha Omega Engineering, Nazareth, Israel). Each such device allows us to control four microelectrodes driven independently. According to the experimental constraints and data acquisition capabilities it is possible to use several multielectrode devices in the same setup. In rat and guinea pig thalamic recordings four electrodes were advanced independently and in cat experiments we used up to six microelectrodes. The distance between the stereotactically oriented guides ranged between 360 and 600 μm. In most cases two microelectrodes were inserted in the same guide.

One electrode aimed at the center of the rostro–caudal extension of mgB was advanced first. Both the activity recorded along the track and the first acoustically evoked activity were used to determine if the region under recording corresponded to the electrophysiologic activity of mgB. The other electrodes were advanced in the auditory thalamus when the first electrode track matched the required criteria and as many as possible single units were isolated on all electrodes. If no acoustically evoked activity could be observed on one electrode, then the signals recorded from that electrode were discarded from the dataset analyzed in this study. The first recording session of an experiment started about 4 hours after the beginning of surgery in guinea pig and rat experiments and after 16 hours in cat experiments. Data were gathered in blocks of 80–400 seconds. Recordings during a total of 300–1000 s without external stimulation, referred to as spontaneous activity, were collected. The stimuli consisted of pure tones and white noise bursts, 200 ms in duration with a rise and fall time of 10 ms. Stimuli were delivered at a rate of 1 Hz through ½-inch earphones (Bruel & Kjaer, type 4134).

Stimulus intensities ranged approximately between 20 and 40 dB above threshold, i.e. close to 60 dB SPL (Sound Pressure Level) for the majority of units. The best frequency (BF) and the width of response ranges were determined by presenting tone bursts, whose frequency was linearly increased from 0.2 to 50 kHz at each stimulus. The bandwidth (BW) for one type of response pattern corresponded to the difference, in octaves, between the highest frequency and the lowest frequency evoking that pattern. These frequency ranges were rarely measured at more than one intensity. Spike intensity curves were computed for the onset response range (i.e. in the interval comprised between 10 and 80 ms after stimulus onset) and the BF was estimated by the strongest excitatory response.

A full protocol of activity characterization was performed prior to cortical inactivation. This protocol lasted on average 45 minutes. During cooling of the primary auditory cortex, a simplified protocol was performed, lasting approximately 30 minutes. After cooling the same simplified protocol was performed in order to check the recovery of the activity. Generally, no injection of drugs was done during this period. If a sign of distress was noticed and a supplementary dose of anesthetic was needed the recording was paused and resumed at least 15 minutes after the injection of the drug. We assume that these recording conditions corresponded to a steady level of anesthesia.

Up to three distinct single units could be recorded from the same microelectrode, using either an analog template matching spike sorter according to a technique described elsewhere (Villa 1990) or using a commercially available digital template-matching spike sorter (MSD, Alpha Omega Engineering, Nazareth, Israel). The overall number of simultaneously recorded single units was up to 8 in cat and up to 15 in rat and guinea pig experiments. The spike firing times of each unit were given by interrupts generated by a digital acquisition board driven by an external clock with accuracy of 1 ms, and stored digitally for off-line analyses. Dot rasters of the spike trains were displayed in real time. The local field potential (LFP) from each electrode was measured by band pass filtering the neural signal at 7–100 Hz (MCP-8000, Alpha Omega Engineering, Nazareth, Israel) with a notch filter at a 50 Hz cutoff frequency (−34 dB attenuation) and a bandwidth ±2 Hz. The analog LFPs were sampled with 2 ms resolution at 12-bit precision (National Instruments NB-MIO-16H-9 I/O board connected to a NB-DMA2800 board) and stored in files for off-line analyses.

Cooling technique

Separate skull-holes were drilled for the thalamic microelectrodes and for the cortical cooling probe. However, according to the size of the probes and to the rostro–caudal distance of the planes corresponding to auditory thalamic and cortical structures the two holes sometimes formed a contiguous opening. The cooling probes were placed above the cortical area referred to as primary auditory cortex, stereotactically determined following the lambda and bregma landmarks for rats (Zilles and Wree 1985; Paxinos and Watson 1986) and guinea pigs (Redies et al. 1989a) and following the suprasylvian, anterior ectosylvian and posterior ectosylvian sulci in cats (Reale and Imig 1980). The cooling probe was fixed to the skull with dental cement. A different model of probe was used for each species, but all consisted of an aluminum cylindrical core, refrigerated by a circulating mixture of chilled ethanol and ice-cold water, in tight contact with the dura mater. Figure 4.3 illustrates the three setups used in this study. The surface of the probe in contact with the cat brain was circular (diameter 10 mm), whereas with guinea pig (9×6 mm) and rat's brain (5×4 mm) the surface was rectangular. In addition, in the rat probe the surface was slightly curved. In the cat probe the flux of the refrigerant liquid was maintained at 100 ml/min, whereas the flux was 12 ml/min in the other probes, by means of a DC peristaltic pump. This difference in the flux rate was due to a specific design of tubular sleeves around the aluminum core of the cat probe, which resulted in a larger section of the circulating fluid. The tubing was mounted in such a way that the refrigerant flowed from the chilled reservoir to the cooling probe, then from the probe to the peristaltic pump entrance and back to the reservoir.

The temperature of the probe-end proximal to the cerebral cortex was monitored continuously by a thermocouple and the degree of reversible inactivation of cortical activity was assessed by means of microelectrodes (at least one) monitoring the auditory evoked responses in the cortex (Fig. 4.4). Cortical rewarming was achieved by interrupting circulation of the cooling fluid. The cooling and rewarming kinetics were observed to be similar in all experiments. The steady state was reached in 15–20 minutes. During cooling the temperature of the probe was near 5 °C and the temperature of the deep cortical layers in the range 16–22 °C, low enough to inactivate cortical synapses (Brooks 1983). Although portions of surrounding cortical fields would have probably been affected by a lateral spread of cooling or by a partial cooling if the probe was slightly overlapping these areas, we will refer to the cooling as primary auditory cortex inactivation throughout this article.

Data Analyses

This article will describe several results based on time domain analyses of electrophysiologic recordings. These analyses are used to characterize single unit activities during spontaneous and acoustically driven activity. In addition, the analysis of simultaneously recorded neural data allows to study the influence of corticofugal activity on the degree of synchronicity and precisely timed activity within the thalamus. Further assessment of the degree of coordinated activity within a localized population of neurons may be achieved by applying frequency domain analyses, i.e. partial coherence and bicoherence analyses. Additional experiments are currently performed in order to gather additional data required for an in-depth evaluation of these analyses, in particular during auditory stimulation. Preliminary results about corticofugal modulation of spontaneous activity, based on frequency domain analyses, were recently presented (Villa et al. 1999a) but they will not be discussed here.

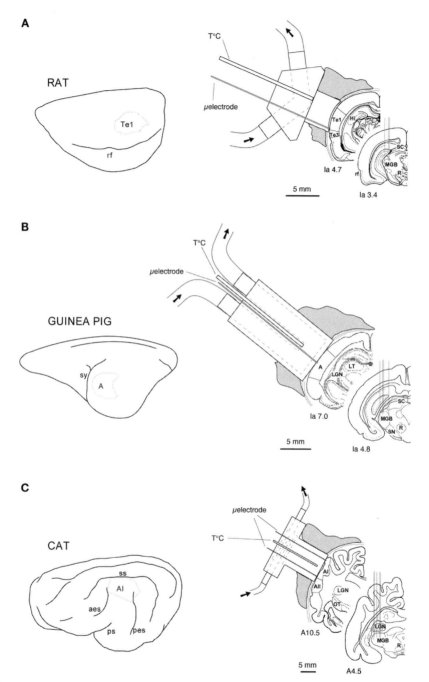

Fig. 4.3 Schematic representation of the anatomical location of the regions of interest and of cooling devices used in rat (A), guinea pig (B) and cat (C). The *left panels* represent a view of the left hemisphere of the cerebral cortex for each species. The scales are different. The *right panels* show two frontal sections, for each species, representative of the

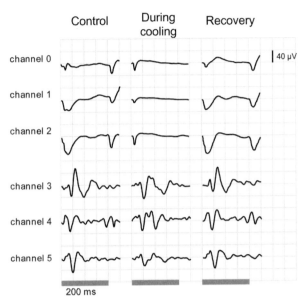

Fig. 4.4 Auditory evoked potentials recorded before, during and after cooling of the primary auditory cortex. Channels 0, 1 and 2 correspond to electrodes located at the level of the dura mater, just beneath the cooling probe. Channels 3, 4 and 5 correspond to electrodes located in the mgB. All electrode traces correspond to averages of 100 sweeps of binaural white noise bursts lasting 200 ms, at an intensity of 60 dB SPL. The grid subdivisions correspond to 40 μV in the abscissa and 50 ms in the ordinate. A thick horizontal tick indicates the stimulus presentation. Note during cooling the transient onset evoked response in the traces recorded in the inactivated primary auditory cortex. This response indicates that the electrical activity is preserved in the thalamocortical fibers. Note that the evoked responses in the thalamus are rather complex and correspond to the vast set of responses that may be observed in the thalamus (see also Fig. 4.8).

Fig. 4.3 (continued)

rostro–caudal levels (interaural coordinates are indicated near the corresponding sections) of the auditory cortex and auditory thalamus. The most rostral section illustrates also the cooling probe fixed to the skull with dental cement (in gray). See text for more details on the cooling probes. Arrows indicate the direction of the refrigerant flow. The thermocouple (T°C) used to monitor the probe temperature and the microelectrode (μelectrode) used to monitor the auditory evoked potentials are also indicated. The scale bar on the right panels corresponds to 5 mm. Abbreviations: A: anterior auditory cortex in guinea pig; AI: primary auditory cortex in cat; AII: secondary auditory cortex in cat; aes: anterior ectosylvian sulcus; Hi: hippocampus; GN: lateral geniculate nucleus; LT: lateral nucleus of the thalamus. mgB: medial geniculate body; OT: optic tract; pes: posterior ectosylvian sulcus; ps: pseudosylvian sulcus; R: red nucleus; rf: rhinal fissure; SC: superior colliculus; SN: substantia nigra; ss: suprasylvian sulcus; sy: sylvian sulcus; Te1: temporal area 1 (rat primary auditory cortex); Te3: temporal area 3 (rat non-primary auditory cortex). Adapted from Villa et al. (1999a).

Spike trains were analyzed with the help of time series renewal density histograms: the peristimulus time (PST) histograms, auto renewal density (ARD) histograms and cross renewal density (CRD) histograms were calculated according to Abeles (1982). Using this technique all histograms were scaled in rate units (spikes/s) and smoothed after convolution with a moving Gaussian-shaped bin (usually with a 10 ms bin width). Quantitative features as well as the qualitative evaluation of the ARD and CRD were based on three histograms (Gerstein and Perkel 1972): (a) "regular" histograms computed on simultaneously recorded spike trains, (b) "shift predictor" histograms obtained by correlating one spike train with another one shifted by exactly one interstimulus period; (c) "difference" histograms obtained by subtracting the shift predictor CRD from the regular CRD.

During spontaneous activity the computation of the shift predictor histogram corresponds to a random Poisson process having the same average as the one obtained for the regular histogram. This means that the difference histogram has zero average and that any significant deviations are signs of a peculiar temporal structure of the spike train. We use the ARD to characterize the bursting pattern (Fig. 4.5a): a hump near the origin indicates that a cell shortly after firing a spike is more likely to fire again. The duration of such hump corresponds to the time of cell firing deviating from a random Poisson process, hence this period can be viewed as the average burst duration ABD. The area under the hump corresponds to the number of spikes exceeding the one expected for a random Poisson process.

Because of the complex PSTs obtained for the majority of units (Fig. 4.5b) the response pattern (for the stimuli lasting 200 ms) was characterized by subdividing the post-stimulus time into five periods: "early-on" (0–30 ms after stimulus onset), "late-on" (30–80 ms), "sustained" (80–200 ms), "early-off" (200–250 ms) and "late-off" (250– 500 ms). The limits of these periods were set according to particularly frequent changes observed in the PSTs at those latencies and were consistent across all experiments with different species.

The functional interaction between single units in the time domain was assessed by computing the cross renewal densities (CRD), often referred to as cross-correlograms. Peaks in the CRDs were identified as crossing the 99% confidence limits, calculated assuming that a Poisson distribution underlay the spike train discharges. Peaks spanning time zero (bilateral peaks) were interpreted as synchronous firing of the pair of units due to a shared input, referred to as "common input," CI. Peaks near to but on one side only of time zero (unilateral peaks) were interpreted as one cell increasing the probability of firing of the other cell, referred to as "direct excitation," Exc. Unilateral troughs, bilateral troughs, peaks far from the zero delay and more complex features of the correlograms were observed in only a few cases and will not be discussed further in the present report (Fig. 4.6). Pairs of spike trains were differentiated if they were recorded from the same electrode (SE) or from different electrodes (DE) in the cross correlation analysis.

Cross-correlograms cannot detect recurrent activity in a cell assembly because complex spatiotemporal patterns of firing are generated. On the other hand, statistically

A   ARD
autocorrelogram

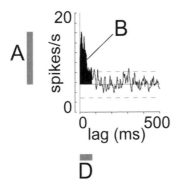

B   PST
peri-stimulus histogram

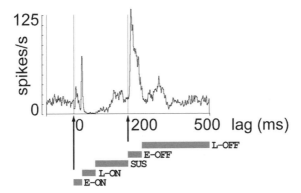

Fig. 4.5 (A) Auto renewal density (ARD) histogram of a thalamic unit during spontaneous activity. Abscissa: lag (ms). Ordinate: rate (spikes/s). Gaussian bin width: 10 ms. The average burst duration (D), the height of the hump (A) and the hump area (B) are indicated. (B) Evoked activity by white noise bursts, presented binaurally at 40 dB above threshold. Peristimulus (PST) histogram. Abscissa: lag (ms). Ordinate: rate (spikes/s). Gaussian bin width: 10 ms. The arrows indicate the start and end times of the stimulus whereas the horizontal ticks indicate the limits of the periods of time chosen for the analysis of the response pattern: "early-on" (E-ON), "late-on" (L-ON), "sustained" (SUS), "early-off" (E-OFF), "late-off" (L-OFF). Broken lines correspond to 99% confidence levels computed according to Poisson distribution.

crosscorrelograms

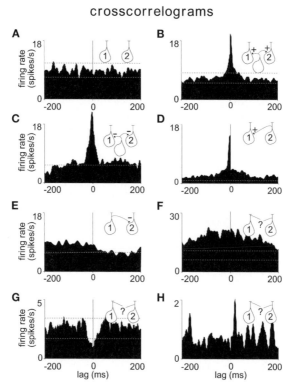

Fig. 4.6 Examples of cross renewal densities (CRDs) during spontaneous activity. Abscissa: lag (ms). Ordinate: instantaneous firing rate (spikes/s) of the follower cell (cell 2) at variable delays before (negative times on the abscissa, up to −200 ms) and after (positive times, up to 200 ms) the firing of the trigger cell (cell 1). Gaussian bin width: 10 ms. Broken lines indicate 99% confidence limits. On the top right corner of each correlogram an oversimplified cartoon illustrates the possible mechanism of the interaction, given that cell 1 and cell 2 represent the cells recorded simultaneously and whose spike trains were used to construct the cross-correlogram. (A) *No Interaction*. Cell 1 was recorded in mgB and cell 2 in RE. (b) *Common Input* (sharp). Both cells were recorded in mgB, same electrode. (C) *Common Input* (broad). Both cells were recorded in mgB, same electrode. (D) *Direct interaction* (excitation). Both cells were recorded in mgB, same electrode. (E) *Direct interaction* (inhibition). Cell 1 was recorded in RE and cell 2 in mgB. (F) *Other*. Cell 1 and cell 2 were recorded in mgB from different electrodes. Note that the ordinate is scaled to 30 spikes/s. (G) *Other*. Both cells were recorded in RE, same electrode. Note that the ordinate is scaled to 5 spikes/s. (H) *Other*. Cell 1 and cell 2 were recorded in mgB from different electrodes. Note that the ordinate is scaled to 2 spikes/s. Adapted from Villa *et al.* (1996).

significant repeated appearance of an identical firing pattern indicates that the corresponding single units have been repeatedly engaged in some kind of information processing carried out by a single cell assembly. Therefore the existence of an excess, over chance expectancy, of spatiotemporal patterns of firing reveals the presence of

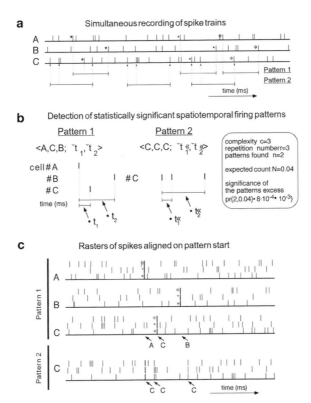

Fig. 4.7 Outline of the general procedure followed by pattern detection algorithms. (A) Analysis of a set of simultaneously recorded spike trains. Three cells, labeled A, B, and C, participate to a patterned activity. Three occurrences of two precise patterns are detected. Each occurrence of the first pattern has been labeled by a specific marker in order to help the reader to identify the corresponding spikes. The spikes belonging to the second pattern are indicated by arrows. (B) Estimation of the statistical significance of the detected patterns. Two patterns, $n=2$, <A,C,B> and <C,C,C> were found. Each pattern was formed by three neurons, $c=3$, and was repeated three times, $r=3$, in the analyzed record. The expected number of patterns of this complexity and repetition number was $N=0.04$. The probability to observe 2 *or more* patterns when 0.04 patterns are expected is noted as pr{0.02, 4}. (C) Display of the pattern occurrences as a raster plot aligned on the patterns start. Adapted from Tetko and Villa (2001a).

very precise temporal coding processed by cell assemblies. The estimation of the number of precise patterns of discharges that occur by chance in records of multiple single unit spike trains was performed by pattern grouping algorithm (PGA) (Tetko and Villa 2001a,b) (Fig. 4.7).

Comparisons between distributions of samples having different sizes were performed using the "bootstrap" method. A reference sample size of $n=20$ was chosen because it was close to the smaller sizes of the observed data samples. For this reason the relative frequencies were often scaled by steps of 5%. In this case significant differences corresponded generally to differences of 15%, otherwise stated.

Spontaneous activity

In the absence of a controlled acoustical stimulation, the activity of single units in the auditory thalamus is referred to as spontaneous. The data presented here refer only to the sample of well-isolated single units maintained throughout the experimental protocol. This refers to single units that recovered their activity after the cooling of AI ($n=288$ in cats, $n=81$ in guinea pigs and $n=48$ in rats), when compared to the control condition, and corresponded to a proportion of 70–85% of the total number of recorded units in our experiments. The locations of the recorded single units were attributed after electrode track reconstruction and were subdivided into ventral mgB ($n=81$, 30% in cats; $n=8$, 10% in guinea pigs; $n=10$, 20% in rats), medial mgB ($n=58$, 20% in cats; $n=16$, 20% in guinea pigs; $n=14$, 30% in rats), dorsal mgB ($n=29$, 10% in cats, $n=17$, 20% in guinea pigs; $n=7$, 15% in rats) and suprageniculate nucleus ($n=25$, 10% in cats; $n=9$, 10% in guinea pigs; $n=5$, 10% in rats). In case the histology was not good enough or the electrolytic lesion was not visible for an accurate localization the unit was attributed to an "other" subdivision of the auditory thalamus ($n=95$, 30% in cats; $n=31$, 40% in guinea pigs; $n=12$, 25% in rats). Note that several data discussed below were also presented in detail elsewhere (Villa 1988; Villa *et al.* 1991, 1996, 1999a).

The criterion for accepting a single unit return to control was no statistical difference (chi-square, $P<0.05$) of three out of four major characteristic parameters of the firing activity. These parameters are the spontaneous firing rate, the average burst duration measured in the auto renewal density histogram, the average burst size, and the signal-to-noise ratio, measured as the square root of the ratio of the peak instantaneous rate of discharges, evoked by a white noise burst lasting 200 ms presented binaurally at 40 dB above threshold, to the spontaneous firing rate. To determine whether a change occurred for one of these characteristic parameters, we compared the combined pre- and postcooling values to the during-cooling value. The deviation was considered significant when it was larger than three times the standard deviation, which means a confidence limit of 99%. The remaining units, which either did not recover the same activity after the cortical inactivation or were lost before the end of the protocol, were not considered further in the analyses of the responses to evoked activity.

During deactivation spontaneous firing rate was not modified in 20% (in rats and cats) to 40% (in guinea pigs) of the units. The relative proportions of units increasing, maintaining, or decreasing the rate of discharges varied among the anatomical subdivisions for all species investigated. In the ventral and dorsal subdivisions of the medial geniculate body the ratio of units characterized by a decreased firing during cortical inactivation varied between 60 and 70%, whereas the ratio of increased firing units was close to 10–15%. The single units recorded in the medial subdivision of mgB and in the suprageniculate nucleus were characterized by a ratio of 40–55% of decreased and

20–35% of increased firing. This difference may account for the result that we observed in our guinea pigs experiments, characterized by a majority of recordings performed in the medial subdivision.

The cortical cooling affected the firing pattern of the units located in the ventral division of mgB, with a tendency to decrease the average burst duration and to decrease the average burst size in a even larger proportion. The units of the suprageniculate nucleus were affected in the opposite way and the cortical inactivation of the primary auditory cortex provoked an increase in the average burst size in about half of the units, whereas in 20–30% of the units the burst size decreased. Despite these regional differences a change of the burst size and duration in the same direction and to a similar extent would lead only to a moderate modification in the intraburst frequency. In addition no significant correlation between the corticofugal effect on the bursting pattern and the firing rate could be found. In all subdivisions and in all experiments that we performed the main result in this respect was that 50–60% of the single units were characterized by an unaffected intraburst frequency. However, we cannot discard the possibility that more accurate measurements of the firing pattern aimed to measure directly the intraburst frequency might reveal some characteristic changes associated with one or two anatomical subdivisions.

Responses to acoustically evoked activity

The responses to white noise bursts were analyzed on the basis of the shape of the peristimulus time histograms. The response pattern tended to be characterized by transient excitatory responses often followed by inhibited activity in the ventral and dorsal divisions of mgB, while more complex patterns were observed in the suprageniculate and medial division of mgB. The response patterns observed in the cat experiments were more complex than those observed in the rats and guinea pigs, probably due to the differences in anesthesia (Zurita *et al.* 1994). The vast majority of units (70–85%) tested to white noise bursts recovered the same pattern of response after the cortical inactivation, even in fine details (Fig. 4.8). The remaining units did not recover exactly the same pattern of response to white noise although the spontaneous activity pattern did (i.e. spontaneous firing rate and bursting parameters).

One of the parameters chosen to describe the responsiveness to white noise bursts is the maximum instantaneous firing rate represented by the highest peak of the peristimulus time histogram. This value was modulated by the auditory cortex for the majority of the units (80%). The square root of the ratio between this peak and the spontaneous firing rate can be considered as an analog of the signal-to-noise ratio. Whenever the corticofugal modulation provoked a variation of the peak in the same direction and to the same extent in the spontaneous firing rate, then no selective effect on the signal-to-noise ratio could be determined. On the opposite, whenever the cortical inactivation provoked an imbalance in the variation of evoked and spontaneous firing rate the signal-to-noise ratio was selectively affected. It is important to notice that in all experiments the majority of units recorded in the ventral division of mgB

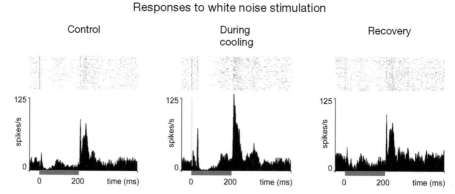

Fig. 4.8 Rasters and peristimulus time histogram of a single unit during acoustically evoked activity by binaural white noise bursts lasting 200ms (horizontal bar) and at an intensity 20dB above threshold for neuron activation. This unit was recorded in the cat suprageniculate nucleus. During cooling note the appearance of two (instead of one during control) onset transient excitatory responses, a prolonged inhibition during stimulus delivery and an increased offset excitatory response, whereas the "background" activity was only moderately affected. The abscissa full scale is 550ms and the ordinate full scale is 125 spikes/s. In the raster display 200 repetitions are stacked.

(55–70%) were characterized by selective effect of cortical cooling on the signal-to-noise ratio. However, in the cat ventral mgB this ratio was predominantly increased during cortical cooling, whereas it was predominantly decreased in the rats and guinea pigs (Fig. 4.9).

In rodents cortical deactivation provoked a generalized increase of the inhibitory components of the response pattern evoked by white noise bursts. This effect could lead to a disappearance (e.g., unit 3 in Fig. 4.9a, unit 4 in Fig. 4.9b) or strong decrease of the onset transient excitatory responses (e.g., unit 1 in Fig. 4.9a). The strengthening of inhibitory onset responses (e.g., unit 2 in Fig. 4.9a, unit 3 in Fig. 4.9b) was sometimes associated with the appearance of a "late-on" response (unit 2 in Fig. 4.9a). Changes in response patterns were observed in 10–15% of the units in either species and in particular in the dorsal division of mgB and in the suprageniculate nucleus (units 1 and 2 in Fig. 4.9b, unit 8 in Fig. 4.10). It is interesting to note that two units recorded from the same electrode may be affected in a very different way by cortical cooling. In normal condition units 1 and 2 in Fig. 4.9b are characterized by a complex excitatory response with multiple components. During cortical deactivation the early onset response is strengthened in unit 1, whereas a very late excitatory response (possibly a rebound of an onset inhibition) is strengthened in unit 2.

In the cat the most frequent response to white noise bursts was characterized by transient excitation followed by a suppression (Fig. 4.10). Corticofugal modulation affected more often the responses at latencies larger than 30ms from the stimulus onset

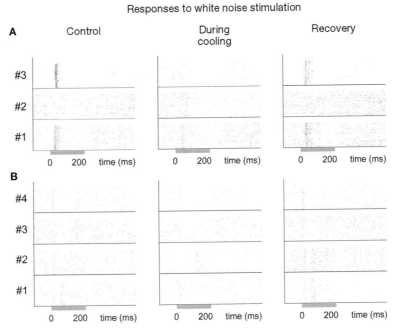

Fig. 4.9 Raster display of single units recorded during acoustically evoked activity by white noise bursts lasting 200 ms (horizontal bar). The abscissa full scale is 600 ms. (A) Recordings performed in the rat thalamus: units 1 and 3 were located in the ventral division of mgB; unit 2 in the medial division of mgB. In the raster display 300 repetitions are stacked. (B) Recordings performed in the guinea pig thalamus: units 1 and 2 were located in the dorsal division of mgB and were recorded by the same electrode; unit 3 in the medial division of mgB; unit 4 in the ventral division of mgB. In the raster display 200 repetitions are stacked.

(e.g., appearance of a late-onset transient excitation followed by a sharp suppression, Fig. 4.8). Early-offset and late-offset responses were seldom observed in normal condition in either species but could be induced by cortical deactivation in the cat (e.g., units 7 and 8 in Fig. 4.10). These differences might be due to species-specific thalamic circuitry, characterized by the presence of local inhibitory interneurons in the cat and not in the rat and guinea pigs, as mentioned in the introduction, but also to different anesthetic conditions.

Out of the total number of units tested with pure tones 5% in cats, 30% in rats and 35% in guinea pigs never responded to tonal stimulation independent of the state of activation of the auditory cortex. The larger proportions of unresponsive units observed in rats and guinea pigs might be related to the limited sample size of tested units and cannot be discussed further. If a unit had a complex temporal pattern of response, its components were considered separately. Such complex response patterns were often dependent on both the pure frequency tone and the cortical state; therefore the width of response ranges (bandwidth, BW) was determined for each component of the response pattern.

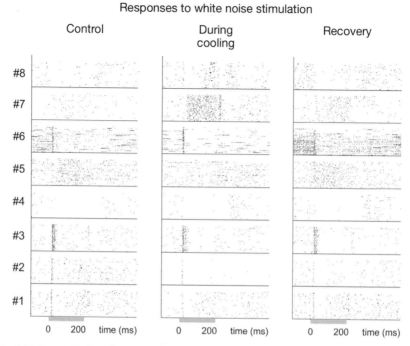

Fig. 4.10 Raster display of eight single units recorded in the cat auditory thalamus during acoustically evoked activity by white noise bursts lasting 200 ms (horizontal bar). The abscissa full scale is 600 ms and 100 repetitions are stacked in the raster. Unit 1 was located in the ventral division of mgB; units 2 and 8 in the suprageniculate nucleus; units 3 and 7 in the medial division of mgB, unit 4 in the brachium of the inferior colliculus; units 5 and 6 were recorded from the same electrode in the auditory sector of the thalamic reticular nucleus.

Excitatory early-onset transient responses, with a latency shorter than 30 ms, were observed in the majority (75%) of the units (e.g., units 1 and 2 in Fig. 4.11). Only about 20% of these units were characterized by responses which remained unchanged during the cortical inactivation (e.g., unit 2 in Fig. 4.11 despite a decreased background activity). Late-onset as well as offset evoked responses to pure tones, observed in less than half of the units, differed by their tendency to be strongly affected during the inactivation of the primary auditory cortex (e.g., prolonged late-onset excitatory response in unit 4 and disappearance of the offset component in unit 5 in Fig. 4.11). A general observation was that the cortical cooling usually induced an increase of the width of excitatory response ranges for long latency responses, whereas it had the opposite effect on short latency responses. Inhibitory responses to pure tones that generally followed an onset excitatory activity could be either strengthened (e.g., unit 1 in Fig. 4.11) or weakened (e.g. unit 5 in Fig. 4.11) during cortical deactivation. It is interesting to note that the response pattern can be completely modified during cortical

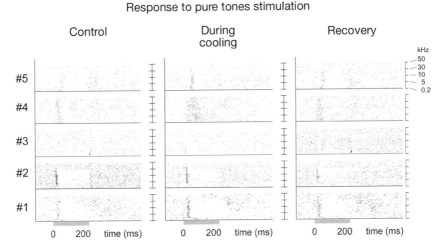

Fig. 4.11 Raster display of single units during pure tones stimulation. Each stimulus lasted 200 ms (horizontal bar) and the frequency was linearly increased from 0.2 to 50 kHz by 200 steps, one per second. The abscissa full scale is 600 ms and 200 seconds are stacked in the raster. Unit 1 was located in the brachium of the inferior colliculus, nearby the ventral subdivision of mgB; unit 2 in the suprageniculate nucleus; unit 3 in the medial division of mgB, units 4 and 5 were recorded from the same electrode in the ventral division of mgB.

cooling and a unit characterized by an offset excitatory response to low frequencies (0.5–2 kHz) during normal conditions responded at the onset of the pure tones (in the frequency range 0.2–5 kHz) during the cryogenic blockade of the primary auditory cortex (unit 3 in Fig. 4.11).

Functional disparity

Considering each functional property separately (like the average burst duration or the bandwidth for a given pattern of response to pure tones) each single unit could be classified as increasing, maintaining, or decreasing the value of that functional property. To determine whether a change occurred for one of the functional properties, we compared the combined pre- and postcooling values to the during-cooling value. The deviation was considered significant when it was larger than three times the standard deviation. Figure 4.12 illustrates one such example applied to the analysis of the responsiveness to pure tones. The single unit presented in the figure is characterized by a complex response pattern with three main components, "onset-excitation," "onset-inhibition" and "offset-excitation" (Fig. 4.12a). All components can be observed during cortical cooling, but their relative bandwidth (BW) is affected to a different extent. The BW of the onset excitation is significantly increased (Fig. 4.12b), the BW of the onset inhibition is significantly decreased (Fig. 4.12c), whereas the BW of the offset-excitation remains unaffected (Fig. 4.12d).

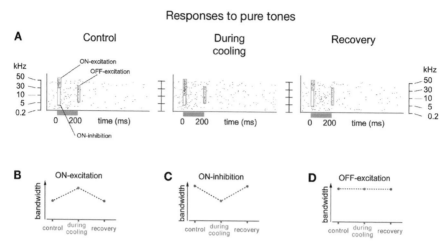

Fig. 4.12 Analysis of bandwidths during pure tones stimulation. (A) Raster display with same legend as Fig. 4.11. Note the three components of the response pattern, ON-excitation, ON-inhibition and OFF-excitation. (B) The bandwidth of the ON-excitation is increased during cortical cooling. (C) The bandwidth of the ON-inhibition is decreased during cortical cooling. (D) The bandwidth of the OFF-excitation is unaffected by corticofugal modulation.

After the assignment of the units into a class ("increasing," "maintaining," "decreasing") the next step was to analyze the units responsiveness according to the anatomical location. Within any given anatomical subdivision, two populations of units were defined according to the tendency of their BW for a given response pattern to increase or to decrease during inactivation of the primary auditory cortex. Average values for the two population of units ("increasing" and "decreasing") are calculated for any given functional property such that a statistical analysis and comparison between the two groups can be performed at all recording conditions (i.e., before, during, and after cortical deactivation). Disparity is characterized by a significant difference between the average BW (in octaves) of these two groups (Mann-Whitney U-test, $p<0.05$) (Fig. 4.13a, b in control condition). In other cases no difference between the two groups may be observed (Fig. 4.13c, d in control condition). The existence of two separate modes in the distribution of a given functional property (e.g. bandwidth of onset-inhibitory responses) could be interpreted as a sign of disparity, coded by the cell assemblies forming the groups of units.

The corticofugal modulation may invert the modal values of the distribution, thus preserving the disparity, termed "functional" because of its dependence on the state of the cerebral cortex, though inverted (Fig. 4.13a). One hypothesis to explain this result might be to consider that clearly distinct modal values correspond to two possible states of activity and that the cortical influence would "switch" between the two states. This case is labeled "XX" (Fig. 4.13a). A second case, labeled "><," would correspond to a disappearance of the disparity (Fig. 4.13b). A third case, labeled "<>," would be the

Functional Disparity

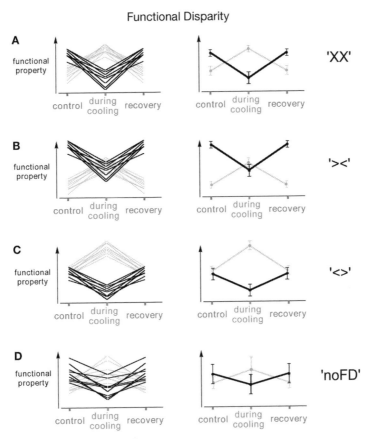

Fig. 4.13 Theoretical model of the functional disparity (FD) for a given functional property. The panels on the left show the effect of cortical cooling on the values of the functional property for several single units. The panels on the right represent the same data grouped into two classes and show the averages and S.E.M. Black lines refer to those single units whose values are significantly decreased and dashed grey lines refer to those single units whose values are significantly increased by cortical deactivation. (A) The two groups are statistically different in normal condition and during cooling, FD is present before and during cooling, labeled "XX." (B) The two groups are statistically different in normal condition but not during cooling, FD is only present before cooling, labeled "><." (C) The two groups cannot be distinguished in normal condition but are statistically different during cooling, FD is only present during cooling, labeled "<>." (D) The two groups cannot be distinguished in either condition, labeled "noFD."

opposite of the previous one, therefore corresponding to a largely overlapping modal values of the groups "increasing" and "decreasing" before the cortical inactivation and to the appearance of the functional disparity (FD) (Fig. 4.13c). The last case, labeled "noFD," appears when there is no disparity in either cortical condition (Fig. 4.13d).

We considered the FD for each subdivision separately and for the following functional properties: firing rate, burst duration and burst size during spontaneous activity; signal-to-noise ratio and peak firing rate evoked by white noise bursts; "onset excitatory," "onset inhibitory," "late-onset excitatory" and "offset excitatory" bandwidths during pure tones stimulation. We observed that only in 10% of cases "no FD" was observed, whereas in 25% of the cases the FD was visible before as well as during the cortical cooling (cases of "XX" type). The inactivation of the primary auditory cortex tended to let the FD appear twice more often than it was allowed to disappear. It is important to notice that the disappearance of FD involves mainly those properties defined for activity driven by pure tones. The meaning of this finding might be that the maximum efficacy of tone discrimination, as determined by the existence of bandwidth disparities, is controlled by cortical activity.

Functional interactions

The previous results are based on the assumption that the firing rate is carrying meaningful information that can be read out by the nervous system. Although we know that rate coding should prevail at levels of processing that are close to sensory input, the auditory thalamus is not simply a relay center and intermediate computations should be based predominantly on the shifting of temporal relations. As these relations, such as synchrony, can only be evaluated by simultaneously recording the activity of different cells, we used multielectrode recordings to reliably detect transient temporal relations among the activities of widely distributed groups of neurons in the thalamus during cortical cooling. The significant cross renewal densities (CRDs) were classified as "common input" (CI) if a symmetrical peak near time zero was observed, thus suggesting a synchronization between the times of firing of the single units, or as "Direct," if an asymmetrical unilateral peak was observed. All other types of significant correlogram features pooled together accounted for 0–5%, according to species, of the significant number of correlograms. Therefore, for statistical reasons and for the sake of comparing the experiments performed on different animal models we limit our study to the two major classes, CI and Direct.

The qualitative effect of reversible deactivation of the primary cortex on the synchronization of the spike trains was determined by counting the correlogram features that were maintained across all experimental conditions ("stable"), those that went away during cooling but reappeared during the recovery period ("disappearing") and those that were only observed during cooling ("appearing"). In several cases the correlogram type was not modified and it was classified in the "stable" class but, an increase or a decrease in strength could be observed. During control and recovery conditions the vast majority of the correlograms computed for pairs of units recorded from the same electrode showed a significant pattern of correlation (56% in cats, 56% in guinea pigs and 77% in rats). These correlograms were predominantly of CI type, but the proportion of Direct vs. CI was higher in guinea pigs and rats (15%) than in cats (3%).

In rats and guinea pigs the number of "disappearing" CI correlograms during cooling, in both samples formed by pairs recorded from the same electrode and from two electrodes, was always larger than the number of "stable" CI. Conversely, the reversible deactivation of cat's primary auditory cortex tended to leave the majority of CI unaltered. Figure 4.14a illustrates a typical effect of cortical deactivation on CI from the same electrode, namely a decrease, or even a disappearance (as shown in Fig. 4.14a), of the functional interaction. There are several ways to interpret such a change in the

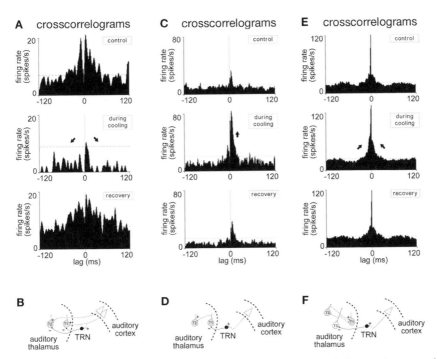

Fig. 4.14 Examples of corticofugal modulation on thalamic crosscorrelations and cartoons for their interpretation. The ordinate corresponds to the instantaneous firing rate of one cell (follower) at variable delays before (negative times on the abscissa) and after (positive times) the firing of the other cell (trigger) of a neuronal pair. TRN: thalamic reticular nucleus. (A) A symmetrical wide hump on both sides of time zero is a typical shape of shared input (CI): this is the most common type of functional interaction. Cortical deactivation provoked a decrease in strength or a disappearance of the central hump; notice also a decrease in firing rate for both units. The cell pair activity was recorded from the same electrode. (B) Model of interpretation of (A): note the shared inhibitory projection from TRN on both thalamocortical cells. (C) The main feature is an asymmetrical peak on one side of time zero, referred to as Direct interaction. Cortical deactivation increased the hump; this is a predominant effect observed across species. The cell pair activity was recorded from the same electrode. (D) Model of interpretation of (C): note the inhibitory projection from TRN on the trigger cell of the correlogram. (E) This example shows a Direct interaction on top of a shared input, two features that were observed during all recording conditions. Note that during cortical cooling the CI feature was increased without a change in the Direct interaction. The increase of CI during cortical deactivation was a peculiar observation of cell pairs recorded in the feline thalamus from different electrodes. (F) Model of interpretation of (E): note the presence of an additional source of shared input labeled by T3.

correlogram, and one possible approach is presented in Fig. 4.14b. Given the relatively little synchronization and long duration of the central hump, we may suggest that the source of synchronization might be a inhibitory neuron of the thalamic reticular nucleus (TRN). This means that during control and recovery conditions a TRN neuron that is projecting to both thalamocortical cells that are being recorded is mainly activated by the corticofugal pathway. During cortical cooling TRN would become less active and its synchronizing effect would decrease or disappear. Notice that in the example reported in Fig. 4.14a both thalamocortical cells decrease the firing rate substantially during cortical cooling, thus suggesting the existence of a direct strong excitatory corticofugal effect. The corticofugal effect on the Direct type of correlogram was uniform across all species and was always characterized by a majority of "appearing" correlations or increase in strength in the "stable" Direct interactions. This tendency was much stronger between cells recorded from the same electrode, and one such example is illustrated by Fig. 4.14c. A model of interpretation would be structured to help consider the major inhibitory effect provoked by the projection of a TRN neuron on the trigger neuron of the pair of thalamocortical cells being recorded by the same microelectrode. During cortical deactivation the TRN neuron would become unable to limit the excitatory effect that a collateral projection of a thalamocortical neuron is producing on its neighbor (Fig. 4.14d).

In the sample formed by correlograms obtained from pairs of units recorded from different electrodes only a minority of graphs (8% in cats, 8% in guinea pigs and 6% in rats) were non flat and suggested the presence of functional interactions. This could be due to the presence of broader polysynaptic paths, whose functional interactions are less likely to be detected by computing CRDs. All data recorded from different electrodes were pooled together. In cat's data a remarkable difference exists between pairs recorded from the same electrode or from different electrodes. In the "same electrode" group we observed as many "appearing" and "disappearing" CI, but in the "different electrode" group the cortical deactivation tended to allow the appearance of, or strengthen, the majority of CI. Figure 4.14e illustrates an increase in synchronization between two cells, recorded by different electrodes, induced by deactivation of the primary cortex, even if one cell was steadily exciting the other cell. The model of interpretation for this example (Fig. 4.14f) raises the possibility that a third neuron, labeled T3, is responsible of the synchrony between the two thalamocortical neurons being recorded. Such a third neuron could be under tonic inhibition of a inhibitory TRN neuron during control and recovery condition. A release of this inhibition would occur when the activation of TRN decreases, i.e. during cortical cooling, thus provoking an increase in the activity of T3. The available data allow us to speculate on the type of T3, which could be either another TRN neuron or another thalamocortical cell (the latter hypothesis is illustrated by Fig. 4.14f). The combination of several features in the same graph were observed in barely 5% of the overall number of significant cross-correlograms. In these cases two separate counts, one for each feature, are reported in the distribution of cross-correlogram types and the total number of cell pairs is increased by one for all such cases. Because of the limited number of these observations, no particular procedure was applied to correct these numbers.

In other cases an additional significant feature of the correlogram could appear during cortical inactivation. Figure 4.15a illustrates one such case with the appearance of a Direct interaction during cooling without a simultaneous modification of the CI. A possible interpretation of this example (Fig. 4.15b) is that the main source of shared input to the pair of units being recorded is not under control of the corticofugal pathway, perhaps lying outside the auditory thalamus. In addition, a collateral projection of one thalamocortical on its neighbor is a potential source of an excitatory influence. However, such functional excitatory projection cannot be observed during control and

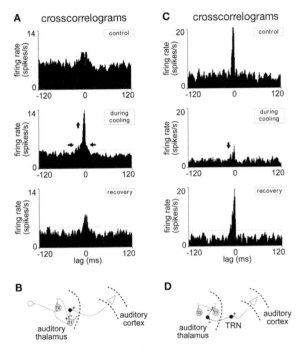

Fig. 4.15 Examples of corticofugal modulation on thalamic crosscorrelations and cartoons for their interpretation. (A) Complex pattern of correlation showing two salient features. The first feature, identified as a nearly symmetrical peak spanning time zero is referred to as a shared input, CI. This feature remained unaltered by cortical deactivation. The second feature was observed only during cooling and was identified as the appearance of a Direct interaction. The cell pair was recorded from the same electrode. (B) Model of interpretation of (A): Note the presence of an external source of shared input and a presynaptic inhibition by a local interneuron on a collateral of a thalamocortical cell. (C) The direct interaction almost disappeared in absence of cortical activity. This cell pair was recorded from the same electrode. (D) Model of interpretation of (A): Note the presynaptic inhibition by a local interneuron on a collateral of a thalamocortical cell and the disinhibitory effect due to the TRN projection on the local interneuron.

recovery because presynaptic inhibition is due to a local interneuron driven by the corticofugal pathway. This is a rather speculative hypothesis, but it has been selected to indicate the kind of inferences that may be drawn from the experimental data. The next example illustrates a decrease in strength of a Direct interaction during cortical deactivation (Fig. 4.15c). The model would suggest that a local interneuron might exert a presynaptic inhibition on a collateral excitatory projection of a thalamocortical cell but, on contrary to the previous model, the local interneuron would be driven by an inhibitory projection from the thalamic reticular nucleus (Fig. 4.15d). This would mean that during normal and recovery conditions the collateral projection is disinhibited. It is important to note that the last two examples have been selected from the cat experiments. They attribute an important role to the local interneurons, in accordance to the known anatomical connections within the cat medial geniculate nucleus.

Precisely timed activity

Further indirect evidence of the corticofugal control on thalamic cell assembly synchronization is provided by the analysis of complex spatiotemporal patterns of spikes. Abeles' synfire chain theory suggests that generation and propagation of precise timing of neuronal discharges in the brain may be achieved by means of feedforward chains of convergent/divergent links and reentry loops between interacting neurons forming an assembly (Abeles 1991). In cell assemblies interconnected in this way, some ordered sequences of intervals will recur within spike trains of individual neurons, and across spike trains from neurons located at different places in the network. Such ordered and precise repetitions (in the order of few ms jitter) of interspike interval relationships are referred to as "spatiotemporal patterns" of discharges and may correspond to complex behaviorally relevant information processes (Villa *et al.* 1999b). A fundamental prediction of such a model is that simultaneous recording of activity of cells belonging to the same assembly involved repeatedly in the same process should be able to reveal repeated occurrences of such spatiotemporal firing patterns. This term encompasses both their precision in time and the fact that they can occur across different neurons, even recorded from separate electrodes.

The number of spikes necessary for a fair statistical evaluation of the significance of the patterns could not be met in all datasets reported here. This is due not only to an insufficient time of recording in certain groups of spike trains, but also to the effect of massive decrease in selected single units firing rate induced by cortical cooling, so that only a limited number of spike trains recorded simultaneously could match the requirements to be analyzed during all experimental conditions. A detailed analysis of the spatiotemporal patterns requires also a systematic evaluation of the complexity of the pattern (i.e., the number of spikes forming the pattern, the number of exact repetitions of the pattern within the record, the number of distinct single units contributing to the pattern and the time interval structure of the significant patterns) by pattern grouping algorithm (PGA) (Tetko and Villa 2001a,b).

PGA was applied to the recordings performed during the control condition, grouped together with recordings during cortical cooling and after the cortical temperature returned back to normal, with window duration equal to 500 ms and jitter equal to 7 ms. The rationale is that patterns associated to a specific state of cortical activation would appear almost exclusively during that condition, but should be searched in the whole data set in order to avoid a circular argument in the searching strategy. We found 10 significant patterns of complexity, 3 repeating at least 7 times in the combined set. Four patterns were characterized by their occurrences only during one recording condition, either before, during or after cortical deactivation. The remaining six patterns were characterized by their occurrences being equally distributed before and after cooling of the auditory cortex. The total number of repetitions per pattern varied between 9 and 20 but only one occurrence, if any, was observed during cortical deactivation. These data show that cortical deactivation can disrupt precisely timed activity within the thalamus in a reversible way.

Figure 4.16 illustrates the pattern $<1,2,2; 263\pm4.5, 307\pm3.5>$ formed by two cells. The significant pattern was observed 9 times in 400 s (i.e. 1.4 pattern occurrences/minute) of spontaneous activity recorded during the control condition. Only one pattern was observed in 300 s of recording time during cooling (0.2 patterns/min) but the same pattern was observed again 6 times in 300 s (1.2 patterns/min) during the recovery period. Note that between the first and the last occurrence of the pattern about 90 minutes had passed. The correlograms of neurons 1 and 2 were almost flat (Fig. 4.16a). This indicated an absence of bursting activity and of any significant synchronous activity between these neurons. The firing rate of these neurons was slightly affected by cortical cooling. It was 3.8, 3.9 and 4.6 spikes/s for neuron number1 and 3.1, 2.2 and 3.1 spikes/s for neuron number 2 before, during and after the cortical cooling, respectively. Thus, the main parameter that was dramatically affected for this pair of neurons during cortical cooling was the disappearance of the spatiotemporal pattern (Fig. 4.16b). The level of significance of this pattern was $p_0<0.001$. This pattern remained significant at level $p_0<0.05$ if data sets recorded before or after cortical cooling were considered separately. The lower level of significance can be attributed to a smaller number of repetitions of this pattern within each dataset separately. With an extended jitter of 11 ms this pattern repeated 12 times at the overall level of significance was $p_0<0.01$. Higher order precise spatiotemporal patterns of activity within the auditory thalamus are only moderately affected by cooling deactivation, generally showing a tendency to become more complex during deactivation of the primary auditory cortex (Villa and Abeles 1990).

A model for thalamocortical processing

Multiple modules characterized by the same basic connectivity may be assumed to work in parallel and include three main components: (i) dorsal thalamic neurons (e.g. from the medial geniculate body for the auditory pathway or from the lateral

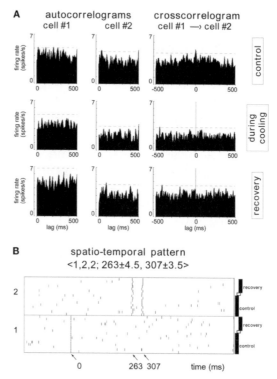

Fig. 4.16 A spatiotemporal firing pattern that is reversibly disrupted by cortical deactivation formed by discharges of thalamic neurons. (A) Autocorrelograms and cross-correlograms of the participating cells recorded before, during and after cooling of the auditory cortex in the rat medial geniculate body. (B) Sixteen occurrences of the pattern <1,2,2; 145±4.5, 225±2.5> are displayed as a special raster aligned on pattern start. The labels on the left indicate the patterns detected before and after inactivation of cortex by reversible cooling, respectively. Notice that only one occurrence of the pattern was detected during the cortical cooling. Adapted from Tetko and Villa (2001b).

geniculate body for the visual pathway) recipient of the sensory input from the periphery; (ii) cells of the thalamic reticular nucleus (RE), a major component of the ventral thalamus; (iii) the cortical area receiving the corresponding thalamic input. The thalamocortical and corticothalamic projections are reciprocal to a great extent, and the scheme of this modular organization is illustrated by Fig. 4.17a.

It is particularly important to stress the strategic position occupied by RE (Villa 1990). This structure receives collaterals from both thalamocortical and corticothalamic fibers and sends its inhibitory projections to the dorsal thalamus, thus regulating the firing mode of the thalamocortical neurons. RE also receives inputs from several forebrain and midbrain areas known to exert modulatory functions (McCormick and Bal 1994). It is worth mentioning that basal forebrain cholinergic fibers containing receptors to the nerve growth factor (NGF), the prototypical neurotrophic factor (Levi Montalcini and Calissano 1986), innervate RE. This nucleus appears as a site of regulation of NGF activity, suggesting that neurotrophic factors might influence thalamocortical neurons through RE, as confirmed by electrophysiologic recordings (Villa *et al.* 1996). The regulation of neurotrophic factors in RE could be selectively related to plastic changes in the NGF-responsive cholinergic terminals of basal forebrain axons and to their role in learning and memory (Bentivoglio *et al.* 1993). The hypothesis is that thalamic cell assemblies could perform adaptive filtering. This processing would allow selective extraction of information from the incoming sensory signal according to the cortical activity. This hypothesis is supported by strong analogies between the thalamocortical neuronal circuitry (Fig. 4.17b) and the engineering technical description (Widrow and Stearns 1985) of adaptive filtering circuits (Fig. 4.17c). Corticofugal activity would regulate the response properties of thalamic units by changing their bandwidth responsiveness to pure tones. The observation of several functionally characterized types of units within the auditory part of RE (Villa 1990) suggest that this structure would play a key role in "setting" the filter's coefficients.

The following explains the functional analogy between the thalamocortical circuit and the adaptive filter. Let us assume that the ascending input from the auditory periphery contains the useful signal s. The reference signal r_0 corresponds to some template activity associated to a learned signal. This reference signal is transmitted by the corticofugal pathway to the medial geniculate body and another reference signal r_1, that is correlated *only* with r_0, is transmitted to RE. Both template signals are uncorrelated with the ascending input, which is driven by the external acoustic signal.

Let us call u the filter's output corresponding to the activity pattern of RE, and w the output activity of the medial geniculate body, we may write $w = s + r_0 - u$ that is equal to $w = s + (r_0 - u)$. The expectation of the product of uncorrelated signals is null. Then, if we square both sides of previous expression we obtain the expectation of the system output w, i.e. $E[w^2] = E[s^2] + E[(r_0 - u)^2]$. When the filter's coefficients change, only the last term of the above equation is affected because the signal s is independent from the filter's processing. Once the mean square error is minimized, we have $\min(E[w^2]) = E[s^2] + \min(E[(r_0 - u)^2])$. Since $E[(r_0 - u)^2]$ is minimized and $(w - s) = (r_0 - u)$ the output activity w represents the best match of the input signal s in the sense of the minimum mean square error (Widrow and Stearns 1985).

The critical physiologic role played by the thalamo–corticothalamic circuit has inspired a number of neural network simulations aimed to understanding the information processing in this circuit. LaBerge and colleagues (LaBerge *et al.* 1992) studied how RE and the pulvinar could be the central element in implementing a neuron-based algorithm for selective filtering within the visual system. For RE cells, due to mutually inhibitory dendrodendritic and axosomatic connections found in this nucleus, a winner-take-all relationship was assumed. The activity of each cell in RE was set to the difference between its output and that of its neighbors only if the neighbors

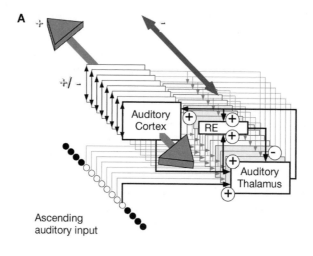

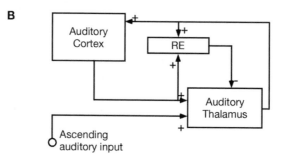

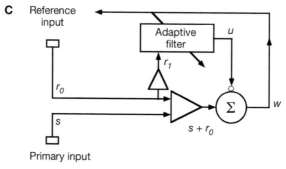

Fig. 4.17 (A) A functional scheme of the modular organization of the thalamocortical auditory pathway. The signs indicate the nature of the connections, (+) excitatory and (−) inhibitory. RE: reticular nucleus of the thalamus. Note the excitatory input from the ascending pathway to the auditory thalamus, the excitatory projection from the thalamus to the cortex with a collateral to RE, and the excitatory projection of the cortex to the thalamus with a collateral to RE. The only output of RE is an inhibitory backprojection to the thalamus. Other intrinsic connections exist within RE (mainly inhibitory) as well as within cortex and thalamus.

output was higher, otherwise the output of the cell was set to zero. In the model of Taylor (Taylor and Alavi 1994) a traveling wave model of RE inhibition was proposed, rather than using the explicit winner-take-all mechanism, and the thalamocortical circuit was suggested to operate as a global competitive network for selective attention and reduction of perceptual redundancy. Detailed cellular models incorporating ionic currents produced specific neuronal behavior such as tonic and bursting modes of firing (Vidal de Carvalho 1994) and could demonstrate that the cortex is likely to activate inhibition from RE which can affect the ascending input at the level of the thalamus, thus suggesting that the cortex opens and closes the thalamus as a gate in an attentional control process. More sophisticated models of the thalamocortical circuitry (Lumer *et al.* 1997a,b) that include multiple cortical layers and distinct populations of excitatory and inhibitory neurons, recurrent connectivity within and between layers and single compartment integrate-and-fire cell models have investigated the critical role of coincident spikes on the dynamics of the network.

Without the need of a strict correspondence between neuronal biophysical properties and phenomenological integrate-and-fire dynamics computational results of simulated thalamocortical neural networks (Villa and Tetko 1995; Hill and Villa 1997) have shown that a wide range of activity patterns and behaviors emerges in a network where only the threshold potential and postsynaptic potential decay vary. These simulations revealed the existence of regions within the parameter space where the balance of postsynaptic excitation and inhibition enables the network to make rapid transitions between different activity states. We suppose that thalamocortical inputs may play a key role for these transitions. The ascending sensory input to the thalamus conveys a large amount of information unevenly distributed in terms of complexity. We found that correlation among outputs of the networks is proportional to the complexity of the input dataset. A functional operational loop between supervised and unsupervised learning algorithms was developed to account for this result (Tetko and Villa 1997). The proposed functional mechanism was able to significantly improve operational speed and accuracy of the neural network ensemble, thus suggesting a tight connection between the adaptive filter hypothesis and attentional mechanisms at the thalamocortical level.

Conclusion

Thalamocortical interactions are based on rich interconnections between the components of this network, and understanding of information processing undergoing in the thalamus necessarily rests on the investigation of corticofugal modulation. Reversible

---

Fig. 4.17 (continued)
(B) Explicit connections within one thalamocortical module. (C) Schematic drawing of adaptive signal filtering with two inputs. The primary input contains the useful signal s and a reference signal r_0 which are uncorrelated. The reference input contains a signal r_1 correlated only with r_0. The filter's output is u and the system's output is w. See the text for more details.

cooling offers the opportunity to investigate the role of cortex by examining thalamic network activity in its absence. However, a firm grounding in the anatomy of connections is essential for adequate interpretations of the effects of deactivating cortical input on thalamic activity. These effects represent the sum of the effects on the composite pathway linking the thalamus and the cerebral cortex, mediated directly via primary projections or indirectly via the thalamic reticular nucleus and corticotectal projections. Because the thalamic reticular nucleus sits between the cortex and the thalamus, activation of this structure by descending projections from the cortex could activate these neurons which could then inhibit relay cells in the thalamus, thereby placing them in the "burst" mode (von Krosigk *et al.* 1993). There are features of the thalamocortical circuitry which are modality- and species-specific, demonstrating the importance of performing such experiments in several species and the advisability to repeat similar experiments for each sensory modality. In addition, the presence of multiple local circuits within the thalamus suggests that the use of simultaneous multisite recording will be of extreme importance. Our study represents an attempt to apply such a global approach to the study of the auditory thalamocortical pathway. We have also demonstrated the complementary information on functional local connectivity that can be obtained by combining single unit and multiple spike train analyses (Villa 2000).

In the auditory system, an excitatory or facilitatory role of the descending cortical projections is now well established in mammals, firstly suggested in cats (Orman and Humphrey 1981) and most recently in bats the corticofugal system has been shown to mediate a positive feedback which, in combination with widespread lateral inhibition, sharpens and adjusts the tuning of neurons at earlier stages in the auditory processing pathway (Zhang *et al.* 1997). Furthermore, a focal electric stimulation of the FM–FM area of the mustached bat auditory cortex (an area formed by delay-tuned combination-sensitive neurons, called FM–FM neurons) evokes changes in the responses of subcortical FM–FM neurons, thus suggesting that corticofugal modulation takes place for frequency domain analysis in exactly the same way as it does in time domain analysis (Suga *et al.* 2000). In addition to changes in the spontaneous firing rates of neurons of the medial geniculate body (MGB, the main thalamic auditory nucleus) cooling deactivation of the primary auditory cortex provokes a remarkable increase in the signal-to-noise ratio to acoustically driven stimulation in the ventral division of mgB units but not in other subdivisions. Even very complex response patterns could be recovered after a steady cortical inactivation lasting 45 minutes. The time course of the response pattern to pure tones and the modulation of the spontaneous activity have suggested that thalamic cell assemblies could perform adaptive filtering. This processing would allow selective extraction of information from the incoming signals according to the cortical activity, so that corticofugal modulation would regulate the response properties of thalamic units by modifying their bandwidth responsiveness to pure tones (Villa *et al.* 1991).

Simultaneous recordings of cell discharges in the cat auditory thalamus prior to, during and after cooling deactivation allowed us to estimate to which extent the thalamic functional connectivity is controlled by the activity of the auditory cortex. Reversible cortical deactivation tended to increase the number of direct interactions between adjacent thalamic neurons (local level, i.e. recorded from the same electrode) as well as from thalamic neurons recorded from different electrodes (areal level). The strength of the interactions was increased twice as often during cooling as it was decreased. Simultaneously, the number of shared inputs tended to decrease in rat and guinea pig but remained moderately unaffected at the local level in cat thalamus. Several scenarios may be proposed to interpret the experimental data but such fast plasticity of the thalamic circuitry can hardly be viewed as "classical" neural compensation in terms of "hard wiring" remodeling. Such a pattern of increased correlated activity within the auditory thalamus is distinct from the increase in synchronization of the auditory thalamus observed after prolonged pharmacologic manipulation of subcortical thalamic afferents (Villa *et al.* 1996).

Under normal conditions, selective activation of auditory cortical assemblies would initiate a feedback influence to the thalamus inducing local processing in mgB, which in turn would enhance the effect of thalamocortical input. Such a selective enhancement of interesting stimulus features while suppressing non-interesting ones (Tetko and Villa 1997), shows that the functional selectivity–adaptive filtering processing, where the gain of filtering is indirectly controlled by the thalamic reticular nucleus, is obtained because the thalamocortical circuit may function as a dynamic temporal filter as well. The suppressed unattended areas may still signal the presence of novel stimuli by triggering a burst of spikes, whereas detailed analysis of the stimulus requires the neurons of the thalamus to be in the tonic mode (Crick 1984; Mukherjee and Kaplan 1995). A diffuse activation of the RE by corticofugal projections would raise the RE firing rate and shift the temporal filtering properties to a lower-frequency mode. At the same time, direct excitatory input on mgB neurons would raise the membrane potential of a specific cell group and place them in a mode suited for analyzing rapid stimulus changes. In this model, a particular pattern of cortical activity ("template feature") could be fed to the thalamus and compared to the pattern elicited by an external sensory stimulus ("test feature"). Consequently, the increased coupling of cortical and thalamic activity in a specific area would amplify the effectiveness of a particular feature of the external sensory input, allowing its detection and binding to higher cognitive processing. Conversely, during cortical deactivation the absence of cortical input would induce an intrathalamic spread of activity, thus characterizing a distributed processing state in which the thalamus speaks primarily with itself.

Acknowledgments

The author wishes to thank A. Audergon, V.M. Bajo Lorenzana, M. Capt, D. Carretta, A. Celletti, F. de Ribaupierre, Y. de Ribaupierre, C. Eriksson, J. Eriksson, C. Haeberli, S. Hill, M. Jadé, F. Rodriguez Nodal, E.M. Rouiller, G.M. Simm, A. Singy, I. Tetko and P. Zurita for their experimental and technical assistance. Several discussions about the role of corticofugal pathway with V. Storozhuk in Kiev and I. Sil'kis in Moscow have contributed to the discussion of this work. This research was partially supported by Swiss NSF 7IP062620 and by INTAS-OPEN 97.0168 grants.

References

Abeles, M. (1982) Quantification, smoothing, and confidence limits for single unit histogram. *Journal of Neuroscience Methods*, **5**:317–25.

Abeles, M. (1991) *Corticonics: Neural Circuits of the Cerebral Cortex*. Cambridge University Press, Cambridge.

Aitkin, L. M. and Dunlop, C. W. (1969) Inhibition in the medial geniculate body of the cat. *Experimental Brain Research*, **7**:68–83.

Allon, N. and Yeshurun, Y. (1985) Functional organization of the medial geniculate body's subdivisions of the awake squirrel monkey. *Brain Research*, **360**:75–82.

Amato, G., LaGrutta, V. and Enia, F. (1969) The control exerted by the auditory cortex on the activity of the medial geniculate body and inferior colliculus. *Archives of Science and Biology*, **53**:291–313.

Andersen, R. A., Knight, P. L. and Merzenich, M. M. (1980) The thalamocortical and corticothalamic connections of AI, AII and the anterior auditory field (AAF) in the cat: evidence for two largely segregated systems of connections. *Journal of Comparative Neurology*, **194**:663–701.

Bajo, V. M., Rouiller, E. M., Welker, E. *et al.* (1995) Morphology and spatial distribution of corticothalamic terminals originating from the cat auditory cortex. *Hearing Reserch*, **83**:161–74.

Bentivoglio, M., Chen, S., Peng, Z.-C. *et al.* (1993) Thalamus, neurotrophins and their receptors. In D. Minciacchi, M. Molinari, G. Macchi *et al.* (eds) *Thalamic Networks for Relay and Modulation*, pp. 309–20. Oxford, UK, Pergamon.

Brooks, V. B. (1983) Study of brain function by local, reversible cooling. *Reviews of Physiology, Biochemistry and Pharmacology*, **95**:1–109.

Calford, M. B. and Aitkin, L. M. (1983) Ascending projections to the medial geniculate body of the cat: evidence for multiple parallel auditory pathways through thalamus. *Journal of Neuroscience*, **3**:2365–80.

Clerici, W. J. and Coleman, J. R. (1990) Anatomy of the rat medial geniculate body: I. Cytoarchitecture, myeloarchitecture, and neocortical connectivity. *Journal of Comparative Neurology*, **297**:14–31.

Crick, F. (1984) Function of the thalamic reticular complex: the searchlight hypothesis. *Proceedings of the National Academy of Sciences USA*, **81**:4586–90.

Desmedt, J. E. and Mechelse, K. (1958) Suppression of acoustic input by thalamic stimulation. *Proceedings of the Society of experimental Biology (NY)*, **99**:772–5.

Gerstein, G. L. and Perkel, D. H. (1972) Mutual temporal relationships among neuronal spike trains. Statistical techniques for display and analysis. *Biophysical Journal*, **12**:453–73.

Hackett, T. A., Stepniewska, I. and Kaas, J. H. (1998) Thalamocortical connections of the parabelt auditory cortex in macaque monkeys. *Journal of Comparative Neurology*, **400**:271–86.

Hill, S.L. and Villa, A. E. P. (1997) Dynamic transitions in global network activity influenced by the balance of excitation and inhibition. *Network*, **8**:165–84.

Jahnsen, H. and Llinas, R. (1984a) Electrophysiological properties of guinea-pig thalamic neurones: an *in vitro* study. *Journal of Physiology*, **349**:205–26.

Jahnsen, H. and Llinas, R. (1984b) Ionic basis for the electro-responsiveness and oscillatory properties of guinea-pig thalamic neurones *in vitro*. *Journal of Physiology*, **349**:227–47.

Jones, E. G. (1975) Some aspects of the organization of the thalamic reticular complex. *Journal of Comparative Neurology*, **162**:285–308.

Jones, E. G. (1985) *The Thalamus*. Plenum Press, New York.

Jordan, H. (1973) The structure of the medial geniculate nucleus (MGN): a cyto- and myeloarchitectonic study in the squirrel monkey. *Journal of Comparative Neurology*, **148**:469–79.

Kvasnak, E., Popelar, J. and Syka, J. (2000) Discharge properties of neurons in subdivisions of the medial geniculate body of the guinea pig. *Physiological Research*, **49**:369–78.

LaBerge, D., Carter, M. and Brown, V. (1992) A network simulation of thalamic circuit operations in selective attention. *Neural Computation*, **4**:318–31.

Levi Montalcini, R. and Calissano, P. (1986) Nerve growth factor as a paradigm for other polypeptide growth factors. *Trends in Neuroscience*, **9**:473–7.

Llinas, R. R., Ribary, U., Jeanmonod, D. *et al.* (1999) Thalamocortical dysrhythmia: A neurological and neuropsychiatric syndrome characterized by magnetoencephalography. *Proceedings of the National Academy of Sciences USA*, **96**:15222–7.

Lumer, E. D., Edelman, G. M. and Tononi, G. (1997a) Neural dynamics in a model of the thalamo-cortical system. II. The role of neural synchrony tested through perturbations of spike timing. *Cerebral Cortex*, **7**:228–36.

Lumer, E. D., Edelman, G. M. and Tononi, G. (1997b) Neural dynamics in a model of the thalamocortical system. I. Layer, loops and the emergence of fast synchronous rhythms. *Cerebral Cortex*, **7**:207–27.

McCormick, D. A. and Bal, T. (1994) Sensory gating mechanisms of the thalamus. *Current Opinion in Neurobiology*, **4**:550–6.

McCormick, D. A. and Huguenard, J. R. (1992). A model of the electrophysiological properties of thalamocortical relay neurons. *Journal of Neurophysiology*, **68**:1384–400.

Morest, D. K. (1964) The neuronal architecture of the medial geniculate body of the cat. *Journal of Anatomy*, **98**:611–30.

Mukherjee, P. and Kaplan, E. (1995) Dynamics of neurons in the cat lateral geniculate nucleus: *In vivo* electrophysiology and computational modeling. *Journal of Neurophysiology*, **74**:1222–43.

Murray, S. and Guillery, R. W. (1996) Functional organization of thalamocortical relays. *Journal of Neurophysiology*, **76**:1367–95.

Orman, S. S. and Humphrey, G. L. (1981) Effects of changes in cortical arousal and of auditory cortex cooling on neuronal activity in the medial geniculate body. *Experimental Brain Research*, **42**:475–82.

Pandya, D. N., Rosene, D. L. and Doolittle, A. M. (1994) Corticothalamic connections of auditory-related areas of the temporal lobe in the rhesus monkey. *Journal of Comparative Neurology*, **345**:447–71.

Paxinos, G. and Watson, C. (1986) *The Rat Brain in Stereotaxic Coordinates*, 2nd edn. Academic Press. San Diego.

Payne, B. R., Lomber, S. G., Villa, A. E. P. *et al.* (1996) Reversible deactivation of cerebral network components. *Trends in Neuroscience*, **19**:535–42.

Reale, R. A. and Imig, T. J. (1980) Tonotopic organization of auditory cortex in the cat. *Journal of Comparative Neurology*, **192**:265–91.

Redies, H., Brandner, S. and Creutzfeldt, O. D. (1989a) Anatomy of the auditory thalamocortical system of the guinea pig. *Journal of Comparative Neurology*, **282**:489–511.

Redies, H., Sieben, U. and Creutzfeldt, O. D. (1989b) Functional subdivisions in the auditory cortex of the guinea pig. *Journal of Comparative Neurology*, **282**:473–88.

Rockland, K. S. (1996) Two types of corticopulvinar terminations: round (type 2) and elongate (type 1). *Journal of Comparative Neurology*, **368**:57–87.

Rose, J. E. and Galambos, R. (1952) Microelectrode studies on medial geniculate body of cat: I. Thalamic region activated by click stimuli. *Journal of Neurophysiology*, **15**:343–57.

Rouiller, E. M. and Welker, E. (2000) A comparative analysis of the morphology of corticothalamic projections in mammals. *Brain Research Bulletin*, **53**:727–41.

Ryugo, D. K. and Weinberger, N. M. (1976) Corticofugal modulation of the medial geniculate body. *Experimental Neurology*, **51**:377–91.

Singer, W. (1977) Control of thalamic transmission by corticofugal and ascending reticular pathways in the visual system. *Physiological Reviews*, **57**:386–420.

Steriade, M. and Llinas, R. R. (1988) The functional states of the thalamus and the associated neuronal interplay. *Physiological Reviews*, **68**:649–742.

Steriade, M., Jones, E. G. and Llinas, R. R. (1990) Thalamic oscillations and signaling. New York, Wiley & Sons.

Steriade, M., McCormick, D. A. and Sejnowski, T. J. (1993) Thalamocortical oscillations in the sleeping and aroused brain. *Science*, **262**:679–85.

Suga, N., Gao, E., Zhang, Y. *et al.* (2000) The corticofugal system for hearing: recent progress. *Proceedings of the National Academy of Sciences USA*, **97**:11807–14.

Taylor, J. and Alavi, F. (1994) A global competitive neural network. *Biological Cybernetics*, **72**:1–16.

Taylor, J. G. (1999) *The Race for Consciousness*. Cambridge, MA, MIT Press.

Tetko, I. V. and Villa, A. E. P. (2001a) A pattern grouping algorithm for analysis of spatiotemporal patterns in neuronal spike trains. 1. Detection of repeated patterns. *Journal of Neuroscience Methods*, **105**:1–14.

Tetko, I. V. and Villa, A. E. P. (2001b) A pattern grouping algorithm for analysis of spatiotemporal patterns in neuronal spike trains. 2. Application to simultaneous single unit recordings. *Journal of Neuroscience Methods*, **105**:15–24.

Tetko, I. V. and Villa, A. E. P. (1997) Efficient partition of learning datasets for neural network training. *Neural Networks*, **10**:1361–74.

Vidal de Carvalho, L. (1994) Modeling the thalamocortical loop. *International Journal of Biomedical Computing*, **35**:267–96.

Villa, A. E. P. (2000) Empirical evidence about temporal structure in multi-unit recordings. In R. Miller (ed.) *Time and the Brain: Conceptual Advances in Brain Research*, vol. 3, pp. 1–51. Harwood Academic Publishers.

Villa, A. E. P. (1988) *Influence de l'écorce cérébrale sur l'activité spontanée et évoquée du thalamus auditif du chat*. Presses Imprivite, Lausanne.

Villa, A. E. P. (1990) Physiological differentiation within the auditory part of the thalamic reticular nucleus of the cat. *Brain Research Review*, **15**:25–40.

Villa, A. E. P. and Abeles, M. (1990) Evidence for spatio-temporal firing patterns within the auditory thalamus of the cat. *Brain Research*, **509**:325–7.

Villa, A. E. P. and Tetko, I. V. (1995) Spatio-temporal patterns of activity controlled by system parameters in a simulated thalamo-cortical neural network. In H. Hermann (ed.) *Supercomputing in Brain Research: From Tomography to Neural Networks*, pp. 379–88. World Scientific Publishing, Singapore.

Villa, A. E. P., Bajo, V. M. and Vantini, G. (1996) Nerve growth factor (NGF) modulates information processing in the auditory thalamus. *Brain Research Bulletin*, **39**:139–47.

Villa, A. E. P., Rouiller, E. M., Simm, G. M. *et al.* (1991) Corticofugal modulation of the information processing in the auditory thalamus of the cat. *Experimental Brain Research*, **86**:506–17.

Villa, A. E. P., Tetko, I. V., Hyland, B. *et al.* (1999b) Spatiotemporal activity patterns of rat cortical neurons predict responses in a conditioned task. *Proceedings of the National Academy of Sciences USA*, **96**:1006–11.

Villa, A. E. P., Tetko, I. V., Dutoit, P. *et al.* (1999a) Corticofugal modulation of functional connectivity within the auditory thalamus of rat, guinea pig and cat revealed by cooling deactivation. *Journal of Neuroscience Methods*, **86**:161–78.

von Krosigk, M., Bal, T., McCormick, D. A. (1993) Cellular mechanisms of a synchronized oscillation in the thalamus. *Science*, **261**:361–4.

Watanabe, T., Yanagiswara, K., Kanzaki, J. *et al.* (1966) Cortical efferent flow influencing unit responses of medial geniculate body to sound stimulation. *Experimental Brain Research*, **2**:302–17.

Widrow, B. and Stearns, S. (1985) *Adaptive Signal Processing.* Englewood Cliffs, Prentice Hall.

Winer, J. A. (1985) The medial geniculate body of the cat. *Advances in Anatomy, Embryology and Cell Biology*, **86**:1–97.

Winer, J. A. and Larue, D. T. (1987) Patterns of reciprocity in auditory thalamocortical and corti-cothalamic connections: study with horseradish peroxidase and autoradiographic methods in the rat medial geniculate body. *Journal of Comparative Neurology*, **257**:282–315.

Winer, J. A. and Larue, D. T. (1996) Evolution of GABAergic circuitry in the mammalian medial geniculate body. *Proceedings of the National Academy of Sciences USA*, **93**:3083–7.

Winer, J. A., Diehl, J. J. and Larue, D. T. (2001) Projections of auditory cortex to the medial geniculate body of the cat. *Journal of Comparative Neurology*, **430**:27–55.

Winer, J. A., Larue, D. T. and Huang, C. L. (1999) Two systems of giant axon terminals in the cat medial geniculate body: convergence of cortical and GABAergic inputs. *Journal of Comparative Neurology*, **413**:181–97.

Zhang, Y., Suga, N. and Yan, J. (1997) Corticofugal modulation of frequency processing in bat auditory system. *Nature*, **387**:900–3.

Zilles, K. and Wree, A . (1985) Cortex: areal and laminar structure. In G. Paxinos (ed.) *The Rat Nervous System*, vol. 1, pp. 375–416. Academic, New York.

Zurita, P., Villa, A. E. P., de Ribaupierre, Y. *et al.* (1994) Changes of single unit activities in the cat's auditory thalamus and cortex associated to different anesthetic conditions. *Neuroscience Research*, **19**:303–16.

Chapter 5

Deactivation of Feedforward and Feedback Pathways in the Visual Cortex of the Monkey

Pascal Girard, Jean Bullier

Introduction

In this chapter we present an overview over our group's long-standing experience with different inactivation methods to investigate the function of corticocortical visual pathways in the macaque monkey. Our studies are mainly centered on the role of feedforward and feedback pathways. Both of these pathways were originally defined on purely anatomical grounds (Van Essen and Maunsell 1983) and a speculative hierarchy of visual areas was derived from this anatomical work. For the past fifteen years we have been examining the functional aspects of this hierarchy with the help of reversible inactivation methods. The advantages and limitations of these methods are provided in the comprehensive overview of Lomber (1999). Many of these points will also be considered in this chapter.

Effect of plasticity upon recovery of cortical lesions

If one seeks to test the role of an afferent signal upon the visual responses of unitary cells in a structure in receipt of these projections, one quickly comes to the realization that this examination is not easily achievable by making permanent lesions of the origin of the projection. This approach only offers the possibility of sampling responses of neurons before the lesion, sampling an equivalent population after the ablation, and then statistically comparing the two populations. This investigation strategy only works when the effects of the lesion are very obvious and profound. For example, the effect of bilateral area V1 lesions that silence all visual responses in inferotemporal cortex (Rocha-Miranda *et al.* 1975). Some studies have successfully tested the properties of a cell population before and after a lesion. For instance, in the cat, Mendola and Payne (1993) recorded the effect of primary visual cortex ablations on the responses of superior colliculus neurons. Using quantitative measurements, they recorded no difference in the direction selectivity indices of these responses, in contrast to earlier studies (Wickelgren and Sterling 1969; Mize and Murphy 1976). However, subtle changes in receptive field properties cannot be identified with this approach. For example, if a neuron undergoes a change in direction tuning, it would most likely go undetected since it is not possible to record from the very same units before and after the lesion.

Besides these considerations, the most difficult aspect in the interpretation of the results from lesion studies is that the experimenter records responses of neurons or behavioral responses in an animal that might have learned to cope with the lesion and that the responses after the lesion reflect *both* the consequences of the lesion and the functional recovery that often follows. Therefore, instead of probing the role of a cortical region, a lesion study may unintentionally address a different topic, namely that of neural plasticity or functional recovery. A vast number of studies have demonstrated that neural or behavioral plasticity occurs following cerebral lesions. One possible mechanism of plasticity is the take-over of the lost function by another cortical region. For instance, in the cat, Baumann and Spear (1977) demonstrated the role of lateral suprasylvian (LS) area in the recovery of visual pattern discrimination abilities following area 17, 18 and 19 lesions: a subsequent lesion of LS cortex counteracted the recovery, whereas a lesion of LS alone had no effect. Another example is found in the motor cortex where the behavioral recovery following a lesion of area M1 on precise grasping movements is abolished by an inactivation of the premotor cortex situated only a few millimeters away from the lesion site (Liu and Rouiller 1999).

The neuronal basis of postlesion behavioral recovery has not often been investigated. Most studies on this kind of plasticity have focused on the consequences of bilateral retinal lesions. Kaas *et al.* (1990) and Gilbert and Wiesel (1992) have shown a reorganization of the cortical receptive fields around the periphery of the lesion. Cortical lesions can also trigger neural plasticity. Results differ, and depend on the locus or extent of the lesion and on the level of training of the animal. Sober *et al.* (1997) have shown expansions of receptive fields (and also shifts and contraction) of neurons in close proximity to a lesion of area MT. They observed the occurrence of such phenomena in as little as three hours following either electrolytic or chemical lesions. Such receptive field expansions may constitute the neuronal basis for the recovery of smooth pursuit eye movements shortly after an ablation of area MT (Yamasaki and Wurtz 1991). On the other hand, after lesions of area 17 in the cat, receptive field sizes only start to increase in close proximity of an ibotenic acid injection site on a time scale of weeks or months, not days (Eysel and Schweigart 1999).

In addition, it is obvious that the brain cannot compensate for every cortical lesion, and some behavioral deficits remain unchanged even over a long period of time. For instance, Rudolph and Pasternak (1999) reported permanent deficits of discrimination thresholds for moving gratings masked by noise after lesions of both areas MT and MST. Another example is that of Schiller (1995), who indicates that lesions of V4 lead to permanent deficits in the identification of masked figures, while discrimination of simpler geometric shapes recovered after several days. Therefore, the effect of the lesion can only be fully assessed after a long lapse and once the system has achieved a stable recovery state. This is the case in the recent study of V4 lesions by Merigan (2000), who showed deficits that are convincingly stable over months in the discrimination of line element grouping.

A similar problem could also potentially occur with reversible inactivation techniques, if there were hints of extremely rapid plastic changes on the systems level. On the molecular level, it is known that MCP-1 message expression in the thalamus begins only one hour after axotomy as a consequence of a cortical ablation (Muessel *et al.* 2000). This could induce retrograde degeneration and modify neuronal responses. However, such rapid effects are unlikely to occur with reversible deactivation, as these techniques do not impair neuronal integrity. To our knowledge, plasticity phenomena at the systems level after a cortical lesion have been demonstrated only within days or at least many hours after inactivation (Sober *et al.* 1997), and they are often increased under the influence of training of the impaired function (Rudolph and Pasternak 1999). This is unlikely to occur within an inactivation cycle that lasts only twenty to thirty minutes, as is the case for reversible deactivation techniques.

General methodologic considerations for our inactivation techniques

We have used two different reversible inactivation methods, depending on the morphology of the cortical region studied; the first was reversible cooling, the second GABA injections (see details below). Some general observations apply to both of them. Reversible inactivation techniques are valuable only if at least two parameters are carefully controlled. First, the extent of the inactivated zone should be assessed. Second, the degree of the inactivation needs to be monitored by use of methods that measure neuronal activity in the inactivated region. This implies mapping of the temperature gradients for the cooling method or measuring of the diffusion of pharmacologic agents combined with electrode recordings (see below). In some cases, partial inactivation of the cortical territory may be sufficient. Moreover, rapid onset and offset of the inactivation is of great value, especially in electrophysiologic studies. The inactivation by cooling is such that cortical temperature stabilizes within a couple minutes in the case of a cryoloop or a Peltier device (Girard and Bullier 1989, Lomber *et al.* 1999). Hupé *et al.* (1999) showed that GABA inactivation by pressure injection is immediate (in the millisecond range) and limited only by the time of diffusion of the agent in the neuropil.

We found no evidence of short-term plasticity in any of our inactivation experiments. For instance, when a cell response was blocked by inactivating another cortical region, we never encountered a recovery of responses during the actual inactivation. Likewise, we did not obtain evidence for behavioral recovery in awake animals during the inactivation period. The rapid stabilization of the cooling temperature (about two minutes) and the immediate onset of GABA blockade in combination with the short duration of the inactivation cycles in both methods (about fifteen minutes) prevented the emergence of plasticity phenomena.

Inactivation of a feedforward pathway

Our first attempt to study the consequences of inactivation of a cortical area on the neuronal responses in an area directly connected to it was with the inactivation of the feedforward pathways from area V1 to several extrastriate areas in the anaesthetized and paralyzed macaque monkey. This work has already been reviewed (Bullier *et al.* 1994) and will be only briefly described here. The purpose of this set of experiments was to explore the neuronal basis of blindsight. This phenomenon occurs in humans who suffer from occipital lesions, which, in some cases, can be confined to area 17. These patients are completely blind as assessed with traditional perimetry measurements. Nevertheless, they can detect and localize a visual stimulus in space when placed in a forced-choice paradigm, although they deny seeing anything consciously (e.g. Weiskrantz 1996). Their performance is particularly impressive for detecting the direction of moving stimuli (Perenin 1991). Similarly, monkeys with a lesion of V1 are able to perform a variety of visuomotor tasks (Cowey and Stoerig 1997), hence this preparation constitutes a suitable model of this phenomenon. Each of the extrastriate areas that we have investigated receives direct connections from area V1 (very weak in the case of V4, Barone *et al.* 2000) and, in addition, receives direct thalamic projections that could drive them in the absence of area V1.

The evidence of residual vision after a lesion of area V1 poses the question of a possible recovery of function following the lesion. In other words, are the behavioral performances due to the recuperation of visual responses in extrastriate visual areas, or is activity in these areas possible even when area V1 stops responding for a short period? We immediately understand how crucial the choice of methodology was. In the case of a complete V1 lesion, unconscious vision can only be sustained by anatomical routes that bypass area V1. If one wants to replicate this situation with a blocking of the activity in V1, one critically needs to completely inactivate the full depth of area V1.

We inactivated a region two centimeters in diameter on the operculum of V1 with a cooling plate extension of a Peltier device (Girard and Bullier 1989). With the help of numerous thermocouple and microelectrode penetrations, we made extensive measurements of the temperature gradients, isotherms and temperature at which the neuronal activity ceased under the cooling plate. These experiments revealed that temperature gradients in the cortex depend on the temperature applied on the cortical surface. They range between 2.3 and 5.5 °C/mm. Once gradient curves are established, it was possible to measure the blocking temperature (since one cannot easily lower a thermocouple and an electrode at the same time). Stimulus-evoked responses began to shut off below 20 °C, with the most resistant ones disappearing only at 6°. Such low blocking temperatures have also been observed in slices of rat visual cortex by Gähwiler *et al.* (1972), with spontaneous activity identified to 5 °C, and by Volgushev *et al.* (2000), where electrically-evoked action potentials were found below 10 °C. In our experiments, in addition to the aforementioned measurements, an electrode was left in layer VI of area V1 during cooling to verify the completeness of the inactivation for each cooling cycle.

The main result of our V1 cooling deactivation experiments is that spared visual responses can be recorded in cortical areas that belong to the dorsal occipitoparietal visual processing stream. On the contrary, virtually no visual responses remain in areas of the ventral occipitotemporal pathway. In detail, we first investigated area V2, which contains subterritories (the cytochrome oxidase bands) that are linked to one or the other above-mentioned pathways. Nonetheless, area V2 is very strongly interconnected with area V1 (as compared with other extrastriate areas) which may explain why we were virtually unable to record visual responses (3/209) in the absence of V1, even in the thick cytochrome oxidase bands which are thought to be more connected to the dorsoparietal pathway (DeYoe and Van Essen 1988; Shipp and Zeki 1985). Other areas that are dramatically affected by the inactivation of V1 are V3 and V4 (Girard *et al.* 1991a,b). Both areas had respectively 1/37 and 7/77 cells that remained (weakly) visually responsive. Interestingly, for both areas, the receptive fields were sometimes so large that they could only be partly contained in the visual field perimeter corresponding to the receptive fields of the inactivated cells in V1. In such cases, we observed only partial blocks of activity restricted to this perimeter. These cases also constitute an important proof that our reversible inactivation method does not lead to nonspecific blocking of neuronal activity by metabolic or blood flow impairments.

A different picture appears from the study of areas V3a and MT that retain many more visually active cells in the absence of V1 (Girard *et al.* 1991a; 1992). Respectively, 23/76 and 46/57 cells were still active. In contrast to the very weak residual responses in V2, V3 and V4, the receptive fields in V3a and V5 could easily be hand-plotted and the response selectivity could clearly be assessed during inactivation of V1. In the case of MT, some changes of direction selectivity were observed: in most cases, the cells tended to become less direction selective, whereas the main axis of optimal direction in space did not change substantially. This is a good example of the advantages of a reversible inactivation method in which responses from the same neuron can be continuously recorded throughout a cycle of control–inactivation–recovery. Other examples of cells remaining direction selective in a similar experiment can be found in Rodman *et al.* (1989).

Inactivation of feedback pathways

Although it is commonly assumed that feedback pathways have a late modulatory action, there has been hardly any direct assessment of this dogma. To our knowledge, the first study using reversible inactivation to investigate the role of a feedback connection between cortical areas (V2 and V1) was done by Sandell and Schiller (1982) in the lissencephalic squirrel monkey. They observed some changes of activity (mostly decreases) and some changes of direction selectivity in the responses of V1 neurons. However, the conclusion of that study was weakened by the possibility of a direct spread of the cooling to the tested area, or insufficient cooling (to prevent the direct spread).

In the macaque monkey, the inactivation of feedback sources can be difficult. The difficulty lies in the fact that the intricate anatomy of the areas buried in the cortical sulci does not allow a straightforward application of the inactivation techniques described so far.

Inactivation of V5/MT

In the case of area V5/MT, we used the cryoloop technique originally developed by Salsbury and Horel (1984) and refined by Lomber *et al.* (1999). The experiments described here were done in collaboration with Drs Stephen Lomber and Bertram Payne. The Peltier device that we had used in the V1 deactivation studies had no advantage over the cryoloop technique. The cryoloop is superior because it can be permanently implanted. Moreover, it has a higher efficiency than the Peltier device, which requires a cumbersome radiator to evacuate the heat removed from the cold plate by the circulating current. In addition, a perfect thermal contact between the Peltier device and the extension cooling plate is not always as straightforward as it seems. Such drawbacks suggest that the cryoloop is ideal for cooling within sulci and deeper brain structures such as the superior colliculus. The only possible disadvantage of the cryoloop is that its fine, narrow tubing could block if carelessly manipulated. So far, in our hands, no experiment has been discontinued due to such a situation.

Under general anesthesia, we carefully dissected the superior temporal sulcus (STS) to lower one or two cryoloops into the fundus of the sulcus, directly over the surface of area V5/MT. The loops were insulated along the shaft in order to prevent cooling along the track. Previous studies (Payne and Lomber 1999) have used 2-deoxyglucose measurements to show that the extent of the cooling with similar devices is well restricted to the sulcus, in which the loop was embedded. This finding was confirmed by our own data since a cryoloop laying in a region of the STS anterior to area V5/MT did not produce any effect, indicating that the cooling did not spread beyond a few millimeters dorsomedially. Furthermore, when two cryoloops were side by side along the STS, if one is lowered down to 10 °C while the other is not activated, the temperature measured by the thermocouple at the base of the inactive loop was 30 °C (measured 2.5 mm away from the edge of the cold probe). This confirms the steep temperature gradients (about 10 °C/mm) measured by Lomber *et al.* (1999).

Knowing the relatively small volume of area MT (its surface is about 80 mm^2) (Gattass and Gross 1981), we can be sure that one loop was sufficient to completely inactivate the representation of the contralateral central visual field. This saved us the tedious work of searching in areas V1, V2 or V3 for a region corresponding to the visual field regions in the inactivated cortical area. The first important result we obtained with this methodology was that the feedback projection of MT to V1, V2 and V3 reinforces the detectability of a low-contrast moving bar on a noisy background (Hupé *et al.* 1998; Bullier *et al.* 2001). In the anesthetized monkey, we tested the effect of cooling MT upon neuronal responses evoked by light bars that moved over a textured background that was static or moving at the same speed. In the control situation, the response to the bar moving with the background was generally suppressed (background suppression) compared to the response of the bar moving alone on the static background. The suppression arises from the interaction between the inhibitory surround and the excitatory center. The mechanisms underlying these interactions have been attributed to horizontal connections (Gilbert *et al.* 1996). However, as the large receptive fields of MT cells could cover both the center and surround of a V1, V2 or V3 cell, the feedback from MT could theoretically play an important role in such interactions.

In these experiments the stability of recording was found to be critical. By definition, the reversible method allows to test neuronal responses of the same units before, during and after the inactivation unless the units are lost by cortical instability. Thus, we must ensure that the effect of the inactivation is genuine by recording two consecutive control runs that do not differ statistically. This would prove that the response variability is sufficiently low to be able to detect small changes due to the inactivation of area MT. Another important issue is the stability of the recorded action potentials. In some cases, a slight change in the action potential size occurs, probably due to some displacement in the brain due to changes in blood circulation. Because of this, it was essential to use a spike sorting device in order to ascertain that the spikes recorded during inactivation were identical to those recorded during control and recovery.

One obvious effect of MT inactivation was a decrease of responsiveness in 33% of all tested cells in V1, V2, and V3. Response increases were observed in only 6.5% of the neurons. This effect is by no means a nonspecific effect; in many neurons we observed response decreases to a moving bar activating the receptive field center and response increases to a flashed bar or the same bar moving together with the background. All these stimuli were randomly interleaved. At low salience (i.e. when the contrast of the bar and the background were similar), the bar was made visible only when it moved over the static background. In this situation, for most cells recorded in area V1, V2 and V3 that exhibited background suppression, cooling V5/MT decreased the response to the bar moving alone and did not change or increase when the bar and background moving conjointly. Hence background suppression was decreased in such a way that both responses become nearly indistinguishable. This effect is particularly striking in area V3, and present to a lesser extent for V2 and V1 cells (not significant for V1). Decreases in background suppression were also present for all areas to a lesser extent at middle and high salience. Figure 5.1 shows an example of a neuron in V3 exhibiting a clear reduction in background suppression as a consequence of V5/MT inactivation. This figure also shows the particularly marked decrease of background suppression at low salience for the whole population of neurons.

The mechanisms of a decrease in background suppression are different depending on the visual area. In areas V1 and V2, the effect is mainly due to a decrease of the response to a low salience moving bar, whereas the response to the background remains constant. The observation that the V5/MT inactivation has a different effect on each area examined may be expected from cortical connectivity. MT projects directly back to V3, V2 and V1 and, in addition, there is a cascade of back projections from V3

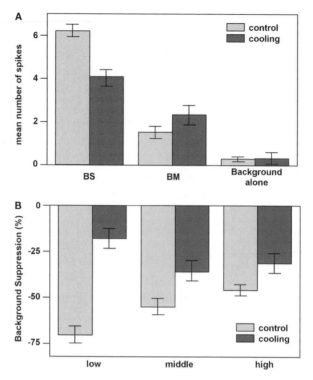

Fig. 5.1 (A) Example of the responses of a single neuron of V3 during cooling of MT. BS stands for response to a bar moving alone on a background, BM stands for response to bar and background moving at the same speed in the same direction. Background suppression is reduced during cooling as a consequence of a combined decrease of BS and increase of BM. (B) Effect of cooling of MT on background suppression indices for the whole population of background suppressed neurons (71 for V1, V2 and V3). Different levels of salience (low, middle and high) are indicated. Background suppression index is defined as $100*(BM- BS)/BSc$, where BSc stands for response to the bar moving on the static background during control. Cooling MT has a major effect at low salience. Reprinted from Hupé *et al*. The role of feedback connections in shaping the responses of visual cortical neurons, *Progress in Brain Research*, 2001, p. 196, with permission of Elsevier Science.

to V2, from V3 to V1 and V2 to V1. Since center–surround interactions are already known to be present in the receptive fields of MT cells (Allman *et al.* 1985; Xiao *et al.* 1997), V3 (our own observations), V2 (Foster *et al.* 1985) and V1 (Knierim and Van Essen 1992), the effect of MT cooling cannot be predicted in a straightforward fashion. For example, a significant decrease of suppression for high salience was observed for ten units in V2 (Bullier *et al.* 2001). It could hypothetically be explained by the summation of nonsignificant decreases at high salience in V3 and V1 transmitted, respectively, back to V2 via feedback connections and up to V2 by feedforward connections.

In conclusion, our results demonstrate that feedback from V5/MT to V1, V2 and V3 helps to enhance the detection (or discrimination) of the motion of a visual stimulus that is hardly visible. Although we do not have direct evidence, feedback connections could play a role in a nonlinear mechanism such as a gain control of the center activation and of the center–surround interactions. This mechanism is not based on modified levels of spontaneous activity, as this is largely independent of the effect of cooling deactivation (Hupé *et al.* 2001a). As no response arises from the surround of a receptive field during cooling, one can conclude that feedback boosts the response in the center that is originally initiated by feedforward activity. We are confident that our results form an electrophysiologic counterpart to the behavioral consequences of a V5/MT lesion (Newsome and Pare 1988; Pasternak and Merigan 1994; Rudolph and Pasternak 1999). These authors observed a profound deficit in the discrimination of motion direction in the presence of noise. Our results suggests that the neural basis of this deficit is not limited to processing steps in area MT but that it also involves neural mechanisms in lower order areas that are normally influenced by MT neurons. Motion detection ability is of particular behavioral significance. Camouflage is broken when an object (more often an animal) moves on a background that has the same texture and contrast. By integration of the whole visual scene throughout larger receptive fields, MT neurons convey this signal back to lower visual processing stages.

Early actions of feedback revealed by reversible inactivations

If V5/MT feedback connections are involved in breaking camouflage, an obvious adaptive inference could be drawn. Monkeys must react immediately to the panther crawling through the undergrowth. Feedback from V5/MT must urgently signal a sudden move of coherent spots. Indeed, the second important result of our studies is that the action of the feedback is extremely rapid (Hupé *et al.* 2001a).

Using the same experimental setup described earlier, we examined the time course of the feedback influences from area MT in the anaesthetized monkey. We measured the time course of this influence on the visual responses of V1, V2 and V3 neurons to stimuli moving, or flashed, over a textured background as above (Hupé *et al.* 2001a). We computed the latencies to both moving and flashed stimuli using the method of Maunsell and Gibson (1992), where latency is defined as the time of the first bin that exceeds the background activity with a probability of $p=0.005$ (0.01 for flash) if this bin is followed by a second one with the same p level and a third one which exceeds $p=0.025$ (0.05). Because of the small number of stimulus repetitions, population PSTH were computed from several neuronal responses similarly affected by cooling to be able to compute statistical differences in latencies. We found that the effects of cooling MT were significant within the first 10 ms of the response.

Responses to a bar flashed in the center of a receptive field allows for a more precise measurement of latencies because neurons in MT, and in lower order areas, are activated by a stimulus striking all receptive fields simultaneously while, in the case of moving stimuli, neurons with large receptive fields tend to be activated earlier than neurons with small overlapping receptive fields. Considering individual neuronal responses, we observed a decrease of the response to a bar flashed on a steady background for fifteen neurons. Except for three cells that showed a delayed effect, the response decrease was observed on the very earliest part of the visual responses. Fourteen units displayed an increase that, again, for the majority (eleven out of fourteen) appears in the first 20 ms of the response. In some cases, the latency could even become shorter during cooling of V5/MT. Furthermore, even neurons with short latencies were affected in the early part of the response. We could detect a decrease of activity due to the inactivation as soon as the response began in one of the shortest latency neurons of our sample (42 ms). Interestingly, this neuron was located in layer 4B of area V1 and is likely to be reciprocally connected with MT (Ungerleider and Desimone 1986; Shipp and Zeki 1989). This case is illustrated in Fig. 5.2. It should be pointed out that this precocious effect is not correlated with changes in spontaneous activity. Indeed, eleven cells with no change in spontaneous activity during the inactivation cycle displayed effects in the early part of the response. Figure 5.3 shows a population histogram that exemplifies the early effects of cooling upon the visual responses to flashed bars. It also shows that inactivation has the tendency to decrease the responses, an effect which continues throughout the entire response period. The same situation is true when inactivation leads to an increase of the responses.

At first glance, our findings seem counterintuitive considering the theoretical framework of the hierarchy of corticocortical connections. Many authors expected a late action of feedback connections because figure-ground coding in V1 is late. We cannot deny that this possibility is important for attention modulated feedback, for example in visual search tasks (Lamme and Roelfsema 2000). However, our results on early feedback action from MT are not too surprising when two points are taken into consideration. First, MT/V5-neurons have extremely short response latencies and can be found among the earliest cortical visual responses (about 30 ms; Raiguel *et al.* 1989; Nowak and Bullier 1997; Schmolesky *et al.* 1998). Second, the conduction velocity of action potentials evoked by electrical stimulation is very fast along corticocortical axons (around 3.5 m/s, Girard *et al.* 2001). Hence, it is quite conceivable that V5/MT feedback can influence early phases of visual responses in lower visual areas.

Fig. 5.2 Decrease of the response to a flashed bar for a neuron of V1, layer 4B during cooling of MT. The decrease occurs already in the beginning of the response although the latency is short (42 ms). Reprinted from Hupé *et al.* (2001a) Feedback connections act on the early part of the responses in monkey visual cortex. *Journal of Neurophysiology,* **85**:134–141.

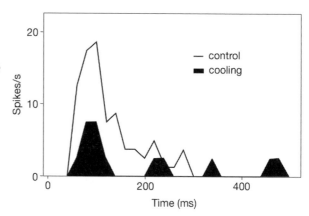

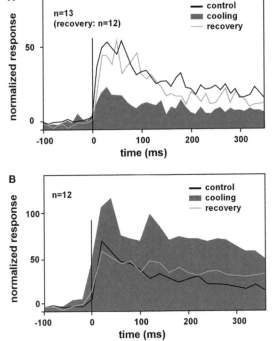

Fig. 5.3 Decrease (A) and increase (B) of the responses to cooling of MT for the whole population. The stimulus is a flashed bar (at time 0). The effect is present with the onset of the responses and is maintained throughout the whole response period. Reprinted from Hupé *et al.* (2001a) Feedback connections act on the early part of the responses in monkey visual cortex. *Journal of Neurophysiology*, 85:134–141.

An interesting perspective emerging from these data would be to test attentional effects in an awake monkey: Reynolds *et al.* (2000) have demonstrated that the contrast sensitivity curves of area V4 neurons are displaced when the animal pays attention to the stimulus. Interestingly, the effects of attention are strongest at low contrast and weak at high contrast. This parallels our results showing that the effects of MT inactivation are strongest on low salience stimuli. Such attentional effects may easily be disrupted by an inactivation of feedback connections (in the study of Reynolds *et al.* (2000), a feedback pathway from inferotemporal cortex to V4 could come into play).

Reversible inactivation of area V2

Another sequence of studies involved the inactivation of area V2 and recording in V1. Due to the convoluted aspect of the lunate sulcus in the macaque, and the proximity of area V1, lowering a cryoloop was not feasible. Therefore, we selected GABA application as the inactivation technique of choice (Hupé *et al.* 1999). Area V2 is nearly as large as area V1; thus it is impossible to completely inactivate the entire area. However, it is possible to restrict the inactivation in V2 to the respective region (convergence zone) that projects to a given point in area V1 (Salin *et al.* 1992; Angelucci *et al.* 2000).

The efficiency of GABA is well established and there is no doubt about the completeness of the blockade that can be achieved at appropriate concentrations (Hupé *et al.* 1999). GABA inactivation is eminently suitable for electrophysiologic studies because it does not affect fibers of passage, allows for complete recovery, and produces extremely rapid inactivations.

Several methods of injection are available. Hupé *et al.* (1999) discarded iontophoresis because it delivers volumes that are too small for a complete inactivation of the entire convergence zone. A better choice was the pressure injection of GABA at 100 mM that allowed for inactivation of up to 500 micrometers lateral to the tip of the pipette. Hupé and collaborators (1999) built a model of the spatiodynamic characteristics of GABA inactivation derived from direct measurements of neuronal activity around the pipettes in cat visual cortex. As with any other method, the possibility of direct effects of a remote inactivation has to be considered. The measurements of Hupé predict an elliptical inactivation volume centered above the pipette tip. Electrode recordings indicated that inactivation does not spread to V1 directly. Experimental recordings and the model were both used to devise a system that could optimally inactivate the convergence zone of V2 upon V1. This analysis produced a system comprised of a compound arrangement of six pipettes (0.58 mm ID, 10–25 microns at the tip)

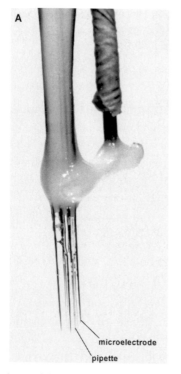
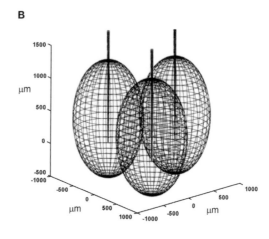

Fig. 5.4 (A) Photograph of the multi-pipette and microelectrode device used to inactivate area V2. (B) Three dimensional estimation of the volume of diffusion of the GABA around the pipette tips, note that it is slightly eccentric (more diffusion upwards). Reprinted from Hupé *et al.* (1999) Spatial and temporal parameters of cortical inactivation by GABA. *Journal of Neuroscience Methods*, **86**:141 with permission of Elsevier Science.

separated by less than 1 mm. This device can inactivate along a diameter of gray matter 2 mm laterally and 1.5 mm deep. Figure 5.4 shows an illustration of the device together with a sketch of the spatial extent of inactivation.

The remaining difficulty was to lower the device to the proper depth in V2 (the upper third of the cortical depth of V2 cortex since GABA flows back along the pipettes) with a correct penetration angle taking into account the angled shape of the lunate sulcus, in order to ensure that every pipette is in the gray matter. Preliminary electrode penetrations were done to map the V2 region to optimize the position of the device.

The Symphony® software program controlled the precise delivery of GABA by a pump (Harvard Apparatus, model PHD 2000). Electrodes glued to the device monitored the activity of the neurons surrounding the microelectrodes. The completeness of the blocking was confirmed for each injection. Regular injections of GABA, 100 mM (25 or 50 nl), were performed to maintain a steady, complete block since neuronal activity could recover quickly. Due to the need to inactivate the convergence zone, we had to match receptive field locations in V1 retinotopically to those at the inactivation site in V2. Electrical stimulation studies have shown that a perfect register is mandatory to obtain antidromic drive between V1 and V2 (Girard *et al.* 2001). This maneuver is particularly difficult, because both sites are usually very close to each other and because of the space restrictions posed by the electrode and pipette holders.

In the anesthetized macaque monkey, we tested the role of feedback from V2 to V1 in figure-ground interactions. The stimuli were similar to the ones used by Knierim and Van Essen (1992) and consisted of concentric patches of small bars flashed in the surround of the receptive field, whereas one central bar was flashed in the classical receptive field. The condition of having all bars with the same orientation yields a strong decrease in the response for most tested neurons, as compared to that to the central bar only. A weaker suppression was observed in cases with a 90° orientation difference between center and surround bars. This differential response is supposed to represent the underlying mechanism of pop-out in visual search (Nothdurft *et al.* 1999). We employed a series of stimuli in which the orientation and occurrence of the surround bars, as well as the presence of the central bar, randomly varied.

We discovered that it was critical to carefully monitor both EEG and blood pressure in order to gain confidence in the stability of the recordings. Indeed, receptive fields sizes can vary according to the state of EEG in the anesthetized animals (Wörgötter *et al.* 1998). Preliminary results in our group (Bullier *et al.* 1996) revealed apparition of responses in the surround (which is by definition unresponsive to visual stimulation) of the receptive fields of V1 during GABA inactivation. Such increases could simply reflect an increase of the classical receptive field during EEG instability, which was not monitored at that time.

Contrary to our expectations and our earlier results without EEG monitoring (Bullier *et al.* 1996), we were unable to see any effect of V2 inactivation on center–surround interactions in a subsequent and better controlled study (Hupé *et al.* 2001b).

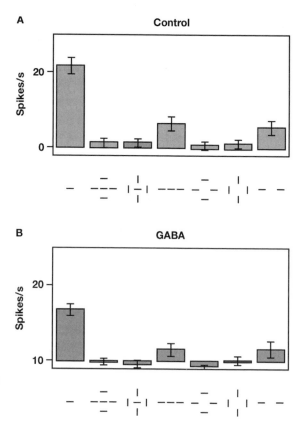

Fig. 5.5 Absence of an effect of the inactivation of V2 upon the center–surround interactions within the receptive field of a single neuron. Stimuli are represented below the histogram of the responses. Reprinted from Hupé, J. M. James, A. C., Girard, P. *et al.* (2001b) Response modulations by static texture surround in area V1 of the macaque monkey do not depend upon feedback connections from V2. *Journal of Neurophysiology,* **85**:146–63.

Similar to what we observed with V5/MT cooling, a decrease of the response for 6/64 V1 units occurs during GABA blockade. Unlike for MT inactivation, an overall decrease of response occurs for each configuration of stimuli, for central stimulation as well as for center–surround stimulation (Fig. 5.5). Consequently, the center–surround modulation is maintained. As in the case of MT inactivation, these decreases are observed in the early part of the responses, during the first 20 ms.

As the result was globally negative, we needed to be more specific in our analysis to be sure that the effect was true for all cell classes. Therefore, we split neurons into different categories according to the influence of the surround in the control condition (general suppression, orientation biased suppressions). These features were maintained during the inactivation for each neuron. However, we had to prove the completeness of the blockade. With our device, no clogging of the pipettes could occur, since overpressure would have led to an unplugging of the tubing on the pipette. Nevertheless, it is quite difficult to control that every single neuron in V2 had been sufficiently blocked, as there is no technology available that would allow for the monitoring of the activity levels in the whole population of neurons. Still, there is no doubt that the region covered by

GABA spread was large and that V2 cortex was massively blocked. However, because of the tortuous configuration of the lunate sulcus, we cannot be certain that we blocked the entire cortical depth below each pipette. If the block was incomplete, it would indicate that the center–surround interactions in V1 are highly nonlinearly depending on back projections from V2. Considering these technical difficulties, it would be interesting to consider doing these experiments in a lissencephalic monkey such as the marmoset, in which cooling V2 is feasible. However, because of the proximity of areas V1 and V2, V1 should be artificially warmed to prevent spread of the cooling (Wang *et al.* 2000).

When we compared the results obtained with inactivation of area MT and inactivation in V2, the lack of effect of V2 inactivation on center–surround interactions appears to contrast with our results in the MT experiments. However, these differences depend on the respective stimulation conditions. The strongest effects observed in the MT experiments were with low salience stimuli, whereas little effect was observed with high salience stimuli (see Fig. 5.1, which indicates that the surround suppression does not change by more than 15% with high salience). Our experiments with V2 inactivation were all done with high salience stimuli. This could be the main reason for the absence of an effect in our experiments. It would be interesting to replicate the V2 experiments with low salience stimuli and a more complete inactivation of the area to see if under those conditions center–surround interactions can be modified by inactivation of feedback inputs. Concerning our hypothesis of breaking camouflage in the case of the V5/MT deactivation experiments, it is the sudden motion of the bar that triggers the response. The stimulus employed in the V2 study may be considered as quite different as it is presented a succession of flashed patterns with blank screens in between. Therefore, a better analog would be a sudden tilt of the central bar embedded in surrounding elements. An obvious follow up would be to test this hypothesis in the awake animal with any kind of sudden change in the visual scene that could drive a behavioral response.

Reversible inactivation of area V4 in the awake monkey

We have also investigated the behavioral effects of reversibly cooling area V4 using the same method as that employed to inactivate V5/MT. Lesions of area V4 have been studied by several investigators. Using an oddity task paradigm, Schiller (1993) found that monkeys were particularly impaired in the detection of stimuli with low saliency, but this was due to size or luminance. Because of the aforementioned disadvantages of lesion techniques, we reinvestigated some aspects of this with a reversible deactivation technique. We positioned a cryoloop on the surface of the prelunate gyrus in the parafoveal representation of V4. The loop was implanted on the left side of the brain, corresponding to the representation of the inferior right quadrant of the visual field. As the loop was unilateral, the animal could serve as its own control.

With this setup, we tested behaving macaque monkeys on a match-to-sample task. The monkey sat in a primate chair, with a fixed head, in front of a video monitor. While the animal fixated a central dot on the screen, one of the two samples used in one session was presented randomly in the right or left inferior quadrant. The sample then turned off, and after a short delay of about 20 ms, two matches are presented in the upper quadrants. When the fixation spot turned off, the monkey was required to make a saccade to the stimulus that was identical to the sample (the nonmatch being the other sample).

The course of the cooling deactivation sessions was stereotyped. Before any stimulus presentation, the protective cap above the loop was removed and the tubing for the cryoloop was connected. The monkey then worked a series of control trials. Without stopping the animal's testing, the cryoloop was activated and reached effective temperature within two minutes. Records of the performance during cooling were recorded for 15–20 minutes after temperature stabilization. As soon as the pump is turned off, the next block of trials constituted the rewarm period. Sham inactivations were also performed. To this end, everything was set up as usual with the pump running, but not circulating any fluid. These recordings show no indication that the monkeys were disturbed by the background noise of the pump because the performance of the animal remained unimpaired.

First, we tested the simple detection of a small bar (24'×7.8'), presented at random positions in the visual field. Monkeys could perform the task of making a saccade to the bar without any error during V4 inactivation. This experiment demonstrates the lack of a gross visual perception impairment and normal saccadic generation to any part of the visual field during V4 inactivation. However, the animals were impaired on matching-to-sample tasks with several kinds of stimuli of equal salience. Figure 5.6 shows the percentage of correct responses in pooling ten cooling sessions obtained in one monkey. Match and nonmatch stimuli differed in shape, or a combination of shape and color (for instance a green circle vs. a white square). A clear deficit occurred when the match was presented in the right inferior quadrant (cooled region). Furthermore, the

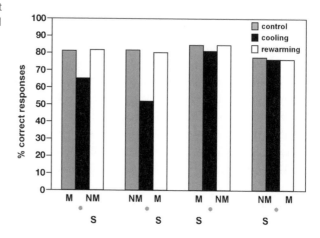

Fig. 5.6 Percentage of correct responses obtained in several sessions of cooling of V4 in an awake monkey. The configuration of the stimuli (randomly presented) is represented below the axis: S: Sample, M: Match, NM: Non Match. The cooling loop inactivates the inferior right quadrant. No effect is seen when the sample is presented in the quadrant contralateral to the cooling loop.

deficit was pronounced when the match was ipsilateral to the appropriate sample. But in every case, errors always consisted in choosing the stimulus on the wrong side.

We should emphasize that reversible cooling reveals deficits that appear to be more severe than a permanent lesion. In a match-to-sample configuration in which the sample was displayed in the fovea and four possible matches in the surround, Schiller (1995) also observed a deficit with stimuli of equal salience but they recovered within about one week of testing. A persisting deficit occurred only for masked stimuli. A tentative explanation for this difference between the outcome of V4 lesions and our reversible inactivation could be found in our results in the anesthetized animals. If we assume that feedback pathways are required for visual perception of low salience stimuli, a lesion of V4 will cut the feedback chain from V4 to V2 to V1 and disrupt it permanently, leading to the deficit observed with low salience stimuli. Without area V4, V2 and V1 may be able to recover visual performance only to high salience stimuli since they do not receive any more feedback. This speculative hypothesis remains to be tested in the awake animal using electrophysiologic recordings.

Conclusions

Reversible inactivation can be helpful to test other important questions that remain open. Our results indicate that feedforward connections have a driving function while feedback connections modulate the responses of neurons in lower order areas in a nonlinear way. Furthermore we found that this modulation is important in improving the responses of neurons in low-order areas to stimuli that are poorly visible. To our knowledge, the role of other feedforward connections between extrastriate areas in the macaque has not yet been tested. The respective role of, for instance, V2 to V3, V2 to MT and V3 to MT connections remain completely unknown. However, this is not a straightforward task due to the geometrical configuration of some of these areas.

The role of feedback connections in a more active visual paradigm remains to be investigated in the awake animal. For instance, it is puzzling that we obtained mainly a negative result with the inactivation of V2 upon center–surround interactions in V1. Feedback connections from V2 to V1 are indeed extremely dense compared to those coming from the lateral geniculate nucleus to V1. We have shown that one possible role of the V2 feedback is the perception of low salience stimuli. However, it is unlikely that such a massive array of connections is devoted only to this function. Therefore, several other possibilities need to be explored when the animal is involved in an active task of discrimination or visual search. For instance, Roelfsema et al. (1998) have shown that in a curve-tracing task, the firing rate of V1 neurons increases simultaneously along the path of the curve that is attentively selected from a distractor curve. Such a modulation of firing rates requires an integration over the large portion of visual space which is covered by the large receptive fields of neurons that send feedback to V1.

Acknowledgments

We wish to thank Frédérique Sarrato for help with the figures.

References

Allman, J., Miezin, F. and McGuinness, E. (1985) Stimulus specific responses from beyond the classical receptive field: neurophysiological mechanisms for local-global comparisons in visual neurons. *Annual Review of Neuroscience*, **8:**407–30.

Angelucci, A., Levitt, J. B., Hupé, J. M. *et al.* (2000) Anatomical circuits for local and global integration of visual information: intrinsic and feedback connections in macaque visual cortical area V1. *European Journal of Neuroscience*, **12:**285.

Barone, P., Batardiere, A., Knoblauch, K. *et al.* (2000) Laminar distribution of neurons in extrastriate areas projecting to visual areas V1 and V4 correlates with the hierarchical rank and indicates the operation of a distance rule. *Journal of Neuroscience*, **20:**3263–81.

Baumann, T. P. and Spear, P. D. (1977) Role of the lateral suprasylvian visual area in behavioral recovery from effects of visual cortex damage in cats. *Brain Research*, **138:**445–68.

Bullier, J., Girard, P. and Salin, P. A. (1994) The role of area 17 in the transfer of information to extrastriate visual cortex. In A. Peters and K. S. Rockland (eds) *Cerebral Cortex, vol. 10, Primary Visual Cortex in Primates*, pp. 301–30. Plenum Press, New York.

Bullier, J., Hupé, J. M., James, A. *et al.* (1996) Functional interactions between areas V1 and V2 in the monkey. *Journal of Physiology (Paris)*, **90:**217–20.

Bullier, J., Hupé, J. M., James, A. C. *et al.* (2001) The role of feedback connections in shaping the responses of visual cortical neurons. *Progress in Brain Research*, **134:**193–204.

Cowey, A. and Stoerig, P. (1997) Visual detection in monkeys with blindsight. *Neuropsychologia*, **35:**929–39.

DeYoe, E. A. and Van Essen, D. C. (1988) Concurrent processing streams in monkey visual cortex. *Trends in Neuroscience*, **11:**219–26.

Eysel, U. T. and Schweigart, G. (1999) Increased receptive field size in the surround of chronic lesions in the adult cat visual cortex. *Cerebral Cortex*, **9:**101–9.

Foster, K. H., Gaska, J. P., Nagler, M. *et al.* (1985) Spatial and temporal frequency selectivity of neurones in visual cortical areas V1 and V2 of the macaque monkey. *Journal of Physiology (London)*, **365:**331–63.

Gähwiler, B. H., Mamoon, A. M., Schlapfer, W. T. *et al.* (1972) Effects of temperature on spontaneous bioelectric activity of cultured nerve cells. *Brain Research*, **40:**527–33.

Gattass, R. and Gross, C. G. (1981) Visual topography of striate projection zone (MT) in posterior superior temporal sulcus of the macaque. *Journal of Neurophysiology*, **46:**621–38.

Gilbert, C. D., Das, A., Ito, M. *et al.* (1996) Spatial integration and cortical dynamics. *Proceedings of the National Academy of Sciences (USA)*, **93:**615–22.

Gilbert, C. D. and Wiesel, T. N. (1992) Receptive field dynamics in adult primary visual cortex. *Nature*, **356:**150–2.

Girard, P. and Bullier, J. (1989) Visual activity in area V2 during reversible inactivation of area 17 in the macaque monkey. *Journal of Neurophysiology*, **62:**1287–302.

Girard, P., Hupé, J. M. and Bullier, J. (2001) Feedforward and feedback connections between areas V1 and V2 of the monkey have similar rapid conduction velocities. *Journal of Neurophysiology*, **85:**1328–31.

Girard, P., Salin, P. A. and Bullier, J. (1991a) Visual activity in areas V3a and V3 during reversible inactivation of area V1 in the macaque monkey. *Journal of Neurophysiology*, **66:**1493–503.

Girard, P., Salin, P. A. and Bullier, J. (1991b) Visual activity in macaque area V4 depends on area 17 input. *Neuroreport*, **2:**81–4.

Girard, P., Salin, P. A. and Bullier, J. (1992) Response selectivity of neurons in area MT of the macaque monkey during reversible inactivation of area V1. *Journal of Neurophysiology,* **67:**1437–46.

Hupé, J. M., Chouvet, G. and Bullier, J. (1999) Spatial and temporal parameters of cortical inactivation by GABA. *Journal of Neuroscience Methods,* **86:**129–43.

Hupé, J. M., James, A. C., Payne, B. R. *et al.* (1998) Cortical feedback improves discrimination between figure and background by V1, V2 and V3 neurons. *Nature,* **394:**784–7.

Hupé, J. M., James, A. C., Girard, P. *et al.* (2001a) Feedback connections act on the early part of the responses in monkey visual cortex. *Journal of Neurophysiology,* **85:**134–45.

Hupé, J. M., James, A. C., Girard, P. *et al.* (2001b) Response modulations by static texture surround in area V1 of the macaque monkey don not depend on feedback connections from V2. *Journal of Neurophysiology,* **85:**146–63.

Kaas, J. H., Krubitzer, L. A., Chino, Y. M. *et al.* (1990) Reorganization of retinotopic cortical maps in adult mammals after lesions of the retina. *Science,* **248:**229–31.

Knierim, J. J. and van Essen, D. C. (1992) Neuronal responses to static texture patterns in area V1 of the alert macaque monkey. *Journal of Neurophysiology,* **67:**961–80.

Lamme, V. A. and Roelfsema, P. R. (2000) The distinct modes of vision offered by feedforward and recurrent processing. *Trends in Neuroscience,* **23:**571–9.

Liu, Y. and Rouiller, E. M. (1999) Mechanisms of recovery of dexterity following unilateral lesion of the sensorimotor cortex in adult monkeys. *Experimental Brain Research,* **128:**149–59.

Lomber, S. G. (1999) The advantages and limitations of permanent or reversible deactivation techniques in the assessment of neural function. *Journal of Neuroscience Methods,* **86:**109–17.

Lomber, S. G., Payne, B. R. and Horel, J. A. (1999) The cryoloop: an adaptable reversible cooling deactivation method for behavioral or electrophysiological assessment of neural function. *Journal of Neuroscience Methods,* **86:**179–94.

Maunsell, J. H. and Gibson, J. R. (1992) Visual response latencies in striate cortex of the macaque monkey. *Journal of Neurophysiology,* **68:**1332–44.

Mendola, J. D. and Payne, B. R. (1993) Direction selectivity and physiological compensation in the superior colliculus following removal of areas 17 and 18. *Visual Neuroscience,* **10:**1019–26.

Merigan, W. H. (2000) Cortical area V4 is critical for certain texture discriminations, but this effect is not dependent on attention. *Visual Neuroscience,* **17:**949–58.

Mize, R. R. and Murphy, E. H. (1976) Alterations in receptive field properties of superior colliculus cells produced by visual cortex ablation in infant and adult cats. *Journal of Comparative Neurology,* **168:**393–424.

Muessel, M. J., Berman, N. E. and Klein, R. M. (2000) Early and specific expression of monocyte chemoattractant protein-1 in the thalamus induced by cortical injury. *Brain Research,* **870:**211–21.

Newsome, W. T. and Pare, E. B. (1988) A selective impairment of motion perception following lesions of the middle temporal visual area (MT). *Journal of Neuroscience,* **8:**2201–11.

Nothdurft, H. C., Gallant, J. L. and Van Essen, D. C. (1999) Response modulation by texture surround in primate area V1: correlates of "popout" under anesthesia. *Visual Neuroscience,* **16:**15–34.

Nowak, L. G. and Bullier, J. (1997) The timing of information transfer in the visual system. In J. H. Kaas, K. L. Rockland and A. Peters (eds) *Cerebral Cortex, vol. 12, Extrastriate Visual Cortex in Primates,* pp. 205–41. Plenum Press, New York.

Pasternak, T. and Merigan, W. H. (1994) Motion perception following lesions of the superior temporal sulcus in the monkey. *Cerebral Cortex,* **4(3):** 247–59.

Payne, B. R. and Lomber, S. G. (1999) A method to assess the functional impact of cerebral connections on target populations of neurons. *Journal of Neuroscience Methods,* **86:**195–208.

Perenin, M. T. (1991) Discrimination of motion direction in perimetrically blind fields. *Neuroreport,* **2:**397–400.

Raiguel, S. E., Lagae, L., Gulyas, B. *et al.* (1989) Response latencies of visual cells in macaque areas V1, V2 and V5. *Brain Research,* **493:**155–9.

Reynolds, J. H., Pasternak, T. and Desimone, R. (2000) Attention increases sensitivity of V4 neurons. *Neuron,* **26:**703–14.

Rocha-Miranda, C. E., Bender, D. B., Gross, C. G. *et al.* (1975) Visual activation of neurons in inferotemporal cortex depends on striate cortex and forebrain commissures. *Journal of Neurophysiology,* **38:**475–91.

Rodman, H. R., Gross, C. G. and Albright, T. D. (1989) Afferent basis of visual response properties in area MT of the macaque. I. Effects of striate cortex removal. *Journal of Neuroscience,* **9:**2033–50.

Roelfsema, P. R., Lamme, V. A. and Spekreijse, H. (1998) Object-based attention in the primary visual cortex of the macaque monkey. *Nature,* **395:**376–81.

Rudolph, K. and Pasternak, T. (1999) Transient and permanent deficits in motion perception after lesions of cortical areas MT and MST in the macaque monkey. *Cerebral Cortex,* **9:**90–100.

Salin, P. A., Girard, P., Kennedy, H. *et al.* (1992) Visuotopic organization of corticocortical connections in the visual system of the cat. *Journal of Comparative Neurology,* **320:**415–34.

Salsbury, K. G. and Horel, J. A. (1984) A cryogenic implant for producing reversible functional brain lesions. *Behavioral Research Methods and Instrumentation,* **15:**433–36.

Sandell, J. H. and Schiller, P. H. (1982) Effect of cooling area 18 on striate cortex cells in the squirrel monkey. *Journal of Neurophysiology,* **48:**38–48.

Schiller, P. H. (1993) The effects of V4 and middle temporal (MT) area lesions on visual performance in the rhesus monkey. *Visual Neuroscience,* **10:**717–46.

Schiller, P. H. (1995) Effect of lesions in visual cortical area V4 on the recognition of transformed objects. *Nature,* **376:**342–4.

Schmolesky, M. T., Wang, Y., Hanes, D. P. *et al.* (1998) Signal timing across the macaque visual system. *Journal of Neurophysiology,* **79:**3272–8.

Shipp, S. and Zeki, S. (1985) Segregation of pathways leading from area V2 to areas V4 and V5 of macaque monkey visual cortex. *Nature,* **315:**322–5.

Shipp, S. and Zeki, S. (1989) The organization of connections between areas V5 and V1 in macaque monkey visual cortex. *European Journal of Neuroscience,* **1:**308–31.

Sober, S. J., Stark, J. M., Yamasaki, D. S. *et al.* (1997) Receptive field changes after strokelike cortical ablation: a role for activation dynamics. *Journal of Neurophysiology,* **78:**3438–43.

Ungerleider, L. G. and Desimone, R. (1986) Cortical connections of visual area MT in the macaque. *Journal of Comparative Neurology,* **248:**190–222.

Van Essen, D. C. and Maunsell, J. H. R. (1983) Hierarchical organization and functional streams in the visual cortex. *Trends in Neuroscience,* **6:**370–5.

Volgushev, M., Vidyasagar, T. R., Chistiakova, M. *et al.* (2000) Synaptic transmission in the neocortex during reversible cooling. *Neuroscience,* **98:**9–22.

Wang, C., Waleszczyk, W. J., Burke, W. *et al.* (2000) Modulatory influence of feedback projections from area 21a on neuronal activities in striate cortex of the cat. *Cerebral Cortex,* **10:**1217–32.

Weiskrantz, L. (1996) Blindsight revisited. *Current Opinion in Neurobiology,* **6:**215–20.

Wickelgren, B. G. and Sterling, P. (1969) Influence of visual cortex on receptive fields in the superior colliculus of the cat. *Journal of Neurophysiology,* **32:**16–23.

Worgotter, F., Suder, K., Zhao, Y. *et al.* (1998) State-dependent receptive-field restructuring in the visual cortex. *Nature,* **396:**165–8.

Xiao, D. K., Raiguel, S., Marcar, V. *et al.* (1997) The spatial distribution of the antagonistic surround of MT/V5 neurons. *Cerebral Cortex,* **7:**662–77.

Yamasaki, D. S. and Wurtz, R. H. (1991) Recovery of function after lesions in the superior temporal sulcus in the monkey. *Journal of Neurophysiology,* **66:**651–73.

Chapter 6

Examining the Basis of Neural Plasticity Using Chronic Pharmacologic Applications

Ralf A. W. Galuske, Dae-Shik Kim,
Kerstin E. Schmidt

Imaging the global patterns of neural activation

The most common method to assess neural activity in the brain is to extracellularly record the discharges of neurons during sensory stimulation. Generally, this approach permits the measurement of responses from a single neuron per electrode. This technique is the method of choice for the basic exploration of neuronal properties. However, for many sensory cortical areas it is well established that neurons with particular functional properties are not randomly distributed over the entire area, but are clustered together into small groups with similar functional properties forming ordered two-dimensional representations or maps of different stimulus features (e.g. Hubel and Wiesel 1962; Hubel *et al.* 1978; Bonhoeffer and Grinvald 1991). Moreover, representations of different stimulus attributes are superimposed within the same population of neurons. For example, in primary visual cortex the same popu-lation of neurons represents the visual field, ocular dominance, and preferences for orientation, direction of movement, spatial frequency and even spatial disparity (e.g. Tootell *et al.* 1988; Obermayer and Blasdel 1993; Shmuel and Grinvald 1996; Weliky *et al.* 1996; Hübener *et al.* 1997; Ohzawa *et al.* 1997; Löwel *et al.* 1998; Kim *et al.* 1999). To visualize these representations it is desirable to record the activation patterns of large populations of neurons rather than the responses of individual cells. This can be achieved by monitoring the global pattern of cortical metabolism during stimulation with different stimuli. One technique that allows such an approach is the optical imaging of intrinsic signals (Grinvald *et al.* 1986; Bonhoeffer and Grinvald 1993). In the following paragraphs theoretical and practical principles of this method are briefly described. The information given here provides a broad overview and further details should be extracted from more specialized reviews of the technique (e.g. Bonhoeffer and Grinvald 1996).

Optical imaging of intrinsic signals exploits the fact that active and inactive cortical regions can be separated from each other by monitoring oxygen consumption. When cortical tissue is illuminated with light at a wavelength of 600–620 nm, light absorption differences between active and inactive cortical regions can be detected due to the higher concentration of deoxyhemoglobin in the active and oxygen consuming cortical sites (Fig. 6.1a) (Frostig *et al.* 1990; Vanzetta and Grinvald 1999). An appropriate system to detect these absorption differences consists of a highly sensitive low-noise CCD camera in combination with a macroscope as described by Ratzlaff and Grinvald (1991; Fig. 6.1b, c). Usually, such a system can monitor the metabolic activity over a cortical region of approximately $1 \, cm \times 1 \, cm$, but with different combinations of lenses, other magnifications and resolutions can be achieved. The so-called intrinsic signals are slow in relation to the time course of the actual neuronal activity exhibiting a delay of $0.5–1 \, s$ to the electrical discharges (Fig. 6.1d) (Frostig *et al.* 1990). The magnitude of the intrinsic signal is low compared to the total amount of reflected light from cortex. The activity dependent component in this light is usually in the range of $0.1–2\%$. Therefore, it is difficult to detect the actual spatial patterns of cortical activation in the raw images.

Data collected under a particular stimulation condition must be averaged (usually between 8–16 times) to reduce the signal-to-noise ratio and have to be further processed to extract the activity dependent component of the total reflection. This is achieved by normalizing the images to a so-called "blank" image. Two different approaches can be applied here. First, as the "blank" condition we assign an image taken from the cortex in the absence of sensory stimulation. This is the most intuitive way of normalizing the images. It eliminates the global signal-independent part of the reflection and ameliorates inhomogeneities in the images caused by large epicortical blood vessels and uneven illumination. The "blank" images are averaged over several trials to reduce their noise level. Ideally, there should be the same number of blank conditions as there are different stimulation conditions within a trial. A second way of normalizing the images is the so-called "cocktail blank" method. This "blank" is not an image taken without sensory stimulation, but the average of the images taken under all different stimulation conditions. This normalization is based on the consideration that global circulation parameters in the completely inactive cortex, in the absence of sensory stimulation, differ from when the cortex is activated partially. An example of this is that during stimulation with an oriented stimulus that activates the respective system of orientation columns but leaves columns representing other orientations inactive. Therefore, the signal range in this case is defined by the reflection differences between active and inactive cortical regions and not, as for the former normalization, between globally inactive and active states.

In theory, this method should be better suited to separate the activity dependent components of the signal from global changes caused by the increases in blood perfusion due to sensory stimulation. However, the "cocktail blank" method also relies on the assumption that with the respective set of different stimuli applied, the recorded cortical region is more or less homogeneously activated. This requirement can be tested by comparing the "cocktail blank" to the "blank" images obtained in the absence of sensory stimulation (see Issa *et al.* 2000 for a comparison of both methods).

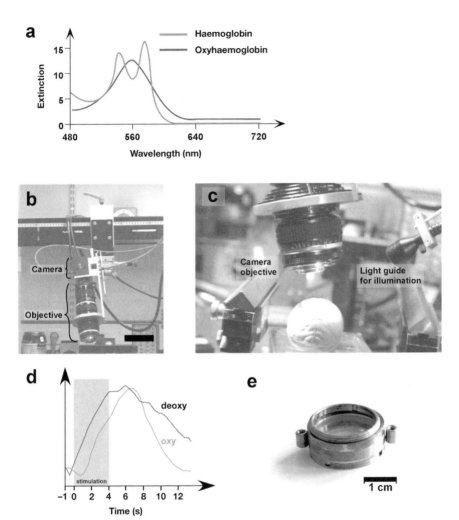

Fig. 6.1 (A) Light absorption spectra of hemoglobin and deoxyhemoglobin (modified from Frostig *et al*. 1990). (B) Photograph of the setup used for the detection of intrinsic signals. Note that the camera and the objective are mounted on a slider to facilitate positioning in almost any position and angle above the preparation. It is important to have a strong support for the camera in any position to obtain stable recordings. The scale bar indicates 10 cm. (C) Higher magnification to illustrate the relation between the objective, the light guides and the surface of the brain. With the objectives used the focal distance is about 5 cm. (D) Temporal relation of the intrinsic signals (note in particular the curve for deoxyhemoglobin) to the actual neuronal activation (black trace below the x-axis). Note the temporal delay between the two signals (modified from Bonhoeffer and Grinvald 1996). (E) Titanium chamber for optical imaging. For recording, this chamber is mounted onto the skull. It is filled with mineral oil through the two filling holes on the sides and closed with a glass plate.

Further improvements of the image quality can be achieved by digital filtering of the images. Usually, low pass filtering (Gaussian or Lee filters) helps to reduce the high-frequency noise. Additionally, images can be high pass filtered to remove gradients caused by uneven illumination and large artifacts. However, care has to be taken not to interfere with the properties of the actual signal. Precautions regarding high pass filtering will be discussed below. Having once calculated the activity maps related to the different stimulation conditions, the so-called "single condition maps," further evaluation of the data can be performed by extracting different parameters from these individual maps. Details on this issue are also provided in the subsequent paragraphs.

Imaging the consequences of local manipulations

Reversible deactivation techniques consist of a broad variety of different approaches to interfere with the performance of neurons and neuronal populations in acute or chronic ways. The principle idea behind these deactivations is to reversibly "switch off" groups of neurons in order to investigate how the nervous system behaves without these components. In this chapter we will describe and discuss how far activation and deactivation techniques can be used to study long-term reorganization processes and identify factors that are involved in these processes. We will describe which actions have to be taken in order to detect the consequences of these manipulations with optical imaging techniques.

The experiments presented here were designed to study the influence of neurotrophins on developmental plasticity. This was done by optical imaging and extracellular single unit electrophysiology following chronic minipump infusion of different neurotrophins and manipulation of the visual experience of the animals. This is a different perspective on how to use reversible deactivation and activation techniques. Here, the principle design is not to monitor the acute consequences of the manipulation, but to study the long-term effects of it. Furthermore, we will discuss the problems one faces when interfering chronically with the neural environment and examining the specific consequences of these manipulations in the same substrate. Furthermore, we will try to point out how the application of both optical and electrophysiologic recording techniques can complement each other in order to permit a clear interpretation of the obtained results.

Background of the experiment

One of the best studied examples of experience-dependent plasticity is the process of segregation of thalamic afferents into ocular dominance (OD) columns which is susceptible to visual experience during a critical period of postnatal development (Stryker 1991). If one eye is deprived of vision or inactivated completely during this period, its afferents lose their ability to drive cortical neurons (Wiesel and Hubel 1963; Hubel and Wiesel 1970) and synaptic terminals and terminal arbors are lost (Shatz and Stryker 1978; Antonini and Stryker 1994). These use-dependent changes follow a Hebbian modification rule (Rauschecker and Singer 1981; Fregnac et al. 1988; Stryker 1991) and are gated by neuromodulators such as norepinephrine (Kasamatsu and Pettigrew 1976), acetylcholine (Bear and Singer 1986; Gu and Singer 1993) and serotonin (Gu and Singer 1995).

The exact mechanisms through which neuronal activity is translated into the observed structural changes are still unknown. One possibility is that different sets of axons compete for factors whose availability depends on a specific pattern of neuronal activity (Barde 1989; Domenici *et al.* 1991; Thoenen 1995). Two members of the neuro-trophin family, brain derived neurotrophic factor (BDNF) (Leibrock *et al.* 1989) and nerve growth factor (NGF) (Levi-Montalcini 1987), might play an important role in this process (Castrén *et al.* 1992, Schoups *et al.* 1995; Rossi *et al.* 1999; Lein and Shatz 2000; Pollock *et al.* 2001; for review see McAllister *et al.* 1999).

Realization of the experiment

In order to investigate the role of different neurotrophins in the experience-dependent synaptic rearrangement of the developing visual cortex, we continuously infused BDNF or NGF into the primary visual cortex of 4–6 week old kittens during monocular deprivation. At the end of the infusion period and after reopening of the deprived eye the effects of this long term manipulation were examined by means of optical imaging of intrinsic signals and extracellular unit recording techniques. To ensure a constant supply of neurotrophins we used osmotic minipumps (Fig. 6.2b). These pumps were implanted beneath the skin of the neck. The functional principle of these pumps is that after the implantation their outer walls will start to swell due to the uptake of extracellular fluids.

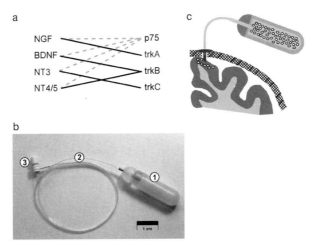

Fig. 6.2 (A) Schematic drawing of the affinities of the different members of the neurotrophin family to the respective receptors. Dashed lines indicate affinities to the low-affinity p75 receptor. (B) Schematic drawing of the minipump infusion. The pump is connected to a needle which is inserted into the cortex and fixed on the skull of the animal. (C) Photograph of the minipump (1) and the infusion tools, flexible sterile tubing (2) and the needle (3) that is finally inserted into the brain and fixed on the skull of the animal.

This swelling of the outer walls continuously decreases the inner lumen of the pump and results in a constant release of the substance inside over a period of several days (Fig. 6.2b). In each animal, two osmotic minipumps (Alzet, model 2001, pump rate 1 ml/h), were implanted and connected with flexible tubing to stainless steel cannulae (Brain Infusion Kit, Alzet; Fig. 6.2c). The minipumps contained either BDNF (Regeneron Pharmaceuticals, Tarrytown, NY, concentration: 1 mg/ml), NGF (2.5 S from mouse submandibular gland, Promega, Madison, WI, concentration: 1 mg/ml) or cytochrome-C at the same concentration in phosphate buffered saline (PBS) with 0.1% bovine serum albumin as control. The tips of the cannulae were inserted 1–2 mm deep into area 18 and secured to the skull with dental cement (Fig. 6.2b). In the same surgical session most of the animals were monocularly deprived by eyelid suture. In the following 6 to 7 days neurotrophins were infused into the cortex at a rate of 12 mg/day.

After infusion, the animals were reanesthetized and prepared for optical (Bonhoeffer and Grinvald 1996) and single cell (Gu and Singer 1993) recording. For optical recording area 18 was exposed between Horsley-Clarke P2 and A8. A recording chamber (Fig. 6.1e) was cemented onto the skull, the dura removed, the chamber filled with silicone oil and closed with a glass plate. During recording, anesthesia was maintained by artificial ventilation with halothane (0.5–1.0%) and N_2O/O_2 (70:30%). Usually, optical and electrophysiologic recordings were initiated 5 hours after removal of the minipumps. Moving, high-contrast (black=0.2 cd/m^2; white=8 cd/m^2), square-wave gratings of four different orientations (0°, 45°, 90°, 135°) with a spatial frequency of 0.15 cycles/degree and a drift velocity of 15 degree/sec were presented monocularly for 3 s on a 19 inch computer screen (screen distance 30 cm). In each stimulation period, five camera frames were taken at a length of 600 ms each.

For analysis of optical data, averaged images of individual stimulation conditions were normalized to the cocktail blank. Subsequently, images were slightly low pass filtered (Gaussian filter, kernel size 3 pixel). The use of high-pass filters was strictly avoided in order to preserve reflectance gradients caused by local changes in cortical activity due to the neurotrophin infusion. In order to quantify OD-distributions the relative signal content for each eye was calculated pixelwise and the resulting data were sorted with respect to their distance from the infusion site. These relative activity distributions were then averaged across experiments performed under the same paradigm to obtain grand averages. For quantification of the optically recorded orientation responses preferred orientations were calculated by pixelwise vectorial addition of the responses to differently oriented gratings and the selectivity of the responses was characterized by the normalized length of the resulting vector (vector strength; Batschelet 1981). Local effects of the neurotrophin infusion were determined by plotting the vector strength as a function of distance from the infusion site. Additionally, orientation preference and degree of selectivity were visualized by computing polar maps in which the color of each pixel represents the respective angle of preferred orientation and the brightness of each pixel the magnitude of the vector strength.

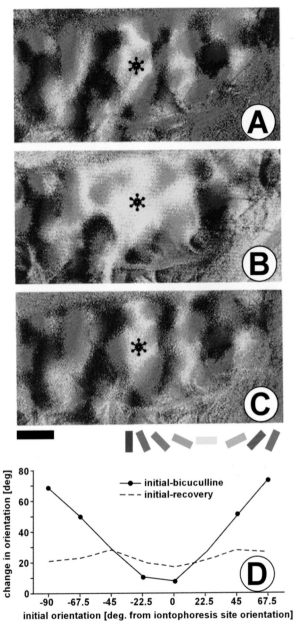

Plate 1 Orientation angle maps in cat V2 and the effect of disinhibition with focal iontophoresis of bicuculline. For full caption, see p. 44-45.

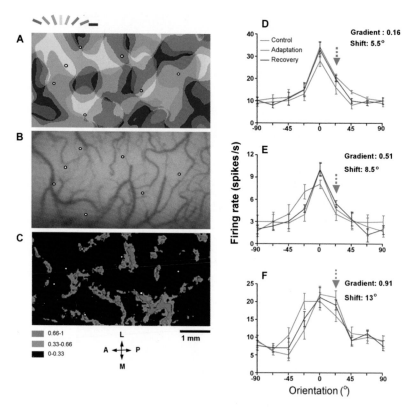

Plate 2 Adaptation-induced plasticity of orientation tuning and the orientaton architecture of V1. For full caption, see p. 48.

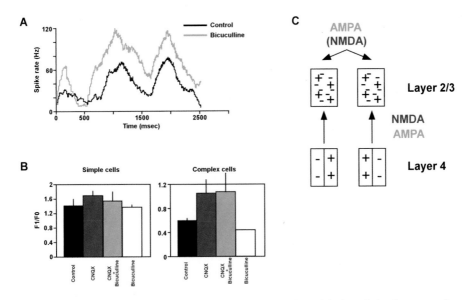

Plate 3 Blockade of inhibition does not affect the temporal modulation of simple or complex cell responses. For full caption, see p. 55.

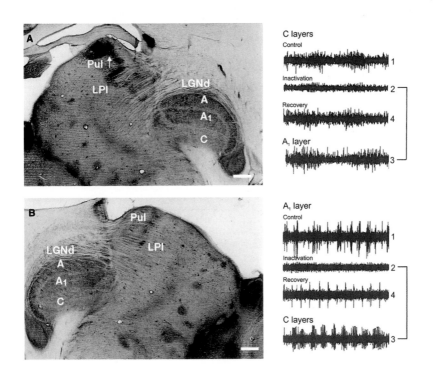

Plate 4 Deactivation can be restricted to specific layers in the lateral geniculate nucleus. For full caption, see p. 69.

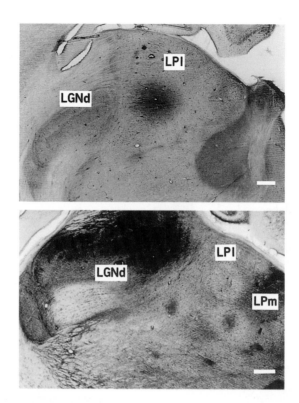

Plate 5 Injection of the deactivating drug can be made to shut down large regions in the LP—pulvinar complex. For full caption, see p. 70.

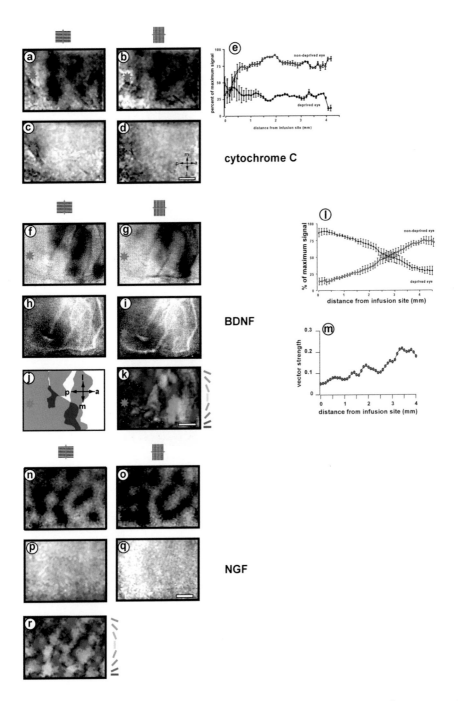

cytochrome C

BDNF

NGF

Plate 6 The effect of monocular deprivation for one week on orientation preference maps in kitten visual cortex after infusion of cytochrome-C at a rate of 12mg/day. For full caption, see p. 148—149.

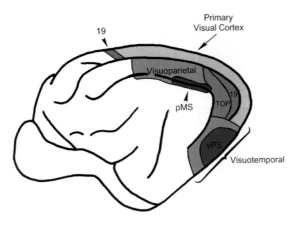

Plate 7 Lateral view of the cat left cerebral hemisphere to show positions of major visual regions. For full caption, see p. 165.

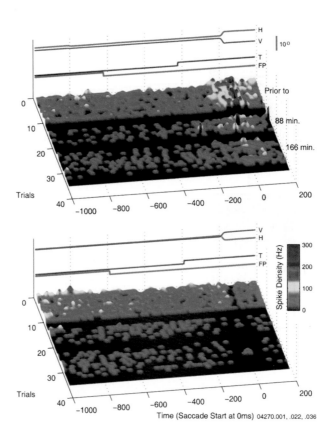

Plate 8 Activity of superior colliculus burst neuron prior to and after inactivation of its frontal eye field input. For full caption, see p. 230.

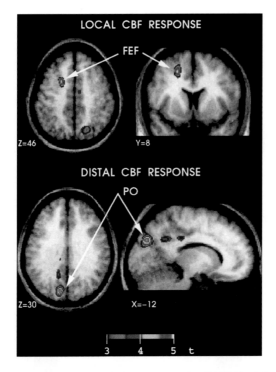

Plate 19 Changes in regional cerebral blood flow as a result of TMS. For full caption, see p. 275.

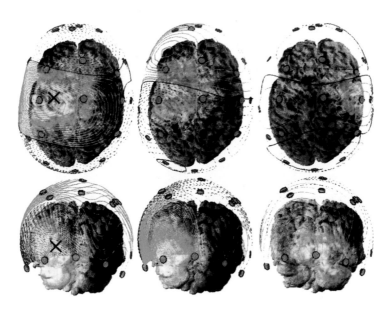

Plate 20 Duration of changes in neural activity induced by TMS. For full caption, see p. 276.

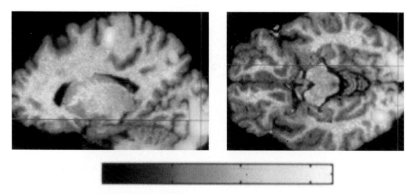

Plate 21 Activation of occipital, striate cortex (in addition to somatosensory cortex) during Braille reading in congenitally or early blind subjects during PET.

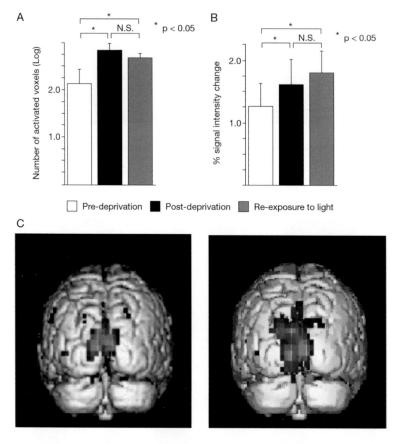

Plate 22 (A) Number of activated voxels (log), and (B) mean MR signal intensity change of activated voxels in the occipital cortex to photic stimulation before, 60 minutes after the onset of visual deprivation, and 30 minutes following reexposure to light. Panel (C) is an example of visual cortex activation in one subject. For full caption, see p. 318.

Effects of chronic BDNF and NGF infusion on ocular dominance plasticity revealed by optical imaging

In kittens, cytochrome-C infusion had no effect on the outcome of MD. After MD and infusion periods of 6–7 days stimulation of the nondeprived eye activated iso-orientation domains over the whole recorded area and even in the close vicinity of the infusion site (Fig. 6.3a, b, and e), excluding major disturbances of cortical excitability by the mechanical and osmotic consequences of the infusion. The deprived eye, as expected from previous studies (Wiesel and Hubel 1965; Kim and Bonhoeffer 1994; Crair et al. 1997), failed to activate the cortex over the whole recorded area (Fig. 6.3c, d, e).

BDNF infusion during monocular deprivation (MD) reversed the normally occurring ocular dominance (OD) shift towards the nondeprived eye so that the deprived eye dominated the BDNF treated cortex after MD (Galuske et al. 1996; Fig. 6.3h, i, and l). This effect extended up to 2.5 to 3.5 mm from the infusion site. In the core of this zone maps could be evoked only through the deprived, but not through the nondeprived, eye. In this region, stimuli of different orientation presented to the deprived eye activated the cortex homogeneously (Fig. 6.3j, k). Also, quantitatively orientation selectivity, as measured by the vector strength, was very low in this region (Fig. 6.3m), indicating that neurons had either lost their orientation selectivity or that neurons with similar preferences were no longer clustered together. Within an adjacent transition zone, the cortex could be activated through both eyes. However, iso-orientation domains could be visualized only by stimulation of the nondeprived eye (Fig. 6.3f, g, and j). Stimulation of the deprived eye led again to homogeneous activation irrespective of the stimulus orientation. This suggests that responses to the nondeprived eye were orientation selective, while those to the deprived eye were not. Beyond 4 mm from the infusion site, the pattern of activation resembled that characteristic for MD; the deprived eye failed to activate the cortex and the normal eye evoked the typical pattern of orientation selective responses (Fig. 6.3f–i).

In kittens that underwent MD and were treated with NGF, the normal effect of MD was encountered (Fig. 6.3n–r). The iso-orientation maps obtained in these animals closely resembled those obtained from hemispheres infused with cytochrome-C (Fig. 6.3a–e). Stimulation of the nondeprived eye produced normal orientation maps that appeared undisturbed even in close vicinity of the infusion site, while stimulation of the deprived eye failed to evoke measurable levels of activity. The polar maps also appeared to be normal (Fig. 6.3r), indicating that the orientation tuning of responses was unaffected by the NGF infusion. The diffusion of the neurotrophin was controlled by subsequent immunohistochemistry with antibodies against NGF. This analysis revealed that NGF had effectively diffused into the cerebral cortex over distances of about 3 mm (Galuske et al. 2000). Thus, immunohistochemically detectable quantities of NGF were present in the area in which the effects of monocular deprivation were assessed and found to be normal.

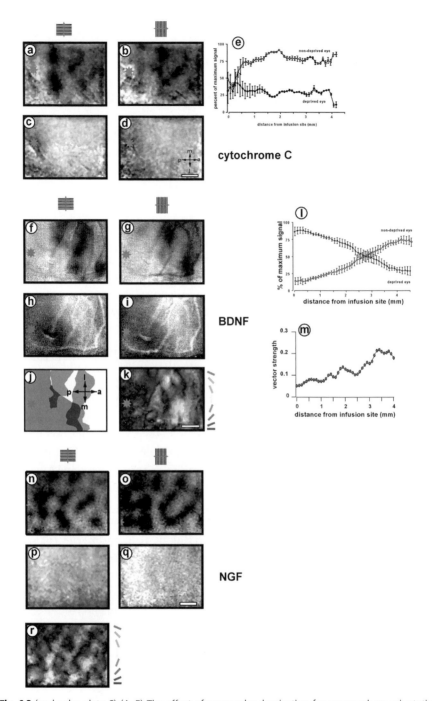

Fig. 6.3 (and color plate 6) (A–E) The effect of monocular deprivation for one week on orientation preference maps in kitten visual cortex after infusion of cytochrome-C at a rate of 12 mg/day. (A–D) Activity patterns evoked from the nondeprived (A, B) and the deprived (C, D) eye with

Technical considerations and electrophysiological validation

The present results indicate that administration of exogenous BDNF has strong effects on the activity dependent reorganization of synaptic connections in the developing visual cortex. These findings are primarily based on optical imaging results. Before going into interpretations of these data it is, therefore, important to ensure that the results seen with optical imaging are clearly based on changes in the neuronal behavior. The issue is particularly important in this case, as long term treatment of cortical tissue with trophic substances may lead to alterations in the cerebral

---

Fig. 6.3 (continued)
horizontal (A, C) and vertical (B, D) gratings, respectively. The dark patches indicate activated regions. Note the absence of activity in (C) and (D) as compared to (A) and (B) (asterisk: infusion site). Scale bar: 1 mm. p=posterior, a=anterior, m=medial, l=lateral. (E) relative strength of cortical activation through either the deprived (filled symbols) or the nondeprived eye (open symbols) as a function of distance from the infusion site (averaged over 5 experiments). The error bars give the standard deviation for each datapoint. (F–M) The effect of monocular deprivation for one week on orientation preference maps in kitten visual cortex after infusion of BDNF at a rate of 12 mg/day. Note that close to the infusion site, stimulation of the normal eye fails to evoke activity (F, G), while stimulation of the deprived eye induces homogeneous activity (H, I). Beyond 3 mm from the infusion site, activation patterns are normal and resemble those in control hemispheres infused with cytochrome-C (A–D). (J) Outlines of cortical territories activated by the deprived eye (red), the nondeprived eye (green) and both eyes (blue) during stimulation with a horizontal grating. Note that in the zone, which is activated by both eyes, the activity of the nondeprived eye (blue) is still confined to iso-orientation domains, while activation of the deprived eye activates the whole area homogeneously. (K) Polar map from the experiment shown above. The angle of the resulting vector is color coded according to the scheme shown on the right edge of the figure, blue represents preference for horizontal orientations, yellow for vertical orientations. Additionally, the orientation tuning is indicated by the brightness of the respective pixel, bright colors indicate a narrow and dark colors a broad tuning. Note that in the area close to the infusion site the normal structure of the map disappeared and most pixels exhibit only a weak or no orientation tuning. (l) Relative strength of cortical activation through the deprived (black filled symbols) or the nondeprived (black open symbols) as a function of distance from the infusion site (averaged over 7 experiments). The error bars give the standard deviation for each data-point. (M) Plot of the vector strength of the orientation tuning as a function of the distance from the BDNF-infusion site. Note the weak orientation tuning close to the BDNF infusion site and the gradual increase with increasing distance. (N–R) The effect of monocular deprivation on orientation preference maps in the kitten visual cortex after infusion of NGF at a rate of 12 mg/day. (N–Q) Activity patterns evoked by the nondeprived (N, O) and the deprived (P, Q) eye with horizontal (N, P) and vertical (O, Q) gratings, respectively. Note the normal layout of iso-orientation domains in (N) and (O) and the absence of activity in (P) and (Q). (R) Polar map from the experiment shown above. Note the normal topology of the polar map even less than 1 mm from the in fusion site, indicating normally structured iso-orientation domains for responses to visual stimulation even close to the infusion site.

microcirculation, which as a consequence might disturb the physiologic basis for the intrinsic signal. Therefore, companion single unit data are required to validate the optical recording results. To this end, we performed extracellular recordings after the optical imaging had been performed. Recording sites were selected according to the optically recorded results.

Electrophysiologic recordings

For the electrophysiologic investigation of cell responses, receptive fields were mapped using a hand-held stimulator. OD (ocular dominance) was quantified in five classes, as described previously (Gu and Singer 1993; Galuske *et al.* 1996). For quantification of orientation tuning, cells were assigned to group 0 if they showed no orientation tuning, cells with wide (>45°) and narrow (<45°) tuning were assigned to groups 1 and 2, respectively. For compilation of orientation tuning histograms we considered only the tuning of responses evoked from the dominant eye. In order to obtain an estimate for the changes in response amplitude and spontaneous activity, these variables were assigned integer numbers, ranging from 1 to 4 and 0 to 3, respectively, as described previously (Gu and Singer 1993; Galuske *et al.* 1996). A response vigor of "1" was assigned to units with very weak light responses, "4" to particularly vigorous responses; lack of spontaneous activity was rated "0" and high activity "3." In binocular neurons, only the responses to the dominant eye were considered for the assessment of response vigor.

The single unit data from the control experiment revealed a close correspondence between optically and electrophysiologically obtained activity patterns. Close to the infusion site (sites 2,3,4 in Fig. 6.4 a, b) most cells were driven by the deprived eye (Fig. 6.4c) as indicated by the optical maps. In the transition zone (site 6 in Fig. 6.4a, b) most of the units were binocular (Fig. 6.4c). Remote from the infusion site (sites 1 and 5 in Fig. 6.4a, b), the units were once again monocular, but driven by the nondeprived eye (Fig. 6.4 c). The single unit data also indicate a close correlation between the paradoxical OD-shift and the loss of orientation selectivity. Orientation tuning of units in the zone close to the infusion site (Fig. 6.4d, left) differed significantly from that of units recorded in the transition zone (Fig. 6.4d, middle) and beyond (Fig. 6.4d, right; $p < 0.0001$, Mann-Whitney U-test). No significant differences could be detected between the orientation tuning of units recorded in the transition zone (Fig. 6.4d, middle) and in the unaffected cortex (Fig. 6.4d, right) (Mann-Whitney U-test, $p = 0.5$). The strongest loss of orientation selectivity was encountered in units exclusively driven by the deprived eye, while those which could still be activated through the nondeprived eye exhibited some degree of orientation preference (ANOVA for orientation selectivity versus OD, $p < 0.001$; Fig. 6.4f). Therefore, we can be certain that the optically observed effects were really based on changes in the neuronal response properties.

In addition, another important question could be resolved by these recordings. When recording a signal based on a large population of neurons, as is the case with optical imaging, a lack of stimulus selectivity may be based on two factors: lack of a topographic organization in the representation of the respective stimulus feature and/or lack of

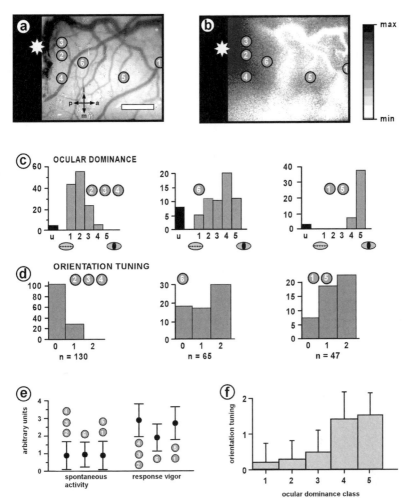

Fig. 6.4 Activity map and single unit responses recorded after 6 days of BDNF infusion (pump rate 12 mg/day) and MD in a kitten that had the pumps in place (modified from Galuske *et al.* 2000). (A) Video image of the examined cortical area. The asterisk and the numbers indicate the position of the infusion cannula and the different recording sites, respectively (scale bar: 1 mm). Note that the infusion site could not be exposed in this case. (B) Activity map computed from the sum of responses to stimulation of the deprived eye with four different orientations. Levels of activity are coded as brightness (dark: high, bright: low). (C) OD distributions and (D) orientation tuning of units recorded at the different sites indicated by numbers in (A) and (B). Note the close correspondence between the OD distributions of neurons and the activity map. (E) Plot of the different response properties of the units recorded at the different recording sites giving the mean value and standard deviation for each parameter in the different recording zones. (F) Diagram of the quality of orientation tuning in relation to the OD-class of units recorded at different distances from the infusion site in this experiment. Note that there is a gradual decrease in the quality of the orientation tuning with the shift of ocularity towards the deprived eye.

selectivity for this stimulus feature on the level of the individual neuron. Our recordings make it very likely that the former possibility can be excluded as a reason for the loss of orientation selectivity in the maps. It is much more likely that the lack of oriented population responses was based on the loss of this property in the individual neurons.

In summary, these results show that optical imaging is an excellent tool to visualize the spatial and qualitative aspects of a local manipulation in the cerebral cortex. Single cell recording alone would not have been sufficient to reveal the global rearrangement, since it provides very limited global information. The extent of the paradoxical OD-shift becomes easily available from the optical data. However, as the basis for this method is the coupling of neuronal and metabolic activity and the resolution of the method is on the population level, a sample of electrical recordings is often needed to validate and better interpret the obtained data. It is also important to emphasize that the processing of optically imaged data can easily lead to wrong conclusions. A good example in this context is the application of high-pass filtering which may have completely obscured the results of the presented study. Therefore, it is very helpful to perform a cursory electrophysiologic analysis of the observed changes, as this might give a second view of the results and help to clarify the issue.

Another point, which must be stressed in the context of validity of the data in general, is the specificity of the observed effects for the infused substance. It is conceivable that the actions observed may be based on either the consequence of infusing large amounts of protein into the cortex or on an unspecific action of molecules from the neurotrophin family. We can discard both of these considerations, because the observed effect could only be achieved with BDNF, but not with cytochrome-C or NGF. The lack of effect of the latter substance is an important finding, as NGF and BDNF are structurally quite similar.

Interpretation of the data

Mechanisms of BDNF-action

BDNF infusion into the kitten visual cortex during periods of MD had three major effects:

1. It prevented the suppression of the deprived afferents;
2. It promoted a paradoxical suppression of the nondeprived afferents;
3. It caused a loss of orientation selectivity.

The paradoxical OD-shift and the complete loss of orientation selectivity occurred only at high concentrations of BDNF reached in the vicinity of the infusion cannula, while the stabilizing effect on the deprived afferents was observed over larger distances. The finding that exogenous addition of BDNF prevented the disconnection of the deprived afferents (Galuske *et al.* 1996, 2000; Gillespie *et al.* 2000) is well compatible with the hypothesis that the effects of MD are based on the competition of the two sets of afferents for a trophic substance whose availability and effect depends on neuronal activity (Domenici *et al.* 1991; Cabelli *et al.* 1995; Hata *et al.* 2000).

Sensory activity regulates the expression of BDNF (Castrèn *et al.* 1992; Rossi *et al.* 1999; Lein and Shatz 2000) and promotes the insertion of trk-B receptors into neuronal membranes (Meyer-Franke *et al.* 1998), which could be a mechanism to enhance the competitive advantage of active afferents in the cortex. However, saturation of a competitive mechanism cannot account for the suppression of the nondeprived afferents at high BDNF concentrations. This effect is also in contrast to anatomical findings indicating an unselective sprouting of both deprived and nondeprived thalamic afferents when BDNF is infused into the cortex (Hata *et al.* 2000). These discrepancies between anatomic and physiologic findings either indicate a dissociation between axonal outgrowth and synaptic efficiency at the level of thalamic afferents or imply further effects of BDNF at the level of intracortical circuits. Evidence indicates that short periods of MD also strongly affect intracortical circuits that relay activity from layer IV to nongranular layers (Kossut and Singer 1991).

The present data do not permit us to identify the mechanisms underlying the BDNF-induced loss of responses to the nondeprived eye, but analogous findings from previous experiments with drug infusion narrow the range of possibilities. The same paradoxical shift of OD towards the deprived eye has been observed with infusion of the $GABA_A$-receptor agonist muscimol and the NMDA-receptor antagonist APV (Reiter and Stryker 1988; Bear *et al.* 1990). Both manipulations bias the equilibrium between excitatory and inhibitory interactions towards inhibition. OD changes can be accounted for by a biphasic synaptic modification rule (Bienenstock *et al.* 1982; Rittenhouse *et al.* 1999). If the product of presynaptic and postsynaptic activity exceeds a first threshold T1 but remains below a second threshold (T2), the respective synapses weaken, but if the product exceeds T2 the synapses strengthen. Augmentation of cortical inhibition by BDNF in a certain range, therefore, could alter these thresholds and induce a paradoxical shift of OD. Recent data indicate that exposure of dissociated cortical tissue cultures to BDNF does strengthen inhibition by reduction of quantal size at excitatory synapses on pyramidal cells and enhancement of quantal size at excitatory synapses on inhibitory interneurons (Rutherford *et al.* 1998), and overexpression of BDNF enhances the maturation of inhibition *in vivo* (Huang *et al.* 1999).

Another line of argument addresses a problem which has to be faced in all experiments that chronically interfere with the neural environment. High concentrations of BDNF cause a downregulation of trk-B receptors (Carter *et al.* 1995; Knüsel *et al.* 1997) that, as a consequence, can block the BDNF-related signal transduction. In this scenario the paradoxical OD-shift could be explained through the inability of the respective afferents to receive the actual signal that is required for them to stabilize at their current position. With some consideration, this could also be the reason for the paradoxical OD-shift observed with muscimol treatment (Reiter and Stryker 1988) because the inactivated postsynaptic sites would be unable to transmit a respective (activity dependent) neurotrophin signal to the active presynaptic sites. However, this is speculative, as the missing link in this cascade is currently the evidence for the hypothesis that active afferents would need higher neurotrophin levels to stabilize than inactive afferents. Still, an impairment of the receptor function after long term treatment needs to be considered, especially as another study using trk-B antibody infusion (Cabelli *et al.* 1997) described similar effects of antibodies blocking these receptors on the development of OD-columns as they have been described earlier after treatment with exogenous BNDF (Cabelli *et al.* 1995).

The finding that BDNF abolished orientation selectivity is consistent with the interpretation that this neurotrophin interferes with activity dependent circuit selection. The development and maintenance of orientation selectivity is influenced by activity (Freeman *et al.* 1981; Singer *et al.* 1981; Fregnac and Imbert 1984; Chapman and Stryker 1993; Weliky and Katz 1997; Crair *et al.* 1998) and appears to depend on competition in very much the same way as OD-changes (Rauschecker and Singer 1981; Singer *et al.* 1981). Therefore, the loss of orientation selectivity could be the result of the undirected outgrowth of thalamocortical afferents (Hata *et al.* 2000) as the selective convergence of thalamic afferents on simple cells is thought to determine the orientation selectivity of these neurons (Chapman *et al.* 1991; Reid and Alonso 1995; Ferster *et al.* 1996).

Mechanisms of NGF action

NGF has been demonstrated to play an important role in the experience dependent maturation of visual cortical function (Maffei *et al.* 1992). NGF has also been reported to counteract the effects of MD during development (Carmignoto *et al.* 1993). These studies are in conflict with our results, which find that NGF infusion failed to rescue deprived afferents. However, our data (Galuske *et al.* 1996, 2000) are supported by similar data from another laboratory (Gillespie *et al.* 2000) and are consistent with the observations that NGF has no effect on the segregation of OD columns (Cabelli *et al.* 1995) and on the shrinkage of thalamic relay cells after MD (Riddle *et al.* 1995). This discrepancy may partially be accounted for by species differences. However, the mode of neurotrophin administration in the different studies must also be considered: Maffei *et al.* (1992) and Carmignoto *et al.* (1993) injected the neurotrophin into the ventricles, while in the other studies NGF was applied intracortically. This suggests that intraventricularly applied NGF might have acted on structures other than the thalamic afferents or their cortical target cells and, thus, might have affected OD-plasticity only indirectly. Two lines of evidence support this possibility. First, trkA, the high affinity receptor for NGF, could not be detected in the LGN and the visual cortex (Holtzman *et al.* 1992; Allendoerfer *et al.* 1994; but see Sala *et al.* 1998). Second, cholinergic neurons in the basal forebrain, which have been shown to play a crucial role in gating developmental plasticity (Bear and Singer 1986; Gu and Singer 1993), express trkA at a high level (Holtzman *et al.* 1992) and react to external and especially intraventricular administration of NGF with an increased expression of cholinacetyltransferase (ChAT).

The interpretation that NGF acts indirectly via modulation of cholinergic pathways could account for the unexpected finding that intracortical NGF infusion failed to affect OD distributions in kittens but did so in adults (Gu *et al.* 1994; Galuske *et al.* 2000). Intracortical application is likely to affect only cholinergic terminals and not the parent cells in the basal forebrain, and there is evidence that these terminals are more susceptible to NGF in the adult than during development (Li *et al.* 1995). During development, trkA receptors redistribute from the soma of cholinergic cells to their distal processes (Li *et al.* 1995), which could enable these neurons to respond to NGF even when applied to target tissue. Evidence that a surplus of ACh can facilitate use-dependent synaptic plasticity in the adult visual cortex is available (Greuel *et al.* 1988).

Concluding remarks

In summary, the complex dose dependent effects of BDNF and NGF observed in this study cannot be accounted for by a single mechanism such as saturation of activity dependent competition for growth factors at the level of thalamocortical synapses. This exemplifies that the physiologic action of neurotrophins is based on a very tightly tuned equilibrium of their synthesis, release and site of action. The analysis of previous experiments leads to several implications for the planning of future experiments which interfere chronically with the investigated neural substrate. First, long term receptor activation may have complex effects on the involved neural circuitry and produce side effects which are eventually hard to control and oversee. A particular aspect of this is the dynamic regulation of receptors for the applied substance which may eventually result in a downregulation and functional loss instead of the desired functional enhancement, causing an inactivation rather than a hyperactivation of the receptor system under examination. The opposite is also conceivable, as a long term deprivation of certain components can easily result in hypersensitivity of the respective receptor system. This is an important issue which implies that at least for long term activation or deactivation experiments precautions have to be taken. Appropriate control experiments and a close monitoring of changes, such as variations of the treatment duration are required and, of course, this issue has to be considered in the interpretation of gained data. Second, as we suspected in the case of NGF, one needs to be aware of the complication that an intentionally local interference might involve complex and quite remote interactions. These facts should be kept in mind when planning an experiment which is meant to test the functional role of certain substances and receptor families in long term adaptive processes, in particular in the developing brain.

The combination of optical imaging and single unit electrophysiology has proven to overcome some of the difficulties with this kind of experiments. Optical data revealed the global alterations induced by the local manipulation which might have been missed by single unit recording at selected sites within the affected cortical area. On the other hand, the companion electrophysiologic data helped to decide what kind of local changes were responsible for the disturbed population response.

Outlook

The experiment presented in this chapter used the approach of chronically interfering with the physiologic properties of the developing brain. So far, most of the studies using this paradigm have studied the effects that external infusion of agonists and antagonists to receptor families that were suspected to play a role in the respective developmental process. This is, of course, a very crude manipulation as compared to the spatially and temporally fine tuning of the physiologic activation patterns of these receptors. These complications have to be considered in the interpretation of the results of such experiments. For the future, we seek more subtle tools to perform such experiments. Certainly, comparison of the chronic treatment by manual injection and the use of osmotic minipumps is already a step toward a finer tuning of the interference. But eventually, one would like to get closer to the actual release or receptor sites for the respective molecules and perhaps affect only certain receptors in certain parts, subcompartments or even cell classes. To this end, we can expect challenging new developments from the use of transgenic animals, in which certain genes can be regulated externally e.g. by antibiotics or by temperature. Also the converse is an interesting approach, namely to have an animal with certain deficits and then examine by which kind of substitution functions can be reinstated. These experiments are already in progress as documented by the exciting work of several laboratories (e.g. Hensch *et al.* 1998; Fagiolini and Hensch 2000) and future work along these lines will provide important new insights, especially into questions of neural development and plasticity.

Acknowledgments

We wish to thank Dr. E. Castren for participation in these experiments and Drs. W. Singer and H. Thoenen for their support during the initiation and realization of this study.

References

Allendoerfer, K. L., Cabelli, R. J., Escandon, E. *et al.* (1994) Regulation of neurotrophin receptors during the maturation of the mammalian visual system. *Journal of Neuroscience,* **14:**1795–811.

Antonini, A. and Stryker, M. P. (1994) Rapid remodelling of axonal arbors in the visual cortex. *Science,* **260:**1819–21.

Barde, Y.-A. (1989) Trophic factors and neuronal survival. *Neuron,* **2:**1525–34.

Batschelet, E. (1981) *Circular Statistics in Biology.* Academic Press, London.

Bear, M. F. and Singer, W. (1986) Modulation of cortical plasticity by acetylcholine and noradrenaline. *Nature,* **320:**172–6.

Bear, M. F., Kleinschmidt, A., Gu, Q. *et al.* (1990) Disruption of experience-dependent modifications in the striate cortex by infusion of a NMDA-receptor antagonist. *Journal of Neuroscience,* **10:**909–25.

Bienenstock, E., Cooper, L. N. and Munro, P. W. (1982) Theory for the development of neuron selectivity: orientation specificity and binocular interaction in visual cortex. *Journal of Neuroscience,* **2:**32–48.

Bonhoeffer, T. and Grinvald, A. (1993) Optical imaging of the functional architecture in cat visual cortex: the layout of direction and orientation domains. *Advances in Experimental Medicine and Biology*, **333**:57–69.

Bonhoeffer, T. and Grinvald, A. (1991) Iso-orientation domains in cat visual cortex are arranged in pinwheel-like patterns. *Nature*, **353**:429–31.

Bonhoeffer, T. and Grinvald, A. (1996) Optical imaging based on intrinsic signals. In A. W. Toga and J. C. Mazziotta (eds) *Brain Mapping, The Methods*, pp. 55–97. Academic Press, San Diego.

Cabelli, R. J., Hohn, A. and Shatz, C. J. (1995) Inhibition of ocular dominance column formation by infusion of NT4/5 or BDNF. *Science*, **267**:1162–6.

Cabelli, R. J., Shelton, D. L., Segal, R. A. *et al.* (1997) Blockade of endogenous ligands of trkB inhibits formation of ocular dominance columns. *Neuron*, **19**:63–76.

Carmignoto, G., Canella, R., Candeo, P. *et al.* (1993) Effects of nerve growth factor on neuronal plasticity of the kitten striate cortex. *Journal of Physiology*, **464**:343–60.

Carter, B. D., Zirrgiebel, U. and Barde, Y. A. (1995) Differential regulation of p21ras activation in neurons by nerve growth factor and brain-derived neurotrophic factor. *Journal of Biological Chemistry*, **270**:21751–7.

Castrén, E., Zafra, F., Thoenen, H. *et al.* (1992) Light regulates the expression of brain-derived neurotrophic factor mRNA in rat visual cortex. *Proceedings of the National Academy of Sciences (USA)*, **89**:9444–8.

Chapman, B. and Stryker, M. P. (1993) Development of orientation selectivity in ferret visual cortex and effects of deprivation. *Journal of Neuroscience*, **13**:5251–62.

Chapman, B., Zahs, K. R. and Stryker, M. P. (1991) Relation of cortical cell orientation selectivity to alignment of receptive fields of the geniculocortical afferents that arborize within a single orientation column in the ferret visual cortex. *Journal of Neuroscience*, **11**:1347–58.

Crair, M. C., Gillespie, D. C. and Stryker, M. P. (1998) The role of visual experience in the development of columns in cat visual cortex. *Science*, **279**:566–70.

Crair, M. C., Ruthazer, E. S., Gillespie, D. C. *et al.* (1997) Relationship between the ocular dominance and orientation maps in visual cortex of monocularly deprived cats. *Neuron*, **19**:307–18.

Domenici, L., Berardi, N., Carmignoto, G. *et al.* (1991) Nerve growth factor prevents amblyopic effects of monocular deprivation. *Proceedings of the National Academy of Sciences USA*, **88**:8811–5.

Fagiolini, M. and Hensch, T. K. (2000) Inhibitory threshold for critical-period activation in primary visual cortex. *Nature*, **404**:183–6.

Ferster, D. (1987) Origin of orientation selective EPSPs in simple cells of cat visual cortex. *Journal of Neuroscience*, **7**:1780–91.

Ferster, D., Chung, S. and Wheat, H. (1996) Orientation selectivity of thalamic input to simple cells of cat visual cortex. *Nature*, **380**:249–52.

Freeman, R. D., Mallach, R. and Hartley, S. (1981) Responsivity of normal kitten striate cortex deteriorates after brief binocular deprivation. *Journal of Neurophysiology*, **45**:1074–84.

Fregnac, Y. and Imbert, M. (1984) Development of neuronal selectivity in primary visual cortex of the cat. *Physiological Reviews*, **64**:325–433.

Fregnac, Y., Shulz, D., Thorpe, S. *et al.* (1988) A cellular analogue of visual cortical plasticity. *Nature*, **333**:367–70.

Frostig, R. D., Lieke, E. E., Ts'o, D. Y. *et al.* (1990) Cortical functional architecture and local coupling between neuronal activity and the microcirculation revealed by *in vivo* high-resolution optical imaging of intrinsic signals. *Proceedings of the National Academy of Sciences USA*, **87**:6082–6.

Galuske, R. A. W., Kim, D. S., Castrén, E. *et al.* (1996) Brain-derived neurotrophic factor reverses experience-dependent synaptic modifications in kitten visual cortex. *European Journal of Neuroscience*, **8:**1554–9.

Galuske, R. A., Kim, D. S., Castren, E. *et al.* (2000) Differential effects of neurotrophins on ocular dominance plasticity in developing and adult cat visual cortex. *European Journal of Neuroscience*, **12:**3315–30.

Gillespie, D. C., Crair, M. C. and Stryker, M. P. (2000) Neurotrophin-4/5 alters responses and blocks the effect of monocular deprivation in cat visual cortex during the critical period. *Journal of Neuroscience*, **20:**9174–86.

Greuel, J. M., Luhmann, H. J. and Singer, W. (1988) Pharmacological induction of use-dependent receptive field-modifications in the visual cortex. *Science*, **242:**74–7.

Grinvald, A., Lieke, E., Frostig, R. D. *et al.* (1986) Functional architecture of cortex revealed by optical imaging of intrinsic signals. *Nature*, **324:**361–4.

Gu, Q. and Singer, W. (1995) Involvement of serotonin in developmental plasticity of kitten visual cortex. *European Journal of Neuroscience*, **7:**1146–53.

Gu, Q., Liu, Y. and Cynader, M. S. (1994) Nerve growth factor-induced ocular dominance plasticity in adult cat visual cortex. *Proceedings of the National Academy of Sciences USA*, **91:**8408–12.

Gu, Q. and Singer, W. (1993) Effects of intracortical infusion of anticholinergic drugs on neuronal plasticity in kitten striate cortex. *European Journal of Neuroscience*, **5:**475–85.

Hata, Y., Ohshima, M., Ichisaka, S. *et al.* (2000) Brain-derived neurotrophic factor expands ocular dominance columns in visual cortex in monocularly deprived and nondeprived kittens but does not in adult cats. *Journal of Neuroscience*, **20:**RC57, 1–5.

Hensch, T. K., Fagiolini, M., Mataga, N. *et al.* (1998) Local GABA circuit control of experience dependent plasticity in developing visual cortex. *Science*, **282:**1504–8.

Holtzman, D. M., Li, Y., Parada, L. F. *et al.* (1992) P140trk mRNA marks NGF-responsive forebrain neurons: evidence that trk gene expression is induced by NGF. *Neuron*, **9:**465–78.

Huang, Z. J., Kirkwood, A., Pizzorusso, T. *et al.* (1999) BDNF regulates the maturation of inhibition and the critical period of plasticity in mouse visual cortex. *Cell*, **98:**739–55.

Hubel, D. H. and Wiesel, T. N. (1962) Receptive fields, binocular interaction and functional architecture in the cat's visual cortex. *Journal of Physiology*, **160:**106–54.

Hubel, D. H. and Wiesel, T. N. (1970) The period of susceptibility to the physiological effects of unilateral eye closure in kittens. *Journal of Physiology*, **206:**419–36.

Hubel, D. H., Wiesel, T. N. and Stryker, M. P. (1978) Anatomical demonstration of orientation columns in macaque monkey. *Journal of Comparative Neurology*, **177:**361–80.

Hübener, M., Shoham, D., Grinvald, A. *et al.* (1997) Spatial relationships among three columnar systems in cat area 17. *Journal of Neuroscience*, **17:**9270–84.

Issa, N. P., Trepel, C. and Stryker, M. P. (2000) Spatial frequency maps in cat visual cortex. *Journal of Neuroscience*, **20:**8504–14.

Kasamatsu, T. and Pettigrew, J. D. (1976) Depletion of brain catecholamines: failure of ocular dominance shift after monocular occlusion in kittens. *Science*, **194:**206–9.

Kim, D. S. and Bonhoeffer, T. (1994) Reverse occlusion leads to a precise restoration of orientation preference maps in visual cortex. *Nature*, **370:**370–2.

Kim, D. S., Matsuda, Y., Ohki, K. *et al.* (1999) Geometrical and topological relationships between multiple functional maps in cat primary visual cortex. *Neuroreport*, **10:**2515–22.

Knüsel, B., Gao, H., Okazaki, T. *et al.* (1997) Ligand-induced down-regulation of trk messenger RNA, protein and tyrosine phosphorylation in rat cortical neurons. *Neuroscience*, **78:**851–62.

Kossut, M. and Singer, W. (1991) The effect of short periods of monocular deprivation on excitatory transmission in the striate cortex of kittens: a current source density analysis. *Experimental Brain Research*, **85**:519–27.

Leibrock, J., Lottspeich, F., Hohn, A. *et al.* (1989) Molecular cloning and expression of brain derived neurotrophic factor. *Nature*, **341**:149–52.

Lein, E. S. and Shatz, C. J. (2000) Rapid regulation of brain-derived neurotrophic factor mRNA within eye-specific circuits during ocular dominance column formation. *Journal of Neuroscience*, **20**:1470–83.

Levi-Montalcini, R. (1987) The nerve growth factor 35 years later. *Science*, **237**:1154–62.

Li, Y., Holtzman, D. M., Kaplan, D. R. *et al.* (1995) Regulation of TrkA and ChAT Expression in developing rat basal forebrain: Evidence that both exogenous and endogenous NGF regulate differentiation of cholinergic neurons. *Journal of Neuroscience*, **15**:2888–905.

Löwel, S., Schmidt, K. E., Kim, D. S. *et al.* (1998) The layout of orientation and ocular dominance domains in area 17 of strabismic cats. *European Journal of Neuroscience*, **10**:2629–43.

Maffei, L., Berardi, N., Domenici, L. *et al.* (1992) Nerve growth factor (NGF) prevents the shift in ocular dominance distribution of visual cortical neurons in monocularly deprived rats. *Journal of Neuroscience*, **12**:4651–62.

McAllister, A. K., Katz, L. C. and Lo, D. C. (1999) Neurotrophins and synaptic plasticity. *Annual Review of Neuroscience*, **22**:295–318.

Meyer-Franke, A., Wilkinson, G. A., Kruttgen, A. *et al.* (1998) Depolarization and cAMP elevation rapidly recruit TrkB to the plasma membrane of CNS neurons. *Neuron*, **21**:681–93.

Obermayer, K. and Blasdel, G. G. (1993) Geometry of orientation and ocular dominance columns in monkey striate cortex. *Journal of Neuroscience*, **13(10)**:4114–29.

Ohzawa, I., DeAngelis, G. C. and Freeman, R. D. (1997) Encoding of binocular disparity by complex cells in the cat's visual cortex. *Journal of Neurophysiology*, **77**:2879–909.

Pollock, G. S., Vernon, E., Forbes, M. E. *et al.* (2001) Effects of early visual experience and diurnal rhythms on BDNF mRNA and protein levels in the visual system, hippocampus, and cerebellum. *Journal of Neuroscience*, **21**:3923–31.

Ratzlaff, E. H. and Grinvald, A. (1991) A tandem-lens epifluorescence macroscope: Hundred-fold brightness advantage for wide-field imaging. *Journal of Neuroscience Methods*, **36**:127–37.

Rauschecker, J. and Singer, W. (1981) The effects of early visual experience on the cat's visual cortex and their possible explanation by Hebb synapses. *Journal of Physiology (London)*, **310**:215–39.

Reid, R. C. and Alonso, J. M. (1995) Specificity of monosynaptic connections from thalamus to visual cortex. *Nature*, **378**:281–4.

Reiter, H. and Stryker, M. P. (1988) Neural plasticity without postsynaptic action potentials: less active inputs become dominant when kitten cortical cells are pharmacologically inhibited. *Proceedings of the National Academy of Sciences USA*, **85**:3623–7.

Riddle, D. R., Lo, D. C. and Katz, L. C. (1995) NT4-mediated rescue of lateral geniculate neurons from effects of monocular deprivation. *Nature*, **378**:189–91.

Rittenhouse, C. D., Shouval, H. Z., Paradiso, M. A. *et al.* (1999) Monocular deprivation induces long-term depression in the visual cortex. *Nature*, **397**:347–50.

Rossi, F. M., Bozzi, Y., Pizzorusso, T. *et al.* (1999) Monocular deprivation decreases brain-derived neurotrophic factor immunoreactivity in the rat visual cortex. *Neuroscience*, **90**:363–8.

Rutherford, L. C., Nelson, S. B. and Turrigiano, G. G. (1998) BDNF has opposite effects on the quantal amplitude of pyramidal neuron and interneuron excitatory synapses. *Neuron*, **21**:521–530.

Sala, R., Viegi, A., Rossi, F. M. *et al.* (1998) Nerve growth factor and brain-derived neurotrophic factor increase neurotransmitter release in rat visual cortex. *European Journal of Neuroscience,* **10:**2185–91.

Schoups, A. A., Elliot, R. C., Friedman, W. J. *et al.* (1995) BDNF and NGF are differentially modulated by visual experience in the developing geniculocortical pathway. *Developmental Brain Research,* **86:**325–34.

Shatz, C. J. and Stryker, M. P. (1978) Ocular dominance in layer IV of the cat's visual cortex and the effects of monocular deprivation. *Journal of Physiology (London),* **281:**267–83.

Shmuel, A. and Grinvald, A. (1996) Functional organization for direction of motion and its relationship to orientation maps in cat area 18. *Journal of Neuroscience,* **16:**6945–64.

Singer, W., Freeman, B. and Rauschecker, J. (1981) Restriction of visual experience to a single orientation affects the organization of orientation columns in cat visual cortex. *Experimental Brain Research,* **41:**199–215.

Stryker, M. P. (1991) Activity-dependent reorganization of afferents in the developing mammalian visual system. In D. M. Lam and C. J. Shatz (eds) *Development of the Visual System,* pp. 267–87. MIT Press, Cambridge, MA.

Thoenen, H. (1995) Neurotrophins and neuronal plasticity. *Science,* **270:**593–7.

Tootell, R. B. H., Switkes, E., Silverman, M. S. *et al.* (1988) Functional anatomy of macaque striate cortex. II. Retinotopic organization. *Journal of Neuroscience,* **8:**1531–68.

Weliky, M., Bosking, W. H. and Fitzpatrick, D. (1996) A systematic map of direction preference in primary visual cortex. *Nature,* **379:**725–8.

Weliky, M. and Katz, L. C. (1997) Disruption of orientation tuning in visual cortex by artificially correlated neuronal activity. *Nature* **386:**680–5.

Wiesel, T. N. and Hubel, D. H. (1963) Effects of visual deprivation on morphology and physiology of cells in the cat's lateral geniculate body. *Journal of Neurophysiology,* **26:**978–93.

Part II

Investigating behavior in animals

Chapter 7

The Use of Cooling Deactivation to Reveal the Neural Bases of Lesion-induced Plasticity in the Developing and Mature Cerebral Cortex

Bertram R. Payne, Stephen G. Lomber

Introduction

Cerebral lesions often produce specific deficits in neural performance and behavior. However, they are also characterized by a subsequent attenuation in the severity of the deficits. According to Kolb and Whishaw (1995) factors described as contributing to recovery of function include regeneration of connections to the area that was previously innervated, sprouting of fibers to innervate new targets structures, denervation supersensitivity to application of the same stimulus, disinhibition of potential compensatory zones and the activation of so-called "silent synapses." Moreover, functional recovery is more likely for complex behaviors that are composed of many components, and it is more pronounced after incomplete lesions. However, recovery is severely limited for neural functions that are highly localized. For example, a lesion of primary motor cortex induces paralysis of voluntary movement and a lesion of primary visual cortex abolishes conscious vision.

In this chapter, we compare the functional outcomes of two types of cerebral lesions. In the first, the lesion was incurred when the brain was mature. Over time, this type of lesion demonstrates postlesion recovery of function. For the second, the lesion was sustained shortly after birth, when the brain is immature, and the brain demonstrates sparing of functions that are otherwise lost following equivalent lesion sustained in adulthood. We make a distinction between the lesions sustained at the two ages because we consider that the term "recovery of neural function" describes the capacities that emerge from, and are superior to, initial postlesion performance when neural function is most debilitated. In contrast, we consider that the term "spared neural function" describes the performance that is present after lesions incurred in the earlier part of life before faculties have fully matured. For technical reasons linked to the identification of spared neural functions, spared performance is always greater than recovered performance, and it results from the altered development of neural pathways.

Embodied in the concept of "sparing" is a prior *absence* of a given behavior and the notion that the lesion triggers a redirection of pathway development. In contrast, embodied in the concept of "recovery" is a prior *presence* of a given behavior, and there is little or no overt rewiring of brain pathways and recovery of function must depend upon other types of neural changes. Thus, the concept of "sparing" differs in fundamental ways from the concept of "recovery."

For the focus of this article, we test cerebral regions for the contributions they make to the recovery and sparing of functions by using limited degrees of cooling to selectively deactivate specific cerebral regions. In the first section we concentrate on our work examining the repercussions of lesions of middle suprasylvian (MS) cortex, a visuoparietal region, and the impact the lesions have on the ability of cats to disengage their attention from a fixated visual locus and redirect it to a new locus in the visual field. We also briefly discuss plasticity of neural systems following lesions of ventral posterior suprasylvian (vPS) cortex in the visuotemporal region. In the second part, we test the contributions pMS and vPS cortices make to the sparing of visually guided behaviors following lesions of primary visual cortex sustained early in life.

Lesions in the mature cerebral hemispheres and the basis for recovery

As a prelude to describing the use of cooling to dissect compensatory circuits following lesions within visuoparietal cortex, it is useful to identify the region in cat, and to recapitulate the repercussions of unilateral and bilateral cooling deactivations of middle suprasylvian (MS) cortex on a task that requires the cat to disengage its attention from a central target (cynosure), and to redirect its attention to a stimulus that is moved into the periphery of the visual field. This work in itself provided some surprising, and even paradoxical results, that are of great interest.

Middle suprasylvian cortex is a large region that covers an expanse of the cerebrum bounding the middle suprasylvian gyrus and the two banks of the middle suprasylvian sulcus, and it forms the visuoparietal field (Fig. 7.1). For the current topic, the most interesting region consists of cortex lining the posterior end of the MS sulcus, which we abbreviate to pMS cortex (Fig. 7.1). It is immediately anterior to the region at the junction of the temporal, occipital and parietal (TOP) fields. pMS cortex includes the visuotopically defined areas PMLS and PLLS of Palmer *et al.* (1978), and TOP junctional cortex corresponds to the retinotopic area termed areas 21a and 21b by Tusa and Palmer (1980). This region is not readily definable because both its architectural and visual maps have numerous features that blend with the maps of areas in the adjacent fields (Sanides and Hoffmann 1969; Tusa and Palmer 1980; Grant and Shipp 1991; Mulligan and Sherk 1993; Sherk and Mulligan 1993). Nevertheless, the core of the combined area 21 is readily distinguishable from the core of the pMS areas by the high abundance of orientation selective neurons and a dearth of neurons that are highly direction selective (Wimborne and Henry 1992; Dreher *et al.* 1996). In contrast, pMS

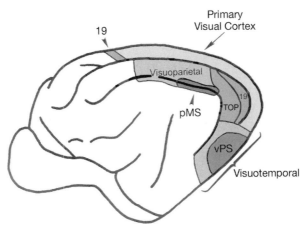

Fig. 7.1 (and color plate 7) Lateral view of the cat left cerebral hemisphere to show positions of major visual regions. Anterior is to the left. Yellow indicates primary visual cortical areas 17 and 18 (see review of Payne and Peters 2002). Purple indicates area 19, which flanks the primary visual areas and comprises the remainder of the occipital field. It is interposed between the primary areas and the spatially distinct visuoparietal and visuotemporal cortices (green), which are separated by the temporo–occipito–parietal (red, TOP) junctional cortex. The position of the posterior middle suprasylvian (blue, pMS) region, which forms the banks of the middle suprasylvian sulcus, is located within the visuoparietal field. The position of the ventral posterior suprasylvian (blue, vPS) region within the visuotemporal field is also shown.

cortex is characterized by neurons that are both highly orientation selective and highly direction selective (Hubel and Wiesel 1969; Spear and Bauman 1975; Zumbroich and Blakemore 1987; von Grunau *et al.* 1987; Gizzi *et al.* 1990; Grant and Shipp 1991; Danilov *et al.* 1995; Dreher *et al.* 1996; Sherk *et al.* 1997).

We deactivated pMS cortex by inserting a cooling loop (Lomber *et al.* 1999) into the sulcus to contact both the medial and lateral banks. To insert the loop, arachnoid and pia maters that bridge the opening to the sulcus were carefully dissected away without compromise of the vasculature. The lateral bank was gently retracted to expose the fundus of the sulcus, and the cooling loop was inserted into the sulcus, and its foot was secured to the skull with dental acrylic that was anchored by screws turned into the skull. One of these cooling loops is shown *in situ* in Fig. 7.2, in contact with the medial bank of the sulcus in the post-mortem, fixed brain. In this instance, the lateral bank was removed to permit visualization of the cooling loop.

The loop is cooled by circulating chilled methanol through the lumen of the tubing. Loop temperature is monitored with a microthermocouple attached to the union of the inlet and outlet tubes (μTC, Fig. 7.2; Lomber *et al.* 1999). Temperature of the loop depends on the interplay of three factors: (1) the temperature of the methanol when it reaches the cryoloop; (2) the rate of methanol flow; and (3) the ability of the brain's vascular system to resist the fall in temperature of the loop. Temperature can be kept

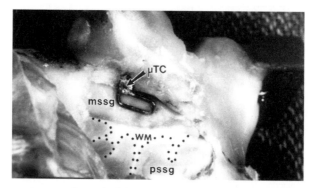

Fig. 7.2 Cryoloop at the posterior end of the MS sulcus of the post-mortem, fixed brain. The cooling loop is resting against the middle suprasylvian gyrus (mssg) that forms the medial bank of the MS sulcus. Cortex lateral to the cryoloop was removed following tissue fixation to reveal the cooling loop. Left is anterior. Pssg, posterior suprasylvian gyrus cut in the horizontal plane; μTC, microthermocouple at the base of the cooling loop; WM, white matter. Scale bar = 10mm. From Lomber and Payne (1996) and reprinted with permission of Cambridge University Press.

constant at a desired level, +1.0°C, by monitoring loop temperature and then increasing or decreasing flow rate in the appropriate direction. Deactivation temperatures of the loop are reached within moments of methanol pumping, with stable deactivation temperatures of the brain reached in 2–5 minutes. The actual time depends upon the closeness of the apposition of the loop to cortex and the level of cooling desired.

Cortex is cooled by direct export of cooled blood in vessels in contact with the cooling loop along penetrating arterioles into the underlying gray matter. Loop temperatures of 8–12°C, typically are sufficient to lower temperatures of the supragranular cortical layers below 20°C and silence the neurons (Fig. 7.3, left and center of trace; Lomber *et al.* 1999; Lomber and Payne 2000). These temperatures are sufficient to severely impair discrimination of small differences in movement direction, but they are without impact on the reorienting of attention (Lomber and Payne 2000). At these temperatures, most deep layer neurons remain active (Schwark *et al.* 1986); a point that is verified by our experiments which show that the temperature of the cooling loop must be reduced to the range of 1–5°C to effect a block of neuronal activity in the deep layers and to block the reorienting of attention (Lomber and Payne 2000). The slight variation in loop temperatures necessary for the deactivations reflects the closeness of the apposition of the cooling loop to cortex, the size of the cooling loop, and its position within the MS sulcus. For example, cooling of loops positioned anterior in the sulcus (aMS cortex) between coronal levels A4 and A16 have virtually no impact on orienting performance (*cf* Fig. 7.4A, D), whereas cooling of loops positioned between A1 and A11 noticeably reduces orienting into the contracooled hemifield by 13% to 48%, and cooling of loops positioned between P2 and A8 virtually abolishes orienting performance altogether, reducing it by between 91% and 100% (Fig. 7.4B, E) (Payne *et al.* 1996a). In this way, cooling of loops positioned at the posterior end of the

Fig. 7.3 Action potentials generated by three neurons in pMS cortex before, during, and after cooling of the cryoloop placed in the middle suprasylvian sulcus (Fig. 7.2). Prior to cooling, action potentials were generated by a bright bar moved back and forth across the aggregate receptive field of the three neurons. When the cooling loop was activated (ON), the numbers of evoked action potentials diminished until the neurons were silenced. The neurons remained silent for the duration of the cooling. When operation of the cryoloop was discontinued (OFF), temperature climbed rapidly, and neuronal activity quickly returned and reached normal levels within one minute as warm blood reperfused the region. From Lomber *et al.* (1994).

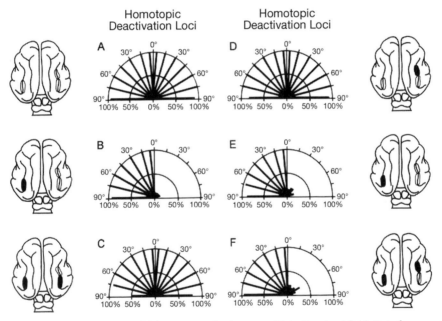

Fig. 7.4 Visual orienting to a high contrast stimulus moved into the visual field. Data from a cat with bilateral pMS cryoloops and an additional aMS cryoloop in the right hemisphere. Data collected: (A) Prior to and after cooling deactivation. (B) Cooling of the left pMS cryoloop. Note neglect of stimuli presented in the right visual hemifield. Orienting to stimuli presented in the left hemifield is completed unimpaired. (C) Bilateral cooling of pMS cryoloops (homotopic loci). Note restoration of visual orienting responses into right hemifield. (D) Cooling of the right aMS cryoloop. Note absence of impact on orienting behavior. (E) Cooling of left pMS cryoloop, as in B. (F) Cooling of the left pMS cryoloop and right aMS cryoloop. Note that cooling of the heterotopic aMS locus did not restore visual orienting responses into the neglected hemifield. From Lomber and Payne (2001b) and reprinted with permission of Cambridge University Press.

MS sulcus to 1–5 °C abolished orienting to stimuli presented in the contralateral visual hemifield. The cooling is without impact on orienting to stimuli presented in the ipsilateral visual hemifield. In effect, the unilateral cooling of pMS cortex induces a profound contracooled neglect of visual stimuli compared to the highly proficient orienting to all positions in the visual field under normal conditions. Cooling deactivations of area 7 on the crown of the middle suprasylvian gyrus (much of the remainder of the visuoparietal field), or dorsal suprasylvian cortex (TOP junction) or ventral posterior suprasylvian cortex in the visuotemporal field have no impact whatsoever on orienting performance (Fig. 7.1) (Lomber *et al.* 1996a; Lomber and Payne 2001a,b).

The impact of the cooling is completely reversed within minutes of switching off the methanol pump (Fig. 7.3, right of trace). Following the cessation of cooling, temperatures initially rise very rapidly, and then gradually reach asymptotically normal temperatures as newly arrived warm blood reperfuses from the cortical surface into the parenchyma of the brain. Orienting performance returns to a high level of proficiency that is characteristic of performance in the absence of any cooling (Fig. 7.4A). Repeated cooling deactivations carried out over a period of 2.8 years remain completely effective and completely reversible (Lomber *et al.* 1999), and subsequent post-mortem analyses reveal that neither the surgical procedures to implant the cooling loops nor the large number of deactivations have any impact on brain structure and overall neural activity (Fig. 7.5A, B). The only evidence of the presence of the cooling loop are small impressions in the cortical surface where the cortex became molded by the hypodermic tubing as the sulcal walls closed around the loop to surround it and ensure close contact.

The extent of the cooling impact can be realized by using electrophysiologic methods to map the cortex adjacent to the cooling loop, and assay responsiveness to visual stimuli. However, there are severe limitations to this approach. One major limitation is the time that is required to carry out a large number of cooling cycles; another is that any damage induced by the assay electrode obscures subsequent visual inspection of the integrity of the cortex in histological sections. The same consideration can be applied to multiple penetrations with microthermocouples to assay the position of the 20 °C thermocline, which demarcates the boundary between functioning and non-functioning cortex (Lomber *et al.* 1996b, 1999).

The most effective way to assay the extent of the deactivated cortex is to cool the cortex and administer C^{14}-2 deoxyglucose (2DG) intravenously for the duration of the deactivation. 2DG is taken up voraciously by active neurons because it is indistinguishable from other glucose molecules. However, once it has entered the cell the molecule is phosphorylated, which prevents the molecule from entering the glycolytic chain of reactions, and the phosphorylated molecule becomes trapped within the neuron (Sokoloff *et al.* 1977; Sokoloff 1981a,b). The presence of the 2DG is assayed post-mortem by fixing, freezing and sectioning the brain (Payne and Lomber 1999), and apposing the sections to X-ray film. Following development, dark regions on the film identify regions with high uptake of 2DG, and levels of uptake are positively correlated

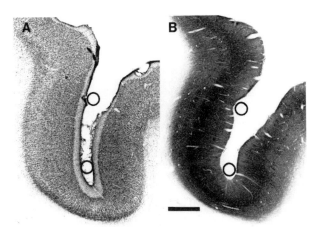

Fig. 7.5 Structure of MS cortex following cryoloop implantation and repeated cooling deactivations over a 2.8 year period. (A) Nissl-stained coronal section to show normal cytoarchitecture. The only evidence of the presence of the cooling loop is the small molding impressions in the cortical surface. (B) Section reacted for the presence of cytochrome oxidase. Cytochrome oxidase activity is at normal levels, and there is no evidence for any long-term impact of either the surgical procedure to implant the cooling loop, or of the repeated deactivations. Circles represent a cross section through the cooling loop. Left is medial. Scale bar: 2 mm. From Lomber *et al.* (1999) and reprinted with permission from Elsevier Science.

with levels of neuronal activity (e.g. Schoppmann and Stryker 1981). It is readily evident in Fig. 7.6 that 2DG uptake on the banks of the MS sulcus (MSs) is reduced almost completely by the cooling, and that the region of reduced uptake is limited to the medial and lateral banks of the sulcus. 2DG uptake is high in all other regions, and extremely high in the lateral geniculate body (LGB) and in primary visual cortical areas 17 and 18. We conclude that: (1) the cooling effects a highly localized deactivation of cortex; (2) unilateral cooling of pMS cortex induces a profound neglect of stimuli presented in the contracooled hemifield; and (3) pMS cortex is an essential component in the visual network for guiding the reorienting of attention, and movements, to new stimuli introduced into the visual field.

On the surface, we have a straightforward link between a brain region and a behavior. However, bilateral cooling of pMS cortex leads us to another conclusion. We expected that bilateral deactivation would induce a neglect of stimuli presented anywhere in the visual field. In fact the exact opposite result was obtained. Once a contralateral neglect was induced by unilateral cooling of pMS cortex (Fig. 7.4B), the additional cooling of pMS cortex in the opposite hemisphere reversed the neglect, and paradoxically reinstated orienting into the previously neglected hemifield (Fig. 7.4C; Lomber *et al.* 1996; Lomber and Payne 2001b). Moreover, the induction of neglect by unilateral cooling and its reversal by bilateral cooling could be repeated many times in the same testing session, and in either the left to right, or the right to left directions. These

Fig. 7.6 Radiogram to reveal C¹⁴-2-deoxyglucose (2DG) uptake during operation of a middle suprasylvian sulcus (MSs) cooling loop (filled circles). The cryoloop was first cooled to 1 °C. Beginning five minutes later, 2DG was administered intravenously over a period of 30 minutes prior to brain fixation. Radiogram shows that 2DG uptake, and hence neural activity, is markedly depressed in both the medial and lateral banks of the MS sulcus. 2DG uptake levels are high in all other regions. Aud=auditory cortex; LGB=lateral geniculate body; 17=area 17; 18=area 18. Left is medial. Scale bar=5mm. From Payne *et al.* (1996c) and reprinted with permission from Elsevier Science.

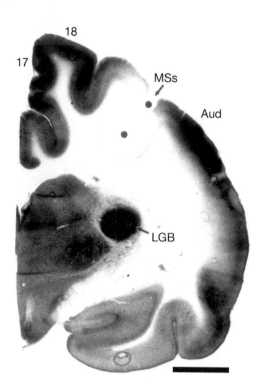

interactions are limited to pMS cortex deactivations because paired asymmetric deactivations of pMS and aMS cryoloops induces the hemineglect characteristic of pMS cortex, and there is no reversal of the pMS cortex-induced hemineglect (Fig. 7.4E, 4F; Lomber and Payne 2001b). We conclude from these data that pMS cortex has virtually no discernible effects on orienting and, in this instance, we conclude that pMS cortex is not essential for guiding this type of orienting behavior. Based on the data from the unilateral and bilateral cooling deactivations, we must conclude that the cerebral network is dynamic, and that the effects of deactivating one node in the network cannot be safely predicted without taking into consideration processing elsewhere in the network.

We have hypothesized that when the cerebral circuits are thrown into imbalance by the unilateral deactivation, there is not only an elimination from target structures of excitatory drive from pMS cortex, but also a removal of inhibition from the contralateral pMS cortex, which becomes superactive. In so doing, the uncooled pMS cortex captures control over regions controlling attention and movement and, consonant with the neglect of the contralateral hemifield, there is more vigorous orienting into the ipsilateral hemifield. This above normal activity is eliminated, and the visuomotor system is brought back into balance by the additional deactivation of pMS cortex in the opposite hemisphere. This explanation is supported by anatomical and electrophysiologic data (Lomber and Payne 1996), and by mathematical descriptions of the system

(Hilgetag *et al.* 1999). Regardless of interpretation of the data, it is worth recognizing that during the bilateral deactivations of pMS cortex, effective reorienting of attention remains possible, and it must rely completely on circuits other than those including pMS cortex (Lomber and Payne 1996).

We now have the basis on which we can return to the central theme of this chapter; the use of cooling deactivation to investigate lesion-induced neural compensations in the mature brain. We have investigated the impact of a permanent deactivation, a lesion, of pMS cortex on the reorienting of attention, and shown that the neural system for reorienting of attention is highly plastic. Because it is not possible to make an aspiration lesion of MS cortex without interrupting at least some fibers of passage in the underlying optic radiation, we injected microvolumes of a solution of ibotenic acid into both banks of the right pMS sulcus. Ibotenic acid remains highly localized and kills neurons in the vicinity of the injection sites, and we injected sufficient amounts over several millimeters of cortex to mirror the extent of a cooling deactivation. In the same surgical procedure we also implanted cooling loops anterior to the lesion, in the right MS sulcus, and in the mirror-symmetric position to the lesion, in the posterior portion of the left MS sulcus.

Figure 7.7 shows a coronal section stained for cytochrome oxidase to verify the presence of a lesion and a permanent deactivation of pMS sulcal cortex. The virtual absence of cytochrome oxidase reaction product on the banks of the middle suprasylvian sulcus

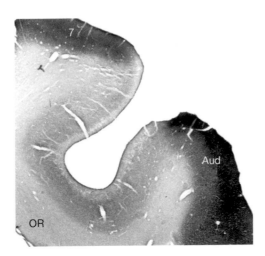

Fig. 7.7 Coronal section through the medial and lateral banks of MS sulcus (MSs) to show the extent of the neurotoxic lesion created by injection of ibotenic acid. The section was reacted for the presence of cytochrome oxidase, which is a sensitive marker for long-term changes in neural activity. The virtual absence of cytochrome oxidase reaction product reveals the absence of neurons and neuropil, and confirms the lesion of both banks of the pMS sulcus. Note rich cytochrome oxidase staining on the crowns of the flanking middle suprasylvian gyrus (area 7) and auditory region of the middle ectosylvian gyrus (Aud), and the absence of damage of the underlying optic radiation (OR).

(MSs) compared to the dense cytochrome oxidase reaction product of the flanking middle suprasylvian (area 7) and auditory region of the middle ectosylvian (Aud) gyri confirms the permanent silencing of neural activity in both banks of the middle suprasylvian sulcus (MSs). Adjacent sections stained for Nissl substance reveal an absence of neurons and a high incidence of glial cells in the neurotoxic scar (not shown), which account for any residual cytochrome oxidase activity. In this way, left pMS cortex was permanently silenced.

Prior to the injection of ibotenic acid we trained the cats on the visual orienting task, and ensured that they were highly proficient at orienting to stimuli presented anywhere in the two visual hemifields. Performance is consistently high (Fig. 7.8A, Days -2, -1). For convenience in the illustration, we summed all orienting positions in the left (dark grey) and right (light grey) hemifields. The impact of the lesion of right pMS cortex was immediately evident when the cat was tested on the day following injection of ibotenic acid. For stimuli presented in the left (dark grey) hemifield no orienting movements could be evoked (absence of dark grey bar), yet interleaved presentation of stimuli into the right (light grey bars) hemifield continued to evoke strong orienting responses. In this instance the impact of the lesion parallels exactly the impact of a cooling deactivation of the same region of cortex (Fig. 7.4B, E).

However, this parallel in the impact of the pMS lesion and pMS cooling was not maintained. In subsequent days, the deficit in orienting proficiency to targets presented in the left hemifield first became incomplete (appearance and growth of the dark grey column), and then progressively attenuated over subsequent days (Fig. 7.8A). By the twelfth day postlesion, orienting into the left (dark grey) hemifield was indistinguishable from the right (light grey) hemifield or normal performance established prior to the lesion (Days -2, -1). After day 12, orienting remained at a high level. Throughout these periods orienting into the right hemifield was completely normal. In other words, the ibotenic acid lesion of right pMS cortex induced a massive initial deficit in orienting proficiency, but the deficit attenuated over the subsequent days. From these results we conclude that the cat strengthened the functional contribution of circuits within the visual network of the right hemisphere to compensate for the debilitating effects of the lesion of right pMS cortex.

One might argue that the depressed orienting and subsequent recovery was merely a general side effect of the surgical procedure and not related to the direct effects of the lesion. The high proficiency of orienting into the ipsilesional (light grey bars) hemifield rules out lingering effects of the anesthesia, impact of analgesia, or general after effects of surgery as an explanation for the depressed orienting responses into the left hemifield. Furthermore, we identified that cooling of left pMS cortex, even on day 1 following surgery, reinstated orienting (dark grey bar, Fig. 7.8B) into the contralesional field, and orienting is at high normal levels as if the brain is behaving with balanced bilateral pMS deactivations (cf Fig. 7.4C). Because reversals of unilateral neglect only occur during bilateral deactivation of pMS cortices, and not of heterotopic loci (cf Fig. 7.4F; Lomber and Payne 2001b), the reversal of pMS lesion-induced neglect by contalateral

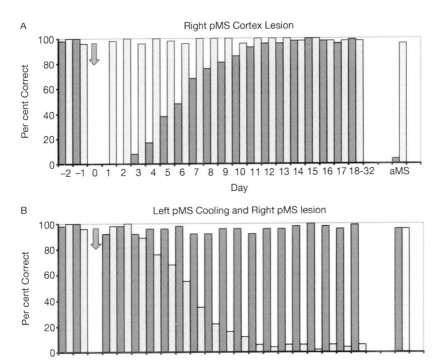

Fig. 7.8 (A) Histograms to show percent correct orienting responses before (Days: -2, -1) and on sequential days (day 1 … day 32) following ablation of right pMS cortex alone on day 0 (arrow). Note: (1) Days: -2, -1: High proficiency in orienting into both left (dark grey bars) and right (light grey bars) visual hemifields prior to ablation. (2) Day 0 (arrow): Lesion of right pMS and implants of cooling loops in right aMS and left pMS sulci. (3) Day 1: induction of profound neglect of the left hemifield (absence of dark grey bar) by the right pMS ablation whereas orienting into the right, calibration hemifield (light grey bar) is normal. (4) Day 3: the magnitude of the neglect starts to attenuate (appearance of small dark grey bar), and continues to attenuate on subsequent days (increasing height of dark grey bar). (5) Days 12–2: Recovery of orienting is complete and maintained. (B) With concomitant cooling of left pMS cortex on day 1, orienting into the left hemifield was restored (dark grey bar). From day 3 onwards there was a sequential decrease in the number of trials in which the cat oriented to stimuli presented in the right hemifield during cooling of left pMS cortex (decreasing size of the light grey bar) that became maximal on days 11/12. At first, the cat occasionally missed stimuli, and then those errors increased in frequency as the neglect grew in strength. On Days 11/12 the cooling induced a profound neglect on all subsequent days of testing (days 13–32). Cooling of the right aMS loop on day 35 induced a neglect of the left hemifield (A). This neglect was reversed by cooling the left pMS loop (B).

pMS cooling verifies that the lesion-induced deficit in orienting is a localized effect of the lesion itself.

Just as importantly, and perhaps more interestingly, cooling on subsequent days induced a substantial and incremental neglect of the contracooled hemifield (Fig. 7.8B, declining light grey bars). Moreover, the fall in performance in the contracooled hemifield is almost perfectly and negatively correlated with the natural recovery of orienting into the contralesional field (Fig. 7.8A, ascending dark grey bars). The incremental cooling-induced neglect provides an independent measure of the rate and magnitude of the network compensations following the pMS lesion, and there are now two measures of the impact of the right pMS lesion: the attenuating neglect of the contralesional, left hemifield as the compensations of the lesioned hemisphere gain hold and boost their influence, and the incremental neglect of the contracooled, right hemifield during successive daily cooling deactivations of left pMS cortex. This approach allows for an elegant demonstration of the lesion-induced neglect and recovery, and for a well-designed verification of the recovery process as it gains strength, and the two hemispheres again compete for control over pathways responsible for redirecting attention and goal directed behavior.

Importantly, the two hemispheres reestablish interactions and apparently normal control over reorienting operations. But what regions contribute? We can speculate that the compensations are based in the superior colliculus or some other cortical structure such as substantia nigra or basal ganglia, all regions that have been implicated as playing a role in the reorienting of attention and reaching movement goals (see e.g. Lomber and Payne 1996; Payne *et al.* 1996a; Lomber *et al.* 2001), but the contributions these regions play cannot readily be tested. However, we have tested the contribution of the juxtalesional cortex. By implanting a cooling loop just anterior to the lesion, in the right aMS sulcus, we have been able to test its contribution to proficient orienting performance following the postlesion recovery. Remember that in the intact cat unilateral cooling deactivation of aMS cortex has no direct impact on orienting proficiency during unilateral cooling (Fig. 7.4D), and it cannot restore orienting into a hemifield neglected as a result of pMS cooling (Fig. 7.4F). However, following postlesion recovery in orienting performance (Fig. 7.8A), cooling of the right aMS loop reinstated a profound neglect of orienting to stimuli presented in the contralesional hemifield (Fig. 7.8A, short dark grey bar, far right). Just as importantly, contemporaneous cooling of the left pMS cortex reversed the impact of aMS cooling (*cf* Fig. 7.8A, B, dark grey and light grey bars, far right). The reversal works also when the order of the aMS and pMS deactivations is reversed. These results are particularly noteworthy because we have obtained a result that is never obtained from the intact cat (Lomber *et al.* 1999; Lomber and Payne 2001b). These results show, and confirm, that the right aMS region is essential for postlesion recovery of orienting behavior, and that the region has taken over the neural operations normally ascribed to pMS cortex.

These data provide further evidence that the cerebral network is dynamic, and they show that other nodes and linkages in the cerebral network have a substantial capacity to compensate for lesion-induced deficits. Since the recovery of orienting performance reaches completion within two weeks, or less, following smaller lesions (Payne and Lomber 1996c), it is likely that the compensation is based upon dynamic reorganization of function in existing circuitry, and not on frank rewiring of visual pathways. To our knowledge no anatomic studies have provided any significant evidence for major rewiring following cerebral lesions in the mature cat visual system (e.g. Payne *et al.* 1996b). However, our data show that juxtalesional regions of cortex are important players in the functional reorganization. Experiments of the kind we have just summarized could not be carried out without the use of the reversible cooling deactivation technique, and experiments that employ our strategy of using reversible deactivation to test the veracity of conclusions on postlesion recovery greatly extend both the strength of the conclusions reached and the power of the knowledge gained.

Cooling deactivation has also provided insights into the bases of the neural compensations following lesions of vPS cortex in the visuotemporal region. For example, cooling deactivation of vPS cortex results in an inability of cats to learn new three-dimensional object discriminations (Lomber *et al.* 1996a,b). This type of discrimination is relatively straightforward for the cat to learn normally and it is a cerebral attribute that survives ablation of the same region of cortex (Campbell 1978; Cornwell and Warren 1981; Cornwell *et al.* 1998). The difference between the cooling- and ablation-based results indicates that existing, but poorly used, secondary circuits are activated or strengthened in the absence of vPS cortex and that they contribute to the successful learning of object discriminations. Such circuits cannot be utilized and strengthened during short cooling periods of ~1 hour. A similar plasticity becomes evident in monkey inferotemporal cortex when the effects of cooling deactivation are compared with the effects of lesions (Iwai and Mishkin, 1969; Cowey and Gross 1970; Gross 1973; Horel *et al.* 1984, 1987; Cirillo *et al.* 1987; Horel 1992).

Why are neural compensations induced by permanent lesions and not by temporary cooling? According to Payne *et al.* (1996c), a dominant factor is likely to be the duration of the deactivation. Following lesions, animals live permanently with the neural defect and there is considerable opportunity for prolonged interactions between the animal with the defect and the environment. These interactions may result in modifications of the remaining circuitry that reduce the severity of the handicap. In contrast, these same influences have little time to act on the nervous system during cooling, which occupies only 5–10% of each day, and there is little or no strengthening of secondary circuits. Furthermore, any compensatory changes initiated during brief cumulative cooling periods do not seem to accumulate over repeated cooling sessions, because either the changes are very minor or they are reversed during the much longer intervals when the brain is functioning normally. However, it is important to recognize that there are exceptions to this generalization that have been identified in studies of learning and memory. For example, if the engram for certain types of form discriminations is firmly established by long periods of training prior to cooling, it is possible for the cats to reestablish high levels of performance on the discriminations during cooling (Lomber *et al.* 1996b). In this instance, the initial cooling deficit may be one of access to the engram, and it is this initial access difficulty that is overcome with training during cooling, and it should not be confused with new learning, *per se*, of the form discriminations. Regardless of interpretation, these results provide evidence for plasticity in the cerebral network in the absence of frank rewiring of pathways. Factors involved in the recovery of function likely include: sprouting of nearby afferent fibers to innervate aMS cortex, or sprouting of aMS efferent fibers in target structures, denervation hypersensitivity to application of the same stimulus, disinhibition of potential compensatory zones, and the activation of synapses that under normal circumstances have no detectable role in orienting behavior, the so-called 'unmasking effect.' A markedly different type of plasticity, one that involves obvious expansion of neural pathways, characterizes the response to lesions of the immature cerebral cortex, and the sparing of neural processes and behavior. That plasticity, and tests for the neural bases of spared operations and organized behaviors, forms the topic of the next section.

Lesions in the young cerebral hemispheres and the basis for recovery

The repercussions of early damage of cat primary visual cortex, designated areas 17 and 18[1] (see review of Payne and Peters 2002), spread throughout the entire visual system, and shape pathways and circuits into new and useful forms that contribute to structured behaviors in adult life (Payne and Cornwell 1994; Payne *et al.* 1996b; Payne and Lomber 2002). These behaviors optimize the individual's interactions with the environment under the new conditions, and they epitomize the plastic capacities of the brain. They should be distinguished from the nonspecific, disordered or deleterious alterations in pathways and function that may also be induced by lesions, but that have no useful function. The lesions may also induce permanent deficits that can be linked to degeneration of specific sub-systems within the visual system (e.g. Payne *et al.* 1996b; Payne and Lomber 2002). To provide a foundation for the behavioral studies on sparing and the use of cooling to test for contributing loci, we summarize the repercussions of the lesion on visual pathways.

Anatomic and physiologic consequences

The anatomic consequences of lesions of cat primary visual cortex sustained during the first postnatal week spread to all other major components of the highly interconnected visual system from retina, through nuclei in thalamus (LGN, LP/Pulvinar complex), and regions of visuoparietal and visuotemporal cortices (compare Fig. 7.9A, B). The repercussions include death of neurons normally highly connected with the damaged region, and consequent reduction or elimination of brain pathways, as well as permanent degradations in neural and behavioral performance (unshaded in Fig. 7.9B). The deaths include many neurons in the lateral geniculate nucleus (LGN), of β retinal ganglion cells (the origin of X signals), and of selected neurons in extrastriate

---

[1] While the lesions always include areas 17 and 18, they also include portions of area 19 to ensure completeness of the removals of areas 17 and 18. For the sake of brevity we will refer to the lesions as being of primary visual cortex.

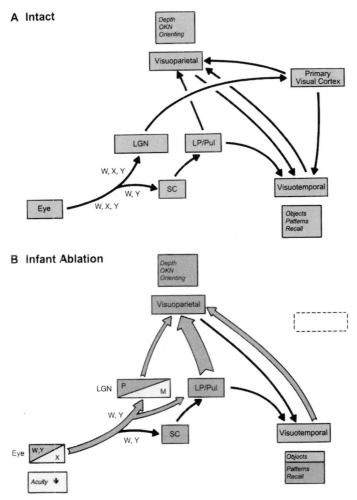

Fig. 7.9 Summary diagram of major ascending visual pathways to and within cerebral cortex. (A) Intact adult cat. (B) In cats that incurred lesions of primary visual cortex during the first post-natal week. Repercussions on functional measures are also identified. Dark grey=no change or no identified change of parameter relative to intact brain; light grey=sparing of function (activity levels, receptive field properties, behavior), or sparing of neurons or expansion of pathways; unshaded=impaired function or degeneration of neurons. LGN=dorsal lateral geniculate nucleus (P=parvocellular layers; M=magnocellular layers), LP/Pul=lateral posterior/pulvinar complex, SC=superior colliculus. W, X, and Y streams emanating from eye and major central destinations are represented. Note elimination of the X system in part B. Data are drawn from Berman and Cynader (1976); Callahan *et al.* (1984); Cornwell and Payne (1989); Cornwell *et al.* (1978, 1989); Doty (1961, 1973); Guido *et al.* (1990a,b, 1992); Kalil *et al.* (1991); Labar *et al.* (1981); Lomber *et al.* (1993, 1995); Long *et al.* (1996); MacNeil *et al.* (1996, 1997); Mendola *et al.* (1993); Murphy and Kalil (1979); Payne and Lomber (1996, 1998); Payne *et al.* (1984, 1991, 1993, 1996b); Rowe (1990); Spear and Baumann (1979); Spear *et al.* (1980); Sun *et al.* (1994); Tong *et al.* (1982, 1984); Tumosa *et al.* (1989) amongst others. From Payne and Lomber (2002). Permission to reprint modified figure has been requested from Sage Science Press.

cortex (not shown). Importantly, the repercussions also include expansion of pathways that bypass damaged cortex and degenerated regions in thalamus (light grey arrows in Fig. 7.9B) and they form the substrate for neural compensations that result in sparing of neural performance and behavior. It is on these pathways that we will focus.

Many of the surviving neurons expand their projections to established and to new target structures (Fig. 7.9B). For example, surviving W and Y ganglion cells increase the density of their projections to the parvocellular layers of LGN and establish a new projection to the lateral posterior nucleus (LP). In addition, the spared neurons in the magno- (M) and parvo- (P) cellular layers of LGN contribute to increased projections to visuoparietal cortex, which includes the middle suprasylvian (MS) region. Their numbers, though, are surpassed by the expansion of an already significant projection from the lateral posterior/pulvinar (LP/Pul) nucleus, to provide, in toto, a massive expansion of projections from visual thalamus into visuoparietal cortex. These expansions have a parallel in the increased numbers of neurons in the vPS region of visuotemporal cortex that project to visuoparietal cortex, and probably in the reciprocal pathway. Lastly, the projection from visuoparietal cortex to the superior colliculus, which is a major conduit for the outflow of signals from the cerebral cortex, also expands its territory and field of influence over collicular neurons (not shown). All of these expansions are accompanied by at least maintenance, if not an increase in overall level of neural activity in brain pathways (dark grey and light grey shading, respectively), and they provide another measure of neural compensations induced by early lesions of primary visual cortex. Retinal activity of W and Y ganglion cells appears to be unmodified (dark grey) because the death of massive numbers of β retinal ganglion cells eliminates the X-signals from the brain, and any sparing of visual functions must be based upon W and Y signals transmitted out of the eye by γ and α ganglion cells, respectively. Neuronal compensations have been identified in both visuoparietal cortex and superior colliculus (light grey shading in Fig. 7.9B).

Behavioral consequences

The anatomic and physiologic repercussions of the early lesions of primary visual cortex have a major impact on overall neural performance and behavior. These repercussions are summarized in Table 7.1, which identifies both permanent impairments that parallel the severity of impairments induced by equivalent lesions sustained in adulthood and the sparing of a number of visually guided behaviors. For example, visual performance based on acuity, and form-learning and -memory tasks that require discrimination of patterns with surround masking distractors are very poor, and no better in the cats with early lesions than in cats that sustained the same lesion in adulthood (Table 7.1, column 4, rows 1 and 5, unshaded cells). However, the very same cats are highly proficient at discriminating simpler forms or figures partially obscured by an overlain masking grid, and their performance is superior to the greatly impaired performances of cats that sustained primary visual cortex lesions as adults (rows 4 and 6, light grey cells), especially when a training paradigm is used in which the number of lines comprising the

Table 7.1 Spared and Impaired Behaviors. Summary of spared and impaired visual performance following lesions of primary visual cortex sustained during the first postnatal week. Tasks are grouped according to neural structure that contributes most fully to the neural operations. ++++=High level of performance; ↓↓↓ =great reduction in performance (severe deficit); ↓↓ lesser reduction in performance (moderate deficit); ↓=slight reduction in performance (minor deficit). Dark grey shading represents normal high levels of proficiency on tasks. Unshaded represents impaired performance. Light grey shading represents partial or complete sparing of behavioral performance. Modified table from Payne and Lomber (2002). Permission to reprint has been requested from Sage Science Press.

Column →	1	2	3	4
Row ↓	Visual Region	Visual Property	Intact	P1 Lesion
		BASIC PROPERTY		
1	Retina	Acuity[1]	++++	↓↓↓
		FORM, LEARNING, MEMORY		
2		Objects	++++	++++
3	Temporal	Patterns		
4	Cortex	Simple[2,3]	++++	++++
5		Masked – Surround[2,3]	++++	↓↓↓
6		Overlain[2,3]	++++	↓
		REFLEX, ACTION, SPACE		
7		Depth[4,5]	++++	↓
8	Parietal	OKN[5]	++++	↓
9	Cortex	Orienting		
10		Visual[5–7]	++++	↓
11		Auditory[6,7]	++++	++++

*=no or lesser deficit following two stage lesions. OKN=Optokinetic nystagmus.

Studies cited are limited to those that employed comparable stimuli and testing procedure in assays of performance of the different groups of cats. 1. Mitchell (2002); 2. Cornwell et al. (1989); 3. Cornwell and Payne (1989); 4. Cornwell et al. (1978); 5. Shupert et al. (1993); 6. Payne et al. (2000); 7. Payne and Lomber (2001).

masking grid is gradually increased in number, and the cat is allowed to master each stage prior to moving on to the next stage. Sparing on this set of pattern discriminations with overlain grids is also complete, or almost complete, if the lesions incurred in infancy are made in two stages with three days between operations. No special behavioral shaping procedures are then needed to reveal the spared neural operations (Table 7.1, row 6 '*'). These tasks are normally associated with visuotemporal cortex (Table 7.1, column 1).

There is also overall superior performance on tasks normally associated with visuoparietal cortex such as judging depth, optokinetic nystagmus (OKN) and reorienting of attention (Table 7.1, rows 7–10). On some tasks, such as the orienting task, the same cats can benefit enormously from additional training (Payne and Lomber 2001). The superior performance by cats on these visuotemporal and visuoparietal tasks, compared to cats with lesions sustained in adulthood, is strong evidence for sparing of a constellation of visually guided behaviors and neural functions. This extensive sparing must be accompanied by significant structural and functional neural adjustments in the cat brain. Like cats with lesions sustained in adulthood, there is little detectable impact of earlier lesions on the ability to discriminate between highly dissimilar objects or on auditory orienting (Table 7.1, rows 2 and 11).

Finally, the performance of cats that sustained large lesions of visual cortex extending from primary visual cortex to include visuoparietal and visuotemporal regions, in addition to primary visual cortex, is very poor on all tasks (Cornwell *et al.* 1978; Shupert *et al.* 1993). The poor performance is understandable because these larger lesions eliminate all, or virtually all, of the cerebral cortical machinery for the processing of visual signals. These data show that the expanded pathways into and out of visuoparietal cortex (Fig. 7.9B), and possibly visuotemporal cortex, are obligatory components of the neural compensations. This conclusion prompts a number of questions about the contributions modified pathways and cerebral regions make to the spared visually guided behaviors. These questions are the topic of the next section.

Modified regional contributions and basis for neural compensations

In the intact brain, each region of the cerebral cortex is unique in terms of its architecture, connectional signature, functional maps, inventory of receptive field properties, and its contributions to neural processing and behavior. The multiple repercussions of the early lesions of primary visual cortex modify all of these attributes, and we are prompted to ask: Is there a redistribution of functions across the modified expanse of cerebral cortex? For example, functions normally localized to one region may become dispersed across a broader region of cerebral cortex as signals are redistributed. Anatomical evidence to support this view is provided by the expanded projection from visuotemporal cortex to visuoparietal cortex and possibly in the reciprocal direction (Fig. 7.9B), as well as the expanded projection from visuoparietal cortex that reaches visuotemporal cortex via the superior colliculus and LP/Pul (not shown). Thus, it may be that the processing of signals in visuoparietal cortex is altered in significant ways by the signals arriving from visuotemporal cortex and viceversa.

Here, we return to the central topic of this article, and we summarize the first experiments to test for redistribution of functions across cortex following restricted cortical lesions based upon the above question and resulting speculations (Lomber and Payne 2001a). The tests have used localized cooling, via subdurally-implanted cooling loops to reversibly deactivate the visuoparietal and visuotemporal cortices in behaving cats in conjunction with four tasks: (1) visual orienting; (2) complex pattern recognition; (3) object recognition; and (4) auditory orienting (Fig. 7.10). As noted for intact cats in the previous section, visual orienting is completely abolished by cooling deactivation of the pMS region of visuoparietal cortex, but is completely unaffected by cooling deactivation of other regions including vPS cortex in the visuotemporal region (Fig. 7.10A, column 2) (Lomber *et al.* 1996a; Lomber and Payne 2001a,b,c). In the reverse direction, the ability to recall differences in complex patterns and objects is critically dependent upon visuotemporal cortex, with no apparent involvement of visuoparietal cortex (Fig. 7.10A, columns 3 and 4) (Lomber *et al.* 1996a,b), and deactivation of neither viusoparietal nor visuotemporal cortices has an impact on orienting to a sound stimulus (Fig. 7.10A, column 5) (Lomber and Payne 2001a,b). As indicated previously, the early lesion of primary visual cortex largely spares the visual orienting, and pattern and object recognition, and has no impact on auditory localization. Cooling deactivations reveal that visual orienting remains strongly dependent upon visuoparietal cortex (Fig. 7.10B, column 2, row 3). However, the dependence is not complete, because full deactivations, as revealed by modified 2DG uptake (Fig. 7.11), do not completely abolish orienting, as it does in intact cats. In the very same cats, independent cooling deactivation reveals a new essential contribution of visuotemporal cortex to high proficiency on the task (Fig. 7.10B, column 2, row 4). Moreover, the impact of combined visuoparietal and visuotemporal deactivations matches the impact of pMS deactivation alone in the intact cat (Fig. 7.10B, column 2, row 5). This result suggests that no region other than vPS cortex acquires a significant role in guiding orienting movements.

In the opposite direction, visuotemporal unique representations spread to visuoparietal cortex. For example, cooling deactivation of visuotemporal cortex in cats that sustained early lesions of primary visual cortex impairs recall of differences in complex patterns (partially masked I and O patterns) as it does in intact cats (Fig. 7.10B, column 3, row 3). However, the impairment is not complete because performance is not reduced to chance levels of reporting, which is characteristic of visuotemporal cooling in intact hemispheres (Fig. 7.10A, column 3, row 4), even though 2DG uptake is markedly depressed and indicative of complete deactivation (Fig. 7.11). However, in the very same cats there is also a reduction in proficiency of performance on recognition of differences in complex patterns when visuoparietal cortex is deactivated (Fig. 7.10B, column 3, row 3). Moreover, during the visuoparietal deactivation, the cats can relearn the task, whereas there is no evidence that performance can improve during visuotemporal deactivation. Visuoparietal cortex does not contribute to recognition of either three-dimensional objects (Fig. 7.10B, column 4) or simple two-dimensional patterns (I and O patterns without masking; not shown), which remain critically dependent upon visuotemporal cortex alone, as they do in intact cats. Thus, following the early lesion of primary visual cortex, visuoparietal cortex also contributes to the recognition and discrimination of complex, masked patterns. Presumably, such complex patterns must be processed across extensive regions of cortex. In intact cats, a significant fraction of this essential processing appears to be carried out in primary visual cortex (Hughes and Sprague 1986). Overall, these observations demonstrate a functional reorganization of neural substrates contributing to visually guided behaviors with the role of visuoparietal cortex in reorienting of attention muted and the role of visuotemporal cortex heightened, with the converse pertaining for the neural bases of recognition of complex patterns. Nevertheless, of the two regions, visuotemporal cortex remains critical for the relearning of overlearned and simple pattern discriminations.

A Intact

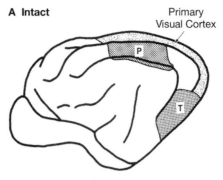

	Visual Orienting	Pattern Recognition	Object Recognition	Auditory Orienting
Performance	++++	++++	++++	++++
Parietal Deactivation	↓↓↓↓	0	0	0
Temporal Deactivation	0	↓↓↓↓	↓↓↓↓	0

B Infant Ablation

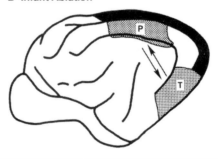

	Visual Orienting	Pattern Recognition	Object Recognition	Auditory Orienting
Performance	+++	+++	+++	++++
Parietal Deactivation	↓↓	↓	0	0
Temporal Deactivation	↓	↓↓	↓↓↓	0
Parietal & Temporal Deactivation	↓↓↓	↓↓↓	↓↓	0

These data show that at least two highly localizable functions of normal cerebral cortex are remapped across the cortical surface as a result of the early lesion of primary visual cortex. Moreover, the redistributions have spread the essential neural operations underlying orienting behavior from visual parietal cortex to a normally functionally distinct type of cortex in the visual temporal system, and in the opposite direction for

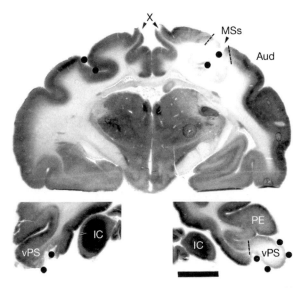

Fig. 7.11 2-deoxyglucose (2DG) radiograms showing regions of diminished ^{14}C-2DG uptake in cortex deactivated by the MS or vPS cooling loops (filled circles). Note very low levels of 2DG uptake throughout the full thickness of the right MS sulcal (MSs) cortex and high uptake levels in adjacent auditory cortex (Aud). Note low uptake levels throughout right vPS cortex and high uptake levels in adjacent PE cortex. Also note high uptake of 2DG in MS and vPS regions in the left hemisphere adjacent to the nonoperational cryoloops (filled circles). "X" marks the position of the removed primary visual cortices in the right and left hemispheres (cf Fig. 7.1). IC, inferior colliculus. Scale bar=5mm. From Lomber and Payne (2001a).

Fig. 7.10 Performance of intact (A) early-visual cortex-ablation cats (B) cats on (1) visual orienting, (2) complex pattern recognition, (3) object recognition, and (4) auditory orienting tasks, and the impact of cooling deactivation of visuoparietal and visuotemporal cortices. Conventions are summarized in Table 7.1. Data drawn from: Lomber (2001), Lomber et al. (1996a,b), Lomber and Payne (2001a), and unpublished data. Behavioral performance: +++=highly proficient performance, +++=competent performance, ++=modest performance, +=poor performance. Impact of cooling: ↓↓↓↓ = Proficiency on task is abolished or reduced to chance levels, ↓↓↓=severe, but incomplete, reduction in performance, ↓↓ modest reduction, ↓=minor reduction. In B, note should be made of initial proficiency prior to cooling. For example, on the orienting task there is considerable sparing of function, but performance is not at normal levels, and it is designated "+++." During combined cooling of visuoparietal and visuotemporal regions the cat is unable to reorient its attention, and the reduction in performance has a matching symbolized reduction of "↓↓↓."

complex pattern recognition. This conclusion could not have been reached without the use of cooling deactivation to test for functional contributions cerebral regions make to spared neural operations. However, we have not gleaned if there is a 'price' to pay for the redistribution of functions, and that neural operations normally associated with respective regions are reduced, displaced, or 'crowded out' as proposed by Teuber (1975), as the regions make contributions to new aspects of visually guided behavior not normally represented. This change in function is a possibility because it is known that visuospatial abilities are reduced when sparing of language functions can be demonstrated in humans (Milner 1974; Teuber 1975).

Summary

In summary, we have compared the outcome of two cerebral lesions; one when the brain was mature and a second when it was developing, and we have shown that cooling deactivation can be used in highly successful ways to examine the cerebral regions that contribute to recovery or sparing of functions. This is a new strategy that can be used in very effective ways to investigate the plastic and dynamic properties of both mature and immature cerebral systems, and it is a technique that has a bright future. Conclusions reached on loci contributing to recovered and spared functions based on the cooling deactivation method are extremely robust, and the approach should be encouraged in efforts to identify cerebral regions contributing to neural processes spared by or that recover after lesions.

Acknowledgments

This work is supported by funds from the National Institute of Neurological Diseases and Stroke and the National Science Foundation.

References

Berman, N. and Cynader, M. (1976) Early versus late visual cortex lesions: Effects on receptive fields in cat superior colliculus. *Experimental Brain Research*, **25**:131–7.

Callahan, E. C., Tong, L. and Spear, P. D. (1984) Critical period for the loss of retinal X-cells following visual cortex damage in cats. *Brain Research*, **323**:302–6.

Campbell, A. (1978) Deficits of visual learning produced by posterior temporal lesions in cats. *Journal of Comparative and Physiological Psychology*, **92**:45–57.

Cirillo, R. A., George, P. J., Horel, J. A. *et al.* (1987) An experimental test of the theory that visual information is stored in the inferotemporal cortex. *Behavioural Brain Research*, **34**:43–53.

Cornwell, P., Herbein, S., Corso, C. *et al.* (1989) Selective sparing after lesions of visual cortex in newborn kittens. *Behavioral Neuroscience*, **103**:1176–90.

Cornwell, P., Nudo, R. J. Staussfogel, D. *et al.* (1998) Dissociation of visual and auditory pattern discrimination functions within the cat's temporal cortex. *Behavioral Neuroscience*, **112**:800–11.

Cornwell, P., Overman, W. and Ross, C. (1978) Extent of recovery from neonatal damage to the cortical visual system. *Journal of Comparative and Physiological Psychology*, **92**:255–70.

Cornwell, P. and Payne, B. R. (1989) Visual discrimination by cats given lesions of visual cortex in one or two stages in infancy or in one stage in adulthood. *Behavioral Neuroscience*, **103**:1191–9.

Cornwell, P. and Warren, J. M. (1981) Visual discrimination defects in cats with temporal or occipital decortications. *Journal of Comparative and Physiological Psychology*, **95**:603–614.

Cowey, A. and Gross, C. G. (1970) Effects of foveal prestriate and inferotemporal lesions on visual discrimination by rhesus monkeys. *Experimental Brain Research*, **11**:128–44.

Danilov, Y., Moore, R. J., King, V. R. *et al.* (1995) Are neurons in cat posteromedial lateral suprasylvian visual cortex orientation sensitive? Tests with bars and gratings. *Visual Neuroscience*, **12**:141–51.

Doty, R. W. (1961) Functional significance of the topographical aspects of the retinocortical projection. In R. Jung and H. Kornhuber (eds) *The Visual System: Neurophysiology and Psychophysics*, pp. 228–47. Springer-Verlag, Heidelberg.

Doty, R. W. (1973) Ablation of visual areas in the central nervous system. In R. Jung (ed.) *Handbook of Sensory Physiology, vol. VII/3B, Central Processing of Visual Information, Part B*, pp. 483–541. Springer-Verlag, Berlin.

Dreher, B., Wang, C., Turlejski, K. J. *et al.* (1996) Areas PMLS and 21a of cat visual cortex: two functionally distinct areas. *Cerebral Cortex*, **6**:585–99.

Gizzi, M. S., Katz, E., Schumer, R. A. *et al.* (1990) Selectivity for orientation and direction of motion of single neurons in cat striate and extrastriate visual cortex. *Journal of Neurophysiology*, **63**:1529–43.

Grant, S. and Shipp, S. (1991) Visuotopic organization of the lateral suprasylvian area and of an adjacent area of the ectosylvian gyrus of cat cortex: a physiological and connectional study. *Visual Neuroscience*, **6**:315–38.

Gross, C. G. (1973) Visual functions of inferotemporal cortex. In R. Jung (ed.) *Handbook of Sensory Physiology, vol. VII/3B. Central Processing of Visual Information*, pp. 451–82. Springer-Verlag, Berlin.

Guido, W., Spear, P. D. and Tong, L. (1990a) Functional compensation in the lateral suprasylvian visual area following bilateral visual cortex damage in kittens. *Experimental Brain Research*, **83**:219–24.

Guido, W., Tong, L. and Spear, P. D. (1990b) Afferent bases of spatial- and temporal-frequency processing by neurons in the cat's posteromedial lateral suprasylvian cortex: Effects of removing areas 17:18, and 19. *Journal of Neurophysiology*, **64**:1636–51.

Guido, W., Spear, P. D. and Tong, L. (1992) How complete is the physiological compensation in extrastriate cortex after visual cortex damage in kittens? *Experimental Brain Research*, **91**:455–66.

Hilgetag, C. C., Kötter, R. and Young, M. P. (1999) Inter-hemispheric competition of sub-cortical structures is a crucial mechanism in paradoxical lesion effects and spatial neglect. *Progress in Brain Research*, **121**:125–46.

Horel, J. A. (1992) Retrieval of active visual discriminations while temporal cortex is suppressed with cold. *Behavioural Brain Research*, **51**:193–201.

Horel, J. A., Pytko-Joiner, D. E., Voytko, M. L. *et al.* (1987) The performance of visual tasks while segments of inferotemporal cortex are suppressed by cold. *Behavioural Brain Research*, **23**:29–42.

Horel, J. A., Voytko, M. L. and Salsbury, K. (1984) Visual learning suppressed by cooling the temporal lobe. *Behavioral Neuroscience*, **98**:310–24.

Hughes, H. C. and Sprague, J. M. (1986) Cortical mechanisms for local and global analysis of visual space in the cat. *Experimental Brain Research*, **61**:332–54.

Hubel, D. H. and Wiesel, T. N. (1969) Visual area of the lateral suprasylvian gyrus (Clare-Bishop area) of the cat. *Journal of Physiology (London)*, **202**:251–60.

Iwai, E. and Mishkin, M. (1969) Further evidence on the locus of the visual area in the temporal lobe of the monkey. *Experimental Neurology*, **25**:585–94.

Kalil, R. E., Tong, L. L. and Spear, P. D. (1991) Thalamic projections to the lateral suprasylvian visual area in cats with neonatal or adult visual cortex damage. *Journal of Comparative Neurology*, **314**:512–25.

Kolb, B. and Whishaw, I. Q. (1995) *Fundamentals of Human Neuropsychology*, 4th edn. W. H. Freeman, New York.

Labar, D. R., Berman, N. E. and Murphy, E. H. (1981) Short- and long-term effects of neonatal and adult visual cortex lesions on the retinal projection to the pulvinar. *Journal of Comparative Neurology*, **197**:639–59.

Lomber, S. G. (2001) Behavioral cartography of visual functions in cat parietal cortex: areal and laminar dissociations. *Progress in Brain Research*, **134**:265–84.

Lomber, S. G., Cornwell, P., Sun, J. S. *et al.* (1994) Reversible inactivation of visual processing operations in middle suprasylvian cortex of the behaving cat. *Proceedings of the National Academy of Sciences USA*, **91**:2999–3003.

Lomber, S. G., MacNeil, M. A. and Payne, B. R. (1995) Amplification of thalamic projections to middle suprasylvian cortex following ablation of immature primary visual cortex in the cat. *Cerebral Cortex*, **5**:166–91.

Lomber, S. G. and Payne, B. R. (1996) Removal of the two halves restores the whole: Reversal of visual hemineglect during bilateral cortical or collicular inactivation in the cat. *Visual Neuroscience*, **13**:1143–56.

Lomber, S. G. and Payne, B. R. (2000) Translaminar differentiation of visually guided behaviors revealed by restricted cerebral cooling deactivation. *Cerebral Cortex*, **10**:1066–77.

Lomber, S. G. and Payne, B. R. (2001a) Perinatal-lesion-induced reorganization of cerebral functions revealed by reversible cooling deactivation and attentional tasks. *Cerebral Cortex*, **11**:194–209.

Lomber, S. G. and Payne, B. R. (2001b) Task-specific reversal of visual hemineglect during reversible deactivation of posterior parietal cortex: A comparison with deactivation of the superior colliculus. *Visual Neuroscience*, **18**:487–99.

Lomber, S. G., Payne, B. R., Cornwell, P. *et al.* (1993) Capacity of the retinogeniculate pathway to reorganize following ablation of visual cortical areas in developing and mature cats. *Journal of Comparative Neurology*, **338**:432–57.

Lomber, S. G., Payne, B. R. and Cornwell, P. (1996a) Learning and recall of form discriminations during reversible cooling deactivation of ventral–posterior suprasylvian cortex in the behaving cat. *Proceedings of the National Academy of Sciences USA*, **93**:1654–8.

Lomber, S. G., Payne, B. R., Cornwell. P. *et al.* (1996b) Perceptual and cognitive visual functions of parietal and temporal cortices of the cat. *Cerebral Cortex*, **6**:673–95.

Lomber, S. G., Payne, B. R. and Horel, J. A. (1999) The cryoloop: An adaptable reversible cooling deactivation method for behavioral and electrophysiological assessment of neural function. *Journal of Neuroscience Methods*, **86**:179–94.

Lomber, S. G., Payne, B. R. and Cornwell, P. (2001) Role of the superior colliculus in analyses of space: superficial and intermediate layer contributions to visual orienting, auditory orienting, and visuospatial discriminations during unilateral and bilateral deactivations. *Journal of Comparative Neurology*, **491**:44–57.

Long, K. D., Lomber, S. G. and Payne, B. R. (1996) Increased oxidative metabolism in middle suprasylvian cortex following removal of areas 17 and 18 from newborn cats. *Experimental Brain Research*, **110**:335–46.

MacNeil, M. A., Einstein, G. E. and Payne, B. R. (1997) Transgeniculate signal transmission to middle suprasylvian extrastriate cortex in intact cats and following early removal of areas 17 and 18: A morphological study. *Experimental Brain Research*, **114**:11–23.

MacNeil, M. A., Lomber, S. G. and Payne, B. R. (1996) Rewiring of transcortical projections to middle suprasylvian cortex following early removal of cat areas 17 and 18. *Cerebral Cortex*, **6**:362–76.

Mendola, J. D. and Payne, B. R. (1993) Direction selectivity and physiological compensation in the superior colliculus following removal of areas 17 and 18. *Visual Neuroscience*, **10**:1019–26.

Milner, B. (1974) Sparing of language function after unilateral brain damage. *Neuroscience Research Program Bulletin*, **12**:213–7.

Mitchell, D. E. (2002) Behavioral analyses of primary visual cortex contributions to vision. In B. R. Payne and A. Peters (eds) *Cat Primary Visual Cortex*, pp. 655–694. Academic Press, San Diego.

Mulligan, K. and Sherk, H. (1993) A comparison of magnification functions in area 19 and the lateral suprasylvian visual area in the cat. *Experimental Brain Research*, **97**:195–208.

Murphy, E. H. and Kalil, R. E. (1979) Functional organization of lateral geniculate cells following removal of visual cortex in the newborn kitten. *Science*, **206**:713–6.

Palmer, L. A., Rosenquist, A. C. and Tusa R. J. (1978) The retinotopic organization of lateral suprasylvian visual areas in the cat. *Journal of Comparative Neurology*, **177**:237–56.

Payne, B. R. (1993) Evidence for visual cortical area homologues in cat and macaque monkey. *Cerebral Cortex*, **3**:1–25.

Payne, B. R., Connors, C. and Cornwell, P. (1991) Survival and death of neurons in cortical area PMLS after removal of areas 17:18 and 19 from cats and kittens. *Cerebral Cortex*, **1**:469–91.

Payne, B. R. and Cornwell, P. (1994) System-wide repercussions of damage to the immature visual cortex. *Trends in Neuroscience*, **17**:126–30.

Payne, B. R., Foley, H. and Lomber, S. G. (1993) Visual cortex damage-induced growth of retinal axons into the lateral posterior nucleus of the cat. *Visual Neuroscience*, **10**:747–52.

Payne, B. R. and Lomber, S. G. (1996) Age dependent modification of cytochrome oxidase activity in the cat dorsal lateral geniculate nucleus following removal of primary visual cortex. *Visual Neuroscience*, **13**:805–16.

Payne, B. R. and Lomber, S. G. (1998) Neuroplasticity in the cat's visual system: Origin, termination, expansion and increased coupling in the retino–geniculo–middle suprasylvian visual pathway following early lesions of areas 17 and 18. *Experimental Brain Research*, **121**:334–49.

Payne, B. R. and Lomber, S. G. (1999) A method to assess the functional impact of cerebra connections on target populations of neurons. *Journal of Neuroscience Methods*, **86**:195–208.

Payne, B. R. and Lomber, S. G. (2001) Training ameliorates deficits in visual detection and orienting following lesions of primary visual cortex sustained in adulthood and in infancy. *Restorative Neurology and Neuroscience*, **17**:77–88.

Payne, B. R. and Lomber, S. G. (2002) Plasticity of cerebral cortex after injury: What's different about the young brain. *The Neuroscientist*, **8**:174–185.

Payne, B. R., Lomber, S. G., Geeraerts, S. *et al.* (1996a) Reversible visual hemineglect. *Proceedings of the National Academy of Sciences USA*, **93**:290–4.

Payne, B. R., Lomber, S. G. and Gelston, C. D. (2000) Graded sparing of visually-guided orienting following primary visual cortex ablations within the first postnatal month. *Behavioral Brain Research*, **117**:1–11.

Payne, B. R., Lomber, S. G., MacNeil, M. A. *et al.* (1996b) Evidence for greater sight in blindsight following damage of primary visual cortex early in life. *Neuropsychologia*, **34**:741–74.

Payne, B.R., Lomber, S. G., Villa, A. E. *et al.* (1996c) Reversible deactivation of cortical network components. *Trends in Neurosciences*, **19**:535–42.

Payne, B. R., Pearson, H. E. and Cornwell, P. (1984) Transneuronal degeneration of beta retinal ganglion cells in the cat. *Proceedings of the Royal Society of London*, **B222**:15–32.

Payne, B. R. and Peters, A. (2002) The concept of cat primary visual cortex. In B. R. Payne and A. Peters (eds) *Cat Primary Visual Cortex*, pp. 1–130. Academic Press, San Diego.

Rowe, M. H. (1990) Evidence for degeneration of retinal W cells following early visual cortex removal in cats. *Brain, Behavior and Evolution*, **35**:253–67.

Sanides, F. and Hoffmann, J. (1969) Cyto- and myeloarchitecture of the visual cortex of the cat and the surrounding integration cortices. *Journal für Hirnforschung*, **1**:79–104.

Schoppmann, A. and Stryker, M. P. (1981) Physiological evidence that the 2-deoxyglucose method reveals orientation columns in cat visual cortex. *Nature*, **293**:574–6.

Schwark, H. D., Malpeli, J. G., Weyand, T. G. *et al.* (1986) Cat area 17. II. Response properties of infragranular layer cells in the absence of supragranular layer activity. *Journal of Neurophysiology*, **56**:1074–87.

Sherk, H. and Mulligan, K. A. (1993) A reassessment of the lower visual field map in striate-recipient lateral suprasylvian cortex. *Visual Neuroscience*, **10**:131–58.

Sherk, H., Mulligan, K. A. and Kim, J. N. (1997) Neuronal responses in extrastriate cortex to objects in optic flow fields. *Visual Neuroscience*, **14**:879–95.

Shupert, C., Cornwell, P. and Payne, B. R. (1993) Differential sparing of depth perception, orienting and optokinetic nystagmus after neonatal versus adult lesions of cortical areas 17:18 and 19 in the cat. *Behavioral Neuroscience*, **107**:633–50.

Sokoloff, L. (1981a) The deoxyglucose method for the measurement of local glucose utilization and the mapping of local functional activity in the central nervous system. *International Review of Neurobiology*, **22**:287–333.

Sokoloff, L. (1981b) The F.O. Schmitt Lecture in Neuroscience 1980. The relationship between function and energy metabolism: its use in the localization of functional activity in the nervous system. *Neuroscience Research Program Bulletin*, **19**:159–207.

Sokoloff, L., Reivich, M., Kennedy, C. *et al.* (1977) (^{14}C) Deoxyglucose method for the measurement of local cerebral glucose utilization: theory, procedure, and normal values in the conscious and anesthetized albino rat. *Journal of Neurochemistry*, **44**:295–311.

Spear, P. D. and Baumann, T. P. (1975) Receptive field characteristics of single neurons in lateral suprasylvian visual area of the cat. *Journal of Neurophysiology*, **38**:1403–20.

Spear, P. D. and Baumann, T. P. (1979) Effects of visual cortex removal on the receptive field properties of neurons in lateral suprasylvian visual area of the cat. *Journal of Neurophysiology*, **42**:31–56.

Spear, P. D., Kalil, R. E. and Tong, L. (1980) Functional compensation in lateral suprasylvian visual area following neonatal visual cortex removal in cats. *Journal of Neurophysiology*, **43**:851–69.

Sun, J.-S., Lomber, S. G. and Payne, B. R. (1994) Expansion of suprasylvian cortex projections in the superficial layers of the superior colliculus following damage of areas 17 and 18 in developing cats. *Visual Neuroscience*, **11**:13–22.

Teuber, H.-L. (1975) Recovery of function after brain injury in man. In *Outcome of severe damage to the nervous system*, Ciba Foundation Symposium 34, Elsevier North-Holland, Amsterdam.

Tong, L., Kalil, R. E. and Spear, P. D. (1984) Critical periods for functional and anatomical compensation in the lateral suprasylvian visual area following removal of visual cortex in cats. *Journal of Neurophysiology*, **52**:941–60.

Tong, L., Spear, P. D., Kalil, R. E. *et al.* (1982) Loss of retinal X cells in cats with neonatal or adult visual cortex damage. *Science*, **217**:72–5.

Tumosa, N., McCall, M. A., Guido, W. *et al.* (1989) Responses of lateral geniculate neurons that survive long-term visual cortex damage in kittens and adult cats. *Journal of Neuroscience*, **9**:280–98.

Tusa, R. J. and Palmer, L. A. (1980) Retinotopic organization of areas 20 and 21 in the cat. *Journal of Comparative Neurology*, **193**:147–64.

von Grünau, M. W., Zumbroich, T. J. and Poulin, C. (1987) Visual receptive field properties in the posterior suprasylvian cortex of the cat: a comparison between the areas PMLS and PLLS. *Vision Research*, **27**:343–56.

Wimborne, B. M. and Henry, G. H. (1992) Response characteristics of cells of cortical area 21a of the cat with special reference to orientation specificity. *Journal of Physiology (London)*, **449**:457–78.

Zumbroich, T. J. and Blakemore, C. (1987) Spatial and temporal selectivity in the suprasylvian visual cortex of the cat. *Journal of Neuroscience*, **7**:482–500.

Chapter 8

Dissecting the Organization of Cortical and Subcortical Circuits for Skilled Limb Movement Control in Development and Maturity with Reversible Inactivation

John H. Martin, Claude Ghez

Introduction

Production of even the simplest movement recruits into action the multiple components of the supraspinal motor systems, including many cortical areas and subcortical motor nuclei, as well as the various descending motor pathways. The task of elucidating the contributions of the different components of the motor systems is complex. Knowledge of the anatomical organization of neural systems has traditionally provided important insights into function. Numerous anatomical studies in mature animals have shown a high degree of connectional specificity within the motor systems. However, the connections of the components of the motor systems are not sufficiently distinct from one another to provide clear insight into their particular roles in limb movement control or posture. For example, several frontal premotor areas each have direct spinal projections to the intermediate zone and ventral horn (He *et al.* 1993). On the basis of termination patterns this information provides little insight into the particular sets of function of one area compared with another, apart from a role in limb or trunk control.

An important experimental tool for the analysis of the functions of the supraspinal motor systems is the reversible lesion technique: cooling or pharmacological inactivation. Performance can be compared immediately before, during, and following inactivation, thereby allowing animals to serve as their own controls. In addition, by examining performance immediately after the start of the inactivation, insufficient time is available for the motor system to engage adaptive mechanisms. The ensuing behavioral changes produced by inactivation may thus more closely reflect the lost function of the inactivated structure rather than a compensatory response of the remaining intact structures (Brooks 1990; Lomber 1999). Reversible inactivation is also a more practical approach than irreversible lesions because it can be routinely applied to multiple sites.

Study of the functional organization of the motor systems has traditionally focused on the analysis of neural circuitry and behavior in mature animals and humans. However, as we have seen for various sensory systems (Goodman and Shatz 1993), study of the changing anatomical and functional organization of the immature brain also can be a fruitful approach for elucidating functional organization. Motor behavior lacks precision and refinement in immaturity (Lawrence and Hopkins 1976; Konczak et al. 1995; Konczak et al. 1997) and development of the skills needed for task efficacy occurs only after a prolonged period (Napier 1980). Reversible inactivation also can be exploited in the developing motor systems to gain insight into the role of *activity-dependent* processes in shaping the changes in motor system connections and functions that occur during early postnatal life. Neural inactivation of circumscribed portions of the developing brain and can be maintained for several weeks, as the motor systems mature and as motor skills normally develop.

In this chapter, we will first briefly review an established method for producing acute reversible pharmacological inactivation of cortical areas and subcortical nuclei, and then consider several key technical issues. We will next examine application of this approach to the motor cortical and cerebellar control of prehension in the cat. Finally, we will describe a novel use of chronic reversible inactivation for studying the anatomical and functional development of the cortical motor systems (Martin et al. 1999; Martin et al. 2000b). Since pharmacological inactivation can be maintained for extened periods of time, it is well suited for examining the role of activity-dependent plasticity during development of the motor systems and in the long-term acquisition of motor skills. While continuous blockade has been used in the visual system (Reiter and Stryker 1988; Shatz and Stryker 1988), this is the first application of the approach for the motor cortex (Martin et al. 1999; Martin and Lee 1999).

Drug injection methodology

Acute pharmacological inactivation has been used successfully to analyze the neural mechanisms involved in limb motor control. We have developed an injection cannula with an indwelling electrode (Fig. 8.1) (Martin et al. 1993, 2000a; Martin and Ghez 1993; Cooper et al. 2000). The cannula is connected to an infusion pump with flexible polyethylene or teflon tubing. Other groups have developed similar approaches for injecting drugs (Dias and Segraves 1997); for review, see (Martin and Ghez 1999). Because of its narrow outside diameter (200 μm), this cannula produces minimal tissue damage. The presence of an electrode in the cannula allows for concurrent recording of neural activity and for microstimulation in the region of the injection.

A common problem with drug microinjection is cannula blockage. The lumen of an injection cannula is small, which can lead to clogging, and the injection pressure is low, which may not overcome an occlusion. Without adequate monitoring of injection volume, failure to inject the drug can go unnoticed. This situation develops because most injection systems can accommodate the small increase in volume that would occur if the cannula were to become blocked during an injection. Consider, for example, a 1 μl injection. The volume of this injection is equal to 1 mm³, which is approximately 0.1% of the total volume of 0.5 m of polyethylene tubing (PE 240). We monitor volume by tinting the drug with a dye and tracking movement of the interface between the drug and the oil used for filling the injection system. This is accomplished through the viewing port, located distal to the flexible tubing, just before the metal cannula (see Fig. 8.1). Another check for the absence of a blockage is noting the reduction in recorded neural activity that occurs when a fluid is injected into the brain, as neural tissue is displaced from the electrode tip.

Several classes of drugs are effective as inactivating agents: sodium channel blockers, inhibitory neurotransmitters, and excitatory neurotransmitter antagonists. Sodium channel blockers inactivate tracts and nuclear regions, whereas drugs that promote synaptic inhibition or prevent excitation are selective for nuclear regions. Sodium channel blockers prevent action potential initiation and conduction both in neuronal cell bodies and axons (Hille 1992), because Na^+ channels are located there. Moreover, Na^+ channels are abundant in neurons in virtually all parts of the nervous system. Sodium channel blockers are the only agents suitable for inactivating neural pathways in the white matter (Sandkühler et al. 1987). The two commonly used Na^+ channel blockers are local anesthetics (e.g., lidocaine) and tetrodotoxin (TTX).

Inhibitory neurotransmitters and their agonists hyperpolarize neurons thereby preventing action potential generation. These agents selectively inactivate neuronal cell bodies, where their receptors are located, and not passing axons. The major inhibitory neurotransmitters in the central nervous system are GABA—through actions primarily on the $GABA_A$ and $GABA_B$ receptors—and glycine. Since the glycine and the $GABA_B$ receptors have a limited distribution in supraspinal structures, such as an absence in several diencephalic and telencephalic regions (e.g., Araki et al. 1988; Chu et al. 1990; Sato et al. 1991), we and others have mainly used GABA and $GABA_A$ agonists. $GABA_A$ agonists increase chloride conduction (Hille 1992). GABA (and its agonists) hyperpolarizes neurons because the chloride equilibrium potential is negative relative to the resting membrane potential. Excitatory neurotransmitter blockade also can be effective for nuclear inactivation. When excitatory transmission is dominated by a particular transmitter such a glutamate, blockade ought to effectively inactivate the injected structure.

The duration of pharmacological actions of inactivating drugs varies. Only short-acting drugs permit collection of post-inactivation data during the same behavioral session. Local anesthetics have short duration behavioral effects (15–60 min. in nuclei and 1–2 hours in tracts; (Sandkühler et al. 1987), while TTX can have effects that last up to several days (Zhuravin and Bures 1991; Beloozerova and Sirota 1993). GABA itself also has a short duration behavioral effect (Fig. 8.2) (Martin et al. 1993). By contrast, the behavioral effects of muscimol can persist for up to 24 hours depending on the dose (Martin et al. 1993). The duration of any drug's effect depends on several factors, including receptor binding affinity (e.g., muscimol has a much greater affinity for

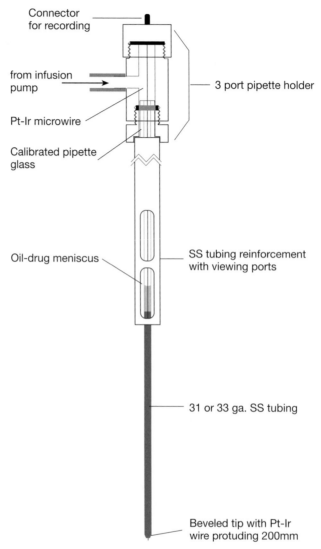

Connector for recording

from infusion pump

Pt-Ir microwire

Calibrated pipette glass

Oil-drug meniscus

3 port pipette holder

SS tubing reinforcement with viewing ports

31 or 33 ga. SS tubing

Beveled tip with Pt-Ir wire protuding 200mm

Fig. 8.1 Microinjection cannula. Inactivation probe for pressure injection of drug with capacity for concurrent visual monitoring of injected volume and electrophysiologic testing. Stainless steel hypodermic tubing (33 ga., OD: 200 µm, ID: 100 µm or 31 ga., OD: 260 µm, ID: 130 µm) is glued to a short length of glass pipette with a calibrated internal diameter. The pipette is reinforced using wide diameter stainless steel tubing. Large windows are ground into the tubing, using a Dremel drill, to create a viewing port for monitoring movement of the meniscus (i.e., drug flow into the cannula). The tip of the cannula is beveled concentrically to facilitate piercing the pia. The cannula is protected by a 26 ga. guide tube (not shown), which is used to pierce the dura but does not penetrate the brain. By using a calibrated pipette with a narrow inner diameter, 1 µL of drug can correspond to 1 or more cms of travel. The cannula is connected to a microsyringe by 0.5–1.0 m length of polyethylene tubing. The system is first filled

the $GABA_A$ receptor than GABA) and the method of degradation or glial uptake (Krogsgaard-Larsen and Johnston 1978).

The spatial distribution of injected drug, both spread and volume, can be determined by injecting radioactive isotopes of inactivating drugs (Fig. 8.3) (Martin 1991). We have found that the distributions of injected lidocaine and muscimol are different (Martin 1991). The radius of a lidocaine (1 μL) injection decreases quickly (Fig. 8.3A1). By contrast, the radius of a muscimol injection (1 μL) changed minimally over a

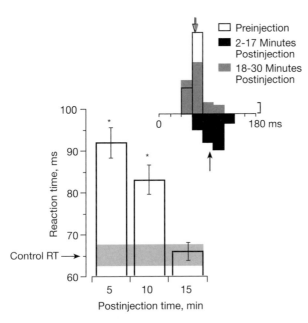

Fig. 8.2 Short duration of action of GABA. The bar graph shows the time course of reaction time prolongation during red nucleus inactivation produced by GABA. Mean reaction time for successive 5 min blocks following injection (26 μg GABA in 1 μL saline). Asterisks indicate blocks in which reaction time was significantly different from control values. The horizontal gray bar shows the mean preinjection control reaction time (65 ms ± 1 SD). Inset shows the distributions of reaction times during the preinjection control period (open bars; open arrow at mean, 64 ± 9 ms), the immediate postinjection period (black bars; black arrow at mean, 95 ± 18 ms), and the late postinjection (recovery) period (gray bars; gray arrow at mean, 63 ± 9 ms). See Martin *et al.* (1993) for details regarding behavioral paradigm and results.

Fig. 8.1 (continued)
with mineral oil and the aqueous drug solution is backfilled into the cannula. In this injection system, which we developed, one can visually monitor the movement of the meniscus at the aqueous drug-oil interface through a pipette (with a calibrated internal diameter) mounted between the hypodermic needle cannula and the polyethylene tubing. The drug is injected by controlled advance of the syringe plunger, either by using an infusion pump or manually.

A1 Lidocaine

B1 Muscimol

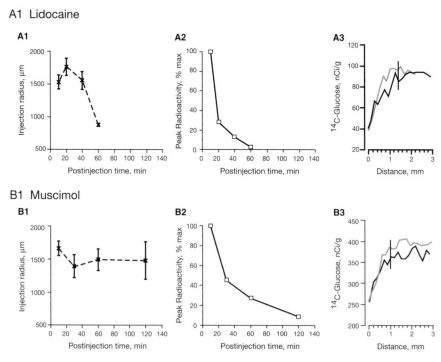

Fig. 8.3 Autoradiographic estimation of spread of ^{14}C-lidocaine (A) and ^{3}H-muscimol (B). In separate experiments, we injected tracer amounts of ^{14}C-lidocaine and ^{3}H-muscimol, together with unlabeled drug (40 μg/μL lidocaine; 1 μg/μL muscimol) into sensorimotor cortex of anesthetized rats. (A1, B1) The injection radius, measured to background radioactivity levels, in relation to postinjection time. The maximal radius of the lidocaine injection was 1,775 μm (at 10 min) and for muscimol, 1,660 μm. (A2, B2) The decline in peak radioactivity at the injection center. (A3, B3) The averaged glucose radioactivity (across 4 sections) through layer 5 through the center of the injection site. The black and grey line plot show radioactivity values lateral and medial to the injection center. The short vertical black lines mark the extrapolated radius of hypometabolism surrounding the center of the injection. Maximal reduction for lidocaine was 48%, which was below white matter levels (30 nCi/g compared with 51 nCi/g for white matter). Maximal reduction for muscimol was 43%, which was within 22% of white matter (275 nCi/g compared with 224 nCi/g for white matter). Data are replotted from Martin (1991).

2-hour test period (Fig. 8.3B1). Peak radioactivity, corresponding to the injection center, diminished over 1–2 hours after injection for both drugs (Fig. 8.3A2, B2), although muscimol (which has long-duration physiological and behavioral effects) radioactivity level remained significantly above background.

The physiological effects of inactivating drugs can be determined by recording the reduction in unit activity or glucose metabolism following injection. Glucose is the sole source of energy for neurons and measured glucose (or deoxyglucose) utilization correlates well with neuronal firing in many systems (Schwartz *et al.* 1979; Mata *et al.* 1980). We have used the metabolic approach (Martin 1991), which has the advantage of providing a high-resolution spatial image of drug effects. Figure 8.3 (A3 and B3) shows ^{14}C-glucose uptake in the region of a lidocaine (A3) and muscimol (B3) injection. Both lidocaine and muscimol reduced glucose metabolism; maximal hypometabolism was consistently observed at the injection center. Glucose metabolism increases progressively from the injection center, reaching a plateau within 2 mm. The vertical bars mark the radius of hypometabolism extrapolated from the injection center. This distance may correspond to the direct actions of the inactivating drug on local neurons. For lidocaine, this distance was 1.4 mm, which is less than the width of the injection monitored using radiolabeled lidocaine. The extrapolated radius for muscimol was 1.0 mm, also less than the radius measured using radiolabeled drug (1.66 mm). These findings suggest that the radius of inactivation may be slightly less than the radius of drug spread. We also found that glucose metabolism was reduced by approximately 5%–10% for several mm beyond the extrapolated radius of hypometabolism (Martin 1991). This reduction may have been due to disfacilitation of local cortico-cortical connections induced by focal injection of lidocaine or muscimol. The results of our drug spread and glucose metabolic studies show that the injection technique is effective in applying drug to a circumscribed area of the brain and producing a focal decrease in function.

We have described drug injection parameters (volume, rate, etc.) for acute inactivation in detail elsewhere (Martin and Ghez 1999). Here we briefly consider three critical methodological issues that are relevant in designing reversible inactivation experiments to analyze functional localization.

Inactivation induction time and stability of effects

Simple blockade of sodium channels or the synaptic effects described above should have an immediate effect, after one takes into account injection time and local diffusion. Therefore, the onset of behavioral changes induced by the inactivation should occur within minutes of the onset of the injection (see Fig. 8.2). When an immediate effect does not occur it cannot be explained by drug spread, since the maximal injection width is achieved within minutes after injection (see Fig. 8.3A1, B1). Such delayed behavioral changes produced by the injection could reflect more complex effects on the circuits of which these neurons are part. For example, a delayed response may reflect the time needed to disfacilitate a sufficiently large population of neurons that are the targets of those at the injection site. Such transsynaptic effects at a distance from the injection site have been observed using metabolic mapping following intrastriatal (Kelly and McCulloch 1984) and intranigral (Dermon et al. 1990) muscimol injection.

A related issue is whether the phenotype of the defect produced by drug injection remains stable during the post-injection period. We have reported that inactivation of the forelimb representation of the caudal subregion of motor cortex with muscimol produces an immediate slowing of prehension, but without impairing performance. However, significant aiming (and trajectory adaptation) defects occur only an hour or more later (Martin and Ghez 1993). The phenotype of this late effect is similar to that seen immediately after inactivation of the adjoining rostrolateral subregion (Fig. 8.4).

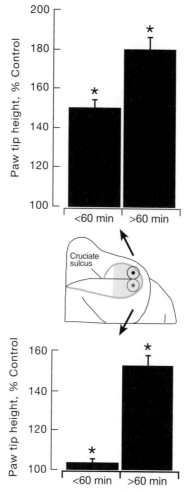

Fig. 8.4 Effects of prolonged inactivation of the lateral portions of the rostral and caudal sub-regions of motor cortex. Histograms show increase in paw tip height (as percent control) during rostral (black bars) and caudal (gray bars) motor cortex inactivation. The grayed region over the lateral portion of the motor cortex corresponds approximately to the portions of the forelimb representations on the surface of the frontal lobe. The histograms show that less than 60 min after injection, inactivation of caudal motor cortex did not produce overreaching, while at times greater than 60 min, overreaching was present, and similar to that seen during the first 60 min of inactivation of rostral motor cortex. Asterisks indicate significant increases ($p < 0.001$).

It is therefore difficult to ascribe the same motor control functions on the basis of defect phenotype to these two motor cortex subregions when the time course of effects is so different. This late effect of caudal motor cortex inactivation cannot be explained by spread because muscimol radioactivity drops to background levels at about 1.5 mm from the injection center (see Fig. 8.3B3). Considering the similarity of deficits, this late effect could be due to disfacilitation of neurons in rostral motor cortex resulting from the reduced activity of cortico-cortical projections from caudal motor cortex (Yumiya and Ghez 1983; Keller 1993). This finding also shows that spatial localization using muscimol inhibition can be less precise at long postinjection intervals (see section on effect of inactivation of adjoining structures, below).

Neural inactivation versus neurotransmitter receptor subtype blockade

With pharmacological inactivation, it is necessary to determine if the effect is due to blocking a structure's ability to initiate and/or conduct action potentials or to blocking excitation of input paths to the structure. Muscimol is routinely used to hyperpolarize neurons because the $GABA_A$ receptor is ubiquitous throughout the central nervous system and it tightly binds to its receptor and produces strong hyperpolarization. Glutamatergic blockade may be more difficult to interpret. For example, while blockade of non-NMDA glutamate action will certainly depress firing, this may not inactivate the injected structure, allowing some non-NMDA-mediated excitation (Miller *et al.* 1989). Moreover, the action of other excitatory neurotransmitters, such as acetylcholine, would be unaffected.

Effect of inactivation of adjoining structures

Spatial localization of drug effects is key to interpreting the results of inactivation. Since an injection width is several mm (Fig. 8.3), it is essential to ascertain that the observed effects result from inactivation of the targeted structure and not to inactivation of adjacent sites. Autoradiographic methods measuring drug spread, described above, define the upper limits of the direct effects of the injected compound on neural tissue. Drug injection into adjoining structures is an effective way of determining the localization of effects of inactivation. Both the absence of an effect of inactivating an adjoining structure, or production of a different effect, confirm the spatial specificity of behavioral changes during inactivation.

Differential contributions of cortical and subcortical structures to the control of skilled arm movements

Reversible inactivation is well suited for elucidating the contributions of the various components of the motor systems to movement control. Behavioral data can be collected before, during, and, depending on the drug used, immediately after inactivation (i.e., recovery). This allows each animal to serve as its own control. In addition, multiple structures, or adjacent regions within the same structure, can be inactivated in the same animal. The ability to dissociate the effects of inactivation at one site from those of other sites makes it possible to verify the spatial specificity of changes in performance produced by inactivation.

We have used reversible inactivation to address the question of the differential contributions of cortical motor areas and subcortical nuclei to controlling skilled forelimb movement in the cat (Martin and Ghez 1993). We have focused on inactivation of the forelimb representations of the anterior and posterior interpositus (IP) nuclei and the primary motor cortex, which receives its major subcortical input, via the lateral thalamus, from these cerebellar nuclei (Rispal-Padel and Latreille 1974; Shinoda *et al.* 1985; Jörntell and Ekerot 1999).

The forelimb representations in subcortical nuclei are small, approximately 1 to 2 mm in diameter (Ghez 1975, Robinson *et al.* 1987). Thus, the drug injection we described above (Fig. 8.3) would be expected to completely inactivate such representations. This is apt not be the case for the forelimb areas of motor cortex because the representations are larger. Indeed, within the motor cortex there are functionally distinct rostral and caudal subregions that are separated by several millimeters (Pappas and Strick 1981a,b; Strick and Preston 1982; Martin and Ghez 1993). Within each subregion, a given muscle or joint is represented at multiple sites (Pappas and Strick 1981a,b; Sato and Tanji 1989; Schmidt and McIntosh 1990; Martin and Ghez 1993). The practical significance of this organization is that focal inactivation of a single site in which particular forelimb muscles and joints are represented could spare other sites in motor cortex where those parts are also represented.

Role of primary motor cortex in trajectory control during reaching

The motor cortex subregions receive differential inputs (Yumiya and Ghez 1983) and have differential spinal projections (Martin 1996). Within rostral motor cortex, lateral and medial sites are differentially influenced by the anterior and posterior interpositus nuclei (Rispal-Padel and Latreille 1974; Shinoda *et al.* 1985; Jörntell and Ekerot 1999). We used reversible inactivation to elucidate whether sites in rostral MC, where forelimb muscles are represented, have different motor control functions (Martin and Ghez 1993). The behavior we used to study this problem is prehension. Animals were trained to reach into a narrow tube to grasp and retrieve a small piece of beef (Gorska and Sybirska 1980; Alstermark *et al.* 1981; Martin *et al.* 1995; Ghez *et al.* 1996; Cooper *et al.* 2000). We showed that cats use visuo-spatial information from the target to scale elbow joint excursions and velocity to control reach height during task performance. The strategy that the cats use to scale movement height is similar to multijoint strategies that have been described in other prehension tasks in cats (Pettersson *et al.* 1997; Perfiliev *et al.* 1998) as well as humans (e.g., Jeannerod 1984; Jakobson and Goodale 1991). Control of scaled elbow excursions is coordinated with motions at the other forelimb joints, which keeps the paw path straight as the limb is lifted to the height of the target (Martin *et al.* 1995; Ghez *et al.* 1996; Cooper *et al.* 2000). Straight distal joint and hand paths are general characteristics of reaching in our task as well as reaching in humans (Morasso 1981).

The small size of the inactivated region, 2–3 mm radius from the injection center (Fig. 8.3), enables selective inactivation of discrete portions within the forelimb representation. Within motor cortex, sites representing the paw are located laterally (Pappas and Strick 1981b; Armstrong and Drew 1985), while sites representing the wrist, elbow, and shoulder are located throughout the entire forelimb region, both medially and laterally.

Our studies of motor cortex have shown that only inactivation of sites within the rostral subregion produce immediate, and distinctive prehension impairments. As briefly described above (Fig. 8.4), inactivation within the caudal subregion produces delayed prehension defects that may be due to indirect actions on sites in rostral motor cortex. Immediately following muscimol injection at sites in *rostrolateral motor cortex*, where the paw and proximal forelimb joints are co-represented, there was a systematic aiming defect and impaired grasping. A characteristic result of inactivations in this subregion is that the animal reached above the tube (Fig. 8.5A1; note the black paw-tip and wrist paths are higher than the control gray paths). Overreaching is due to impaired control of the elbow joint in raising the wrist and paw to the height of the tube (Kably *et al.* 1996).

In animals trained to reach around an obstacle (bar) that was placed unexpectedly in the movement path (Martin and Ghez 1993), rostrolateral motor cortex inactivation also produced an impairment in trajectory adaptation (Fig. 8.5A2). Wrist paths for obstructed reaches correspond to the thick lines; the small circle corresponds to the location of the bar. Unobstructed trials before and during inactivation (thin gray and black lines) are shown for comparison. For the control (pre-inactivation), obstructed trials (thick, gray), the limb hits the bar during the first obstructed reach (not shown) but on all subsequent reaches, the wrist clears the obstruction with a safety margin. By contrast, during inactivation the wrist bumps into the bar and is subsequently dragged over it on the first and all subsequent obstructed trials. Note the absence of clearance on the wrist paths.

Inactivation of sites in *rostromedial motor cortex*—where only the shoulder, elbow, and wrist are represented (and not the paw)—produce paw paths that were hypometric. Note reduced height of black wrist and tip path compared with controls. The paths also showed an increase in curvature during the latter part of the reach due to impaired control at the wrist joint. These sites were located approximately 2.5 mm medial to the sites where the paw is represented, and where overreaching was produced during inactivation. Hoffman and Strick (1995) have reported that irreversible motor cortex lesions in monkeys also produced systematic wrist trajectory errors. Inactivation of rostromedial motor cortex did not produce a trajectory adaptation impairment (Fig. 8.5B2). While wrist paths were more variable during than prior to inactivation, the safety margin between the obstacle and the wrist was maintained for most trials.

Pharmacological inactivation permitted systematic exploration of the functional organization of the forelimb areas of motor cortex. In this way, the effects of inactivating the two motor cortex regions were dissociated from each other and from those at

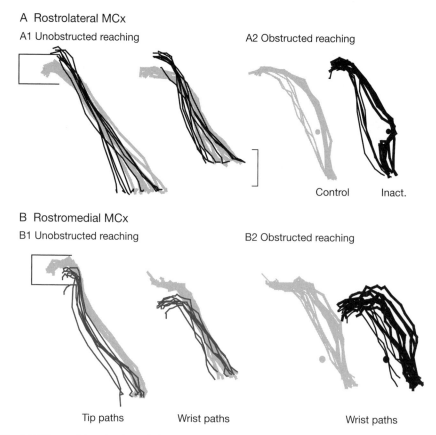

A Rostrolateral MCx

A1 Unobstructed reaching

A2 Obstructed reaching

Control   Inact.

B Rostromedial MCx

B1 Unobstructed reaching

B2 Obstructed reaching

Tip paths   Wrist paths   Wrist paths

Fig. 8.5 Effects of inactivation of sites in the forelimb representations of motor cortex. (A) Lateral portion of rostral subregion, where all forelimb joints are represented. (B) Medial portion of rostral subregion, where only the proximal forelimb joints are represented. Each part of the figure shows wrist and paw paths for preinjection control (gray) and postinjection test (black) trials. (A1, B1) Unobstructed reaches. (A2, B2) Wrist paths of obstructed reaches are shown as thick lines and unobstructed reaches (for comparison), are shown as thin lines. Calibration: 5 cm.

adjacent caudal sites. The presence of distinctive effects of inactivation of the various forelimb representations in motor cortex is strong evidence for localization of different movement control functions. For example, overreaching produced by rostrolateral motor cortex inactivation could reflect a role for this sector in aiming (Martin and Ghez 1993), while the path curvature changes produced by rostromedial motor cortex inactivation points to a role in interjoint coordination (Martin *et al.* 1995). We also dissociated the roles of lateral and medial sectors in trajectory adaptation (Martin and Ghez 1993). The trajectory changes produced by inactivation of medial and lateral portions of rostral motor cortex (overreaching, under-reaching, increased path curvature) are due to impaired control of muscles/joints that are represented throughout rostral motor cortex. The presence of differential effects of inactivation in rostral motor cortex shows that the multiple sites in this region that represent the same muscle are not redundant but rather participate in controlling different trajectory features (e.g., aiming, coordination).

Functional output channels from the interposed nuclei to the motor cortex

The forelimb representations of motor cortex (both rostrally and caudally) receive their major subcortical inputs from the anterior and posterior interpositus nuclei, via ventral thalamic relays (Rispal-Padel and Grangetto 1977; Rispal-Padel and Latreille 1974; Anderson and DeVito 1987). We used reversible inactivation of anterior and posterior interpositus to determine if the different effects of inactivation of the rostro-medial and rostrolateral sectors of motor cortex reflect different patterns of functional connections from these nuclei. Correlating impairment phenotypes produced by inactivation of the cerebellar nuclei with those produced by inactivation of different motor cortex sectors could provide insight into how subcortical control signals from these nuclei are routed to different motor cortex subregions for controlling different aspects of movement.

We compared the effects of selective inactivation of the anterior and posterior inter-positus nuclei on reaching with those produced by rostral motor cortex inactivation, which we described above. While inactivation of these structures has diverse effects on prehension, including increased curvature, terminal inaccuracy, and ataxia (Martin *et al.* 1995, Ghez *et al.* 1996, Cooper *et al.* 2000), we have focused on defects in control-ling the height of the reach and trajectory adaptation. Posterior interpositus inactiva-tion (Fig. 8.6A1) produced overreaching (black tip and wrist paths), similar to that produced by inactivating the lateral portion of rostral motor cortex (Fig. 8.5A). On the other hand, anterior interpositus inactivation produced under-reaching (Fig. 8.6B1), which is similar to that produced by inactivating the medial portion of rostral motor cortex (Fig. 8.5B). These distinctive effects of cerebellar nuclear inactivation occurred when injection sites were as close as 2 mm, suggesting that the width of the zone of inactivation is less than that of drug spread, based on autoradiography.

When we looked at trajectory adaptation, we found that inactivation of anterior (Fig. 8.6B2) but not posterior (Fig. 8.6B1) interpositus produced a trajectory adapta-tion impairment. Thus, the trajectory changes produced by anterior interpositus inac-tivation were similar to those produced by rostromedial motor cortex inactivation, but the adaptation defect was similar to rostrolateral motor cortex inactivation. Figure 8.7 summarizes the kinds of defects produced at the different sites. Our findings suggest that posterior and anterior interpositus nuclei could influence different rostral motor cortical sectors in complex, but limited, ways to play distinctive roles in trajectory control. The presence of similarities in impairment phenotypes produced by cerebellar and motor cortex inactivation is consistent with the hypothesis that there are distinct

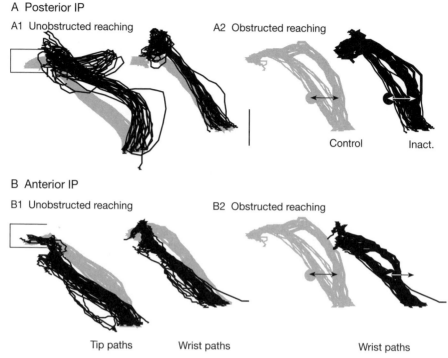

A Posterior IP

A1 Unobstructed reaching

A2 Obstructed reaching

Control   Inact.

B Anterior IP

B1 Unobstructed reaching

B2 Obstructed reaching

Tip paths   Wrist paths   Wrist paths

Fig. 8.6 Effects of inactivation of sites in the forelimb representations of posterior (A) and anterior (B) interpositus (IP) nuclei. Layout is similar to Fig. 8.5. (A1, B1) Unobstructed reaches. (A2, B2) Obstructed reaches. Calibration: 5 cm.

functional cerebellar output channels that link cell groups in the anterior and posterior interpositus with interconnected downstream targets in motor cortex. Overreaching is common to inactivation of posterior interpositus and rostrolateral motor cortex, implying a functional link from one to the other. Under-reaching is associated with inactivation of anterior interpositus and rostromedial motor cortex, which also imply a link, but the trajectory adaptation defect is associated with anterior interpositus and rostrolateral motor cortex, implying a different link.

Electrophysiological studies provide support for this idea. For example, Jörntell and Ekerot (1999) have shown that stimulation of anterior interpositus nucleus produced extracellular field potentials in a territory that overlapped the medial and lateral rostral motor cortex sites. The projection to more medial sites could be important in inter-joint coordination for trajectory control and, to lateral sites, for trajectory adaptation. By contrast, stimulation of posterior interpositus nucleus produced extracellular field potentials selectively in lateral cortex, helping to explain why inactivation of either site produces overreaching. By mapping the sites that produce other impairments, other patterns of functional connections could be revealed.

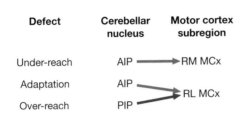

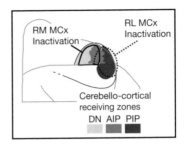

Fig. 8.7 Summary of defects (left) produced by anterior (AIP) and posterior (PIP) interpositus nucleus inactivation, base on finding of Martin *et al.* (2000), and by inactivation of rostromedial motor cortex (RM MCx) and rostrolateral motor cortex (RL MCx), based on findings of Martin and Ghez (1993). Semi-schematic representation (right) of cerebello–cortical projection zones in area 4 of the cat (based on Rispal-Padel and Latreille 1974; Shinoda *et al.* 1985; Jörntell and Ekerot 1999) together with ensemble locations of inactivation sites in motor cortex (Martin and Ghez 1993). RM MCx injections are represented by thick solid black line, and RL MCx motor cortex injections by the dashed line. Cerebello–cortical receiving zone for AIP is based on Fig. 9 of Jörntell and Ekerot (1999). PIP and dentate nucleus (DN) zones are more schematic and are also based on published findings (Rispal-Padel and Latreille 1974; Shinoda *et al.* 1985; Jörntell and Ekerot 1999). Overlap between adjacent zones is not shown. Thin solid (and dashed) line is the approximate border between area 4 and adjoining somatic sensory and premotor areas. Jörntell and Ekerot (1999) reported that short latency cutaneous inputs are received primarily rostral to the AIP area as well as lateral and caudal to the PIP area. (Modified from Martin *et al.* 2000).

Use of prolonged inactivation to probe activity-dependent development of the corticospinal system and skilled limb movement

Pharmacological inactivation, while typically used acutely for studying motor control processes, also can be used to block activity continuously to examine long-term control functions. This approach has been used to examine activity-dependent development of the visual system, with blockade of retinal ganglion cells, and the primary visual cortex (for review, see Shatz, 1990; Goodman and Shatz 1993). Activity-dependent processes are much less well understood in the developing motor systems. We have recently used continuous reversible inactivation to examine activity-dependent processes governing the early postnatal development of corticospinal connections and development of prehension skills (Martin *et al.* 1999, 2000b). Here we describe use of continuous blockade of the sensory-motor cortex to examine features of corticospinal system development that depend on neural activity (Martin *et al.* 1999). The same techniques that we describe for continuous neural blockade during development also could be applied to the study of acquisition of motor skills in maturity.

Although methods for acute inactivation offer fine control of the inactivated region, they are impractical for long-term blockade because they require daily injections. We produced long-term blockade of a circumscribed portion of motor cortex by

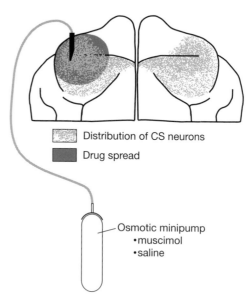

Fig. 8.8 Method for continuous intracortical drug or saline infusion. Osmotic pump (Alza Corp.) is implanted between the scapulae and connected to an implanted cannula (27 gauge) centered in the forelimb area of motor cortex. Dark gray form corresponds to approximate region of drug spread. The approximate distribution and density of corticospinal neurons is shown by the light gray stippling.

continuous infusion of the $GABA_A$ agonist muscimol, using an osmotic pump (Alza Corp.; Fig. 8.8). This method, which has also been used in the visual system, produces a much larger inactivated region than with acute injections (Fig. 8.8; dark gray territory) The pump was connected to an intracortical cannula (28 ga. hypodermic tubing) with vinyl tubing. The cannula was implanted at a depth of 3 mm below the pial surface, and the mounting assembly was fixed to the bone with screws and dental acrylic. The cannula tip was beveled, with the lumen oriented medially to facilitate flow in that direction (M. Stryker, pers. comm.). A more detailed description of the implantation procedure has been published (Martin *et al.* 1999). In our developmental studies, we initially used a high infusion rate (2.2 µL/hour) but have since begun to use a slower rate (0.56 µL/hour), with similar results. A key control in these experiments is saline infusion at the same sites and at the same rates and durations.

Long-term muscimol infusion did not produce a specific lesion, but in the neonatal animal, did produce morphological changes in cortex (Martin *et al.* 1999). There were quantitative changes in the local sulcal patterns, and at the microscopic level, changes in the thickness of, and density of neurons in, certain laminae (Fig. 8.9A, B). We estimated the spread of muscimol by monitoring local metabolic changes as reflected in the levels of the mitochondrial enzyme cytochrome oxidase (Wong-Riley 1979). Cytochrome oxidase activity levels, detected histochemically by monitoring substrate oxidation using a peroxidase reaction, change over the course of a week or more after cessation of neural activity (Wong-Riley 1979). Significant reductions in staining were observed up to 8 mm caudal and 7 mm rostral to the site of injection (Fig. 8.9C, D). These distances are comparable to those reported by Hata and Stryker (1994) for loss of visually-evoked activity in the primary visual cortex.

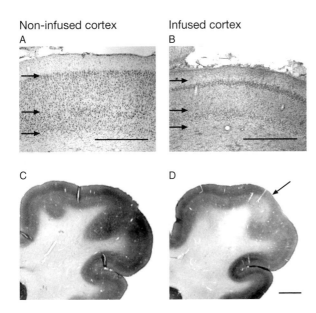

Non-infused cortex   Infused cortex

A   B

C   D

Fig. 8.9 Morphological changes following muscimol infusion between postnatal days 21 and 50 (see Martin *et al.* 2000 for details). (A) Sagittal Nissl-stained section through cortex contralateral to infusion site in PD 55 animal. (B) Similar to (A) but within 1 mm of the infusion site. (C, D) Cytochrome oxidase staining through the noninfused (C) side of cortex and (D) within 1 mm of the infusion site. Arrow points to the site of maximally-reduced cytochrome oxidase staining at the injection site. Calibrations: A, B 1 mm; C, D 2 mm.

The topography of corticospinal terminations is shaped by activity-dependent competition

Several studies have shown that the laterality of corticospinal terminations is refined postnatally (Theriault and Tatton 1989; Alisky *et al.* 1992). At postnatal day (PD) 21, when corticospinal terminations are well-established in the cord, the sensory motor cortex on one side projects bilaterally to the spinal gray matter in the intermediate zone and ventral horn. By PD 49, terminations from the sensory motor cortex are predominantly in the contralateral gray matter. Thus, when corticospinal terminations first become established in the cord, the sensory-motor cortical areas in each hemisphere project in an overlapping fashion in the spinal gray matter. We asked the question if neural activity is necessary for refinement of the laterality of corticospinal terminations. We blocked neural activity in the sensory-motor cortex on one side during this refinement period. After cessation of activity blockade, the tracer wheat germ agglutinin conjugated to horseradish peroxidase (WGA-HRP) was injected into either the silenced or the contralateral active cortex and we examined the distribution of labeled terminations. We also examined projections from control subjects.

Unilateral blockade of neural activity in sensory-motor cortex between postnatal day 21 and 49 had robust bilateral effects on the pattern of corticospinal terminations (Fig. 8.10; Martin *et al.* 1999). While control animals show a predominantly contralateral termination pattern (Fig. 10A), projections from the silenced cortex are sparse and limited to the most lateral portion of the gray matter (Fig. 8.10B). Those from the active side

A Control

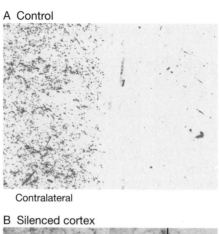

Contralateral

B Silenced cortex

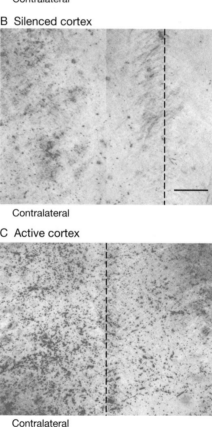

Fig. 8.10 Corticospinal axon terminations from cortex of control (noninfused) animal (A), silenced cortex (B), and active sensorimotor cortex (i.e., side contralateral to the infusion) (C). Inactivation was produced by muscimol infusion. Images are digitally-inverted dark-field images, sites of HRP reaction product were shaded black using the an automatic algorithm of the program Photoshop (Adobe). Dashed vertical line indicates the midline. Note that the image in (B) is skewed to contralateral side to show the minimal labeling that was present. No additional labeling was present on the ipsilateral side. (See Martin *et al.* 1999 for details). Calibration: 200 μm.

Contralateral

C Active cortex

Contralateral

are dense and bilateral (Fig. 8.10C). Thus, the silenced side failed to maintain terminations, either contralaterally or ipsilaterally. The active side, by contrast, had strong terminations bilaterally. This shows that refinement of the laterality of the developing corticospinal terminations depends on neural activity in sensory-motor cortex. When activity blockade is produced after postnatal day 49, the laterality of corticospinal terminations is not changed thus demonstrating the existence of a critical period (Martin *et al.* 1999).

This reciprocal effect suggests that the developing terminations are competing for space in the gray matter of the cord in which to project. Activity would confer a competitive advantage. The terminations could be competing for limited amounts of trophic substances, as suggested for the primary visual cortex (Cabelli *et al.* 1995). The question of activity independence vs activity-dependent competition can be addressed by comparing the effects of unilateral and bilateral inactivation. With bilateral inactivation, neither side has a competitive advantage. When we blocked activity bilaterally (Fig. 8.11) (Martin and Lee 1999) there was significantly more label than following unilateral inactivation. This shows that activity-dependent competition between projections from the two sides was important in shaping the density of terminations rather than activity alone.

Prehension impairments produced by early postnatal sensory-motor cortex activity blockade

Since unilateral sensory-motor cortex inactivation produced robust changes in the anatomical organization of the corticospinal projection, we next determined the effect of this treatment on the development of motor skills. To examine this question, we trained kittens to reach and grasp a small cube of beef (Martin *et al.* 2000b) beginning several days after cessation of sensory-motor cortex activity blockade. Training began approximately at the age when we examined the topography of corticospinal terminations (Fig. 8.10). When tested 2–3 weeks later, after training, we found that animals that received saline infusion, like untreated animals, aimed their movements accurately to the food targets (Fig. 8.12A). However, muscimol-treated animals showed severe

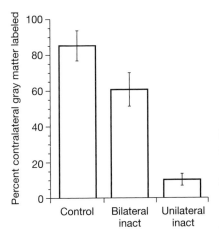

Fig. 8.11 Comparison of percent of contralateral gray matter labeled from cortex silenced unilaterally or bilaterally and in controls. Data replotted from Martin and Lee (1999).

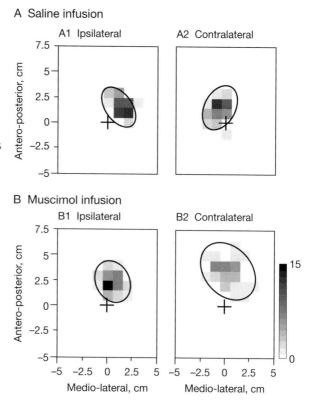

Fig. 8.12 Endpoints of reaches to a single target (6 cm from cage aperture) for an animal that received unilateral saline infusion (A) and one that received unilateral muscimol infusion (B). Gray scale indicates number of reaches that ended at a given coordinate. Plus signs correspond to target locations. Data for each cat are from a single daily session. Number of trials: A1. $n=57$; A2. $n=50$; B1. $n=50$; B2. $n=44$. (See (Martin *et al.* 2000b) for details).

reaching impairments using the limb contralateral to the infusion (Fig. 12B2). This limb is controlled by the sparse corticospinal projection from the inactivated side and aberrant ipsilateral terminations from the active side (see Fig. 8.10). These animals also showed severe grasping impairments (Martin *et al.* 2000b). For reaching, the severity of effects was slightly less following bilateral than unilateral inactivation, but for grasping, the defects were more severe (Martin *et al.* 2000b).

Laterality of limb control in animals subjected to unilateral sensory-motor cortex activity blockade

Continuous postnatal inactivation produced sparse corticospinal terminations from the silenced side (Fig. 8.10B) but dense bilateral terminations from the active side (Fig. 8.10C). We used reversible inactivation to examine the functional contributions of the aberrant ipsilateral terminations from the active side. Normally, animals use the contralateral sensory-motor cortex to control their forelimbs during prehension (Martin *et al.* 1999). We determined if animals that received unilateral inactivation controlled the impaired limb using the contralateral cortex, via the sparse terminations, or bilaterally, with a contribution from the aberrant ipsilateral terminations.

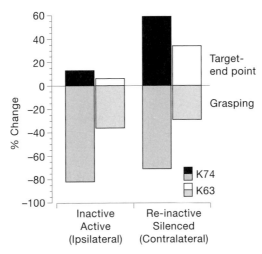

Fig. 8.13 Effect of inactivation (PW 11 for K74; PW 15 for K63) of previously active sensory-motor cortex and re-inactivation (PW 14 for K74; PW 17 for K63) of previously silenced cortex on reaching (upward black and white bars; target-endpoint distance) and grasping (downward gray and stippled bars; trials during which meat was normally grasped) with the impaired (right) forelimb. Data from two cats (K74, K63) are shown. Bars plot the percent change in the measurement in relation to the mean of the values during periods without any cortical muscimol infusion (during baseline periods). Error magnitude did not change systematically for either cat during the period of behavioral testing and late inactivations. Effect of inactivating the previously active cortex was significant (K74: 13%; from 3±1.22 cm to 3.39±1.32 cm; $p<0.04$, K63: 6%; from 4.26±0.98 to 4.52±0.82 cm; $p<0.005$). Inactivation of the previously silent cortex was also significant and had a greater effect (K74: 59%; from 3 cm to 4.78±1.39 cm; $p<0.0001$; K63: 4.26 to 5.72±1.33 cm; $p<0.0001$). (See Martin *et al.* 2000b for details).

After animals were trained, we inactivated the previously active cortex using an indwelling cannula connected to an osmotic pump, like the system used for long-term inactivation (Fig. 8.8). However, this late blockade was only maintained for several days to permit behavioral testing. This inactivation exacerbated the reaching end-point errors by only a small amount (Fig. 8.13; upward-going bars on left), while the grasping errors worsened to a much greater extent (downward-going bars). This is consistent with the hypothesis that the aberrant ipsilateral terminations are rescuing function, since without their contributions, errors increased. It is also possible that projections from the ipsilateral cortex to brain stem sites are assisting in control. Re-inactivation of the previously silenced cortex worsened both reaching and grasping defects in a similar and robust way (Fig. 8.13; right bars), showing that contralateral control still predominates. The results of this experiment show how inactivation can be used to probe the function of novel/aberrant neural pathways.

Conclusions

Our findings suggest that, in mature animals, functionally distinct output channels link portions of the anterior and posterior interpositus nuclei with different sectors of the primary motor cortex. Electrophysiological findings in maturity show a high degree of connectional specificity along these pathways from the cerebellum and motor cortex. Our inactivation studies show that the outputs of both anterior and posterior interpositus nuclei could play different roles in trajectory formation, since the phenotype of behavioral changes during inactivation is different. These output channels from the intermediate cerebellum may be similar in organization, but not in function, to output channels from the dorsal, lateral, and ventral dentate nuclei in the monkey proposed by Middleton and Strick (1997). The function of lateral cerebellar (i.e. dentate) output channels have yet to be explored.

The cerebello–cortical circuits from anterior and posterior interpositus nuclei to motor cortex, in turn, engage topographically specific corticospinal projection systems (Martin 1996) for translating supraspinal control signals into motor actions. Our developmental studies show the importance of neural activity in the corticospinal system during early postnatal life in establishing the precise patterns of connections normally seen in maturity. Neural activity during a postnatal critical period also is essential for development of normal prehension skills. Little is known of the development of the cerebellar output systems that impinge upon the different motor cortex subregions, although, overall connectional specificity of the intermediate cerebellum is less during early postnatal life than in maturity (Song *et al.* 1993). While the mechanisms shaping development of connectional specificity in the cerebellar output systems is not known, it is plausible that activity-dependent processes could play an important role.

Acknowledgments

We thank Scott E. Cooper and Bouchra Kably for participating in many of the inactivation experiments and Antony G. Hacking and Laura Donarummo for expert technical assistance. We also thank Gary Johnson for construction of the apparatus. This work was supported by grants from the National Science Foundation (IBN-9421582), the National Institutes of Health to J. M. (NS36835), and the March of Dimes Foundation.

References

Alisky, J. M., Swink, T. D. and Tolbert, D. L. (1992) The postnatal spatial and temporal development of corticospinal projections in cats. *Experimental Brain Research,* **88:**265–76.

Alstermark, B., Lundberg, A., Norrsell, U. *et al.* (1981) Integration in the descending motor pathways controlling the forelimb in the cat. 9. Differential behavioural defects after spinal cord lesion interrupting defined pathways from higher centers to motoneurons. *Experimental Brain Research,* **42:**299–318.

Anderson, M. E. and DeVito, J. L. (1987) An analysis of potentially converging inputs to the rostral ventral thalamic nuclei of the cat. *Experimental Brain Research*, **68**:260–76.

Araki, T., Yamano, M., Murakami, T. *et al.* (1988) Localization of glycine receptors in the rat central nervous system: an immunocytochemical analysis using monoclonal antibody. *Neuroscience*, **25**:613–24.

Armstrong, D. M. and Drew, T. (1985) Forelimb electromyographic responses to motor cortex stimulation during locomotion in the cat. *Journal of Physiology*, **367**:327–51.

Beloozerova, I. N. and Sirota, M. G. (1993) The role of the motor cortex in the control of accuracy of locomotor movements in the cat. *Journal of Physiology*, **461**:1–25.

Brooks, V. B. P. (1990) Study of brain function by local, reversible cooling. *Review of Physiology, Biochemistry and Pharmacology*, **95**:1–109.

Cabelli, R. J., Hohn, A. and Shatz, C. J. (1995) Inhibition of ocular dominance column formation by infusion of NT-4/5 or BDNF. *Science*, **267**:1662–6.

Chu, D. C., Albin, R. L., Young, A. B. *et al.* (1990) Distribution and kinetics of GABA$_B$ binding sites in rat central nervous system: a quantitative autoradiographic study. *Neuroscience*, **34**:341–57.

Cooper, S. E., Martin, J. H. and Ghez, C. (2000) Effects of inactivation of the anterior interpositus nucleus on the kinematic and dynamic control of multijoint movement. *Journal of Neurophysiology*, **84**:1988–2000.

Dermon, C. R., Pizarro, P., Georgopoulos, P. *et al.* (1990) Bilateral alterations in local cerebral glucose utilization following intranigral application of the GABAergic agonist muscimol. *Journal of Neuroscience*, **10**:2861–78.

Dias, E. C. and Segraves, M. A. (1997) A pressure system for the microinjection of substances into the brain of awake monkeys. *Journal of Neuroscience Methods*, **72**:43–7.

Ghez, C. (1975) Input-output relations of the red nucleus in the cat. *Brain Research*, **98**:93–108.

Ghez, C., Cooper, S. C. and Martin, J. (1996) In P. Haggard, R. Flanagan, and W. Wing (eds) *Hand and Brain: Neurophysiology and Psychology of Hand Movement*, pp.187–211. Academic Press, Orlando, Fl.

Goodman, C. S. and Shatz, C. J. (1993) Developmental mechanisms that generate precise patterns of neuronal connectivity. *Cell*, **10(Suppl):** 77–98.

Gorska, T. and Sybirska, E. (1980) Effects of pyramidal lesions on forelimb movements in the cat. *Acta Experimental Neurobiology*, **40**:843–59.

Hata, Y. and Stryker, M. P. (1994) Control of thalamocortical afferent rearrangement by postsynaptic activity in developing visual cortex. *Science*, **265**:1732–5.

He, S. Q., Dum, R. P. and Strick, P. L. (1993) Topographic organization of corticospinal projections from the frontal lobe: motor areas on the lateral surface of the hemisphere. *Journal of Neuroscience*, **13**:952–80.

Hille, B. (1992) *Ionic Channels of Excitable Membranes*. Sinauer, Sunderland, MA.

Hoffman, D. S. and Strick, P. L. (1995) Effects of a primary motor cortex lesion on step-tracking movements of the wrist. *Journal of Neurophysiology*, **73**:891–5.

Jakobson, L. S. and Goodale, M. A. (1991) Factors affecting higher-order movement planning: a kinematic analysis of human prehension. *Experimental Brain Research*, **86**:199–208.

Jeannerod, M. (1984) The timing of natural prehension movements. *Journal of Motor Behavior* **16**:235–4.

Jörntell, H. and Ekerot, C. F. (1999) Topographical organization of projections to cat motor cortex from nucleus interpositus anterior and forelimb skin. *Journal of Physiology* **514**:551–66.

Kably, B., Martin, J. H. and Ghez, C. (1996) Impairments in trajectory control in reaching produced by inactivation of rostral motor cortex. *Society for Neuroscience Abstracts*, **22**:1830.

Keller, A. (1993) Intrinsic connections between representation zones in the cat motor cortex. *NeuroReport*, **4**:515–8.

Kelly, P. A. T. and McCulloch, J. (1984) Extrastriatal circuits activated by intrastriatal muscimol: a [^{14}C]2-deoxyglucose investigation. *Brain Research*, **292**:357–66.

Konczak, J., Borutta, M. and Dichgans, J. (1997) The development of goal-directed reaching in infants. 2. Learning to produce task-adequate patterns of joint torque. *Experimental Brain Research*, **113**:465–74.

Konczak, J., Borutta, M., Topka, H. *et al.* (1995) The development of goal-directed reaching in infants: Hand trajectory formation and joint torque control. *Experimental Brain Research*, **106**:156–68.

Krogsgaard-Larsen, P. and Johnston, G. A. R. (1978) Structure-activity studies on the inhibition of GABA binding to rat brain membranes by muscimol and related compounds. *Journal of Neurochemistry* **30**:1377–82.

Lawrence, D. G. and Hopkins, D. A. (1976) The development of motor control in the rhesus monkey: evidence concerning the role of corticomotoneuronal connections. *Brain*, **99**:235–54.

Lomber, S. G. (1999) The advantages and limitations of permanent or reversible deactivation techniques in the assessment of neural function. *Journal of Neuroscience Methods*, **86**:109–17.

Martin, J. H. (1991) Autoradiographic estimation of the extent of reversible inactivation produced by microinjection of lidocaine and muscimol in the rat. *Neuroscience Letters* **127**:160–4.

Martin, J. H. (1996) Differential spinal projections from the forelimb areas of the rostral and caudal subregions of primary motor cortex in the cat. *Experimental Brain Research*, **108**:191–205.

Martin, J. H., Cooper, S. C. and Ghez, C. (1995) Kinematic analysis of reaching in the cat. *Experimental Brain Research*, **102**:379–92.

Martin, J. H., Cooper, S. E. and Ghez, C. (1993) Differential effects of local inactivation within motor cortex and red nucleus on performance of an elbow task in the cat. *Experimental Brain Research*, **94**:418–28.

Martin, J. H., Cooper, S. E., Hacking, A. *et al.* (2000a) Differential effects of deep cerebellar nuclei inactivation on reaching and adaptive control. *Journal of Neurophysiology*, **83**:1886–99.

Martin, J. H. and Ghez, C. (1993) Differential impairments in reaching and grasping produced by local inactivation within the forelimb representation of the motor cortex in the cat. *Experimental Brain Research*, **94**:429–43.

Martin, J. H. and Ghez, C. (1999) Pharmacological inactivation in the analysis of the central control of movement. *Journal of Neuroscience Methods*, **86**:145–59.

Martin, J. H., Hacking, A. and Donarummo, L. (2000b) Impairments in prehension produced by early postnatal sensorimotor cortex activity blockade. *Journal of Neurophysiology*, **83**:895–906.

Martin, J. H., Kably, B. and Hacking, A. (1999) Activity-dependent development of cortical axon terminations in the spinal cord and brain stem. *Experimental Brain Research*, **125**:184–99.

Martin, J. H. and Lee, S. (1999) Activity-dependent competition between developing corticospinal terminations. *NeuroReport*, **10**:2277–82.

Mata, M., Fink, D. J., Gainer, H. *et al.* (1980) Activity-dependent energy metabolism in rat posterior pituitary primarily reflects sodium pump activity. *Journal of Neurochemistry*, **34**:213–15.

Middleton, F. A. and Strick, P. L. (1997) Cerebellar output channels. *International Review of Neurobiology*, **41**:61–82.

Miller, K. D., Chapman, B. and Stryker, M. P. (1989) Visual responses in adult cat visual cortex depend on N-methyl-D-aspartate receptors. *Proceedings of the National Academy of Sciences USA*, **86**:5183–7.

Morasso, P. (1981) Spatial control of arm movements. *Experimental Brain Research*, **42**:223–7.

Napier, J. R. (1980) *Hands.* Allen and Unwin, London.

Pappas, C. L. and Strick, P. L. (1981a) Anatomical demonstration of multiple representation in the forelimb region of the cat motor cortex. *Journal of Comparative Neurology*, **200**:491–500.

Pappas, C. L. and Strick, P. L. (1981b) Physiological demonstration of multiple representation in the forelimb region of the cat motor cortex. *Journal of Comparative Neurology*, **200**:481–90.

Perfiliev, S., Pettersson, L. G. and Lundberg, A. (1998) Food-taking in the cat investigated with transection of the rubro- and corticospinal tracts. *Neuroscience Research*, **32**:181–4.

Pettersson, L. G., Lundberg, A., Alstermark, B. *et al.* (1997) Effect of spinal cord lesions on forelimb target-reaching and on visually guided switching of target-reaching in the cat. *Neuroscience Research*, **29**:241–56.

Reiter, H. O. and Stryker, M. P. (1988) Neural plasticity without postsynaptic action potentials: Less-active inputs become dominant when kitten visual cortical cells are pharmacologically inhibited. *Proceedings of the National Academy of Sciences USA*, **85**:3623–7.

Rispal-Padel, L. and Grangetto, A. (1977) The cerebello-thalamo-cortical pathway. Topographical investigation at the unitary level in the cat. *Experimental Brain Research*, **28**:101–23.

Rispal-Padel, L. and Latreille, J. (1974) The organization of projections from the cerebellar nuclei to the contralateral motor cortex in the cat. *Experimental Brain Research*, **19**:36–60.

Robinson, F. R., Houk, J. C. and Gibson, A. R. (1987) Limb specific connections of the cat magno-cellular red nucleus. *Journal of Comparative Neurology*, **257**:553–77.

Sandkühler, J., Maisch, B. and Zimmermann, M. (1987) The use of local anesthetic microinjections to identify central neural pathways: a quantitative evaluation of the time course and extent of the neuronal block. *Experimental Brain Research*, **68**:168–78.

Sato, K., Zhang, J.-H., Saika, T. *et al.* (1991) Localization of glycine receptor a_1 subunit mRNA-containing neurons in the rat brain: an analysis using in situ hybridization histochemistry. *Neuroscience*, **43**:381–95.

Sato, K. C. and Tanji, J. (1989) Digit-muscle responses evoked from multiple intracortical foci in monkey precentral motor cortex. *Journal of Neurophysiology*, **62**:959–70.

Schmidt, E. M. and McIntosh, J. S. (1990) Microstimulation mapping of precentral gyrus during trained movements. *Journal of Neurophysiology*, **64**:1668–82.

Schwartz, W. J., Smith, C. B., Davidsen, L. *et al.* (1979) Metabolic mapping of functional activity in the hypothalamo-neurohypophysial system in the rat. *Science*, **205**:723–5.

Shatz, C. J. (1990) Impulse activity and the patterning of connections during CNS development. *Neuron*, **5**:745–56.

Shatz, C. J. and Stryker, M. P. (1988) Prenatal tetrodotoxin infusion blocks segregation of retinogeniculate afferents. *Science*, **242**:87–9.

Shinoda, Y., Kano, M. and Futami, T. (1985) Synaptic organization of the cerebello-thalamo-cerebral pathway in the cat. I. Projection of individual cerebelar nuclei to single pyramidal tract neurons in areas 4 and 6. *Neuroscience Research*, **2**:133–56.

Song, W.-J., Kobayashi, Y. and Murakami, F. (1993) An electrophysiological study of a transient ipsilateral interpositorubral projection in neonatal cats. *Experimental Brain Research*, **92**:399–406.

Strick, P. L. and Preston, J. B. (1982) Two representations of the hand in area 4 of a primate. I. Motor output organization. *Journal of Neurophysiology*, **48**:139–49.

Theriault, E. and Tatton, W. G. (1989) Postnatal redistribution of pericruciate motor cortical projections within the kitten spinal cord. *Developmental Brain Research*, **45**:219–237.

Wong-Riley, M. (1979) Changes in the visual system of monocularly sutured or enucleated cats demonstrable with cytochrome oxidase histochemistry. *Brain Research*, **171**:11–28.

Yumiya, H. and Ghez, C. (1983) Specialized subregions in cat motor cortex: Anatomical demonstration of differential projections to rostral and caudal sectors. *Experimental Brain Research*, **53**:259–276.

Zhuravin, I. A. and Bures, J. (1991) Extent of the tetrodotoxin induced blockade examined by pupillary paralysis elicited by intracerebral injection of the drug. *Experimental Brain Research*, **83**:687–690.

Chapter 9

Cerebral Control of Eye Movements

Mark A. Segraves

Introduction

As has been the case for all of the functional systems considered in this book, investigations of the role of the cerebral cortex in the control of eye movements with "virtual lesions" were preceded by experiments where surgical removal of a region of cortex was followed by behavioral testing to determine the ability of the subject to make eye movements in the absence of that area. We now understand that studying the behavior of an animal after a region of cortex has been removed is not so much a study of the function of the role of that missing cortex as it is a study of the ability of the brain to compensate for the loss of that cortex (Lomber 1999). Studies of this sort may reveal components of behavior for which a particular cortical area is absolutely essential. The extensive reorganization and compensation that must take place following cortical damage, however, ensures that studies of postlesion behavior provide sparse insight into the role of the damaged region in the normal, intact brain.

A good example of this problem is found in the evidence for a role of the primate frontal eye field in eye movement behavior based upon anatomic and electrophysiologic findings, versus the results of studies where the frontal eye field was damaged. The frontal eye field is a functionally defined area of cortex located on the anterior bank of the arcuate sulcus of the rhesus monkey. Anatomically, the frontal eye field is connected to all cortical oculomotor areas and projects directly to the superior colliculus as well as to the oculomotor regions of the pons (Huerta *et al.* 1986; Segraves and Goldberg 1987; Stanton *et al.* 1988; Segraves 1992). Physiologically, the frontal eye field is defined as the area of the arcuate sulcus region where saccadic eye movements can be evoked by microstimulation with thresholds of $\leq 50\,\mu A$ (Bruce *et al.* 1985). Saccades are voluntary, high velocity eye movements that are used to redirect the line of sight, placing objects of interest on the fovea where visual acuity is highest (for background, see Leigh and Zee 1999). Electrophysiologic experiments have identified a rich diversity of neurons in the frontal eye field that have activity that precedes and is closely correlated with the generation of saccadic eye movements (Bruce and Goldberg 1985; Schall 1991). In spite of this strong electrophysiologic evidence for a role of the frontal eye field in the generation of saccades, the results of surgical removal of the frontal eye field led many to believe that the frontal eye field did not play an essential role in the generation of eye movements. This was because lesions confined to the frontal eye field produced only subtle deficits in eye movement behavior (Latto and Cowey 1971a,b; Schiller *et al.* 1980; Lynch 1992).

Virtual lesion techniques, including cooling and injections of neuroactive drugs, have contributed tremendously to our understanding of the role of the frontal eye field, as well as other areas of cerebral cortex, in the control of eye movements. This chapter reviews a sample of those contributions, providing a description of techniques and experiments performed in my own laboratory, as well as reviewing a selection of the findings reported by other investigators.

Methods for cortical injections

The injection of minute amounts of fluid substances into physiologically defined regions of the cerebral cortex requires a system that enables the investigator to accurately position the tip of an injection cannula at the intended injection site, record cell activity at the site of the injection so that it can be physiologically characterized, and be able to control the precise amount of substance injected. In my own laboratory, we have relied upon the microinjection of various agonists and antagonists of neurotransmitters to investigate the role of the frontal eye field in the control of saccadic eye movements. The following is a description of a method that we have found useful for the injection of substances into the cerebral cortex (for additional details see Dias and Segraves 1997). The most important features of this system are the ability to record neuronal activity at the tip of the injection device as well as apply electrical stimulation to evoke eye movements, and the ability to closely monitor the amount of substance that is injected.

A common problem with making injections in the brain is the inability to accurately monitor the quantity of chemical injected. A microsyringe can become clogged at the tip and still allow movement of its plunger, giving the false impression that material is being ejected from the tip. With iontophoretic injections, where the differential flow of charged ions is involved, it is usually not possible to know the actual quantity of substance injected. The system described here allows the experimenter to directly observe the actual volume of substance being injected, greatly enhancing the precision of the experiment.

The central component of this system is an injection device made from a glass capillary tube and a 30–gauge stainless steel cannula joined together at the middle with glue (Fig. 9.1). The overall length of an assembled cannula as used in our laboratory for cortical injections is approximately 105 mm. To enable recording of neural activity, a piece of enamel-coated stainless steel wire with outside diameter of 0.05 mm is drawn through the injection cannula. The end of the wire is cut so that only a small segment (~0.2 mm) protrudes from the end of the cannula. The glass and metal cannula, along with the recording wire, are fixed in an electrode holder that has three ports. The bottom port holds the cannula in place. The top port makes the connection with the recording wire, and the side port is used for introducing positive or negative pressure

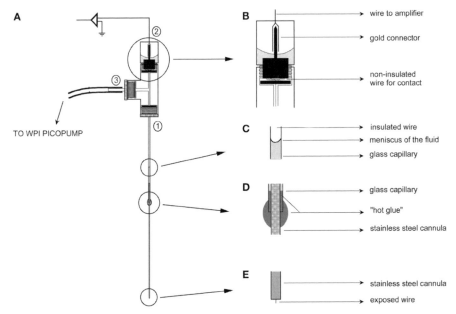

Fig. 9.1 Injection/Recording system. (A) Steel and glass cannula attached to electrode holder with connections to electrode amplifier and pressure source. (B–E) Enlargements of parts in (A). From Dias and Segraves (1997).

to the inside of the cannula. The electrode holder, cannula, and recording wire are completely sealed, so that the only location where it is possible for fluid to leave the injection cannula is through the tip of the cannula. Injection pressures of up to $7\,kg/cm^2$ (100 psi) are possible. The cut end of the recording wire has an impedance of about $0.2\,M\Omega$ at 1 kHz, and is good for recording multiunit activity and occasionally single units. The design of this system allows the recording tip to be renewed by withdrawing the cannula several millimeters into the electrode holder, cutting 1–2 mm off the tip of the wire and then repositioning the cannula so that 0.2 mm of the wire protrudes from the tip of the cannula. The entire wire can also be replaced without having to replace other components of the system.

The glass capillary tubing at the upper end of the cannula allows for the monitoring of fluid movement in and out of the tip of the cannula. Vacuum is used to draw fluid into the cannula until a meniscus of fluid is visible in the glass tube. The position of this meniscus is then used to monitor the amount of fluid injected. An operating microscope with a calibrated vernier scale in one of the oculars is used to measure the distance the meniscus moves during an injection. At the highest total magnification of 17×, the smallest unit division of the vernier scale corresponds to an injection volume of 0.15 µl. Normally, we have used a magnification of 11×, where the smallest division of the scale corresponds to a volume of 0.24 µl.

A pneumatic picopump is connected to the pressure port of the electrode holder. The picopump is attached to both an external vacuum pump and a pressure source. Vacuum applied at a level of about 50 mm Hg is used to fill the cannula. Once the cannula is filled, the vacuum is left connected to the electrode holder port but adjusted to a very low level ≤ 25 mm Hg) to ensure that fluid does not leak out of the cannula.

For accurate positioning of the cannula in the brain, the injection apparatus is used in conjunction with a grid system developed by Crist *et al.* (1988). Briefly, the grid consists of a round plastic cylinder with an array of 256 holes spaced at 1 mm intervals. The grid is positioned inside of a cylindrical metal recording cylinder attached to the monkey's head with dental acrylic. Twenty-three gauge stainless steel guide tubes are introduced into the brain through the grid holes that hold the guide tubes firmly in place until they are removed. The guide tube is used for the introduction of microelectrodes as well as the injection cannula into the brain. Normally, microelectrodes are used to characterize a prospective injection site before the injection cannula is introduced, and to check the viability of the site after an injection has been made. The guide tubes allow one to position an electrode or injection cannula at the same site repeatedly, allowing for multiple electrode penetrations and injections in the same region of neural tissue. For positioning in the brain, the injection apparatus is attached to a hydraulic microdrive.

In a typical experiment, we map the targeted cortical area with the grid and guide tube system using tungsten microelectrodes. This preliminary mapping is done to minimize the damage done by penetrations with the thicker injection cannula and because the microelectrodes have higher impedances and give better recording results. Once we have identified an intended injection site, the filled injection system is substituted for the microelectrode and the injection cannula is positioned in the brain. The guide tube ensures reproducibility so that the tip of the injection cannula can be positioned at the same recording site as the electrode. Location of the tip of the injection cannula is confirmed by recording the activities of cells at the tip of the cannula through the recording wire and by microstimulation to evoke eye movements. When we are convinced that the tip of the injection cannula is at the desired site, we proceed with the injection. Brief pressure pulses applied by the picopump make the injection. Pressure is initially set at 2–3 kg/cm^2 (30–40 psi), and 5 ms pulses are applied while the level of the fluid meniscus is monitored through the operating microscope. If the meniscus does not move, the pressure is increased until a pulse causes it to move. At this point, additional pulses are applied at 15 s intervals until the desired amount is injected. Pressure is never increased beyond 7 kg/cm^2 (100 psi). If we experience difficulty in ejecting fluid from the tip of the cannula, increasing the pulse width by several milliseconds is often an effective means for getting fluid to begin to flow out of the tip of the cannula. The picopump allows one to vent the applied pressure in the cannula to either the room atmosphere or the vacuum system. This ensures that applied pressure is immediately removed when the brief pulse is ended. In our system, we always vent the cannula to the vacuum pressure set initially to prevent movement of fluid in or out of the cannula tip.

This injection system allows one to continue recording cell activity during the injections. This is very useful as changes in cell activity during the injection help to confirm that the substance is having the desired effect. We leave the cannula in place for the duration of the experiment (usually 3–5 hours), injecting additional amounts as needed. At the end of the experiment, we remove the injection apparatus, leaving the guide tube in place. The guide tube can be used on subsequent days to return to the same site to repeat the experiment, make a control injection, test the effects of other drugs, or to make microelectrode recordings.

Spread of injected substances

Of equal importance to the identification of the injection site and the control of the amount of substance injected, is an understanding of the degree of spread of the injected substance from the center of the injection site. This spread determines the functional size of the injection site. The identity and initial concentration of the injected substance, the facility with which it diffuses through neural tissue, and the density of the tissue surrounding the injection site all have an effect upon spread. There are a limited number of studies that have examined this process in detail, particularly in primate cerebral cortex. Tehovnik and Sommer (1997) examined the spread of the short-acting anesthetic lidocaine. In their experiment, 2% lidocaine was injected into rhesus monkey frontal cortex in the vicinity of the supplementary eye field. Microelectrodes positioned eccentric to the injection cannula monitored the spread of lidocaine. Lidocaine takes effect quickly and its action is of relatively short duration. Maximal inactivation of neural activity occurred roughly 8 minutes after the beginning of the injection. By 30 minutes postinjection, neural activity had returned to normal levels. Tehovnik and Sommer found that the volume of cortex that was inactivated by lidocaine injection was spherically shaped, centered on the tip of the injection cannula. The radius of this sphere depended upon the volume of lidocaine injected, with 7 μl of lidocaine required to produce 100% inactivation 1 mm away from the center of the injection site, and 30 μl required to produce full inactivation up to 2 mm away from the center. The effects of changing concentration were not tested, but this could also be expected to have a direct effect upon effective spread.

Martin (1991) examined the spread of the GABA-agonist muscimol in the cortex and brainstem of the rat. By looking at the spread of radioactively labeled muscimol, he found that 1 μl of muscimol at a concentration of 1 μg/μl spread over a region with a radius of about 1.7 mm. Radioactivity indicating the continued presence of muscimol was still present 2 hours after the injection was made. Martin was also able to show, by looking at glucose uptake, that the hypometabolism due to the inactivation of neurons after the injection was strongest at a central core of tissue with a radius of about 1 mm. Using a similar method of analysis to examine the spread of muscimol in both rat and cat cerebral cortex, Martin and Ghez (1999) report that the area of cortex most strongly affected by an injection of muscimol has a radius of 1 mm.

In addition to these direct methods, behavioral assessment of deficits following cortical injections provides an additional means to assess the effective spread of the injected substance. For cortical areas with well-documented functional maps, an estimate of the extent of effective spread may be based upon the observed changes in behavior, for example, the range of eye movement amplitudes and directions that are affected by an injection in the frontal eye field.

Injection of GABA-related substances into the frontal eye field

As pointed out in the Introduction, both anatomic and electrophysiologic evidence suggests that the rhesus monkey frontal eye field is strongly involved in the control of eye movements (for reviews see Goldberg and Segraves 1989; Bruce 1990; Schall 1997; Tehovnik et al. 2000). In contrast to the supportive evidence from anatomy and neurophysiology, lesion studies in monkeys have shown that surgical removal of the frontal eye field has little effect on the animal's oculomotor behavior, as long as other oculomotor structures are left intact (Latto and Cowey 1971a; Schiller et al. 1980; Keating and Gooley 1988; Lynch 1992). The main effect of removing the frontal eye field was an initial neglect of the contralateral visual hemifield, which recovered completely within 2–4 weeks. When more sophisticated forms of behavior were tested, deficits from frontal eye field lesions became apparent. Frontal eye field removal impaired the normal patterns of eye movements used to scan the environment (Latto 1978; Schiller et al. 1980; Collin et al. 1982; Schiller and Chou, 1998). By using a delayed response task, Deng and collaborators (1986), found that monkeys with frontal eye field lesions had difficulty making saccades to the remembered location of a briefly flashed target light. These same monkeys did not show difficulty making saccades to target lights that were present when the saccade was initiated. Together, these results suggest that the frontal eye field may be important for the generation of saccades that require a high level of processing, so-called "cognitive saccades." Based upon this evidence, however, it has been suggested that the frontal eye field is not involved in the generation of simple visually guided saccades.

In contrast to the effects of removal of the frontal eye field alone, simultaneous removal of both the frontal eye field and superior colliculus had severe effects on the generation of eye movements (Schiller et al. 1980), even though superior colliculus lesions alone also had minor effects on the oculomotor performance of the monkeys, mainly an increase in the latencies of saccades and a reduction of express saccades. Also, concomitant removal of both the frontal eye field and parietal oculomotor cortex also increased latencies and saccade initiation, although either lesion alone produced modest deficits (Lynch 1992). These studies using combined lesions suggest that there is a distributed system controlling saccades, and it is likely that remaining oculomotor areas assume the functions of damaged areas, after a recovery period.

In light of the strong anatomic and physiologic evidence supporting a role for the frontal eye field in the control of saccades, and the possibility that the acute effects of frontal eye field removal from the oculomotor system were being masked by plasticity and recovery of function in lesion experiments, we directed our attention to reversible inactivation techniques. Our hope was that the use of short-term, reversible inactivation methods would provide a clearer picture of the role of the frontal eye field in the intact brain. To do this, we made small injections of substances related to the neurotransmitter γ-aminobutyric acid (GABA) into the frontal eye field of monkeys and tested the monkeys' performance on tasks involving saccadic eye movements. We used muscimol, a GABA agonist that has an inhibitory effect in the cerebral cortex to test the effect of inactivation of frontal eye field activity, and we used bicuculline, a GABA antagonist that produces a disinhibition of cortical cells to test the effects of activation of frontal eye field activity (Andrews and Johnston 1979; Lloyd and Morselli 1987). These experiments enabled us to observe reversible acute changes in saccadic eye movement behavior of monkeys. These changes were substantially more robust than the changes produced by surgical ablations.

The details of the methods used in these experiments have been described in detail elsewhere (Segraves 1992; Dias *et al.* 1995; Dias and Segraves 1999). In brief, rhesus monkeys were prepared for chronic recording of eye movements and neuronal activity, and were trained to perform a variety of oculomotor tasks. Electrodes and injection cannulae were introduced into the frontal eye field through guide-tubes placed in the grid system described earlier. In the rhesus monkey, the frontal eye field is defined as the area within the anterior bank and fundus of the arcuate sulcus where saccades can be evoked with thresholds of $\leq 50\,\mu A$ (Bruce *et al.* 1985). Measuring the threshold for electrically elicited saccades provided verification that recording and injection sites were located within the frontal eye field. In addition to measuring thresholds for evoking eye movements, we looked for cell activity that is characteristic of the frontal eye field. This included a predominance of cells with presaccadic activity during visually and memory-guided saccade tasks, including cells with visual and/or movement-related activity (Bruce and Goldberg 1985). The performance of these monkeys in oculomotor tasks was recorded both before and after the injection of muscimol, bicuculline, or saline. Frequently, control data collected in the absence of any injection was recorded one or two days following the day of an injection experiment. Using the injection system described earlier, injections of up to $1.0\,\mu l$, in $0.2\,\mu l$ steps, were made by pressure applied to the injection cannula. The concentration of muscimol used was $5\,\mu g/\mu l$, and of bicuculline $1\,\mu g/\mu l$.

Three basic forms of oculomotor tasks were used to test the effects of the injections:

1. Fixation task. The monkey fixated a central spot of light on a tangent screen, and was rewarded for maintaining fixation at that location;

2. Visually guided saccade task. The monkey made a saccade from the fixation spot to a peripheral target when the fixation spot was turned off;

3. Memory-guided saccade task. The monkey maintained fixation on the central spot while a target was briefly flashed in the periphery and, after a delay of 100 ms, the fixation spot was turned off and the monkey rewarded for making a saccade towards the location where the target flashed.

In both visually and memory-guided saccade tasks, target lights were positioned by mirror galvanometers under computer control so that they could be positioned anywhere on the tangent screen. In addition, the computer controlled the timing of events of the behavioral task and recorded eye movement and neuronal activity. Eye movements were monitored using the magnetic search coil technique (Robinson 1963; Judge *et al.* 1980).

We made a total of twelve injections of muscimol and eight injections of bicuculline in three monkeys. Four additional injections of saline were made as controls. We placed the injections in different subregions of the frontal eye field, choosing sites representing different saccade vectors, ranging from small saccades (e.g. 3° amplitude) to large saccades (e.g. 30° amplitude). Injections of muscimol, bicuculline, and saline were interspersed, usually with a day or more left between injections.

Muscimol is an agonist of the inhibitory neurotransmitter GABA. Injecting muscimol into the frontal eye field effectively inactivated the cortex surrounding the tip of the injection cannula, creating an oculomotor scotoma. After the injection the monkeys had difficulty making saccades corresponding to the amplitude and direction of saccades represented at the injection site, though still making saccades to targets outside of this representation. The activity of the cells recorded from the tip of the injection cannula was shut down and saccades could not be elicited with electrical currents as high as 150 μA. This effect was progressive. Initially, saccades towards the retinotopic representation at the injection site could still be made, but with longer latencies, slower peak velocities and reduced accuracy. Eventually, usually after at least one hour, the monkey was almost never able to saccade to the most affected direction, and the increase in latency expanded to flanking locations.

An example of data obtained for a muscimol injection site is provided in Fig. 9.2. Prior to the injection, electrical microstimulation applied through the wire at the tip of the injection cannula yielded saccades of about 10° amplitude directed rightward and close to the horizontal meridian (Fig. 9.2A). The injection data (Fig. 9.2B, C, left side) were recorded about 2 hours after the injection was made. The most obvious deficit in the monkey's performance of the visually-guided saccade task after the injection was the reduced number of saccades made to the right, particularly at polar angles of 0° and 315° (Fig. 9.2B). Although all targets were presented a similar number of times, the monkey would usually not initiate a saccade towards the retinotopic location represented at the injection site. In addition, the saccades towards regions flanking the affected region, for example down to the right, were slower than normal, and had increased latencies. Visually guided saccades directed towards the ipsilateral hemifield were not as strongly affected by the injection, although they differed from controls in

(A)

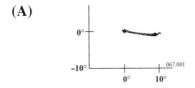

(B) VISUALLY-GUIDED SACCADES

(C) MEMORY-GUIDED SACCADES

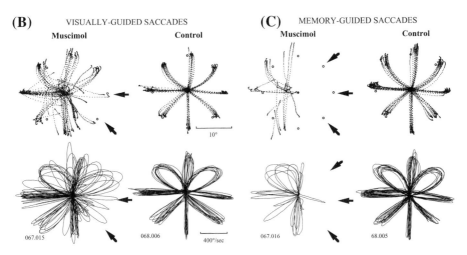

Fig. 9.2 Effects of muscimol injection in the left frontal eye field on visually and memory-guided saccades. (A) Trajectories of the saccades evoked by electrical stimulation at the injection site while the monkey fixated the central fixation light, with dots representing eye position sampled at a rate of 1 kHz. These recordings were made just moments before the injection. (B) Visually guided saccades made two hours after the muscimol injection (left side) compared to control data (right side). The top panel is a plot of the trajectories of saccades. The bottom panel contains a plot of the horizontal and vertical components of eye velocity, plotted for the duration of each saccade, such that the farthest point from the origin represents the peak velocity for each saccade (velocity at origin=0°/s). Saccades were made to one of eight randomly chosen target locations (peripheral *circles*) each located 10° from the central fixation point (central *circle*). *Arrows* in both position and velocity plots point to the targets for which the monkey showed greatest changes in performance after the muscimol injection. (C) Memory-guided saccades recorded immediately following the visually guided movements in (B). Controls were recorded four days after the injection. From Dias and Segraves (1999).

some respects. They reached peak velocities that were comparable to controls, but were less accurate in reaching the target. Plots of control data collected four days after the day of the muscimol injection are included on the right side of Fig. 9.2B and demonstrate that the monkey performed the visually guided task well under normal conditions. It is also possible to note a greater scatter of the endpoints of postinjection saccades when compared to controls. In addition, eye position during fixation before the start of saccades was deviated toward the ipsilateral hemifield and individual fixation positions were scattered, whereas, in the controls, fixation positions overlapped closely and were centered on the fixation spot.

While the monkey was having difficulty in generating visually guided saccades 2 hours after the injection was made, she was completely unable to make memory-guided saccades into the hemifield contralateral to the injection site (Fig. 9.2C, left). She could, however, still make memory saccades into the ipsilateral hemifield, indicating that she was alert and motivated. On first examination of Fig. 9.2C, it would appear that the monkey also had some difficulty making ipsilateral saccades in the memory task. Note that for directions of 180° and 225°, in particular, there are many fewer correct saccades than were made to either 135° or to the vertical directions 90° and 270°. The reason for this is that the monkey tended to make premature saccades for these directions that occurred before the disappearance of the fixation point (cue to make a saccade) and the trial was scored incorrect. Injection of muscimol in the left frontal eye field has produced an imbalance of activity. Whereas the region surrounding the injection site is inactivated by the muscimol, the corresponding region in the right frontal eye field has increased its activity. As a result, the monkey is unable to maintain fixation and suppress a visually guided saccade to the target light when it appears. This finding is similar to what has been reported for humans with unilateral frontal lesions who have difficulty suppressing unwanted saccades to suddenly appearing visual targets (Guitton *et al.* 1985). Dias and Bruce (1994) have described a fixation disengagement signal in the frontal eye field that is carried by about 50% of the cells that are active before saccades. Our results suggest that a localized inactivation of this signal causes an imbalance in this population of frontal eye field cells, resulting in changes in latency and a decrease in the ability to suppress saccades during fixation.

As was the case for the visually guided saccade task, memory-guided saccades made towards regions flanking the affected region were slower than normal, and had increased latencies. Initial fixation positions for the memory task were more scattered in the postinjection group than they were in the control data. Likewise, the injection caused fixation positions to deviate to the ipsilateral side.

It is interesting to note that, outside of the task conditions described above, the monkeys also seemed to have difficulty generating the saccades most affected by the injection site. For example, after the injection described above, trials where the monkey made a leftward eye movement normally required that the monkey make a rightward eye movement during the intertrial interval to return her gaze to the central fixation light to begin the next trial. Unfortunately, this rightward movement was the one most affected by the injection and the monkey would adopt an alternative strategy for returning gaze to the center of the tangent screen. This might include a large downward saccade followed by an oblique saccade up and to the right to place the eyes on the fixation point.

The effects of the muscimol injection outlined above were observed for the duration of the testing session, which lasted for approximately 3–4 hours after the time

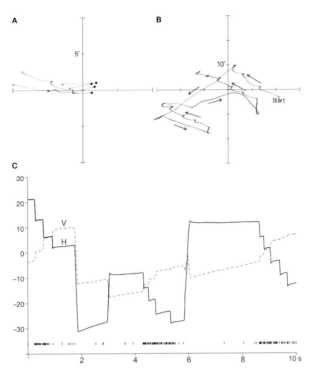

Fig. 9.3 Effects of bicuculline injection in right frontal eye field. These data were collected 45 minutes after the injection was made. Electrical stimulation evoked leftward saccades of about 3° amplitude at this site. (A) Saccades generated during fixation task. Single saccades as well as sequences of several saccades were made while the monkey attempted to maintain gaze on a central fixation light. Large dots mark the starting position of the eyes. (B) Eye movements made in the dark; one hour after injection. Arrows indicate the direction of movement. (C) Same movements plotted in (B) with the horizontal and vertical components of the eye trace plotted against time. Multiunit activity recorded from the injection cannula is represented by vertical tick marks at the bottom of the graph. From Dias *et al.* (1995).

of the injection. By the next day the monkeys were able to make normal saccades in all directions.

Injections of the GABA antagonist bicuculline produced effects that were nearly opposite to those produced by muscimol. The oculomotor scotoma created by the muscimol injection was replaced by a focus of heightened neuronal activity within the frontal eye field (Fig. 9.3). During the time that the injection was being made, cellular activity recorded from the injection cannula began to increase producing bursts of activity that were accompanied by irrepressible saccades equal in amplitude and direction to the saccades represented by the injection site. Shortly after the injection was made, the monkey was unable to suppress the saccades generated by the heightened activity surrounding the injection site (Fig. 9.3A). When the monkey was immersed in darkness without a task to perform, she spontaneously produced rapid series of saccades of approximately the same direction and amplitude as the saccade evoked electrically from the injection site (Fig. 9.3B, C). These "staircases" of saccades are reminiscent of the groupings of saccades elicited by electrical stimulation of the frontal eye field with long trains of electrical pulses (Robinson and Fuchs 1969). The groups of successive saccades produced by the bicuculline injection were accompanied by bursts of cell activity lasting for the duration of each sequence of saccades. An intriguing characteristic of this cell activity is that it occurs in bursts despite the constant presence of bicuculline at the injection site. It is unclear what is responsible for the formation or triggering of these bursts. Their presence suggests that the frontal eye field activity provides more than a constant signal specifying a saccade of the represented vector and might contain dynamic information relevant, perhaps, to the time of initiation of each saccade within a sequence.

After bicuculline injections, the monkeys were hampered in their ability to correctly perform a visually guided saccade task. Frequently, the first saccade made after the fixation point was extinguished was equivalent to the saccades represented by the injection site regardless of the position of the target. After this initial movement, a corrective saccade was made towards the location of the visible target. As was the case for muscimol, fixation was less accurate and deviated toward the side ipsilateral to the injection. The monkeys were incapable of doing the memory-guided saccade task because they could not maintain fixation long enough for the task to proceed to the point where they were allowed to make a saccade to the remembered location of the target. The effects of the bicuculline injection were not as long lasting as those produced by muscimol. Bicuculline effects began to subside 1.5–2 hours after the injection was made. If needed, it was then possible to make an additional injection to help maintain the cellular and behavioral effects of the drug.

Control injections of saline at the same locations where muscimol and bicuculline injections were made had no effect on the monkeys' oculomotor performance.

Inactivation of the frontal eye field by lidocaine injection

In a study similar to our own muscimol work, Sommer and Tehovnik (1997) used injections of lidocaine (18 μl, 2%) to inactivate the frontal eye field. Their results share many similarities to the results of the muscimol experiment. Inactivation with lidocaine affected saccades generated in a task identical to our own memory-guided saccade task, causing increases in latency and saccadic error. As was the case for muscimol, there was an increased frequency of premature saccades that were made before the movement cue for targets in the ipsilateral hemifield. In addition, the eyes were deviated ipsiversively when the monkey was in darkness, in a manner similar to the ipsiversive deviation of fixation seen with muscimol. Remarkably, Sommer and Tehovnik (1997) reported only mild and inconsistent decreases in velocities of memory-guided saccades after frontal eye field inactivation in their paradigm. This may have been a consequence of their keeping the room where the monkey performed the tasks dark. In general, saccades made in the dark are slower than saccades made in the light (Becker 1989). In the muscimol experiments by Dias and colleagues (1995, 1999), the room contained dim background illumination.

The most notable difference between the findings made with muscimol and those with lidocaine is that lidocaine did not appear to affect the ability of the monkey to make saccades in a visually guided saccade task. Memory-guided saccades were affected, but if the target light was visible when the monkey received the cue to make a saccade, those saccades appeared to be normal. It may be that the duration of action of lidocaine prevented it from having an effect upon visually guided saccades. The effects of lidocaine, reported by Sommer and Tehovnik, lasted for about 1 hour whereas the disruption of visually guided saccades following muscimol injections, noted by Dias and Segraves (1999), became evident 1–2 hours after the injection and were even worse at 4 hours. Sommer and Tehovnik (1997) report making two muscimol injections that produced results similar to their findings with lidocaine, and they suggest that the difference between their results and those of Dias and Segraves (1999) may be attributable to differences in stimulus intensity. Background illumination, as well as other parameters of the task may also have contributed to these differences.

Finally, the deficits reported by Sommer and Tehovnik (1997) appeared to affect all saccades to the contralateral hemifield. It is likely that this is due to the amount of muscimol versus lidocaine injected in these experiments. Where injections of 1 μl of muscimol produced effective inactivation of a portion of the frontal eye field, Sommer and Tehovnik found it necessary to inject 18 μl of lidocaine to obtain reliable inactivation of the frontal eye field. Injections of this size tended to inactivate the entire frontal eye field. As the effective spread of lidocaine in these experiments appeared to be greater than it was for muscimol in the injections of Dias and Segraves, this rules out diffusion as a possible explanation for the deficits seen in visually guided saccades with muscimol but not with lidocaine. Based upon the topography of the sites affected by the injections, muscimol appears to have spread less, but the severity of the deficit is greater.

Injection of a cholinergic antagonist into the frontal eye field

A major advantage of the injection method for creating reversible changes in the brain is the ability it provides to test the effects of agonists and antagonists of different neurotransmitters upon the behavioral contribution of a brain region. Since both surgical removal of and muscimol injection in the frontal eye field demonstrate a role for this cortical area in tasks that contain a memory component (memory-guided saccade task), we wanted to test the effects of injections of substances that were more directly linked to cortical memory systems (Dias *et al.* 1996). There is a wealth of evidence suggesting that the cholinergic muscarinic system plays a central role in learning and memory. For example, systemic injection of scopolamine, a cholinergic muscarinic antagonist, impairs memory in a variety of species, including primates. Since frontal cortex receives a massive projection of cholinergic axons originating in the basal fore-brain, we felt that this system might play an important role in the memory component of the eye movement tasks that we used to test our monkeys. To test this possibility, we made injections of scopolamine (0.5–1.0 μl; 10 μg/μl), a cholinergic antagonist, into the frontal eye field. With the exception of the substance injected, the methods and injection system used for this study were identical to those used for muscimol and bicuculline injections. The main effect of the scopolamine injections was to decrease the accuracy of memory-guided saccades. The accuracy of saccades to remembered target positions became even less precise as the length of the memory delay period for the task was increased. For some injection sites, this deficit was mainly for saccades whose amplitude and direction were similar to the optimal saccade vector represented by the injection site. This specificity is similar to what was seen for injections of GABA-related substances. At other injection sites, however, the accuracy of saccades in all directions was reduced. In addition to effects upon accuracy, there was also an increase in saccade latencies and frequently a reduction in saccade velocities. In contrast, there were no observable effects of the injection upon visually guided saccades. In addition to these saccade-related deficits, the monkey had a difficult time maintaining fixation after the injection, and was easily distracted from the task.

These findings are in contrast to those described for muscimol injections. An injection of muscimol into the frontal eye field disrupts both visual and memory-guided saccades. In addition, muscimol silences neuronal activity at the injection site, whereas neurons remained active after a scopolamine injection. The fact that the effects of scopolamine were not as restricted topographically as they were for muscimol and bicuculline suggests that this drug has a much larger effective spread through the cortex. This larger spread would explain the more generalized inattentiveness that was observed later in the experiment. In fact, intracortical microinjections of scopolamine are not required for this drug to have effects upon eye movements. Systemic injections of scopolamine (0.5 mg, injected intramuscularly) in humans affect saccade size, velocity, and latency, and cause instability of fixation (Oliva *et al.* 1993).

Frontal eye field corticotectal connections

One of the primate frontal eye field's strongest projections is to the deep layers of the superior colliculus. This projection provides the superior colliculus with information concerning the maintenance and release of fixation, saccade target location, and the amplitude and direction of an impending eye movement (Segraves and Goldberg 1987; Sommer and Wurtz 2000). In my laboratory, Janet Helminski has used antidromic activation to identify pairs of interconnected frontal eye field and superior colliculus recording sites. Orthodromic stimulation in the frontal eye field site was then used to identify cells in the collicular site that received direct frontal eye field input. We found that frontal eye field neurons focus their projections upon movement-related cells located in the deep layers of the superior colliculus (Helminski and Segraves 1996). These cells include cells with a long-lead buildup of activity prior to the saccade as well as cells with saccade-related burst activity (Mays and Sparks 1980; Munoz and Wurtz 1995). In the course of these experiments, we attempted to use cross-correlation methods to examine the interactions between frontal eye field and collicular cells in more detail. These experiments were not fruitful. The cross-correlation method depends heavily upon the strength of interconnections between individual neurons. It may be that the connections between a single frontal eye field neuron and a single superior colliculus neuron are not sufficient in strength to yield detectable results with this method. As an alternative approach, we decided to use inactivation of the frontal eye field with muscimol as a means to examine the activity of burst and buildup cells whose frontal eye field input has been silenced (Helminski and Segraves 1997).

In these experiments, antidromic excitation was used to identify a frontal eye field site that projected to a particular collicular recording site, and orthodromic stimulation from the frontal eye field site was then used to ascertain that cells at the collicular recording site received monosynaptic input from the frontal eye field site. The frontal eye field was then inactivated with a microinjection of muscimol. Following the injection, multiunit and single unit activity was monitored for several hours while the monkeys performed visuomotor tasks. The changes in activity observed were for trials in which the monkey successfully completed a visually guided saccade task. We found that neurons with burst and buildup activity showed changes in their activity following the injection. Neurons with burst activity alone displayed a progressive reduction in the amplitude of that burst for saccades made in the cell's ON-direction (Fig. 9.4). Conversely, the period when the burst neuron was silent for saccades made in the OFF-direction lengthened. Neurons whose activity contained a combination of buildup and burst activity displayed a broadening of the duration of the burst following the injection accompanied by a reduction of the level of buildup activity.

These are preliminary results from injection/recordings made in two monkeys. Nevertheless, they provide a glimpse of the power that combining reversible activation or inactivation with neuronal recording can provide. There will certainly be problems with interpretation. Whereas the changes seen in the burst neurons appeared to be a relatively straightforward effect of the removal of frontal eye field input, the changes observed in neurons with combined buildup and burst activity appeared to represent, not only the loss of frontal eye field input, but also the response of the remainder of the oculomotor system to the loss of that input. By broadening the length of their saccade-related bursts, these cells appeared to be adopting a new approach to generating a saccade. These changes may have resulted from changes in a number of remaining inputs to the colliculus including extracollicular input from saccade-related areas of the cortex and cerebellum, intracollicular input, or feedback from saccade-related areas of the brainstem.

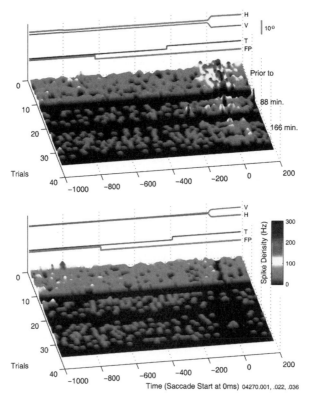

Fig. 9.4 (and color plate 8) Activity of superior colliculus burst neuron prior to and after inactivation of its frontal eye field input. Corresponding frontal eye field and superior colliculus sites were isolated by matching saccade-vector topography and by antidromically exciting frontal eye field cells from the superior colliculus site. The superior colliculus cell illustrated in this figure was orthodromically driven from the frontal eye field site. This cell is a burst neuron, characterized by its strong burst of activity surrounding saccades made into its movement field (Top plot, "Prior to" group of trials). Bottom plot includes activity for eye movements made in the direction opposite to the optimal vector for the cell. The cell's activity sampled at 1 kHz is plotted as spike density ($\sigma = 10$ ms) on the Z-axis. Along the Y-axis, groups of ~ 10 consecutive trials are plotted together for time intervals prior to as well as 88 and 166 minutes after inactivation of the frontal eye field with muscimol. Time in milliseconds during the trial is plotted on the X-axis with the beginning of the saccade at Time=0. The task performed by the monkey was a variation of the visually guided saccade task called the gap task. This gap task included a 400 ms interval between fixation point disappearance and target onset. H, V—horizontal and vertical eye position; FP—central fixation point; T—saccade target. Adapted from Helminski (1998).

In addition to the problems of interpretation, there are substantial technical obstacles with this method. Movement of the electrode and other factors may cause changes in the size and shape of the action potential that may affect the ability of the recording system to maintain isolation of that cell's activity. Therefore it is very important to monitor the isolation of the cell's activity throughout the course of the experiment. In a test of our ability to maintain constant isolation of a neuron's activity, we isolated movement-related superior collicular neurons, in the absence of a frontal eye field injection, and found that single unit traces, cell activity during visuomotor tasks, and saccade parameters during visuomotor tasks could be reliably recorded for test periods of up to four hours.

Chafee and Goldman-Rakic (2000) have used cooling to study the reciprocal inputs between posterior parietal and prefrontal cortex. This method, using a Peltier device placed over the area that was to be inactivated, has advantages over inactivation with muscimol. Most importantly, the effects of cooling take effect and can be removed much more rapidly. This provides better control and verification of cell isolation as discussed above. The speed with which the effects of cooling take place may also reduce the influence of adaptive changes that might occur with the longer lasting effects of muscimol. Cooling cannot be localized as well as a microinjection, and it will not have the specificity that injections of different drugs can provide, but will likely serve as a better first approach for combining inactivation with neuronal recordings. Shorter acting drugs such as lidocaine may combine the fast onset and quick reversibility of cooling with the localization of muscimol (Tehovnik and Sommer 1997). The use of GABA itself could offer these benefits as well as providing the pharmacologic specificity that muscimol provides. The short duration of action of GABA, however, limits its usefulness for studying changes in behavior.

As discussed earlier in this chapter, the frontal eye field has projections that reach the oculomotor centers of the brainstem by way of the superior colliculus, as well as direct projections to these oculomotor centers. In fact, the signals that the frontal eye field sends by way of these two projections are very similar (Segraves and Goldberg 1987; Segraves 1992; Sommer and Wurtz 2000). It has been unclear what the relative contributions of these two pathways are. Although the corticotectal projection of the frontal eye field is much more substantial than its corticopontine projection, surgical ablation of the frontal eye field or superior colliculus has supported the notion that either region alone can function to allow the normal generation of saccades. A recent study using muscimol injections in the superior colliculus has provided a much clearer picture of the relative importance of the frontal eye field's corticotectal and corticopontine projections. Hanes and Wurtz (2001) used microstimulation of the frontal eye field to evoke saccadic eye movements, and examined the effect of muscimol inactivation of a portion of the superior colliculus upon the ability to evoke saccades from the frontal eye field. They found that when the topographies of the cortical and collicular sites were closely matched, saccades could not be evoked by frontal eye field stimulation after the collicular site was inactivated. When the stimulation and injection site did not represent the same saccade vector, saccades evoked by frontal eye field stimulation still reflected the loss of the vector component represented by the inactivated collicular site. This is strong evidence supporting the role of the serial pathway from frontal eye field to colliculus to brainstem in the generation of saccades. These results also reinforce the idea that the ability of the frontal eye field to control the generation of saccades after the colliculus has been surgically removed is the result of adaptive changes that take place after the ablation.

Supplementary eye field

The oculomotor segment of dorsomedial frontal cortex, also known as the supplementary eye field (Schlag and Schlag-Rey 1987), is a cortical eye field located adjacent to the mid-sagittal sulcus, directly rostral to supplementary motor cortex, and dorsal to the frontal eye field (for reviews see Schall 1997; Tehovnik *et al.* 2000). Although the supplementary eye field shares many of the same anatomic connections of the frontal eye field, the results of neuronal recording studies indicate that the supplementary eye field is not as closely linked to the control of saccades as is the frontal eye field. In line with roles proposed for the supplementary motor cortex, with which the supplementary eye field shares its caudal border, it is believed that supplementary eye field plays a role in the planning stages of saccades, particularly for sequences of saccades that include more than one saccade made in series, or for saccades made in new and novel situations.

Sommer and Tehovnik (1999) examined the effects of reversible inactivation of the dorsomedial frontal cortex/supplementary eye field with lidocaine (18 µl, 2%). They found that this inactivation did not affect a monkey's ability to make saccades in both visually guided and memory-guided saccade tasks. Fixation was also intact. The primary deficit produced by the inactivation in this experiment appears to have been a mild problem with a double-step task where the monkey was trained to make a series of two saccades to the locations of two flashed target lights. The target lights appeared briefly, one after the other, and both disappeared before the first saccade of the series was initiated. Only a few injection sites (five) were tested with this task and results varied by site. For two of the sites, the deficit appeared to primarily affect the first saccade in the sequence, whereas for a third site, the second saccade was more affected. For the two remaining sites, the monkey had difficulty performing the double-step task, but the deficit could not be attributed to difficulty with a specific saccade in the sequence. In contrast to the frontal eye field, the deficit produced by inactivation of the supplementary eye field involved difficulty with ipsiversive as well as contraversive saccades. These results emphasize a role for the supplementary eye field in saccadic control that is at a higher level of saccade planning than is the case for the frontal eye field.

Lateral intraparietal cortex

The lateral intraparietal area of posterior parietal cortex is an additional component of the network of cortical areas involved in the control of eye movements (Barash *et al.*

1991a,b; Andersen 1995). The lateral intraparietal area and the frontal eye field both send saccade-related activity to the superior colliculus (Segraves and Goldberg 1987; Paré and Wurtz 1997; Sommer and Wurtz 2000). Inactivation by cooling of either of these cortical areas strongly affects the neuronal activity in the other area (Chafee and Goldman-Rakic 2000).

Li and colleagues (1999) used injections of muscimol (1–2 μl, 8 μg/μl) to investigate the contribution of the lateral intraparietal area to the generation of visually guided and memory-guided saccades. Muscimol injections cause contraversive memory-guided saccades to be reduced in size and have lower than normal velocities. The size and velocity of visually guided saccades were not affected. The latencies of both memory-guided and visually guided contraversive saccades were increased. Unlike the frontal eye field, the effects of these injections did not appear to be topographically localized. Li and colleagues (1999) attribute this to the large receptive fields and course topographic representation in this area. In general, upward saccades appeared to be more affected than downward saccades, which were understood to be the result of a bias for upward movements in this area.

Frontal eye field control of smooth pursuit eye movements

The reversible inactivation method has also been used to study the role of the frontal eye field in the control of smooth pursuit eye movements. In addition to its role in the control of saccadic eye movements, the frontal eye field has been shown to be involved in the control of smooth pursuit movements. Smooth pursuit eye movements are the movements used to track objects moving with velocities of $\leq 80°/s$ (for background, see Leigh and Zee 1999). The smooth pursuit region of the frontal eye field is physically separate from the saccade-related portion, and is located in the fundus and posterior bank of the arcuate sulcus. Neurons in this region are active during smooth pursuit eye movements, and long trains of electrical stimuli can evoke smooth pursuit movements at low thresholds (MacAvoy *et al.* 1991; Gottlieb *et al.* 1993; Gottlieb *et al.* 1994). Surgical lesions of this region also produce long-term deficits in smooth pursuit eye movements (Lynch 1987; Keating 1991).

Shi and colleagues (1998) used microinjections of muscimol (1.0–1.4 μl, 5.0 μg/μl) to reversibly inactivate sites in the smooth pursuit region of the frontal eye field (Fig. 9.5). These injections impaired smooth pursuit primarily in directions toward the side of the injection site. This matches the preferred pursuit directions of cells recorded at the injection sites as well as the direction of pursuit evoked by microstimulation. The effects upon pursuit movements included a reduction in velocity to 10–30% of preinjection velocity, reduced acceleration, and an increase in latency for initiation of pursuit. The ability of the monkey to make saccades was not affected by these injections until late in the experiment, a result attributable to diffusion of muscimol from the injection site. This reinforces the notion that the saccadic and smooth pursuit functions of the frontal eye field are segregated into two separate areas or regions.

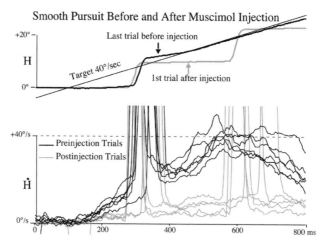

Fig. 9.5 (and color plate 9) Smooth pursuit before (solid lines) and after (dashed lines) an injection of muscimol in the smooth pursuit region of the right frontal eye field. These plots show horizontal eye position (top panel) and velocity (bottom) while the monkey pursued a target that was moving to the right at 40°/s. Before the injection, the monkey acquired the target with a single saccade, and a rapid acceleration brought eye speed equal to target speed within 500–600 ms. Immediately after the injection, the monkey was not able to generate sufficient smooth pursuit acceleration or velocity and followed the moving target with a series of saccadic eye movements. Adapted from Shi *et al.* (1998).

Injections confirmed by recording and microstimulation to be directly into the smooth pursuit region produced immediate changes in smooth pursuit performance. Injections into the adjacent saccade region did produce some deficits in smooth pursuit, but only after 30–60 minutes. This delay was, again, likely due to the time required for muscimol to diffuse from the injection site into the smooth pursuit region.

Conclusions

This chapter has reviewed a number of studies that have used "virtual lesion" methods to investigate the role of cerebral cortex in the control of eye movements. It is clear from these experiments that the lateral intraparietal area, the frontal eye field, and the supplementary eye field each make unique contributions to this process. These findings also reinforce the existence of a network of cortical areas involved in eye movement control. In addition to being interconnected with one another these three cortical areas also project to downstream oculomotor centers, particularly to the superior colliculus. One of the most important problems that we face today is to understand how these areas function together to control eye movements under a variety of conditions. This is a difficult problem to address. The spatial and temporal resolution required is beyond the ability of current brain imaging techniques. One of the most promising approaches requires simultaneous microelectrode recordings made from multiple sites within the network. Virtual lesion methods combined with these multielectrode recordings will provide a means to probe the network on a short-term basis, allowing us to see how the components of the network react to the loss or enhancement of input from a particular cortical site. Virtual lesion methods have replaced surgical ablation as the method of choice for examining the role of individual cortical areas in the control of behavior. In addition, the plasticity and recovery of function issues that plague the ablation method make it unsuitable for studying acute changes within a cortical network (see chapter 7 in this volume). This leaves virtual lesions as the method of choice to use in combination with multielectrode recording techniques to reversibly probe a component of the cortical network. Together, these methods are likely to make a substantial contribution to our understanding of the interactions taking place within a variety of brain systems during the generation of behavior.

Acknowledgments

I'd like to thank Deanne Compaan, Elisa Dias, Janet Helminski, Marin Kiesau, and Marsel Mesulam for their contributions to the work described in this chapter. I am grateful to members of my laboratory group, including Anil Cherian, Janet Choi, Justine MacNeil, Angela Nitzke, and Mike Sherman, for the discussions we have had concerning the material included here. This work was supported by National Eye Institute grant EY08212.

References

Andersen, R. A. (1995) Encoding of intention and spatial location in the posterior parietal cortex. *Cerebral Cortex*, **5:**457–69.

Andrews, P. R. and Johnston, G. A. R. (1979) GABA agonists and antagonists. *Biochemistry and Pharmacology*, **28:**2697–701.

Barash, S., Bracewell, R. M., Fogassi, L. *et al.* (1991a) Saccade-related activity in the lateral intra-parietal area. I. Temporal properties; comparison with area 7a. *Journal of Neurophysiology*, **66:**1095–108.

Barash, S., Bracewell, R. M., Fogassi, L. *et al.* (1991b) Saccade-related activity in the lateral intra-parietal area. II. Spatial properties. *Journal of Neurophysiology*, **66:**1109–24.

Becker, W. (1989) Metrics of saccades. In R. H. Wurtz and M. E. Goldberg (eds) *The Neurobiology of Saccadic Eye Movements, Reviews of Oculomotor Research, vol. III*, pp. 13–67. Elsevier, Amsterdam.

Bruce, C. J. (1990) Integration of sensory and motor signals in primate frontal eye fields. In G. M. Edelman, W. E. Gall, and W. M. Cowan (eds) *Signal and Sense: Local and Global Order in Perceptual Maps*, pp. 261–314. Wiley-Liss, New York.

Bruce, C. J. and Goldberg, M. E. (1985) Primate frontal eye fields: I. Single neurons discharging before saccades. *Journal of Neurophysiology*, **53:**603–35.

Bruce, C. J., Goldberg, M. E., Stanton, G. B. *et al.* (1985) Primate frontal eye fields. II. Physiological and anatomical correlates of electrically evoked eye movements. *Journal of Neurophysiology*, **54:**714–34.

Chafee, M. V. and Goldman-Rakic, P. S. (2000) Inactivation of parietal and prefrontal cortex reveals interdependence of neural activity during memory-guided saccades. *Journal of Neurophysiology*, **83:**1550–66.

Collin, N. G., Cowey, A., Latto, R. *et al.* (1982) The role of frontal eye-fields and superior colliculi in visual search and non-visual search in rhesus monkeys. *Behavioural Brain Research*, **4**:177–93.

Crist, C. F., Yamasaki, D. S. G., Komatsu, H. *et al.* (1988) A grid system and a microsyringe for single cell recording. *Journal of Neuroscience Methods*, **26**:117–22.

Deng, S.-Y., Goldberg, M. E., Segraves, M. A. *et al.* (1986) The effect of unilateral ablation of the frontal eye fields on saccadic performance in the monkey. In D. S. Z. E. Keller (ed.) *Adaptive processes in the visual and oculomotor systems*, pp. 201–8. Pergamon Press, Oxford.

Dias, E. C. and Bruce, C. J. (1994) Physiological correlate of fixation disengagement in the primate's frontal eye field. *Journal of Neurophysiology*, **72**:2532–7.

Dias, E. C., Compaan, D. M., Mesulam, M. M. *et al.* (1996) Selective disruption of memory-guided saccades with injection of a cholinergic antagonist in the frontal eye field of monkey. *Society for Neuroscience Abstracts*, **22**:418.

Dias, E. C., Kiesau, M. and Segraves, M. A. (1995) Acute activation and inactivation of macaque frontal eye field with GABA-related drugs. *Journal of Neurophysiology*, **74**:2744–8.

Dias, E. C. and Segraves, M. A. (1997) A pressure system for the microinjection of substances into the brain of awake monkeys. *Journal of Neuroscience Methods*, **72**:43–7.

Dias, E. C. and Segraves, M. A. (1999) Muscimol-induced inactivation of monkey frontal eye field: effects on visually and memory-guided saccades. *Journal of Neurophysiology*, **81**:2191–214.

Goldberg, M. E. and Segraves, M. A. (1989) The visual and frontal cortices. In R. H. Wurtz and M. E. Goldberg (ed.) *The Neurobiology of Saccadic Eye Movements, Reviews of Oculomotor Research, vol. III*, pp. 283–313. Elsevier, Amsterdam.

Gottlieb, J. P., Bruce, C. J. and MacAvoy, M. G. (1993) Smooth eye movements elicited by microstimulation in the primate frontal eye field. *Journal of Neurophysiology*, **69**:786–99.

Gottlieb, J. P., MacAvoy, M. G. and Bruce, C. J. (1994) Neural responses related to smooth-pursuit eye movements and their correspondence with electrically elicited smooth eye movements in the primate frontal eye field. *Journal of Neurophysiology*, **72**:1634–53.

Guitton, D., Buchtel, H. A. and Douglas, R. M. (1985) Frontal lobe lesions in man cause difficulties in suppressing reflexive glances and in generating goal-directed saccades. *Experimental Brain Research*, **58**:455–72.

Hanes, D. P. and Wurtz, R. H. (2001) Interaction of the frontal eye field and superior colliculus for saccade generation. *Journal of Neurophysiology*, **85**:804–15.

Helminski, J. O. (1998) Macaque frontal eye field input to saccade-related cells in the superior colliculus. Unpublished Ph.D. thesis. Northwestern University, Evanston, IL.

Helminski, J. O. and Segraves, M. A. (1996) Macaque frontal eye field input to saccade-related cells in the superior colliculus. *Society for Neuroscience Abstracts*, **22**:418.

Helminski, J. O. and Segraves, M. A. (1997) Effect of macaque frontal eye field input upon saccade-related cells in the superior colliculus. *Society for Neuroscience Abstracts*, **23**:1296.

Huerta, M. F., Krubitzer, L. A. and Kaas, J. H. (1986) Frontal eye field as defined by intracortical microstimulation in squirrel monkeys, owl monkeys, and macaque monkeys: I. Subcortical connections. *Journal of Comparative Neurology*, **253**:415–39.

Judge, S. J., Richmond, B. J. and Chu, F. C. (1980) Implantation of magnetic search coils for measurement of eye position: an improved method. *Vision Research*, **20**:535–8.

Keating, E. G. (1991) Frontal eye field lesions impair predictive and visually guided pursuit eye movements. *Experimental Brain Research*, **86**:311–23.

Keating, E. G. and Gooley, S. G. (1988) Saccadic disorders caused by cooling the superior colliculus or the frontal eye field, or from combined lesions of both structures. *Brain Research*, **438**:247–55.

Latto, R. M. (1978) The effects of bilateral frontal eye-field, posterior parietal or superior collicular lesions on visual search in the rhesus monkeys. *Brain Research*, **146**:35–50.

Latto, R. and Cowey, A. (1971a) Visual field defects after frontal eye field lesions in monkeys. *Brain Research*, **30**:1–24.

Latto, R. M. and Cowey, A. (1971b) Fixation changes after frontal eye-field lesions in monkeys. *Brain Research*, **30**:25–36.

Leigh, R. J. and Zee, D. S. (1999) *The Neurology of Eye Movements*. Oxford University Press, Oxford.

Li, C. R., Mazzoni, P. and Andersen, R. A. (1999) Effect of reversible inactivation of macaque lateral intraparietal area on visual and memory saccades. *Journal of Neurophysiology*, **81**:1827–38.

Lloyd, K. G. and Morselli, P. L. (1987) Psychopharmacology of GABAergic drugs. In H. Y. Meltzer (ed.) *Psychopharmacology: The Third Generation of Progress*, pp. 183–95. Raven Press, New York.

Lomber, S. G. (1999) The advantages and limitations of permanent or reversible deactivation techniques in the assessment of neural function. *Journal of Neuroscience Methods*, **86**:109–17.

Lynch, J. C. (1987) Frontal eye field lesions in monkeys disrupt visual pursuit. *Experimental Brain Research*, **68**:437–41.

Lynch, J. C. (1992) Saccade initiation and latency deficits after combined lesions of the frontal and posterior eye fields in monkeys. *Journal of Neurophysiology*, **68**:1913–16.

MacAvoy, M. G., Gottlieb, J. P. and Bruce, C. J. (1991) Smooth-pursuit eye movement representation in the primate frontal eye field. *Cerebral Cortex*, **1**:95–102.

Martin, J. H. (1991) Autoradiographic estimation of the extent of reversible inactivation produced by microinjection of lidocaine and muscimol in the rat. *Neuroscience Letters*, **127**:160–4.

Martin, J. H. and Ghez, C. (1999) Pharmacological inactivation in the analysis of the central control of movement. *Journal of Neuroscience Methods*, **86**:145–59.

Mays, L. E. and Sparks, D. L. (1980) Dissociation of visual and saccade-related responses in superior colliculus neurons. *Journal of Neurophysiology*, **43**:207–32.

Munoz, D. P. and Wurtz, R. H. (1995) Saccade-related activity in monkey superior colliculus. I. Characteristics of burst and buildup cells. *Journal of Neurophysiology*, **73**:2313–33.

Oliva, G. A., Bucci, M. P. and Fioravanti, R. (1993) Impairment of saccadic eye movements by scopolamine treatment. *Perceptual and Motor Skills*, **76**:159–67.

Paré, M. and Wurtz, R. H. (1997) Monkey posterior parietal cortex neurons antidromically activated from superior colliculus. *Journal of Neurophysiology*, **78**:3493–7.

Robinson, D. A. (1963) A method of measuring eye movement using a scleral search coil in a magnetic field. *IEEE Transactions in Biomedical Engineering*, **10**:137–45.

Robinson, D. A. and Fuchs, A. F. (1969) Eye movements evoked by stimulation of frontal eye fields. *Journal of Neurophysiology*, **32**:637–48.

Schall, J. D. (1991) Neuronal activity related to visually guided saccades in the frontal eye fields of rhesus monkeys: comparison with supplementary eye fields. *Journal of Neurophysiology*, **66**:559–79.

Schall, J. D. (1997) Visuomotor areas of the frontal lobe. In J. H. Kaas, K. L. Rockland and A. Peters (eds) *Cerebral Cortex, vol. 12, Extrastriate Visual Cortex in Primates*, pp. 527–638. Plenum Press, New York.

Schiller, P. H. and Chou, I. (1998) The effects of frontal eye field and dorsomedial frontal cortex lesions on visually guided eye movements. *Nature Neuroscience*, **1**:248–53.

Schiller, P. H., True, S. D. and Conway, J. L. (1980) Deficits in eye movements following frontal eye field and superior colliculus ablations. *Journal of Neurophysiology*, **44**:1175–89.

Schlag, J. and Schlag-Rey, M. (1987) Evidence for a supplementary eye field. *Journal of Neurophysiology*, **57**:179–200.

Segraves, M. A. (1992) Activity of monkey frontal eye field neurons projecting to oculomotor regions of the pons. *Journal of Neurophysiology*, **68**:1967–85.

Segraves, M. A. and Goldberg, M. E. (1987) Functional properties of corticotectal neurons in the monkey's frontal eye field. *Journal of Neurophysiology*, **58**:1387–419.

Shi, D., Friedman, H. R. and Bruce, C. J. (1998) Deficits in smooth-pursuit eye movements after muscimol inactivation within the primate's frontal eye field. *Journal of Neurophysiology*, **80**:458–64.

Sommer, M. A. and Tehovnik, E. J. (1997) Reversible inactivation of macaque frontal eye field. *Experimental Brain Research*, **116**:229–49.

Sommer, M. A. and Tehovnik, E. J. (1999) Reversible inactivation of macaque dorsomedial frontal cortex: effects on saccades and fixation. *Experimental Brain Research*, **124**:429–46.

Sommer, M. A. and Wurtz, R. H. (2000) Composition and topographic organization of signals sent from the frontal eye field to the superior colliculus. *Journal of Neurophysiology*, **83**:1979–2001.

Stanton, G. B., Bruce, C. J. and Goldberg, M. E. (1988) Frontal eye field efferents in the macaque monkey. I. Subcortical pathways and topography of striatal and thalamic terminal fields. *Journal of Comparative Neurology*, **271**:473–92.

Tehovnik, E. J. and Sommer, M. A. (1997) Effective spread and timecourse of neural inactivation caused by lidocaine injection in monkey cerebral cortex. *Journal of Neuroscience Methods*, **74**:17–26.

Tehovnik, E. J., Sommer, M. A., Chou, I. H. *et al.* (2000) Eye fields in the frontal lobes of primates. *Brain Research Reviews*, **32**:413–48.

Chapter 10

Reversible Impairment of an Auditory–visual Association Task

Germán Sierra-Paredes, Joaquín M. Fuster

Introduction

The dorsolateral prefrontal cortex (DLPC) of the primate plays an essential role in the temporal organization of goal-directed behavior (Fuster 1997). To perform that role, the DLPC engages sensory and motor cortices in complex functional interactions that integrate information from many sources into sequences of purposive action. The most compelling evidence of the temporal integrative role of the DLPC derives from the deficits that lesions of this cortex induce in delay tasks, where a specific sensory item determines a specific action after a delay of a few seconds. The cooling of DLPC has been shown to impair reversibly the performance of visual (Bauer and Fuster 1976; Quintana *et al.* 1993) and tactile (Shindy *et al.* 1994) delay tasks.

Single-unit studies in monkeys performing delay tasks indicate that DLPC cells integrate information across time by supporting two cognitive operations and their underlying mechanisms: the working memory of the sensory cue (Fuster 1973; Niki 1974; Funahashi *et al.* 1989; Miller *et al.* 1996) and the preparation for the forthcoming motor act (Niki and Watanabe 1979; Quintana and Fuster 1999). A recent study, however, indicates that DLPC cells not only integrate information across time by working memory and learning set, but correlate stimuli of two separate modalities (sound and vision) that have been associated behaviorally by learning (Fuster *et al.* 2000). This finding suggests that those cells are component elements of distributed cortical networks that store behavioral associations in long-term memory. The present study examined the effects of cooling DLPC on the performance of a cross-modal audiovisual task. Our objective was to verify that the role of the DLPC in the temporal integration of unimodal—visual or tactile—information extends to the temporal integration of auditory with visual information as well.

Experimental design

The experimental animals were two adult male monkeys (*Macaca mulatta*) also used for a single-unit study (Fuster *et al.* 2000). They were individually housed, with free access to food but restricted access to water on experiment days. The animals were trained to perform an audiovisual matching task (Fig. 10.1). A trial was initiated by the presentation of a 2 sec high-pitch (3000 Hz) or low-pitch (240 Hz) tone (45 db above background) through an overhead speaker. Simultaneously with that tone, or after a delay of 5 or 10 sec, the animal was presented with two colors, red and green, on two side-by-side stimulus–response disks. If the tone was high-pitched, the animal had to touch the red disk; if low pitched, the green disk. Tone pitch and relative position of colors changed randomly between trials. Correct color choices were rewarded with fruit juice. The animals were trained until they reached the criterion of 75% correct responses with 10 sec delays.

Following completion of training, surgery was performed under strictly aseptic conditions and general Nembutal anesthesia. Hollow cylindrical pedestals (17 mm I.D.) were implanted bilaterally in circular skull openings, for later support of Peltier coolers (or a microelectrode drive) over the DLPC—including parts of areas 8, 9, 10, and 46 of Brodmann. In one of the animals, additional pedestals were implanted bilaterally over posterior parietal cortex—including parts of areas 5 and 7. A subdural miniature thermistor was implanted in the center of each pedestal for cortical temperature control. With a cooler in place, the effective cortical cooling surface was 19 mm.

After recovery from surgery, the animals were tested on the task in a succession of alternating control and cooling sessions, one session per day. Up to 150 trials were administered to an animal on a given session, in mixed blocks of simultaneous and

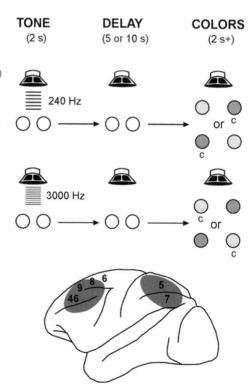

TONE (2 s)   **DELAY** (5 or 10 s)   **COLORS** (2 s+)

Fig. 10.1 (and color plate 10) Above: The audiovisual task. A trial begins with a 2 sec tone, low-pitch or high-pitch. After a delay, two color disks appeared on a panel in front of the animal. The animal is rewarded for choosing the green disk if the tone was low-pitch and the red disk if high-pitch (c, correct response). In the simultaneous—no delay—variant of the task, the tone and the colors are presented simultaneously. Below: Diagram of the monkey's brain showing (in blue) the position of the cooling probes. Numbers refer to approximate location of Brodmann's areas.

delayed sound-color matching. In control sessions, the animal performed the task with the head restrained and two thermoelectric coolers (Hayward *et al.* 1965) inserted in two of the cylinder-pedestals but inactive (that is, with cortex at normal temperature). During cooling sessions, the animal performed the task under identical conditions but with the cooling cylinders activated bilaterally over either prefrontal or parietal cortex. Three levels of cortical cooling were tested on frontal cortex: 25°C, 15°C, and 10°C; one level only—10°C—was tested on parietal cortex. Two measures of behavior were obtained under each experimental condition: (a) percentage of correct-response trials, and (b) reaction time, i.e., time from color presentation to manual choice of color. After normalization by arc-sine transformation, the data were submitted to a two-way ANOVA (main variables: monkey, delay, temperature). All surgery and experiments were conducted by adherence to guidelines from the UCLA Division of Animal Medicine, the Society for Neuroscience and the National Institutes of Health.

Behavior during DLPC deactivation

In the acute monkey preparation (Fuster and Bauer 1974), the temperature gradients under and around a cortical cooling probe of the Peltier-type, as those used in the present experiment, are relatively steep. While cortical surface temperature is at 20°C, for example, the temperature of cortex 10 mm under a cooling probe is almost normal. Consequently, surface cooling, even to a temperature as low as 10°C, cannot be assumed to produce more than a temporary and reversible depression of neural activity in the underlying cortex.

The bilateral cooling of either cortical region, prefrontal or parietal, at any of the temperatures tested, failed to induce any overt effect on the normal behavior of the animals outside of the testing situation. Ocular and manual motility and dexterity appeared unimpaired (e.g., reaching to and grasping with the fingers small cubes of fruit). The motivation of the animals to perform the task also appeared to be unimpaired.

At normal cortical temperature (control condition), the average of correct performance was about 85% on simultaneous tone-color matching, and lower on trials with 5 or 10 sec delay (Fig. 10.2). Under bilateral prefrontal cooling, the percentage of correct performance was significantly lower than at normal temperature (comparing the pooled results at the three levels of hypothermia with those at normal temperature). The effect of cooling was especially apparent at 10°C. Table 10.1 shows the results of the analysis of the effects of the three main variables—monkey, delay, and temperature—on performance and reaction time. The effects of delay and temperature on performance were significant, but not the interaction of those two variables.

The monkey effect on reaction time was significant (one animal generally faster than the other), and so was the effect of delay on reaction time. However, prefrontal cooling did not have a significant effect on the reaction time of either animal.

The bilateral cooling of posterior parietal cortex to 10°C did not induce any significant change on levels of correct performance in any of the task variants—simultaneous,

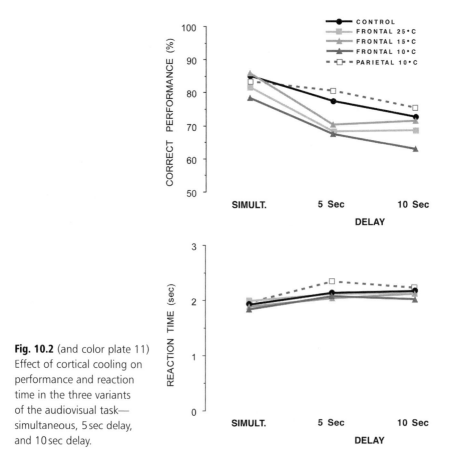

Fig. 10.2 (and color plate 11) Effect of cortical cooling on performance and reaction time in the three variants of the audiovisual task—simultaneous, 5 sec delay, and 10 sec delay.

Table 10.1 ANOVA for prefrontal cooling

	df	Performance		Reaction time	
		F	p	F	p
Monkey	1	1.676	>0.10	6.419	<0.02
Delay	2	27.919	<0.001	13.029	<0.001
Temperature	3	3.461	<0.02	2.461	>0.05
Delay×Temperature	6	0.155	>0.1	0.403	>0.1

5 sec delay, and 10 sec delay (Fig. 10.2). Nor did parietal cooling induce any significant change in reaction time.

Implications

The absence of effects of cortical cooling on reaction time or on the overt behavior of the animal outside of the task indicates that cortical hypothermia did not affect motivation or purposeful movement. Thus, the deficit that prefrontal cooling induced on performance of the task was cognitive. Insofar as this deficit, however modest, could be observed on the simultaneous matching of auditory and visual stimuli, it appeared to stem from faulty perception of the relationship between a sound and the corresponding color. That tone-color association was a rule of performance that the animal had acquired in the process of learning the task. In this respect present findings are in good agreement with the finding (Fuster *et al.* 2000) that, within the frontal region cooled in these experiments, cells fire in correlated fashion to tones and colors that have been associated by learning.

The results induced by prefrontal cooling on performance of the audiovisual delay task complement those observed by use of the same procedure on visual (Bauer and Fuster 1976; Quintana and Fuster 1993) and tactile (Shindy *et al.* 1994) delay tasks. The dorsolateral prefrontal area cooled in the present audiovisual task is almost identical to the area cooled in those tasks. Ablations of DLPC have long been known to induce deficits in performance of spatial delay tasks (Jacobsen 1931; Goldman and Rosvold 1970). Thus, the dorsolateral frontal area cooled in the present study appears to play a supramodal role in working memory. That role applies to the short-term retention of not only visual information, whether spatially defined or not (e.g., color), but tactile information as well. The present study indicates that the role of the DLPC in working memory extends to items of associative auditory–visual information.

A large literature provides evidence of 'working-memory cells' in DLPC (e.g., Fuster 1973; Niki 1974; Funahashi *et al.* 1989; Miller *et al.* 1996; Quintana and Fuster 1999). Those are cells that during the mnemonic retention of a sensory item—that is, in the delay period of a delay task—fire persistently at levels higher than in intertrial baseline conditions (no memorization required). That persistent discharge in the delay period has been found (a) related to the need to perform motor responses in accord with the memorandum, and (b) correlated with the animal's level of performance (efficacy of working memory). A study of unit firing in the present task (Fuster *et al.* 2000) shows cells whose reactions to the tone correlate with their reactions to the associated color after the 10 sec delay; the activity of some of those cells during the delay was correlated with both the tone and the color. Further, both the correlation and the delay–activity were diminished in incorrect response trials. The unit correlation of reactions to the two associated stimuli, auditory and visual, implicates those cells in the network that represents that association in long-term memory. It is reasonable to suppose that, in the present study, the poorer performance of the task under DLPC cooling resulted in part from the cryogenic depression of the discharge of those cells in the retrieval of that memory. In addition, the depression of the working-memory function of DLPC cells may have contributed to the deficit.

In conclusion, the deficit induced by DLPC cooling in the audiovisual cross-modal task appears to be the result of a failure of two related neural processes that mediate the integration of the task: (a) the activation of an associative auditory–visual network, and (b) the maintenance of that activation through the delay or memory period of the task. This interpretation agrees with the notion that the role of the DLPC in so-called working memory consists basically in the temporary, goal-directed, activation of a preestablished memory network (Fuster 1995). The formation of that network during learning, as well as its temporary activation in the cross-modal task, are most likely served by reciprocal connections of the DLPC with cortices of auditory and visual association (Pandya and Yeterian 1985). Functional interactions between DLPC and inferotemporal cortex in the working memory of visual stimuli (colors) have been investigated by the concomitant use of cryogenic and microelectrode methods (Fuster *et al.* 1985). The cooling of either cortex, prefrontal or inferotemporal, induces a deficit in visual working memory; at the same time, the cells in the other cortex show a diminution of their capacity to discriminate the visual memoranda by firing frequency. These observations indicate that working memory engages connection loops between the two cortices in reverberating activity, and the cooling of either cortex interrupts those loops. Comparable loops between DLPC and auditory association cortex may have been disrupted by prefrontal cooling in the audiovisual memory task utilized for the present study.

Acknowledgments

We thank William Bergerson and Bradford Lubell for valuable technical assistance. This work was supported by grants from the National Institute of Mental Health. G. Sierra-Paredes was an International Post-doctoral Fellow of the Xunta de Galicia, Spain.

References

Bauer, R. H. and Fuster, J. M. (1976) Delayed-matching and delayed-response deficit from cooling dorsolateral prefrontal cortex in monkeys. *Journal of Comparative and Physiological Psychology*, **90**:293–302.

Funahashi, S., Bruce, C. J. and Goldman-Rakic, P. S. (1989) Mnemonic coding of visual space in the monkey's dorsolateral prefrontal cortex. *Journal of Neurophysiology*, **61**:331–49.

Fuster, J. M. (1995) *Memory in the Cerebral Cortex—An Empirical Approach to Neural Networks in the Human and Nonhuman Primate*. MIT Press, Cambridge, MA.

Fuster, J. M. (1997) *The Prefrontal Cortex—Anatomy Physiology, and Neuropsychology of the Frontal Lobe*, 3rd edn. Lippincott-Raven, Philadelphia, PA.

Fuster, J. M. and Bauer, R. H. (1974) Visual short-term memory deficit from hypothermia of frontal cortex. *Brain Research*, **81**:393–400.

Fuster, J. M., Bauer, R. H. and Jervey, J. P. (1985) Functional interactions between inferotemporal and prefrontal cortex in a cognitive task. *Brain Research*, **330**:299–307.

Fuster, J. M., Bodner, M. and Kroger, J. (2000) Cross-modal and cross-temporal association in neurons of frontal cortex. *Nature*, **405**:347–51.

Goldman, P. S. and Rosvold, H. E. (1970) Localization of function within the dorsolateral prefrontal cortex of the rhesus monkey. *Experimental Neurology*, **27**:291–304.

Hayward, J. N., Ott, L. H., Stuart, D. G. *et al.* (1965) Peltier biothermodes. *American Journal of Medical Electronics*, **4**:11–9.

Jacobsen, C. F. (1931) A study of cerebral function in learning: The frontal lobes. *Journal of Comparative Neurology*, **52**:271–340.

Miller, E. K., Erickson, C. A. and Desimone, R. (1996) Neural mechanisms of visual working memory in the prefrontal cortex of the macaque. *Journal of Neuroscience*, **16:**5154–67.

Niki, H. (1974) Differential activity of prefrontal units during right and left delayed response trials. *Brain Research*, **70:**346–9.

Niki, H. and Watanabe, M. (1979) Prefrontal and cingulate unit activity during timing behavior in the monkey. *Brain Research*, **171:**213–24.

Pandya, D. N. and Yeterian, E. H. (1985) Architecture and connections of cortical association areas. In A. Peters and E. G. Jones (eds) *Cerebral Cortex*, vol. 4, pp. 3–61. Plenum Press, New York.

Quintana, J. and Fuster, J. M. (1993) Spatial and temporal factors in the role of prefrontal and parietal cortex in visuomotor integration. *Cerebral Cortex*, **3:**122–32.

Quintana, J. and Fuster, J. M. (1999) From perception to action: Temporal integrative functions of prefrontal and parietal neurons. *Cerebral Cortex*, **9:**213–21.

Shindy, W. W., Posley, K. A. and Fuster, J. M. (1994) Reversible deficit in haptic delay tasks from cooling prefrontal cortex. *Cerebral Cortex*, **4:**443–50.

Part III

Probing the Human Brain

Case Studies in Virtual Neuropsychology: Reversible Lesions and Magnetic Brain Stimulation

Vincent Walsh, Alvaro Pascual-Leone

Introduction

Transcranial Magnetic Stimulation (TMS) is now an established technique in cognitive neuroscience. The utility of the technique can be stated simply: the temporary disruption of normal cortical functioning, within a prescribed brain region and/or period of processing, can be used to study the effects of lesions in real time, without the masking effects of the "specter of compensation." These virtual lesion patients produced by TMS can be used as their own controls, unlike real neuropsychological patients and, again unlike in real patients, the temporal resolution of TMS makes a chronometric analysis of the virtual lesion effects possible.

There are several types of virtual patients one can produce and the main ones are shown in Fig. 11.1. TMS can be used to produce errors or deficits by disrupting the primary function of focus either on-line or distally (Fig. 11.1, top), or the effect of stimulating one area may be to disinhibit function in a second area (Fig. 11.1, middle) that may lead to a paradoxical improvement in the task. Double virtual lesions can also be used to assess interactions between areas (Fig. 11.1, bottom). In addition, patients with neuropsychological deficits can be stimulated as a means of assessing interactions between remaining functions of the lesioned area with intact areas. In this chapter we describe experiments from each of these categories and focus on the methodological importance of the experiments as well as the theoretical questions they aimed to address. The technical details of TMS have been provided in several publications and we therefore deal with the empirical findings in the first half of the chapter before outlining the relevant technical aspects in the second half.

Fig. 11.1 Different spatial modes of TMS. The most common use of magnetic stimulation is to apply pulses over a single brain area of interest to directly influence this site (top), or, much more difficult to establish, it can be applied over an area with the intention of changing activity—which might mean disinhibiting as much as disrupting—at a secondary site (middle panel). TMS can also be applied to two sites simultaneously or with some given stimulation onset asynchrony to investigate the timing of the interactions of two areas (e.g. Pascual-Leone and Walsh [2001] bottom panel).

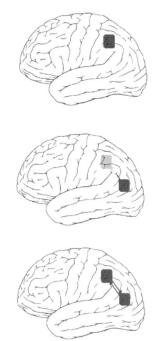

Case studies

The parietal cortex, attention and binding

The function of the parietal cortex is an anchor for many theories of visual attention and binding. Patients with damage to the right parietal cortex may exhibit a range of deficits that include detection of a conjunction target in a visual search array (Arguin *et al.* 1990, 1993; Friedman-Hill *et al.* 1995), inability to attend to the left side of visual space (Weintraub and Mesulam 1987; Bisiach and Vallar 1988) and inaccurate saccadic eye movements. The first two deficits are often linked together and one explanation of these patients' failure to detect conjunction targets is that their spatial attentional problems prevent them from performing what is referred to as "visual binding" (Treisman 1996). The posterior parietal cortex lies on the dorsolateral surface of the cortex and is easily accessible to TMS. In an attempt to model the effects of right parietal lesions a number of single pulse studies have been carried out. Ashbridge *et al.* (1997) stimulated right posterior parietal cortex (PPC) while subjects carried out standard "feature" and "conjunction" visual search tasks (Fig. 11.2). Patients with right PPC lesions are impaired on the conjunction tasks but not the feature tasks. TMS over right PPC replicated these two basic findings but with some important differences. Single pulses of TMS were applied at stimulus-TMS onset asynchronies of between 0 and 200 msecs and subjects showed two patterns of effect. The reaction time to report "target present" was maximally increased when TMS was applied around 100 msecs after visual stimulus onset but to increase the time taken to report "target absent" TMS had to be applied around 160 msecs after visual array onset (Fig. 11.3). Here, then, TMS has replicated the patient data (PPC damage impairs conjunction search) but it adds two further items of information—that the PPC is important for target absent responses and that

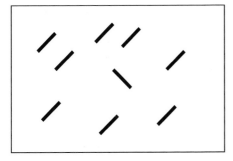

Fig. 11.2 (and color plate 12) Feature and conjunction visual search tasks. In the feature task, the target is defined by a single dimensional difference and in the conjunction tasks, by two dimensions.

Fig. 11.3 The effects of TMS applied to parietal cortex during visual search. The dotted line at 1 on the ordinate indicates the control reaction time in the absence of TMS. The solid line which peaks at 100 msecs represents reaction time, relative to control trials, when a target was present; the dashed line which peaks at 160 msecs represents reaction time, relative to control trials when the target was absent.

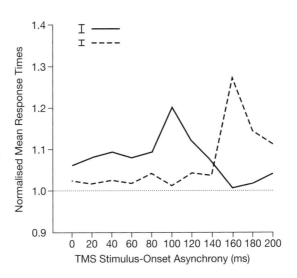

the mechanisms underlying target present and target absent responses occupy different time windows in PPC. Patients often have an array of problems that mean that standard psychological experimental paradigms have to be modified and reaction time studies might be problematic. In studies of visual search the patients are likely to report a high level of false positives and thus we have little knowledge from the patients about how the PPC might contribute to search in the absence of the target. Indeed because of the patients' propensity to report positively, the deficit has been interpreted predominantly as one of visual binding. The target absent data requires that this conclusion be reconsidered. If PPC is important to both target present and target absent trials it is unlikely that its special role in visual search is binding the separate features of the target—in target absent trials there is no target to bind. The answer to the role of PPC lies in the relative timing of the TMS effects on present and absent responses. Target present responses typically occur more quickly than target absent responses (784 ms and 856 ms respectively in the experiment discussed here) and the order of the TMS effects mirror this. This is something observed in many subsequent studies. A parsimonious

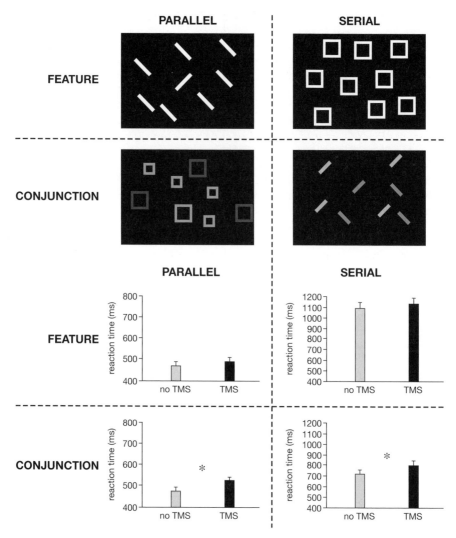

Fig. 11.4 (and color plate 13) Comparison of the effects of TMS on feature and conjunction search tasks independent of whether performance on the task is serial or parallel. TMS was applied over right posterior parietal cortex in seven subjects. TMS caused an increase in RTs when the visual search array presented the subjects with a conjunction task irrespective of task difficulty. TMS did not have any effect on the performance of feature discrimination tasks even when the feature task was harder (defined as taking longer per item in the display) than a conjunction task that was disrupted by TMS.

interpretation of these data is that the PPC contribution to the components of visual search that involve binding of visual attributes, is not predominantly (if at all) visual, for which the extrastriate visual areas seem sufficient (Corbetta *et al.* 1991, 1995), but rather to the response component of search.

Conjunction searches used in experiments to compare performance with feature searches are usually selected to yield a serial search function, likewise the feature searches are selected because they return a flat RT/set size slope. Thus the failure of a patient with damage to the parietal cortex to detect conjunction targets accurately may be due to the difficulty of identifying conjunctions relative to features, rather than to anything intrinsic to feature binding. To investigate this Ellison *et al.* (submitted) gave subjects hard and easy feature and conjunction search tasks to dissociate the importance of binding from difficulty. The easy feature and conjunction tasks were performed with a flat search function and the hard feature and conjunction searches which gave a serial function and longer intercepts than the easy tasks. Figure 11.4 shows the four tasks used. TMS was given over the right posterior parietal cortex at 10 Hz for 500 msecs at approximately 60% of stimulator output at the onset of the visual array. TMS significantly lengthened reaction times on the two serial tasks but had no effect on the two parallel tasks. From this experiment, then it seems that the parietal cortex does have an important role in some element of conjunction searches. In their next experiment, Ellison and colleagues used the same targets and distractors, but presented them as singletons on each trial and the subject was then required to decide whether the stimulus present was a target or a distractor (Fig. 11.5). In one condition the stimulus was always presented in the center of the computer monitor and in the other condition the stimulus could appear anywhere on the monitor. TMS over right PPC did not affect the reaction time for detection of the conjunction target when it was in the center of the monitor, but did slow down the subjects when it could appear anywhere on the screen. The combined results of these two experiments suggest that PPC is important for conjunction detection but only when the spatial location of the appearance of the stimulus is uncertain. This could be taken as consistent with the claim that PPC is necessary for the spatial processing that is a prerequisite of visual binding (Friedman-Hill *et al.* 1995). However, the lack of TMS effects on the conjunction detection task in the center-only condition weakens an account based on binding of features.

A clue to the function of the PPC is in its anatomical location; poised between the visual and motor cortices it would seem that the critical role of PPC in visual search is visuo-motor, perhaps an involvement in initially forming stimulus response associations. An alternative view to Ellison and associates' data therefore would be to interpret the TMS costs incurred when spatial uncertainty is introduced to the task as a cost in deciding where in space to direct one's response. A third experiment also favours a response-based view of the PPC function in search rather than a visual binding account. Figure 11.6 shows the reaction time increases produced by TMS over PPC in a conjunction visual search task with two different set sizes. The increase in reaction time remains relatively constant and is not related to the number of elements in the visual array. Any function disrupted as a function of a visual component of the task might be expected to be increasingly disrupted as the visual component of the task increased.

The parietal cortex and visual neglect

The effects of TMS rarely provide an exact match for patients' deficits and the differences between real and virtual lesion patients can be important. In the first demonstration of attentional effects with rTMS Pascual-Leone and colleagues (1994) applied 25 Hz TMS over the occipital, parietal or temporal cortices. The aim was to study a well-known phenomenon, visual extinction, most often seen following right parietal lesions. Subjects showing extinction can detect and identify targets that are presented singly in one or other of the two visual fields but are unable to detect the stimulus in the field contralateral to the lesion if the two stimuli are presented together. In Pascual-Leone and colleagues' study, stimulation of the right parietal cortex duly reproduced visual extinction of left visual field stimuli when two targets were presented. But left parietal stimulation also produced the phenomenon with equal facility (Fig. 11.7). As expected, occipital stimulation interfered with the perception of any stimuli contralateral to the hemisphere that received TMS and no clear effects were seen with temporal cortex stimulation. The difference between the real and virtual patients can be accounted for by

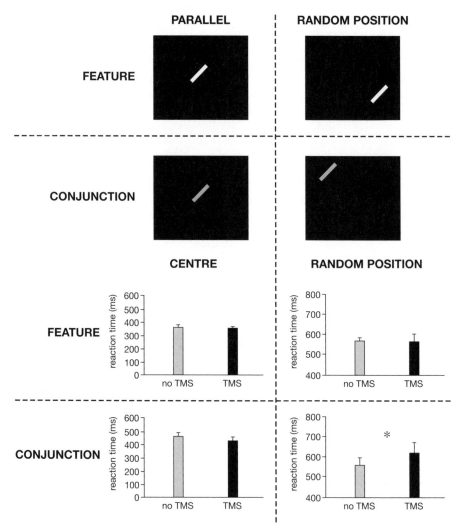

Fig. 11.5 (and color plate 14) The effects of TMS on identifying the presence or absence of a conjunction target are not significant when the spatial location of the discriminanda is known and there are no distractors in the array.

again taking into account reorganization following brain damage. From this experiment one could conclude that both hemispheres are equally balanced in the competition for attention to visual areas and the predominance of the right hemisphere, inferred from extinction studies of neuropsychological patients, is due to an advantage in reorganization of the left hemisphere.

Modeling of visual neglect by Fierro *et al.* (2000) reinforces the common view that the right hemisphere does have a special role in visuospatial orienting. Neglect is widely studied in neuropsychological patients but there are many differences between patients and the tendency is for the phenomenon to be transient (Bisiach and Vallar 1988). By taking a psychophysical approach, Fierro and associates

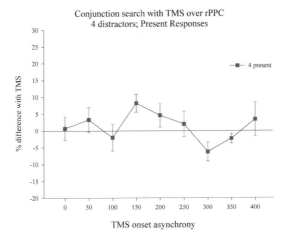

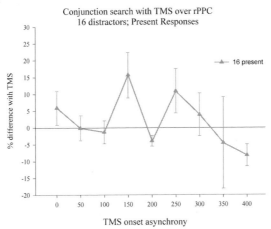

Fig. 11.6 Reaction time increases produced by TMS over PPC in a conjunction visual search task with two different set sizes.

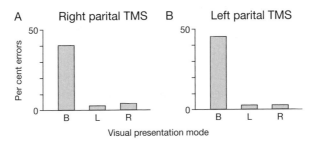

Fig. 11.7 Visual extinction produced by TMS. Data replotted from Pascual-Leone et al. (1994). When two stimuli are presented simultaneously (one in each hemifield indicated as B on the abscissa). TMS over the parietal lobe reduces detection of the stimulus in the contralateral visual field to chance levels. Detection is not reduced when single stimuli are presented to one hemifield (L or R).

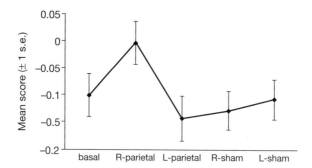

Fig. 11.8 The effect of TMS on the perception of bisected lines. When TMS is applied to the right parietal cortex subjects judged the relative lengths of the two sides of bisected lines relatively well. Without TMS the subjects showed a right "pseudoneglect" and judged the left sides of the lines to be longer than they were. TMS over left parietal cortex had no effect on this pseudoneglect nor did sham TMS over left or right parietal cortex. In principle, this correction of a pseudoneglect may provide a basis for modeling the neglect suffered by neuropsychological patients. From Fierro *et al.* (2000) with permission.

have produced a protocol that may be useful in modeling neglect. Subjects were briefly presented (50 msecs) with prebisected lines and required to judge whether the left, right or neither side was longer. In control trials there was a pseudoneglect tendency, consistent with right hemisphere bias to report the left as longer (Bowers and Heilman 1980; McCourt and Jewell 1999). On TMS trials, pulses were delivered at 115% of motor threshold at 25 Hz for 400 msecs over left or right parietal cortex at the time of stimulus onset. Right parietal stimulation corrected the pseudoneglect but left parietal and sham TMS did not change the subjects' behaviour (Fig. 11.8). The ability to reproduce neglect is an important step in modeling the phenomenon and one wonders whether a reaction time approach might increase the sensitivity of this particular assay.

The parietal cortex and motor attention

Studies of single unit activity in the parietal cortex of monkeys have shown that orienting attention is closely associated with preparation of oculomotor responses. This has led to the proposal that the role of the parietal cortex is best described as intentional (to emphasize the motor role) rather than attentional (Rizzolatti *et al.* 1997; Snyder *et al.* 1997) To address this attention/intention debate Rushworth *et al.* (2001) investigated the possibility that other attentional mechanisms might be tied to a particular response modality. In monkeys the posterior region of the parietal cortex (area 7a) is anatomically connected to visual areas and the frontal eye fields (Paus *et al.* 1997; Goldman-Rakic 1998) whereas another region (area 7b) is connected with somatosensory and motor cortices (Goldman-Rakic 1998). The human homologues of the macaque areas are the posterior parietal cortex (area 7a) and the supramarginal gyrus (area 7b). On the basis of the anatomical connectivity of the supramarginal gyrus (SMG), Rushworth and colleagues hypothesized that rTMS applied here should interfere with motor attention but not visual orienting attention while rTMS to the posterior parietal cortex should have the opposite pattern of effects. Figure 11.9 shows the tasks presented to subjects to test this hypothesis.

The visual orienting task did not require any motor decision component, simply a reflex response when the target red square was detected. Subjects fixated the center of the screen and were presented with a green rectangle that cued the location at which the target red square would appear. Usually the

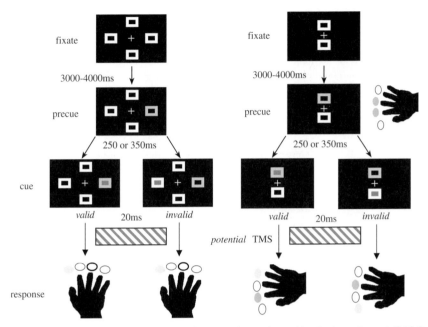

Fig. 11.9 (and color plate 15) Right. Orienting attention task used by Rushworth *et al.* (2001): Subjects maintained fixation of a central cross between four white outline boxes (top). The box outline changing from white to green (middle) was the precue that instructed subjects to orient to one of the four locations. After a gap of 250 ms or 350 ms a target (a box *center* turning red) appeared at one of the four locations (bottom). On 75% of trials the precue was valid and correctly predicted the target position (bottom left). On 20% of trials the precue was invalid and the target appeared in the box on the opposite side of fixation (bottom *center*). On 5% of trials no target was presented (bottom right). The type of response made by the subjects is shown at the very bottom of the figure. Each trial begun once the subject was not pressing any of the four response keys. Whenever a target was presented, at any of the four locations, subjects made the same key press response with the index finger. On the 5% of trials, on which no target was presented, the subjects had to refrain from pressing the button for 2000 ms. rTMS trains were delivered at random on 50% of invalidly cued trials and 10% of the more frequent validly cued trials. Left. Motor attention task used by Rushworth *et al.* (2001). Subjects fixated a central cross between two white boxes (top). In this task the box *centers* were close above and below fixation. At the beginning of each trial the subject used the middle and index fingers of the same hand to press down the central two keys of the keypad (middle finger home button [HM] and the index finger home button [HI]). The box outline turning from white to green (middle) was the cue that allowed subjects to direct motor attention to the response they would make in the final part of the trial (bottom), 450 ms or 800 ms later when a target appeared in one of the boxes. Subjects responded to a lower target (right) by using the index finger to press the lowest key (bottom target [BT]) while simultaneously keeping the middle finger pressed on its home key (HM) at the center. The response to an upper target (left) was to press the middle finger on the upper key (top target, [TT]) while simultaneously keeping the index finger on its home key (HI) at the center. On 80% of trials the cue was valid and correctly warned the subject which response would be made. The cue was invalid on 20% of trials. rTMS trains were delivered at random on 50% of invalidly cued trials and 10% of validly cued trials.

cue correctly indicated the location of the target but on 20% of trials the cue was invalid and incorrectly cued the location. This is a version of the task used by Posner *et al.* (1984) to show that patients with right parietal damage were impaired at switching attention from a cued to an uncued location. In the motor attention task the subjects were cued not for a visual location but for which finger to press in response to the onset of the target. Again the cue was usually correct but was invalid on 20% of trials. This is a motor analogue of the visual orienting response. Repetitive pulse TMS (10 Hz for 500 msecs) was applied over the right or left PPC or the right or left SMG 20 msecs after the onset of the target. The outcome showed that the parietal cortex is critical for both motor intention and visual attention. When rTMS was applied over the right PPC there was an increase in reaction time on the invalid trials of the visual orienting task (Fig. 11.10) but no effect on the motor attention task. When rTMS was applied over the left SMG there was an increase in reaction time on the invalid trials of the motor attention task for left hand (Fig. 11.11) and right hand responses (Fig. 11.12) but not the visual orienting task (Fig. 11.10). The physiological data from non-human primates therefore is consistent with respect to visual and motor attention, but whereas in the monkey the two functions require the intraparietal sulcus, in man they have become lateralised, presumably reflecting the left hemisphere's crucial role in movement selection and execution and the right hemisphere's preeminence in visuospatial function.

Secondary disinhibition and performance enhancements

Brain damage can occasionally result in an improvement of function or a return of a previously compromised ability. The most famous example is the original Sprague effect. Sprague (1966) removed regions of the right occipito-temporal cortex and produced a corresponding hemianopia in the contralateral visual field. By subsequently lesioning the left superior colliculus, Sprague was able to restore responses to visual stimuli in the left visual field and concluded that the original deficit was due to inhibition or suppression of the right colliculus by the left.

There are now many replications and reports of similar effects in the animal literature (Hardy and Stein 1988; Lomber and Payne 1996) and several reports of functional facilitation in human subjects (see Kapur 1996). The two main classes of facilitation have been termed "restorative" wherein a hitherto deficient function has returned (as in the Sprague effect), and "enhancing" in which some damage or loss of function results in the patient performing better than normal subjects at some task. Both classes of facilitation reveal much of interest about the dynamic interactions between different modalities or even components of sensory modalities. Nevertheless, as Kapur notes "such findings have often been ignored or undervalued in the brain-behaviour research literature." Perhaps this is because paradoxical facilitations are less common and less salient than deficits and also more difficult to interpret. Recent neurocomputing work may be useful in imposing some direction and also constraints on the search for and interpretation of facilitatory effects of TMS (Hilgetag *et al.* 1999; Young *et al.* 1999, 2000). One simulation, for example, showed that the connectivity of a cortical area was a strong predictor of the effects of lesions on the rest of the network as well as how that area responded to a lesion elsewhere in the network. This may seem like a truism but the kind of connectivity analysis offered by these models is not really taken into account in

Orienting Attention Task

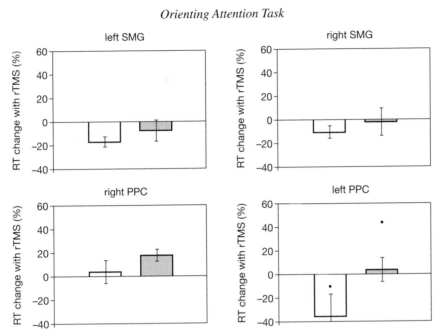

Fig. 11.10 Orienting attention experiment results: The results when rTMS was delivered over the right and left hemisphere sites are shown on the right and the left respectively. The results from when rTMS was delivered over SMG or ANG sites are shown above and below respectively. Hollow and filled bars show the results for non-rTMS control trials and rTMS trials respectively. Data collected on valid and invalid trials are respectively shown on the left and right of each panel. In general rTMS at most sites has little effect or causes some facilitation. At the right ANG site (bottom right) only, however, rTMS caused a significant slowing of RT, by a mean of 68 ms, on invalid trials only.

classical lesion analysis (see also Robertson and Murre, 1999; Rossini and Pauri 2000) and the modelling work has begun to make these predictions explicit and testable.

In the visual system, Walsh *et al.* (1998) stimulated visual area V5 in an attempt to model the "motion blind" patient L.M. (Zihl *et al.* 1983; McLeod *et al.* 1989) and indeed V5 stimulation did impair performance on visual search tasks that involved scanning complex motion displays. On displays in which motion was absent or irrelevant to task performance, subjects were faster with TMS than in control trials (Fig. 11.13). This can be interpreted as evidence that the separate visual modalities may compete for resources and the disruption of the motion system may have liberated other visual areas from its influence. In this experiment the subjects received blocks of trials of a single type and therefore knew whether the upcoming stimulus array would contain movement, color or form as the important parameter. When the types of trials are interleaved such that the subject does not have advance information, the enhancing effects of TMS were not obtained. Therefore, it seems that a combination of priming

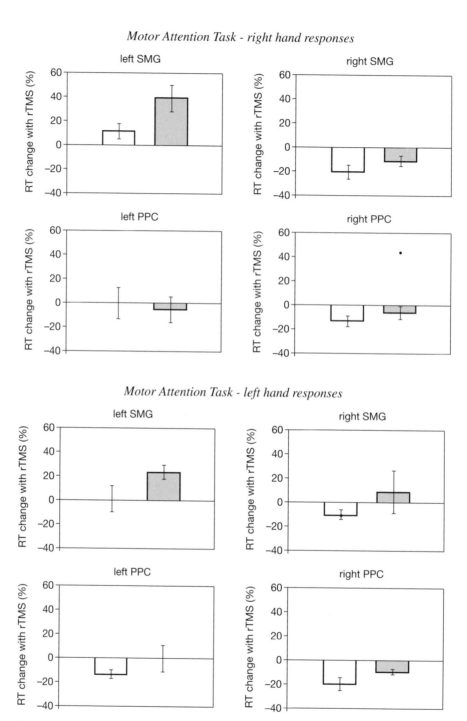

Fig. 11.11 and Fig. 11.12 Motor attention experiment results: The same conventions are used as in Fig. 11.10. The results for subjects using their left hand (Fig. 11.11) or right hand

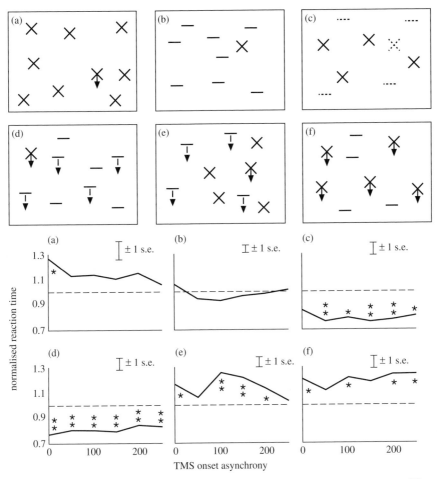

Fig. 11.13 Applying TMS to a region of cortex can enhance or inhibit performance on different tasks. (A) six visual search tasks in which subjects were required to detect the presence or absence of a target. (B) effects of applying TMS to area V5. In two tasks (tasks a and b there is little or no effect of TMS. When TMS is applied to V5 during a search requiring attention to motion (tasks e and f) performance is significantly slower with TMS. Tasks on which attention to attributes other than motion is required are facilitated by TMS over V5. Dotted line at 1 represents reaction times without TMS. Solid lines show reaction times with TMS relative to without. From Walsh *et al.* (1998) with permission.

Fig. 11.11 and Fig. 11.12 (continued)
(Fig. 11.12) are shown separately. In general rTMS at most sites has little effect or causes some facilitation. There was, however, a significant impairment when rTMS was delivered over the left SMG. The effect of left SMG rTMS was significantly greater on invalid trials and RT was significantly slowed on invalid trials only, regardless of whether the right (255 ms effect) or left (131 ms) hand was used.

(due to the advanced knowledge of the stimuli) and weakening of the V5 system (by TMS) were required to enhance performance on color and form tasks. Conceptually similar is the finding of Seyal *et al.* (1995) who observed increases in tactile sensitivity as a result of stimulation of the somatosensory cortex ipsilateral to fingers being tested. The interpretation here is also based on disinhibition of the unstimulated hemisphere.

Imagery and awareness

There are many instances of lesion studies being in apparent conflict with single unit physiology or brain imaging results. These disagreements are often caused by different experimental conditions being used with the two techniques or by a lack of overlap between the spatiotemporal properties of the two techniques and thus a debate being carried out across a divide between two different problem spaces. The solution often has to come from another technical avenue. The role of primary visual area V1 in visual imagery has been one such dispute. When subjects are asked to use depictive imagery, blood flow in area V1 is increased relative to a condition in which no visual stimuli are presented and visual imagination is not required. The question is whether imagery depends upon V1 (Kosslyn 1988, 1993a,b) or if the activity seen is epiphenomenal or not representative of visuotopic processing in imagery. To investigate this, Kosslyn *et al.* (1999) used identical task conditions in an rTMS study and in a PET experiment. In the TMS experiment subjects received 1 Hz stimulation at 90% of motor threshold for ten minutes. They were then required to visualize and compare the properties of memorized images of grating patterns or of real images of the same stimuli. The reaction times of subjects were significantly increased in both real perception and imagery conditions (Fig. 11.14) showing that area V1 was critical for visual imagery as well as real perception.

Another long running debate regarding visual function and primary visual cortex centers around whether area V1 is necessary or whether functionally specialized areas such as V4 and V5 are sufficient for awareness of the visual attribute for which they are specialized. Stimulation over the extrastriate cortical area V5 of sighted subjects yields a perception of movement (Hotson *et al.* 1994; Stewart *et al.* 1999) and stimulation of V1 or, more correctly, occipital pole, produces the sensation of stationary phosphenes. To address the problem of visual awareness Cowey and Walsh (2000) induced phosphenes by TMS to examine the integrity of visual cortex in a totally retinally blind subject and compared the results with those obtained by stimulating the same regions in normally sighted individuals and in an hemianopic subject who possesses blindsight in the impaired field. Vivid phosphenes were easily elicited from the blind subject when TMS was applied to the occipital pole and moving phosphenes when applied to V5 (Fig. 11.15). However, extensive and intensive stimulation of the damaged hemisphere in the blindsight subject did not yield reliable or reproducible phosphenes—even when applied to an intact area V5 on that side.

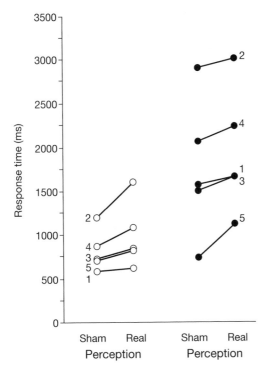

Fig. 11.14 TMS and mental imagery. Results of delivering rTMS over occipital cortex before perception and imagery conditions. "Real" TMS occurred when the magnetic field was directed into area 17 and sham rTMS occurred when the field was diverted away from the head. TMS over visual cortex slowed response times in both perception and imagery conditions in all five subjects. From Kosslyn *et al.* (1999) with permission.

Thus, the experience of motion seems to depend upon the integrity of striate cortex (Cowey and Walsh 2000).

Pascual-Leone and Walsh (2001) probed the timing of the interactions between V5 and V1 by stimulating the occipital pole a few milliseconds after stimulating V5. First of all, phosphenes were elicited in overlapping regions of the visual field by stimulation of V5 or striate cortex and the phosphene threshold for these regions was established. Single pulse TMS was then applied to V5 at 100% of phosphene threshold and over the occipital pole at 80% of phosphene threshold. When the two pulses were delivered together, subjects reliably reported the perception of a moving phosphene, but as the asynchrony of V5 and V1 TMS increased, the confidence of the subjects diminished and they reported either stationary phosphenes or were unsure of the direction of movement when TMS was applied over V1 between 5 and 15 ms after TMS over V5. When TMS was applied over the occipital pole 15–45 ms after the pulse delivered to V5, the perception of the phosphene was abolished. To discount the possibility of the effects being due to disrupting fast feed-forward projections to V5 from V1, Pascual-Leone and Walsh (2001) used the same procedure with double stimulation of V5, and consistent with the backprojection hypothesis, there was no effect of the second TMS pulse on the phosphene produced by the first pulse (Fig. 11.16). This finding reflects the time window of the back projection

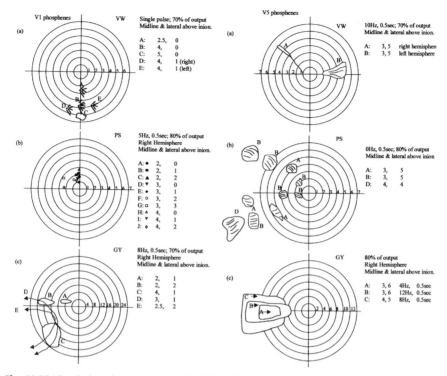

Fig. 11.15 Visual phosphenes produced by TMS (A) in a normally sighted observer (B) in peripherally blind subject P.S. and (C) in hemianopic patient G.Y. The coordinates give the site of stimulation in dorsal-lateral order. For example, 2,1 indicates that the coil was centered 2 cm above the inion and 1 cm lateral. Note that as the coil is moved dorsally away from the inion the phosphenes migrate inferiorly (c.f. A and C in G.Y., Fig. 11.1c), and that as the coil is moved away from the midline the phosphenes migrate further into the contralateral visual field (c.f. A and B in G.Y., Fig. 11.1 bottom). In P.S., Fig. 11.1 bottom, the phosphenes remain resolutely in the central few degrees of the visual field despite stimulation being delivered between 2 and 5 cm above the inion and up to 2 cm lateral. Where there are phosphenes elicited beyond the central two degrees they are in the opposite direction to that predicted by normal retinotopic mapping (stimulating more dorsally yields more superior rather than inferior phosphenes).

from V5 to V1 and is consistent with recent studies of cortical deactivation in monkeys in which cooling of extrastriate areas decreases the sensitivity of neurons in V1 (see Bullier 2001 for review). This experiment is also a good example of the powerful effects even apparently low levels of TMS can have on cortical functioning.

Methodological and technical considerations

In 1985, Barker and colleagues successfully applied a magnetic pulse over the vertex of the human scalp and elicited clear hand movements and accompanying EMG activity recorded from the first dorsal interosseous (FDI) (Barker *et al.* 1985): cortical input

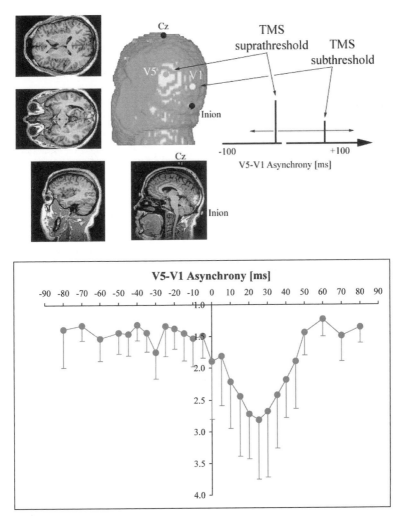

Fig. 11.16 (and color plate 16) Corticocortical interactions. The V5-V1-TMS asynchrony is displayed on the x-axis: negative values indicate that V1 received TMS prior to V5, and positive values indicate that V1 was stimulated after V5. The subjects made one of four judgements. The phosphene elicited by V5 TMS was (1) present and moving, (2) present but not confident to judge whether moving, (3) present but stationary, (4) no phosphene was observed. TMS over V1 between 10 and 30 ms after TMS over V5 affected the perception of the phosphene (see text for details).

had produced a measurable motor output. The basic, generic circuitry of magnetic stimulators is shown in Fig. 11.17. A capacitor charged to a high voltage is discharged into the stimulating coil via an electrical switch called a thyristor. This circuitry can be modified to produce rapid, repetitive pulses that are used in rTMS. Figure 11.18 shows the whole sequence of events in TMS from the pulse generation to cortical stimulation.

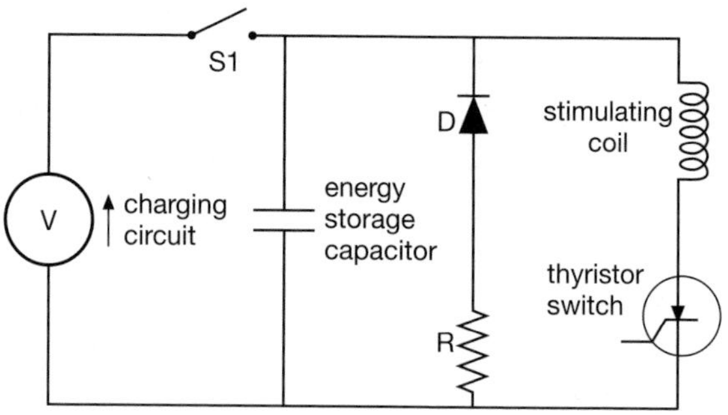

Fig. 11.17 Schematic diagram of a standard (single pulse) magnetic nerve stimulator. From Barker (1999), with permission.

The important points are that a large current (8kA in the example shown) is required to generate a magnetic field of sufficient intensity to stimulate the cortex and that the electric field induced in the cortex is dependent upon the rate of change as well as the intensity of the magnetic field. To achieve these requirements the current is delivered to the coil with a very short rise time (approx. 200 μs) and the pulse has an overall duration of approximately one millisecond. These demands also require large energy storage capacitors and efficient energy transfer from capacitors to coil, typically in the range of 2000 joules of stored energy and 500 joules transferred to the coil in less than 100 μs. The induced field has two sources (Roth *et al.* 1991); 1) the induction effect from the current in the coil (and this is what is usually meant when discussing TMS), and 2) a negligible accumulation of charge on the scalp or between the scalp and the skull. Figures 11.19 and 11.20 show the difference between two types of pulse, monophasic and biphasic, which can be produced by magnetic stimulators. The biphasic waveform required for rTMS machines differs from the monophasic in two ways. First, in the biphasic mode up to 60% of the original energy in the pulse is returned to the capacitor, rendering the rTMS more energy efficient and thus enabling the capacitors to recharge more quickly (Jalinous 1991; Barker 1999). More importantly for the end user, the biphasic waveform seems to require lower field intensities to induce a current in neural tissue (McRobbie and Foster 1984). The reasons for the higher sensitivity of neurons to biphasic stimulation have been examined with respect to the properties of the nerve membrane (Reilly 1992; Wada *et al.* 1996). The rise time of the magnetic field is important because neurons are not perfect capacitors, they are leaky, and the quicker the rise to peak intensity of the magnetic field, the less time is available for the tissue to lose charge. A fast rise time has other advantages in that it decreases the energy requirements of the stimulator and the heating of the coil (Barker 1999).

Neuronal stimulation

In magnetic stimulation, an electric field is induced both inside and outside the axon (Nagarajan *et al.* 1993). To produce neural activity the induced field must differ across

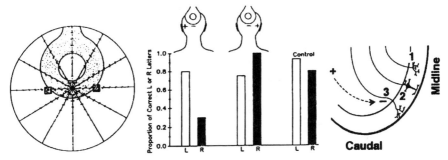

Fig. 11.22 The electric field induced by TMS delivered by a round coil is here modelled (left) in a spherical saline volume conductor. The effect on visual detection of reversing the polarity of the induced electric field is shown (middle) and a schematic of the possible sites of stimulation are shown (left). The clockwise current in the coil (left) induces an anticlockwise electric field and the field intensity diminishes with distance from the peak of stimulation (*center* of spherical saline bath). The results from one subject show that reversing the direction of the induced field differentially suppresses visual performance in the left or right visual hemifield (Amassian *et al.* 1994). The most likely point of stimulation is the bend in the axon (3). Excitation of the axonal arborizations (1) is less likely due to relative high resistance and excitation of the dendritic arbors (2) is less likely due to relative reduced electrical excitability (Reilly 1989). From Amassian *et al.* (1998) with permission.

Stimulation with a figure of eight coil increases the focality of stimulation (Ueno *et al.* 1988). This configuration is of two circular coils that carry current in opposite directions and, where the coils meet, there is a summation of the electric field. Figure 11.23 (bottom) and Fig. 11.24 (bottom) show the induced electric field and the rate of change of the field with respect to a straight neuron. In addition to the new "summated" anode and cathode produced by the figure of eight coil, the two separate windings maintain their ability to induce a field under the outer parts of the windings. However, in experiments where the center of the figure of eight is placed over the region of interest, the outer parts of the coil are usually several cm away from the scalp and thus unlikely to induce effective fields.

"Location, location, location"

From the foregoing discussion one might be forgiven for thinking it impossible to target specific cortical areas with TMS. Several converging lines of evidence now show that there is good reason for confidence in the anatomical, but more importantly in the functional specificity of TMS. One could simply appeal to the surface validity of TMS. Barker's first demonstration of motor cortex stimulation, for example, was itself strongly suggestive of relatively selective, suprathreshold stimulation of the hand area of the cortex. Perhaps there was some spread of current to arm, shoulder and face regions of the motor cortex, but in the absence of movements from these parts of the body one must infer that the stimulation was effectively precise, i.e. stimulation of the other areas was

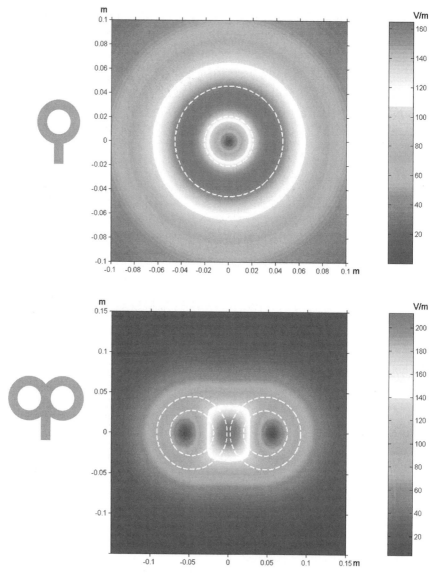

Fig. 11.23 (and color plate 17) Distribution of the induced electric fields by a circular (top) and figure of eight (bottom) stimulating coil. The circular coil has 41.5 mm inside turn diameter, 91.5 mm outside turn diameter (mean 66.5 mm) and 15 turns of copper wire. The figure of eight coil has 56 mm inside turn diameter, 90 mm outside turn (mean 73 mm) and 9 turns of copper wire on each wing. The outline of each coil is depicted with dashed white lines on the representation of the induced fields. The electric field amplitude is calculated in a plane 20 mm below a realistic model of the coil ($dI/dt = 10^8$ A s^{-1}). Figure created by Anthony Barker.

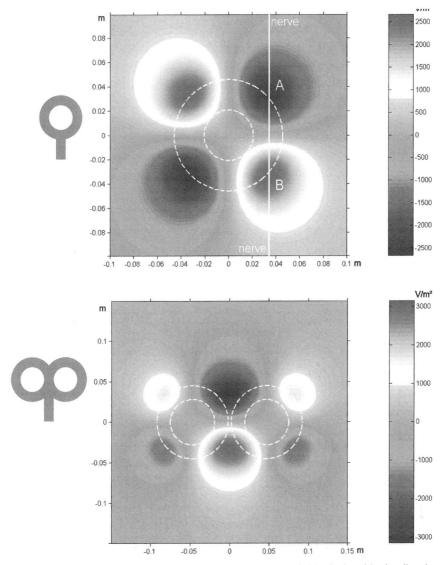

Figure 11.24 (and color plate 18) Rate of change of the electric field calculated in the direction of the nerve along the axis AB. Figure created by Anthony Barker.

subthreshold for producing a behavioural effect. There are many other examples of surface validity: phosphenes are more likely if the coil is placed over the visual cortex (Marg 1991; Meyer *et al.* 1991; Kastner *et al.* 1998; Kammer 1999), speech arrest more likely if stimulation is applied over facial motor or frontal cortex (Pascual-Leone *et al.* 1991; Epstein *et al.* 1996; Stewart *et al.* 2001a), and neglect and extinction-like deficits more likely if the coil targets the parietal lobe (Pascual-Leone *et al.* 1994; Ashbridge *et al.* 1997; Fierro *et al.* 2000). Mapping of motor cortex with EMGs also shows precise mapping of the fingers, hand, arm, face, trunk and legs in a pattern that matches the gross organization of the motor homunculus (Singh *et al.* 1997) sensitive both to coil location and intensity (Brasil-Neto *et al.* 1992a,b). There are also more direct measures of the specificity of TMS. Wassermann *et al.* (1996) mapped the cortical representation of a hand muscle with TMS and coregistered the inferred volumetric fields with anatomical MRIs from each subject, and these were in turn coregistered with PET images obtained while subjects moved the finger that had been mapped with TMS. In all subjects the inferred induced TMS fields met the surface of the brain at the anterior lip of the central sulcus and extended along the precentral gyrus for a few millimeters anterior to the central sulcus. When compared with the PET activations, the MRI locations were all within 5–22 mm, which is an impressive correspondence across three techniques.

A similarly impressive level of correspondence has also been seen in other studies that have correlated TMS with fMRI (Terao *et al.* 1998a,b) and with MEG (Morioka *et al.* 1995a,b; Ruohonen *et al.* 1996). There are reasons for caution in interpreting these data (see Wasserman *et al.* 1996). For example, the hand area activated lies deep in the central sulcus, possibly too deep to be directly activated by TMS and therefore presumably activated transsynaptically. The evidence for transsynaptic activation comes from a comparison of the EMG latencies elicited by electrical or magnetic stimulation (Day *et al.* 1987, 1989; Amassian *et al.* 1990). Magnetically evoked latencies are approximately 1–2 msecs longer than electrically evoked and this can be explained on the basis of which neurons are most likely to be stimulated by each technique (Rothwell 1994): TMS is more likely to stimulate neurons that run parallel to the cortical surface whereas electrical stimulation can directly stimulate pyramidal output neurons that run orthogonal to the cortical surface. Thus the 1–2 msec delay between electrical and magnetic cortical stimulation may be accounted for by the time taken for the stimulation to be transmitted from the interneurons to the pyramidal cells. Knowledge of which kinds of cells are stimulated based on temporal information can inform the interpretation of functional specificity. A clear example comes from the work of Heinen *et al.* (1998) who measured central motor conduction time (CCT) by recording TMS-evoked EMG from the first dorsal interosseous of children (mean age 7 years) and adults (mean age 29 years) in relaxed and facilitated (hand muscle tensed) conditions. The adults' relaxed latencies were significantly faster (by approximately 2 msecs) than the children's but there was no difference between the two groups. The difference between relaxed and facilitated CCT is attributed to the temporal summation of descending corticospinal volleys at the alpha-motoneuron (Hess *et al.* 1987; Chiappa *et al.* 1991) and Heinen and colleagues hypothesised that the difference between the adults and children was "due to an immature synaptic organization at either the first or the second neuron of the pyramidal tract".

Other evidence strengthens the correlation between targeted and activated cortical regions. Paus and colleagues (1997, 1998a,b, 1999) have carried out a number of studies in which TMS has been combined with analysis of PET activations using a method of frameless stereotaxy which aligns MRI landmarks and the center of the stimulating coil with an accuracy within 0.4 – 0.8 cm. The first critical finding of these experiments is that TMS has a major effect under the center of a figure of eight coil, and secondary effects at sites that are known to be anatomically connected (Fig. 11.25). The second finding is that optimal stimulation depends critically on the precise orientation of the coil.

Further evidence of the accuracy of the TMS has been shown by Siebner and colleagues (1998), who compared the changes in regional cerebral blood flow caused by 2 Hz rTMS over the motor cortex, sufficient to elicit an arm movement, with blood flow changes due to the actual movement of the arm. The correspondence was striking. TMS induced movements and voluntary movements both activated SM1 (area 4) ipsilateral to the site of stimulation. Voluntary movement also activated ipsilateral SMA (area 6) and the motor activity associated with the voluntary movement was more extensive than that elicited by rTMS. This could be because the voluntary arm movement was slightly

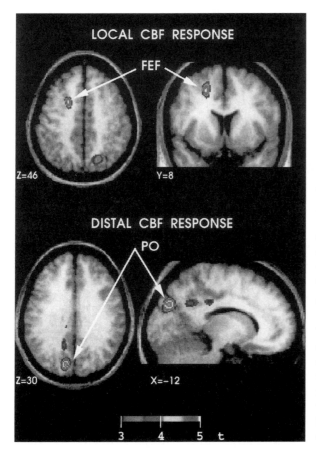

Fig. 11.25 (and color plate 19) Changes in regional cerebral blood flow as a result of TMS. The top figure shows a significant correlation between TMS and rCBF in the vicinity of the frontal eye fields (FEF) i.e. in the regions targeted by the TMS pulses. The bottom figure shows one of the cortical regions that most likely was activated through spread of stimulation effects, namely the parieto-occipital (PO) cortex of the ipsilateral hemisphere—a regions similar to that known to be connected with the FEF in monkeys. From Paus et al. (1997), with permission.

greater than the TMS movement or because voluntary activity would involve more muscles than TMS activity. Whatever the difference, it is a clear example of the specificity of TMS and the physiological validity of TMS effects. These studies are important examples of the spatial specificity of TMS—they do not mean that the induced electric field is limited to the functional units stimulated, nor do they suggest that activation of neurons is limited to the areas seen in PET and fMRI; but they show unequivocally that the theoretical spread of the induced field is not the determinant of the area of effective stimulation and that the functional localization of TMS is under experimenter control.

Studies of EEG responses by Ilmoniemi *et al.* (1997) provide another demonstration of the relative primary and secondary specificity of TMS. As Fig. 11.26 shows, stimulation over the visual or motor cortex elicits EEG around the site of stimulation in the first few msecs after TMS. Within 20–30 msecs this activity is mirrored by a secondary area of activity in the homotopic regions of the contralateral hemisphere. These delays in homotopic areas are a rich source of hypotheses regarding the timing of effects in interhemispheric interactions. The utility and specificity of this combination of techniques was further demonstrated by applying TMS to the motor cortex of a patient who had suffered a lesion to the right basal ganglia and had lost fine finger control in his left hand and some control of his left arm. When the intact hemisphere was

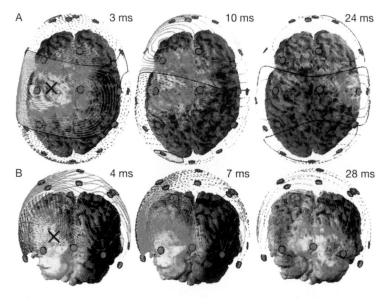

Fig. 11.26 (and color plate 20) Duration of changes in neural activity induced by TMS. Four milliseconds after TMS over the occipital lobe most of the electrical activity recorded with high resolution EEG around the area directly under the TMS stimulation site (marked by the X). By 7 ms this has spread to the midline and by 28 ms there is clearly contralateral activation. From Ilmoniemi *et al.* (1997), with permission.

stimulated EEG responses were seen in both the ipsilateral motor cortices. When the motor cortex ipsilateral to the affected basal ganglia was stimulated, some EEG was seen ipsilaterally but none was transmitted interhemispherically to the intact hemisphere.

The depth of penetration of TMS is another important question and as with the question of lateral specificity there is no easy answer, but again there are good reasons to think that the approximations available are meaningful and can be used to guide interpretation of results. Models of the electric field at different depths from the coil suggest that relatively wide areas are stimulated close to the coil, decreasing in surface area as the field is measured at distances further from the coil. The image offered by these models is of an egg-shaped cone with the apex, which marks the point of the smallest area of stimulation, furthest from the coil. For a standard figure of eight coil, one estimate is that stimulation 5 mm below the coil will cover an area of approximately 7×6 cm. This area decreases to 4×3 cm at 20 mm below the coil, i.e. in the region of the cortical surface (Fig. 11.27). Calculations of induced electric fields as a function of depth can also be used as a guide to specificity because stimulation at points where the fields overlap allows subtraction of the effects. If a coil positioned at site A disrupts performance on a behavioural task, the effective site of stimulation could be said to be anywhere, within, around or connected to the neurons crossed by the induced field. If stimulation at sites B and C situated, say 2 cm dorsal and ventral respectively to site A fails to disrupt the task, then the overlap in fields between A and B and A and C can be said to be ineffective regions of the field and the most effective field is the remaining subregion of A. So, our notion of the effective resolution of TMS can be refined; whereas a single pulse of TMS cannot be said to have a small, volumetric resolution in the cortex, from a functional point of view it can be shown to have a small scalp resolution and an inferred or subtracted volumetric resolution when multiple sites are compared. A comparison might be made here with fMRI and, say, a cortical area such as visual area V5 (Watson *et al.* 1993); it is clearly not the case that moving visual stimuli activate V5 and V5 alone. Rather, the specificity of this area is, quite properly, inferred by subtracting the activations caused by stationary or colored stimuli.

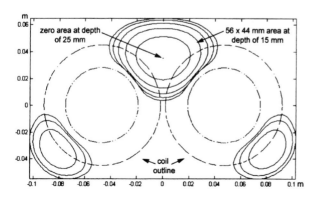

Fig. 11.27 Estimated stimulation areas at depth intervals of 5mm beginning at the cortical surface. From Barker (1999), with permission.

Safety: virtual lesions are virtually safe

The use of TMS is rightly subject to approval by local ethical committees and there are some precautions that must be taken in all studies using the technique. The safety of single pulse stimulation is well established, but further precautions should be taken when using repetitive-pulse TMS. The magnetic field produced by stimulating coils can cause a loud noise and temporary elevations in auditory thresholds have been reported (Pascual-Leone *et al.* 1993). The use of earplugs is recommended in all experiments. Some subjects may experience headaches or nausea or may simply find the face twitches and other peripheral effects of TMS too uncomfortable. Such subjects obviously should be released from any obligation to continue the experiments. More serious are the concerns that TMS may induce an epileptic seizure. There are a number of cases of focal seizures induced by repetitive pulse TMS and caution is necessary. As a guide, any subject with any personal or family history of epilepsy or other neurological condition should be precluded from taking part in an experiment that does not involve investigation of that condition. Pascual-Leone *et al.* (1993) assessed the safety of rTMS and noted that seizures could be induced in subjects who were not associated with any risk factors. Pascual-Leone *et al.* (1993) presents some guidelines for the use of rTMS and familiarity with this paper should be a prerequisite of using rTMS. However, the paper is not exhaustive—it is based on only three sites of stimulation and expresses pulse intensity as a percentage of motor threshold. It has recently been argued that studies which apply rTMS to the prefrontal or occipital visual areas cannot simply lift stimulation parameters and criteria from this paper and assume they transfer to other conditions since there is no necessary relationship between motor cortex excitability and that of any other cortical regions (Stewart *et al.* 2001b). It is also recommended that anyone wishing to use rTMS visit the TMS website (http://pni.unibe.ch/maillist.htm). The TMS community is constantly reviewing safety procedures and this website is a starting point for access to sound information. A more recent paper (Wassermann 1998) summarizes the consensus that exists within the community. The adverse effects recorded include seizures, though these are rare, some enhancement effects on motor reaction time and verbal recall, and effects on affect (some subjects have been reported to cry following left prefrontal rTMS and others to laugh). There is little information about potential longer term problems with rTMS but the issue cannot be ducked. If, on the one hand, rTMS is potentially useful in the alleviation of depression (George *et al.* 1995, 1996) it must be conceded that rTMS can have longer-term effects. It would be disingenuous to suggest that all long-term effects are likely to beneficial rather than deleterious. It should be noted, however, that the improvements in mood as a result of rTMS follow several sessions of magnetic stimulation and the effects were cumulative (George *et al.* 1995, 1996). A simple precaution that may be taken is to prevent individual subjects from taking part in repeated experiments over a short period of time. The use of rTMS should follow a close reading of Pascual-Leone *et al.*'s (1993) and Wassermann's (1998) reports. Studies of neuropsychological functions, such as those discussed in this chapter, seldom approach the safety limits and it is a simple matter to design experiments that use minimal intensities and durations of TMS.

A concern sometimes raised about TMS is that it is in some sense "unnatural" to apply magnetic pulses to people's scalps because the resulting neural activity is "abnormal" and may have long term consequences. If ecological accuracy (rather than validity) were a requirement of psychological experiments, one wonders how spatial frequency gratings, stroop stimuli, adaptation experiments (the McCullough effect, for example can last for months) and many other manipulations could be justified. But the question is still important: if we are to understand the mechanisms of TMS we need to know how the neural noise induced can be compared with real neural activity and with the functional noise introduced in dual task experiments and other psychological interference techniques; an understanding of how cortex responds to TMS is also critical to the interpretation of longer term effects of TMS and to accurate analysis of experiments in which TMS is combined with fMRI.

Niehaus *et al.* (1999) have approached this question using Transcranial Doppler Sonography (TCD, a non-invasive technique that allows blood flow, as velocities, to be recorded from intracranial arteries see Bogdahn 1998) to observe rapid changes in the haemodynamic response to TMS and to compare this with "real" sensory (in this case, visual) stimulation. As Fig. 11.28 shows, TMS produced changes in blood flow that occurred earlier and were larger in the hemisphere ipsilateral to stimulation over the occipital lobe (cf the results of Ilmoniemi *et al.*, above). There was also a close correspondence between blood flow associated with trains of 5 Hz TMS and 5 Hz light flicker (Fig. 11.29), thus supporting the assumption that blood flow changes evoked by TMS are a reflection of neural activity rather than non-specific effects on the vascular system. Importantly, there were no long-term changes associated with the rTMS.

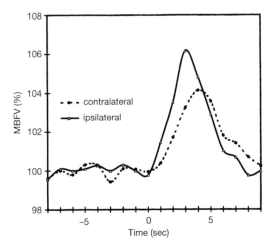

Fig. 11.28 The cerebral haemodynamic response to TMS over the motor cortex in 10 subjects. Five trains of 10 Hz were given to each subject. Time locked average MBFV changes in the middle cerebral artery ipsilateral and contralateral to the stimulation site is shown. From Niehuas *et al.* (1999), with permission.

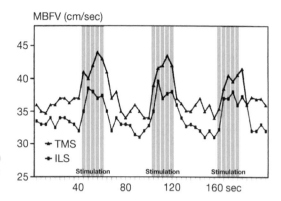

Fig. 11.29 Changes in MBFV in the left posterior cerebral artery during rTMS over the left occipital cortex or visual stimulation with light flicker. Stimulation was performed with rTMS trains of 5 Hz and 20 s duration and intermittent visual stimulation (ILS) with the same frequency and stimulation duration.

Acknowledgments

The authors are grateful to the Royal Society, The Medical Research Council, The Dr. Hadwen Research Trust, The Oxford McDonnell-Pew Centre for Cognitive Neuroscience, The Guarantors of Brain, The National Institute of Mental Health (MH60734, MH 57980) and The National Eye Institute (EY12091).

References

Abdeen, M. A. and Stuchly, M. A. (1994) Modelling of magnetic stimulation of bent neurons. *IEEE Transactions in Biomedical Engineering*, **41**:1092–5.

Amassian, V. E., Quirk, G. J. and Stewart, A. (1990) A comparison of corticospinal activation by magnetic coil and electrical stimulation of monkey motor cortex. *Electroencaphalography and Clinical Neurophysiology*, **77**:390–401.

Amassian, V. E., Eberle, L., Maccabee, P. J. *et al.* (1992) Modeling magnetic coil excitation of human cerebral cortex with a peripheral nerve immersed in a brain shaped volume conductor: the significance of fiber-bending in excitation. *Electroencaphalography and Clinical Neurophysiology*, **85**:291–301.

Amassian, V. E., Maccabee, P. J. and Cracco, P. Q. (1994) The polarity of the induced electric field influences magnetic coil inhibition of human visual cortex: implications for the site of excitation. *Electroencephalography and Clinical Neurophysiology*, **93**:21–6.

Arguin, M., Joanette, Y. and Cavanagh, P. (1990) Comparing the cerebral hemispheres on the speed of spatial shifts of visual attention: evidence from serial search. *Neuropsychologia*, **28**:733–6.

Arguin, M., Joanette, Y. *et al.* (1993) Visual search for feature and conjunction targets with an attention deficit. *Journal of Cognitive Neuroscience*, **5**:436–52.

Ashbridge, E., Walsh, V. and Cowey, A. (1997) Temporal aspects of visual search studied by transcranial magnetic stimulation. *Neuropsychologia*, **35**:1121–31.

Barker, A. T., Freeston, I. L. *et al.* (1985) Magnetic stimulation of the human brain. *Journal of Physiology (London)* **369**: 3P.

Barker, A. T., Freeston, I. L., Jalinous, R. *et al.* (1987) Magnetic stimulation of the human brain and peripheral nervous system: an introduction and the results of an initial clinical evaluation. *Neurosurgery*, **20**:100–9.

Barker, A. T. (1991) An introduction to the basic principles of magnetic nerve stimulation. *Journal of Clinical Neurophysiology*, **8**:26–37.

Barker, A. T. (1999) The history and basic principles of magnetic nerve stimulation. *Electroencephalography and Clinical Neurophysiology supplement*, **51**:3–21.

Bisiach, E. and Vallar, G. (1988) Hemineglect in humans. In F. Boller and J. Grafman (eds) *Handbook of Neuropsychology*, pp. 195–222. Elsevier Science, Amsterdam.

Bogdahn, U. (1998) *Transcranial doppler sonography*. Blackwell Science, New York.

Bowers, D. and Heilman, K. M. (1980) Material-specific hemispheric activation. *Neuropsychologia*, **18**:309–19.

Brasil-Neto, J. P., Cohen, L. G., Panizza, M. *et al.* (1992a) Optimal focal transcranial magnetic activation of the human motor cortex: effects of coil orientation, shape of the induced current pulse and stimulus intensity. *Journal of Clinical Neurophysiology*, **9**:132–6.

Brasil-Neto, J., Cohen, L. G., Pascual-Leone, A. *et al.* (1992b) Rapid reversible modulation of human motor outputs after transient deafferentation of the forearm: a study with transcranial magnetic stimulation. *Neurology*, **42**:1302–6.

Bullier, J. (2001) Cortical connections and functional interactions between visual cortical areas. In M. Fahle (ed.) *Neuropsychology of Vision*. Oxford University Press, Oxford. In press.

Chiappa, K. H., Cros, D., Day, B. L. *et al.* (1991) Magnetic stimulation of the human motor cortex: ipsilateral and contralateral facilitation effects. *Electroencaphalography and Clinical Neurophysiology suppl.*, **43**:186–201.

Corbetta, M., Miezin, F. M., Dobmeyer, S. *et al.* (1991) Selective and divided attention during visual discriminations of shape, color, and speed: functional anatomy by positron emission tomography. *Journal of Neuroscience*, **11**:2383–402.

Corbetta, M., Shulman, G. L., Miezin, F. M. *et al.* (1995) Superior parietal cortex activation during spatial attention shifts and visual feature conjunction. *Science*, **270**:802–5.

Cowey, A. and Walsh, V. (2000) Magnetically induced phosphenes in sighted, blind and blindsighted observers. *Neuroreport*, **11**:3269–73.

Day, B. J., Thompson, P. D., Dick, J. P. *et al.* (1987) Different sites of action of electrical and magnetic stimulation of the human brain. *Neuroscience Letters*, **75**:101–6.

Day, B. L., Rothwell, J. C., Thompson, P. D. *et al.* (1989) Delay in the execution of voluntary movement by electrical or magnetic brain stimulation in intact man. Evidence for the storage of motor programs in the brain. *Brain*, **112**:649–63.

Ellison, A., Rushworth, M. F. S. and Walsh, V. Aspects of visual search and parietal cortex function (submitted).

Epstein, C. M., Lah, J. J., Meador, K. *et al.* (1996) Optimum stimulus parameters for lateralized suppression of speech with magnetic brain stimulation. *Neurology*, **47**:1590–3.

Fierro, B., Brighina, F. and Bisiach, E. (2000) Contralateral neglect induced by right posterior parietal rTMS in healthy subjects. *Neuroreport*, **11**:1519–21.

Friedman-Hill, S. R., Robertson, L. C., Robertson, L. C. *et al.* (1995) Parietal contributions to visual feature binding: evidence from a patient with bilateral lesions. *Science*, **269**:853–5.

Garnham, C. W., Barker, A. T. and Freeston, I. L. (1995) Measurement of the activating function of magnetic stimulation using combined electrical and magnetic stimuli. *Journal of Medical Engineering and Technology*, **19**:57–61.

George, M. S., Wassermann, E. M., Williams, W. A. *et al.* (1995) Daily repetitive transcranial magnetic stimulation (rTMS) improves mood in depression. *Neuroreport*, **6**:1853–6.

George, M. S., Wassermann, E. M., Williams, W. A. *et al.* (1996) Changes in mood and hormone levels after rapid-rate transcranial magnetic stimulation (rTMS) of the prefrontal cortex. *Journal of Neuropsychiatry and Clinical Neuroscience*, **8**:172–80.

Goldman-Rakic, P. S. (1998) The prefrontal landscape: implications of functional architecture for understanding human mentation and the central executive. In A. C. Roberts, T. W. Robbins and L. Weiskrantz (eds) *The Prefrontal Cortex*. Oxford University Press, Oxford.

Hardy, S. C. and Stein, B. E. (1988) Small lateral suprasylvian cortex lesions produce visual neglect and decreased visual activity in the superior colliculus. *Journal of Comparative Neurology*, **305**:543–58.

Heinen, F., Fietzek, U. M., Berweck, S. *et al.* (1998) The fast corticospinal system and motor performance in children: conduction precedes skill. *Journal of Pediatric Neurology suppl.*, **19**:217–21.

Hess, C. W., Mills, K. R. and Murray, N. M. F. (1987) Magnetic stimulation of the human brain: facilitation of motor responses by voluntary contraction of the ipsilateral and contralateral muscles with additional observation on an amputee. *Neuroscience Letters*, **71**:235–40.

Hilgetag, C. C., Kötter, R. and Young, M. P. (1999) Inter-hemispheric competition of sub-cortical structures is a crucial mechanism in paradoxical lesion effects and spatial neglect, *Progress in Brain Research*, **121**:125–46.

Hotson, J., Braun, D., Herzberg, W. and Boman, D. (1994) Transcranial magnetic stimulation of extrastriate cortex degrades human motion direction discrimination. *Vision Research*, **34**:2115–23.

Ilmoniemi, R. J., Virtanen, J., Ruohonen, J. *et al.* (1997) Neuronal responses to magnetic stimulation reveal cortical reactivity and connectivity. *Neuroreport*, **8**:3537–40.

Jalinous, R. (1991) Technical and practical aspects of magnetic nerve stimulation. *Journal of Clinical Neurophysiology*, **8**:10–25.

Kammer, T. and Nusseck, H. G. (1998) Are recognition deficits following occipital lobe TMS explained by raised detection thresholds? *Neuropsychologia*, **36**:1161–6.

Kammer, T. (1999) Phosphenes and transient scotomas induced by magnetic stimulation of the occipital lobe: their topographic relationship. *Neuropsychologia*, **37**:191–8.

Kapur, N. (1996) Paradoxical functional facilitation in brain-behaviour research. A critical review. *Brain*, **119**:1775–90.

Kastner, S., Demmer, I. and Ziemann, U. (1998) Transient visual field defects induced by transcranial magnetic stimulation over human occipital pole. *Experimental Brain Research*, **118**:19–26.

Kosslyn, S. M. (1988) Aspects of a cognitive neuroscience of mental imagery. *Science*, **240**:1621–26.

Kosslyn, S. M., Alpert, N. M. *et al.* (1993a) Visual mental imagery activates topographically organized visual cortex: PET investigations. *Journal of Cognitive Neuroscience*, **5**:263–87.

Kosslyn, S. M., Daly, P. F., McPeek, R. M. *et al.* (1993b) Using locations to store shape: an indirect effect of a lesion. *Cerebral Cortex*, **3**:567–82.

Kosslyn, S. M., Pascual-Leone, A., Felician, O. *et al.* (1999) The role of area 17 in visual imagery: convergent evidence from PET and rTMS. *Science*, **284**:167–70.

Lomber, S. G. and Payne, B. R. (1996) Removal of two halves restores the whole: Reversal of visual hemineglect during bilateral cortical or collicular inactivation in the cat. *Visual Neuroscience*, **13**:1143–56.

Maccabee, P. J., Amassian, V. E., Eberle, L. P. *et al.* (1993) Magnetic coil stimulation of straight and bent amphibian and mammalian peripheral nerve *in vitro*: locus of excitation. *Journal of Physiology (London)*, **460**:201–19.

Marg, E. (1991) Magnetostimulation of vision: direct noninvasive stimulation of the retina and the visual brain. *Optometry and Visual Science*, **68**:427–40.

McCourt, M. E. and Jewell, G. (1999) Visuospatial attention in line bisection: stimulus modulation of pseudoneglect. *Neuropsychologia*, **37**:843–55.

McLeod, P., Heywood, C. A., Driver, J. *et al.* (1989) Selective deficits of visual search in moving displays after extrastriate damage. *Nature*, **339**:466–7.

McRobbie, D. and Foster, M. A. (1984) Thresholds for biological effect of time-varying magnetic fields. *Clinical Physiological Measurement*, **2**:67–78.

Meyer, B.-U., Papke, K. *et al.* (1991) Supression of visual perception by transcranial magnetic stimulation—experimental findings in healthy subjects and patients with optic neuritis. *Electroencephalography and Clinical Neurophysiology*, **86**:259–267.

Morioka, T., Mizushima, A., Yamamoto, T. *et al.* (1995a) Functional mapping of the sensorimotor cortex: combined use of magnetoencephalography, functional MRI, and motor evoked potentials. *Neuroradiology*, **37**:526–30.

Morioka, T., Yamamoto, T., Mizushima, A. *et al.* (1995b) Comparison of magnetoencephalography, functional MRI, and motor evoked potentials in the localization of the sensory-motor cortex. *Neurological Research*, **17**:361–7.

Nagarajan, S. S., Durand, D. M. *et al.* (1993) Effects of induced electric fields on finite neuronal structures: a simulation study. *IEEE Transactions in Biomedical Engineering*, **40**:1175–88.

Niehaus, L., Rorricht, S., Schulz, U. *et al.* (1999) Hemodynamic response to repetitive magnetic stimulation of the motor and visual cortex. *Electroencephalography and Clinical Neurophysiology supplement*, **51**:41–7.

Pascual-Leone, A., Gomez-Tortosa, E., Grafman, J. *et al.* (1994) Induction of visual extinction by rapid-rate transcranial magnetic stimulation of parietal lobe. *Neurology*, **44**:494–8.

Pascual-Leone, A., Gates, J. R. and Dhuma, A. (1991) Induction of speech arrest and counting errors with rapid-rate transcranial magnetic stimulation. *Neurology*, **41**:697–702.

Pascual-Leone, A., Houser, C. M., Reese, K. *et al.* (1993) Safety of rapid-rate transcranial magnetic stimulation in normal volunteers. *Electroencephalography and Clinical Neurophysiology*, **89**:120–30.

Pascual-Leone, A. and Walsh, V. (2001) Backprojections from extrastriate cortex to striate cortex are fast and necessary for visual awareness. *Science*, **292**:510–2.

Paus, T., Jech, R., Thompson, C. J. *et al.* (1997) Transcranial magnetic stimulation during positron emission tomography: a new method for studying connectivity of the human cerebral cortex. *Journal of Neuroscience*, **17**:3178–84.

Paus, T. and Wolforth, M. (1998a) Transcranial magnetic stimulation during PET: reaching and verifying the target site. *Human Brain Mapping*, **6**:399–402.

Paus, T., Jech, R., Thompson, C. J. *et al.* (1998b) Dose-dependent reduction of cerebral blood flow during rapid-rate transcranial magnetic stimulation of the human sensorimotor cortex. *Journal of Neurophysiology*, **79**:1102–7.

Paus, T. (1999) Imaging the brain before, during, and after transcranial magnetic stimulation. *Neuropsychologia*, **37**:219–24.

Posner, M. I., Walker, J. A., Friedrich, F. J. *et al.* (1984) Effects of parietal lobe injury on covert orienting of visual attention. *Journal of Neuroscience*, **4**:1863–74.

Reilly, J. P. (1992) *Electrical Stimulation and Electropathology*. Cambridge University Press, Cambridge.

Rizzolatti, G., Fogassi, L. and Gallese, V. (1997) Parietal cortex: from sight to action. *Current Opinion in Neurobiology*, **7**:562–7.

Robertson, I. H. and Murre, J. M. J. (1999) Rehabilitation of brain damage: Brain plasticity and principles of guided recovery. *Psychological Bulletin*, **125**:544–75.

Rossini, P. M. and Pauri, F. (2000) Neuromagnetic integrated methods tracking brain mechanisms of sensorimotor areas "plastic" reorganisation. *Brain Research Reviews*, **33**:131–54.

Roth, B. J., Saypol, J. M., Hallett, M. *et al.* (1991) A theoretical calculation of the electric field induced in the cortex during magnetic stimulation. *Electroencephalography and Clinical Neurophysiology*, **81**:47–56.

Rothwell, J. C. (1994) Motor cortical stimulation in man. In S. Ueno (ed.) *Biomagnetic Stimulation*, pp. 49–58. Plenum Press, New York.

Ruohonen, J., Ravazzani, P., Ilmoniemi, R. J. *et al.* (1996) Motor cortex mapping with combined MEG and magnetic stimulation. *Electroencephalography and Clinical Neurophysiology supplement*, **46**:317–22.

Rushworth, M. F. S., Ellison, A. and Walsh, V. (2001) Complementary localization of visual attention and motor intention. *Nature Neuroscience*, **4**:656–61.

Seyal, M., Ro, T. and Rafal, R. (1995) Increased sensitivity to ipsilateral cutaneous stimuli following transcranial magnetic stimulation of the parietal lobe. *Annals of Neurology*, **38**:264–7.

Siebner, H. R., Willoch, F., Peller, M. *et al.* (1998) Imaging brain activation induced by long trains of repetitive transcranial magnetic stimulation. *Neuroreport*, **9**:943–8.

Singh, K. D., Hamdy, S. and Aziz, Q. (1997) Topographic mapping of transcranial magnetic stimulation data on surface rendered MR images of the brain. *Electroencephalography and Clinical Neurophysiology*, **105**:345–51.

Snyder, L. H., Batista, A. P. and Andersen, R. A. (1997) Coding of intention in the posterior parietal cortex. *Nature*, **386**:167–9.

Sprague, J. M. (1966) Interaction of cortex and superior colliculus in mediation of visually guided behaviour in the cat. *Science*, **154**:1544–7.

Stewart, L. M., Battelli, L. *et al.* (1999) Motion perception and perceptual learning studied by magnetic stimulation. *Electroencephalography and Clinical Neurophysiology*, **51**:334–50.

Stewart, L. M., Walsh, V., Frith, U. *et al.* (2001a) TMS can produce two different types of speech disruption. *NeuroImage*, **13**:472–8.

Stewart, L., Walsh, V. and Rothwell, J. (2001b) Motor and phosphene thresholds: a TMS correlation study. *Neuropsychologia*, **39**:415–9.

Terao, Y., Fukuda, H., Ugawa, Y. *et al.* (1998a) Visualization of the information flow though the human oculomotor cortical regions by transcranial magnetic stimulation. *Journal of Neurophsyiology*, **80**:936–46.

Terao, Y., Ugawa, Y., Sakai, K. *et al.* (1998b) Localising the site of magnetic brain stimulation by functional MRI. *Experimental Brain Research*, **121**:145–52.

Treisman, A. (1996) The binding problem. Current opinion in *Neurobiology*, **6**:171–8.

Ueno, S., Tashiro, T. *et al.* (1988) Localized stimulation of neural tissues in the brain by means of a paired configuration of time-varying magnetic fields. *Journal of Applied Physics*, **64**:5862–4.

Wada, S., Kubota, H., Battelli, E. *et al.* (1996) Effects of stimulus waveform on magnetic nerve stimulation. *Japanese Journal of Applied Physiology*, **35**:1983–8.

Walsh, V., Ellison, A. *et al.* (1998) Task-specific impairments and enhancements induced by magnetic stimulation of human visual area V5. *Proceedings of the Royal Society of London*, **B265**:537–43.

Wassermann, E. M., Wang, B. *et al.* (1996) Locating the motor cortex on the MRI with transcranial magnetic stimulation and PET. *Neuroimage*, **3**:1–9.

Wassermann, E. M. (1998) Risk and safety of repetitive transcranial magnetic stimulation: report and suggested guidelines from the International Workshop on the Safety of Repetitive Transcranial Magnetic Stimulation. *Electroencaphalography and Clinical Neurophysiology*, **108**:1–16.

Watson, J. D., Myers, R., Frackowiak, R. J. *et al.* (1993) Area V5 of the human brain: evidence from a combined study using positron emission tomography and magnetic resonance imaging. *Cerebral Cortex*, **3**:79–94.

Weintraub, S. and Mesulam, M. M. (1987) Right cerebral dominance in spatial attention. Further evidence based on ipsilateral neglect. *Archives of Neurology*, **44**:621–5.

Young, M. P., Hilgetag, C. *et al.* (1999) Models of paradoxical lesion effects and rules of inference for imputing function to structure in the brain. *Neurocomputing*, **26–27**:933–8.

Young, M. P., Hilgetag, C. and Scannell, J. W. (2000) On imputing function to structure from the behavioural effects of brain lesions. *Philosophical Transactions of The Royal Society of London*, **B355**:147–61.

Zihl, J., von Cramon, D. and Mai, N. (1983) Selective disturbance of movement vision after bilateral brain damage. *Brain*, **106**:313–40.

Chapter 12

Metamodal Cortical Processing in the Occipital Cortex of Blind and Sighted Subjects

Alvaro Pascual-Leone, Roy H. Hamilton

Introduction

We perceive the world by means of an elaborate set of distinct modality-specific receptor systems that feed into the myriad networks of the cerebral cortex. It is the distinctness of these sensory channels that enables us to experience sensations that are uniquely unimodal. The acquisition of information in separate modalities, however, also allows us to process the different elements of sensation in parallel in order to form a unitary multimodal percept. Moreover, information garnered by means of one sense impinges upon, enhances, and alters information acquired via others (Stein and Meredith 1993). Well known perceptual phenomena demonstrate that we are constantly integrating information from different modalities to form richer multisensory experiences. The "ventriloquism effect," for example, refers broadly to the phenomenon by which individuals form intersensory associations between auditory and visual information (Howard and Templeton 1966). In a similar fashion, the "McGurk effect" refers to a remarkable perceptual illusion in which auditory perception of speech sounds influences visual perception of spoken speech, and vice versa (McGurk and MacDonald 1976). Synesthesia, the involuntary joining of information from one sense with perception from another, further illustrates the ability of the senses to trespass freely into each other's domains (Baron-Cohen and Harrison 1997; Cytowic 1989). Such multisensory phenomena clearly illustrate that while sensory information is processed through different "channels," there is widespread communication of information between modalities that plays a major role in our integrated experience of the world.

Speculation about how information is processed between modalities is far from new. The medieval model of the mind contained within it the concept of a "sensus communis," a place in the brain where information from all modalities was summed into an integrated whole that could be utilized by the higher cognitive faculties of reason and memory (Gross 1998). Rene Descartes (Descartes 1972 [1662]) described intersensory neural connections between the olfactory, the tactile, and the visual systems, which he believed converged in the pineal gland. Later that century, the Irish philosopher

William Molyneux pondered if and how knowledge would be communicated between touch and vision in a blind person cured of his or her blindness (Morgan 1977; Degenaar 1996). In some sense this question was approached experimentally in 1728, when William Cheselden, an English surgeon, removed the cataracts from the eyes of a congenitally blind thirteen-year-old boy and noted the marked perceptual difficulties that the child subsequently experienced (Cheselden 1728). These scientists, physicians, and philosophers believed that sensory processing systems were inherently multi-modal, and that information obtained via one sense could inhibit, accentuate, or otherwise alter processing of information from another sense.

In contrast to these early multimodal descriptions of sensory processing, strictly uni-modal models emerged in the nineteenth century. It was soon widely accepted that the brain consisted of multiple spatially and functionally distinct modules, each of which was responsible for processing a different aspect of sensation or cognition. Johannes Müller and his renowned students Hermann von Helmholtz and Emil Du Bois-Reymond popularized the doctrine of specific nerve energies, which stated that modal-ities by which nerve impulses were experienced as sensations depended entirely on which sets of receptors were stimulated and where in the brain these receptor systems terminated (Müller 1965 [1838]). Du Bois-Reymond went so far as to claim that if it were possible to cross-connect the auditory and optic nerves, we would see with our ears and hear with our eyes (Gross 1998). Recent work in M. Sur's laboratory, on an animal model of cross-modal plasticity, provides support for this very notion (Melchner *et al.* 2000; Merzenich 2000; Sharma *et al.* 2000).

Despite a century of revolutionary change and discovery in the neurosciences, the notion that sensory systems are composed of spatially and functionally distinct uni-modal cortical networks acting simultaneously but independently has remained one of the central tenets of brain science as well as neurology. Neuroscientists commonly con-ceive of the brain as being composed of numerous cytoarchitecturally distinguishable areas that have different connectivity and subserve different purposes. Sensory systems are generally characterized as having peripheral receptor systems that transduce infor-mation to precortical neural relay stations. These relays (for instance, the nuclei of the thalamus) direct sensory signals to unimodal sensory cortical areas, thought to be responsible primarily for lower-order processing of data from a single modality. Only after this series of steps, in which sensory information has remained isolated by modal-ity, is information thought to merge in higher-order multimodal association areas of the cortex (Stein and Meredith 1993). It is now widely accepted that these multimodal association areas of the cortex contain multisensory cells, which provide a neural mechanism for integrating sensory experiences, modulating the saliency of stimuli, assigning experiential and affective relevance, and providing the substrate for perceptu-al experience. However, the presence of multisensory neurons does not appear to account for all phenomena that cross the boundaries of unimodality. Recent studies on blind, visually deprived, and even sighted subjects demonstrate that cortical processing for one sensory modality can occur even in primary cortical regions typically dedicated to different modalities, and call into question the strict organization of the brain into parallel unimodal systems that are only integrated in higher-order brain centers (Hamilton and Pascual-Leone 1998; Pascual-Leone and Hamilton 2001). An alternative hypothesis may claim that the brain actually represents a metamodal structure organized as a network of cortical operators that execute given functions or computations regardless of the sensory modality of their inputs (Pascual-Leone and Hamilton 2001). One such operator might have a predilection for a given sensory input based on its relative suitability for the kinds of computations required to process information from that modality. Such predilection might lead to operator-specific selective reinforcement of certain sensory modalities, eventually generating the impression of a brain structured in parallel, segregated systems processing different sensory signals. According to this view, a sense-specific brain region like the "visual cortex" may be visual only because we have sight and because the kinds of computation performed by the striate cortex is best suited for retinal, visual information. Similarly, the "auditory cortex" may only be auditory in hearing individuals and only because the computation performed by the temporal, perisylvian cortex is best implemented in the context of cochlear, auditory signals. However, in the face of visual deprivation or well chosen, challenging tasks, the striate cortex may unmask its tactile and auditory inputs to implement its computational functions on the available nonvisual sensory information.

The study of such phenomena requires the use of appropriate methodologies. Essentially, the requirement is to establish causal links between brain activity and behavioral manifestations. Traditionally, "lesion studies" represent the best way of establishing such a causal link between brain function and behavior. However, this "lesion study approach" is probably hampered by the plastic capabilities of the brain. Following a brain injury, brain function reorganizes in an attempt to compensate for the lost abilities, and therefore the observations might yield inaccurate results. Furthermore, cognitive abilities might be globally impaired after a brain insult, so that the patient might not be suited for extensive and detailed testing of a given ability. Patients will frequently have more than a single brain injury, or the injury might be larger than the brain area under study, making the correlation between regional brain function and disturbed behavior difficult. Finally, lesion studies depend on the opportunity and chance occurrence of a given brain injury and thus cannot be planned in advanced are generally limited to single or few case studies, and cannot be repeatedly tested in different patients for confirmation.

Functional neuroimaging techniques such as positron emission tomography (PET) have convincingly shown the association between certain behaviors and specific patterns of joint activation of cortical and subcortical structures. Functional magnetic resonance imaging (fMRI) studies can add greater anatomical resolution and the temporal profile of the pattern of activation of such neural networks for specific behaviors. However, in the best of circumstances, these neuroimaging techniques only provide supportive evidence of the neural network *associated* with a given behavior rather than direct, *causal* evidence. Activation of a given neural network by a behavior can establish an association between neural activity and behavioral manifestation, but does not provide insight into the role that a given neural structure or its connections play in the behavioral manifestation. In addition, different strategies in behavior are difficult to control for and might induce misleading results in such "associative" approaches of correlation between behavior and brain activity.

Applied as single pulses appropriately delivered in time and space, or in trains of repetitive stimuli at appropriate frequency and intensity, transcranial magnetic stimulation (TMS) can be used to transiently disrupt the function of a given cortical target, thus creating a temporary "virtual brain lesion" (Pascual-Leone *et al.* 1999; Walsh and Rushworth 1999; Walsh and Cowey 2000). This allows the study of the contribution of a given cortical region to a specific behavior. This technique has multiple advantages over lesion studies that are discussed elsewhere in this volume (see Chapter 11). Essentially, TMS provides a novel approach to the scientific study of regional brain function and behavior by the possibility of "creating" virtual patients. Furthermore, TMS can provide chronometric information about the contribution of a given brain region to a given behavior, and is suited for the study of human brain function and behavior on the basis of functional connectivity between brain structures rather than on the basis of localization of a given function to a specific brain structure.

In the present chapter we shall review the contributions of TMS to the study of metamodal processing of information in the occipital, "visual" cortex in blind, visually deprived, and sighted volunteers.

Feeling with the mind's eye: the occipital cortex in the early blind

Because the processing of visual information encompasses a significant portion of the brain, peripheral blindness represents a deafferentation of large portions of the cerebral cortex and imposes great demands on other sensory systems, such as touch or hearing. A particularly complicated compensatory tactile ability acquired by many blind individuals is Braille reading. Faced with the complex cognitive and perceptual demands of Braille reading, it appears that striking adaptive changes occur in the human brain (Hamilton and Pascual-Leone 1998). An emerging body of evidence now suggests that the occipital cortex can be recruited to process tactile information in persons who have been blinded early in life.

Using PET as a measure of cortical activation during tactile discrimination tasks, Sadato *et al.* (1996, 1998) found that blind subjects demonstrated activation of both primary and secondary occipital cortical areas (V1 and V2; Brodmann areas 17, 18, and possibly 19) during tactile tasks (Fig. 12.1), whereas sighted controls showed deactivation in these regions. Studies by Uhl *et al.* (1991, 1993) using event related potentials (ERPs) and cerebral blood flow measures also suggest occipital cortex activation in early blind humans. These findings indicate that, in blind subjects, the occipital cortex appears capable of reorganizing to accept nonvisual sensorimotor information, possibly

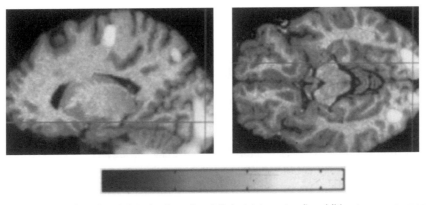

Fig. 12.1 (and color plate 21) Activation of occipital, striate cortex (in addition to somatosensory cortex) during Braille reading in congenitally or early blind subjects during PET. Modified from Sadato *et al.* (1996).

for further processing. However, as mentioned above, functional neuroimaging studies and electrophysiologic measures can only establish correlations between cognitive tasks and changes in brain activity. To confirm that activity in a brain region is actually related to performance of a particular task, one would want to demonstrate that disrupting the activity of that region results in a deficit in performance of the task in question. TMS provides a means of temporarily modifying cortical activity and thereby defining the function of specific cortical regions in a given task (Pascual-Leone *et al.* 1999, 2000; Walsh and Rushworth 1999; Walsh and Cowey 2000).

Cohen *et al.* (1997) found that repetitive TMS (rTMS) applied to the occipital cortex was able to disrupt Braille letter reading and the reading of embossed Roman characters in early blind subjects (subjects born blind or that had become blind before the age of 7; Fig. 12.2). In this study, repetitive rTMS induced errors and distorted the tactile perceptions of blind subjects in both tasks. In the case of the Braille task, subjects knew that they were touching Braille symbols, but were unable to discriminate them, reporting instead that the Braille dots felt "different," "flatter," "less sharp and less well defined." Occasionally, some subjects even reported feeling additional ("phantom") dots in the Braille cell. By contrast, occipital stimulation had no effect on tactile performance in normal sighted subjects, whereas similar stimulation is known to disrupt their visual performance (Kosslyn *et al.* 1999).

We have recently had the opportunity to corroborate these TMS findings with a naturally occurring case of acquired Braille alexia following insult to the occipital cortex in a congenitally blind Braille reader (Hamilton *et al.* 2000a). In this instance the serendipity of nature provides experimental evidence that TMS is creating a transient virtual lesion.

A 63-year-old right-handed woman was blind (with no light perception) since birth due to retrolental fibroplasia. She had been born six weeks prematurely, but the preceding pregnancy had been uncomplicated and aside from severe retinal damage, she

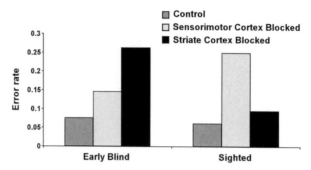

Fig. 12.2 Results of disruption of the somatosensory or striate cortex by repetitive TMS on Braille character recognition or tactile reading of embossed Roman letters in early blind subjects or sighted controls. The graph presents only the critical comparison of baseline (with TMS discharged off the subjects' head) and TMS to the contralateral somatosensory cortex or the occipital pole. For further details on the experimental protocol and control conditions please see original report. Modified from Cohen *et al.* (1997).

did not manifest any other long-term effects of premature birth or of newborn intensive care. She had developed normally, achieving developmental milestones at expected ages. She started to learn to read Braille at age 6, and became a proficient reader. She used Braille extensively in college, graduated with a Bachelor's degree, and had been working for the National Radio Station for the Blind in Spain since age 22. At work, she would use Braille to communicate with colleagues, take notes, and write her reports and memos, which amounted to approximately 4 to 6 hours of Braille use each day. Her reading speed was remarkable, with a rate of 120 to 150 symbols per minute. She used both hands and several fingers in each hand for character recognition.

At age 52, she developed adult onset diabetes, which was controlled to a reasonable degree with diet and hypoglycemic agents, and she had, for several years prior to presentation, required treatment for hypertension. She smoked one pack of cigarettes per day. According to yearly physical exams, she had mild left ventricular hypertrophy, thought to be secondary to the hypertension, but experienced no other consequences from her medical problems. Specifically, there was no documentation of diabetic peripheral neuropathy that might have led to difficulties with Braille reading.

One morning, she complained to her co-workers of light-headedness, difficulty swallowing, and motor incoordination. Despite the patient's complaints, her co-workers reported no objective correlates to her sensations. According to the patient, these vague complaints continued for most of the morning, and around noon she reportedly collapsed. Her secretary did not notice any tonic–clonic activity, and initially felt that the patient might have fainted, since there was no cardiorespiratory arrest noted. She was taken to the university hospital, where she was found to be obtunded, with withdrawal to strong stimuli but no response to verbal orders. Her breathing was shallow, but there was no respiratory compromise. Her pupils were equal and normally reactive to light. No focal signs on the neurological exam were documented in the emergency room evaluation. The patient was admitted to the intensive care unit, where, over the course of the following 24 hours, she became alert and able to interact normally with her surroundings. The physician noted a normal physical and neurologic exam on the second day of her hospitalization. She no longer reported having difficulty swallowing, nor did she feel light-headed. She was able to get up and walk without problems. On the second day, when she tried to read a Braille card sent to her, she was unable to do so. She stated that the Braille dots "felt flat" to her, though she described being able to "concentrate" and determine whether or not there was a raised dot in a given position in an isolated cell of Braille. Nonetheless, when attempting to read Braille normally, she found that she could not "extract enough information" to determine what letters, and especially what words, were written. She likened her impairment to "having the fingers covered by thick gloves." Despite her profound inability to read, she was struck by the fact that she did not notice any similar impairment in touch discrimination when trying to identify the roughness of a surface or locate items on a board. She was able to identify her house key by touch in order to ask a friend to check on her cat at home, and she was similarly able to identify different coins tactually without any difficulty.

Twelve months later she continued to be unable to read Braille and had resorted to the use of a computer with voice recognition software; otherwise she remained active and continued to work at the radio station. An MRI of her brain (Fig. 12.3), revealed extensive bilateral occipital lesions of increased T2 signal, most suggestive of bilateral occipital ischemic strokes. In summary, this patient became alexic for Braille following bilateral occipital strokes, probably secondary to an embolic stroke at the tip of the

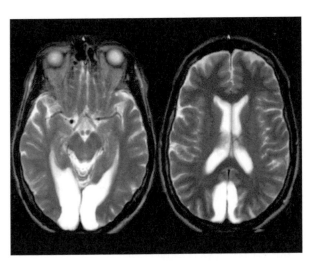

Fig. 12.3 T2-weighted MRI of an early blind patient who was formerly a proficient Braille reader. Following her cerebrovascular accident, the patient developed Braille alexia. Modified from Hamilton *et al.* (2000a).

basilar artery. Her MRI failed to document any lesions to the sensory motor cortices or to their projections. Similarly, imaging of her brain did not reveal damage to language centers, the angular gyrus, or white matter pathways leading to it. Peripheral motor and sensory nerve functions, as well as the sensory afferent pathways, appeared to be normal as documented by the neurologic exam and neurophysiologic studies. There was no discernible difficulty in performing nonspatial tactile perception tasks. The findings strongly support the notion that in this early blind patient, the occipital cortex was indeed responsible for the decoding of spatial and tactile information required for Braille reading skill. Unfortunately, the patient declined further testing, making more detailed examination impossible.

The chronometry of spatial information processing from somatosensory input to occipital cortex

TMS can provide information about the timing of information processing along a neural network (Pascual-Leone *et al.* 2000). TMS can very briefly disrupt the function of a targeted cortical region (Walsh and Cowey 2000) and thus, applied at variable intervals following a given stimulus, it can provide information about the temporal profile of activation and information processing along elements of a neural network. This application has been used in normal volunteers to study the timing of visual information processing in the striate cortex (Maccabee *et al.* 1991) and of somatosensory information in the primary sensory cortex (Cohen *et al.* 1991).

A TMS stimulus appropriately delivered in time and space can transiently disrupt the arrival of the thalamocortical volley into the primary sensory cortex and interfere with detection of peripheral somatosensory stimuli (Cohen *et al.* 1991). This disruptive effect will result in the subject's failure to detect the stimulus. The subject is not aware that he or she received a peripheral somatosensory stimulus prior to TMS. In order to achieve this effect, the TMS cortical stimulus (CS) has to be appropriately timed following the peripheral stimulus (PS) and the current induced in the brain appropriately oriented (Pascual-Leone *et al.* 1994). Detection of PS is disrupted only when the interval between PS and CS is 15 to 35 ms (Cohen *et al.* 1991; Pascual-Leone *et al.* 1994). In addition, topographic specificity can be demonstrated according to the known somatotopic organization of the sensory cortex. TMS must be delivered at the appropriate site for projection of index finger afferences when PS is applied to the index finger pad, and no effect is demonstrable if the site of TMS is displaced by 1 or 2 cm to any direction (Pascual-Leone *et al.* 1994).

These findings provide information about the time course of information arrival to the primary sensory cortex and its processing time there in normal subjects. The same effect of blocking detection of somatosensory stimuli can be demonstrated in blind proficient Braille readers (Pascual-Leone and Torres 1993). Detection of electric stimuli applied to the pad of the index finger can be blocked by properly timed TMS stimuli to the contralateral sensorimotor cortex. Using a specially designed stimulator that resembled a Braille cell, we applied electric stimuli slightly above sensory threshold to the index finger pad of right or left hand in sighted controls and blind subjects. These peripheral stimuli were followed by TMS stimuli at variable intervals and intensities to different scalp positions targeting the sensorimotor cortex. TMS stimuli appropriately delivered in time and space resulted in a block of detection of the peripheral stimuli such that the subjects were unaware of having received a peripheral stimulus preceding the cortical stimulus. In blind subjects, the block of detection of the peripheral stimulus could be achieved by cortical stimuli delivered to a larger cortical area, and at a longer window of intervals between peripheral and cortical stimuli, but required a stronger intensity of the TMS stimuli.

Using a similar approach it is possible to evaluate the timing and contributions of somatosensory and occipital cortex to processing of tactile information in the congenitally blind (Hamilton and Pascual-Leone 1998). The pilot study was conducted on subjects who were blind due to premature retinopathy and had no residual vision with absent responses to visual evoked potentials. All subjects had normal neurologic exams, except for the blindness, and normal brain MRIs. All were proficient Braille readers and used Braille 1 to 6 hours per day. Real or nonsensical Braille stimuli were presented with a specially designed Braille stimulator to the pad of the reading index finger. Subjects used primarily their right index finger for Braille character recognition. Single-pulse TMS stimuli were applied to the left or right sensorimotor cortex and the striate cortex at variable intervals following the presentation of the Braille stimuli. The site of stimulation was determined by correlating the scalp position of the TMS coil with the subject's 3D reconstructed MRI using a frameless stereotactic targeting device. The study was conducted in blocks of 360 trials. Each subject completed three blocks of 360 trials that differed in the cortical area targeted by TMS. In each block three Braille stimulation conditions were tested (no Braille stimulus, real Braille stimulus, and nonsensical Braille stimulus). In addition, in each block 12 different TMS conditions were tested (no TMS and 10–110 ms interstimulus intervals between Braille stimulus and TMS). Figure 12.4 summarizes schematically the experimental design and the results of a representative subjects.

This study revealed that TMS to the left somatosensory cortex disrupted detection of Braille stimuli at interstimulus intervals of 20 to 40 ms in congenitally blind subjects using their right index for the task. In fact, when TMS was applied to the contralateral somatosensory cortex at these intervals the subjects often did not realize that a peripheral stimulus had been presented to their finger. In the instances in which they did realize the presentation of a peripheral stimulus, they were able to correctly identify whether it was real Braille or not, and what Braille symbol was presented. It would appear that the somatosensory cortex was engaged in *detection* of the tactile stimulus.

Furthermore, we found that TMS to the striate cortex disrupted the processing of the peripheral stimuli at interstimulus intervals of 50 to 80 ms. Contrary to the findings after sensorimotor TMS, the subjects generally knew whether a peripheral stimulus had been presented or not, therefore no interference with detection was demonstrated. However, the subjects were unable to discriminate whether the presented stimuli were

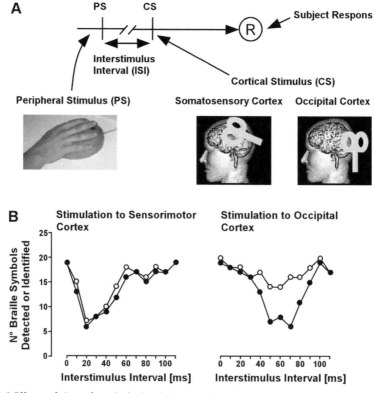

Fig. 12.4 Effects of sites of cortical stimulation on detection and identification of Braille symbols. Summarizes the experimental design (top) and the results for a representative early blind subject (bottom). The graph displays in open symbols the number of stimuli detected and in filled symbols the number of stimuli correctly identified (perceived) depending on TMS condition and regardless of whether real or nonsensical Braille stimuli were presented. Modified from Hamilton and Pascual-Leone (1998).

real or nonsensical Braille or what Braille symbol might have been presented (interference with perception).

Therefore, in early blind subjects, the interval between a tactile stimulus to the finger pad and a cortical stimulus that interferes with processing of tactile information is different for cortical stimulation of the somatosensory and the striate ("visual") cortex. This time difference provides insight into the temporal profile of information processing and transfer in early blind subjects between somatosensory and striate cortex. Theoretically, two main alternative routes could be entertained: thalamocortical connection to sensory and visual cortex; and corticocortical connections from sensory cortex to visual cortex.

Thalamic somatosensory nuclei could send input to both the somatosensory cortex and the striate cortex from multimodal cells in the geniculate nuclei. These theoretical multiple projections might be masked or even degenerate in the postnatal period given normal vision. However, in early blind subjects, these somatosensory thalamo–striatal projections might remain and be responsible for the participation of the striatal cortex in tactile information processing. Murata *et al.* (1965) demonstrated the existence of weak nonvisual input to cells of the newborn cat primary visual cortex. Such tenuous multimodal pathways might be unmasked in the case of early injury and visual deprivation. Unfortunately, further studies on such multimodal input into the visual cortex in the adult or blind animals or humans are few and uncertain (Morell 1972; Pascual-Leone and Hamilton 2001).

Further support for a subcortical origin of the recruitment of the visual cortex for tactile information processing in the early blind can be seen in the changes induced by blindness in the neuronal populations of the geniculate nucleus. Rauschecker *et al.* (1995) found that early visual deprivation results in an increase in the number of multimodal neurons in the geniculate nucleus. Such multimodal neurons receive and process auditory and tactile information and are presumed to retain their projection to visual cortex.

Nevertheless, corticocortical connections between sensory cortex and visual cortex seem the more likely route of recruitment of the striate cortex for tactile spatial information processing in the early blind. A sequential striate–prestriate–inferior temporal cortical pathway (ventral visual pathway) is known to serve visual discrimination functions (Ungerleider and Mishkin 1982). In macaque monkeys, ablation of the posterior part of the inferior temporal cortex (area TEO) leads to severe visual pattern discrimination deficits. Recent PET studies in humans show activation in the fusiform gyrus in occipital and occipitotemporal cortex during tasks that require attention to form such as processing of pictures, faces, letter strings, and geometric shapes (Corbetta *et al.* 1990, 1991; Haxby *et al.* 1991). These reports support the notion that the ventral visual pathway is used for visual shape discrimination and that there might in fact be an analogy between pathways of visual and tactile shape discrimination (Mishkin *et al.* 1983; Murray and Mishkin 1984). The secondary sensory cortex (SII) for touch discrimination may be analogous to the posterior region of the inferior temporal cortex (area TEO) for visual pattern discrimination, and the insula may be analogous to the anterior part of the inferior temporal cortex (area TE). Early visual deprivation in the monkey makes most neurons in area 7 and 19 responsive to somatic exploration (Hyvarinen *et al.* 1981), and diffuse reciprocal projections link area 19 to the primary visual cortex (Shipp and Zeki 1989). These findings suggest that somatosensory input could be transferred to the primary visual cortex through the dorsal visual association areas during spatial tactile information processing by blind subjects. The spatial information originally conveyed by the tactile modality in the sighted subjects (SI—SII—insular cortex—limbic system) might be processed in the blind by the neuronal networks usually reserved for the visual, shape discrimination process (SI—BA 7—dorsolateral BA 19—V1—occipitotemporal region—anterior temporal region—limbic system). This plasticity through corticocortical connections would explain the fact that tactile information processing in the somatosensory and occipital cortex in early blind is not only different in timing but also in the type of contribution, detection versus discrimination or perception respectively.

Changes in occipital activity correlate with tactile performance

It is often said of the blind, the deaf, or other persons suffering from sensory loss, that in the absence of one sense the other senses "grow sharper." Anecdotally, this would seem to be true of blind individuals, who often appear to be possessed of outstanding nonvisual sensory abilities. In his remarkable autobiographical book, *Touching the Rock*, John Hull, a formerly-sighted individual documenting his journey into blindness, describes the development of dramatic changes in his sensory perception (Hull 1992). These include the ability to discern environments by the sound of rainfall and the ability to navigate obstacles via a combination of echolocation and vibratory sensation that he refers to as "facial vision." Even the ability to read Braille fluently by touch, a relatively common skill among the blind, represents a remarkable act of tactile perception. Is it, however, truly the case that blind individuals have heightened sensory acuity, or are they simply more attentive to nonvisual information than sighted individuals? If there are real compensatory adaptive sensory and behavioral changes that take place in the presence of blindness, could these be related to the changes in cortical processing of sensory information demonstrated in prior functional neuroimaging, lesion, and TMS studies?

Lesion studies are not optimal tools for delineating the actual behavioral benefit of activity in a particular brain region. Loss of a behavioral or perceptual ability induced by a lesion implies but does not denote that enhanced activity in the lesioned area would lead to gains in that ability. It could be the case that the occipital cortex assumes the role normally subserved by other cortical areas without yielding any demonstrable difference in perception. Were this the case, tactile processing in the occipital cortex would be necessary for adequate tactile perception in the blind, but would provide no advantage in tactile perception relative to sighted individuals. Therefore, while lines of evidence may suggest that the tactile performance of blind persons suffers when they experience either transient or enduring lesions of the occipital cortex, these investigations do not establish whether the participation of the functioning occipital cortex in nonvisual tasks actually leads to adaptive perceptual changes in the blind.

However, when early blind subjects and sighted controls are tested using a grating orientation task (GOT) in order to compare tactile acuity between these two populations, it is possible to show that blind subjects do indeed have a heightened tactile acuity (van Boven *et al.* 2000). Remarkably, this improved tactile performance of blind subjects in the GOT tactile task appears correlated with increased blood oxygen level dependent (BOLD) activation on functional magnetic resonance imaging (Kiriakopoulos *et al.* 1999). TMS would provide a unique tool to take such results further and explore whether disruption of striate cortex activity leads to worsening GOT acuity in this blind subjects.

Taken together, our findings suggest that in blind Braille readers, the occipital cortex is activated during tactile tasks and processes information in a behaviorally beneficial way. Furthermore, the perceptual role of occipital tactile processing in the blind appears to be complex and can be differentiated from simple detection or low-level representation of tactile stimuli by means of TMS. Is this elaborate processing of nonvisual sensory information in the occipital cortex limited to the tactile domain? It may, for example, be the case that auditory information can also be processed in the occipital cortex of early blind individuals. If this were the case, one would predict that adaptive auditory abilities might be demonstrable in the blind, and that these may be related to plastic cortical changes in these individuals. Consistent with this hypothesis, a fortuitous discovery that has emerged from our work with early blind subjects is that blind musicians appear to have dramatically altered pitch perception abilities compared to their sighted counterparts (Hamilton *et al.* 2000b).

Occipital cortex contribution to tactile object recognition in the sighted

Using the same logic as discussed above, Kris Sathian and colleagues have tested the contribution of visual imagery (and hence visual cortex [Kosslyn 1996; Kosslyn *et al.* 1999]) to tactile processing in the sighted. In fact, using the same GOT mentioned before, they have shown that tactile discrimination may lead to increased metabolic activity in parieto-occipital areas in PET in the sighted (Sathian *et al.* 1997), and that occipital TMS can actually interfere with performance on the GOT (Zangaladze *et al.* 1999).

Other recent studies have confirmed the capacity of the occipital cortex to process nonvisual information. For example, Diebert and colleagues have used fMRI to demonstrate that the neural substrates for tactile object recognition in sighted humans involves the calcarine fissure and extrastriatal cortex, as well as the inferior parietal lobule, inferior frontal gyrus, and superior frontal gyrus–polar region (Deibert *et al.* 1999). Macaluso and colleagues have used fMRI to demonstrate that tactile stimulation enhances activity in the visual cortex when on the same side of as a visually presented target. Analysis of effective connectivity between brain regions further suggests that touch impacts the primary visual cortex by means of back projections from parietal areas (Macaluso *et al.* 2000).

Here again, TMS could be favorably used to further extend the neuroimaging results. For example, TMS could be applied to the occipital or parietal cortex during PET or fMRI recording, in order to study the functional connectivity between brain regions depending on the tactile stimulation state.

Crossmodal plasticity or metamodal cortical processing

Until one can make and test models about the mechanisms underlying crossmodal cortical activation, the changes in cortical function seen in early blind persons must remain in the realm of phenomenology. Although one could postulate many explanations for how nonvisual sensory processing takes place in the occipital cortex of the blind, two main hypotheses emerge as the most likely mechanisms for such processing. One model involves the presence of true cross-modal plasticity. This would imply that the occipital cortex, which is normally responsible solely for visual processing would take on the functional and possibly structural characteristics of other cortical regions through the influence of cross-modal connections. In keeping with this hypothesis, one would need to argue that different mechanisms account for the activation of occipital cortex in sighted subjects during specific tasks and in congenitally blind subjects. An alternative to the existence of true cross-modal plasticity in primary sensory cortical models would be that areas like the striate cortex are part of distributed metamodal structures. This would mean that sensory cortical networks do not process information strictly from single modalities, but are instead capable of performing certain sets of computations and transformations on data irrespective of the sensory modalities from which that data is received.

In other words, with the prolonged deafferentation of early blindness the functional and structural identity of the occipital cortex may change from visual cortex to tactile or auditory cortex. On the other hand, it may be the case that the occipital cortex is normally capable of the kinds of functions and computations required by the processing of nonvisual information, and that this activity is unmasked by the state of blindness. One way to differentiate these two possibilities and to reveal which of them truly characterizes the occipital cortex would be to investigate the possibility of transiently inducing nonvisual processing in the occipital cortex in a population of individuals who had not experienced long-standing deafferentation. To that end, we have been conducting an involved study in which we attempt to elicit nonvisual processing in the visual cortex of sighted individuals who are visually deprived for five days. These subjects stay at the General Clinical Research Center (GCRC) at Beth Israel Deaconess Medical Center throughout the study, and functional and behavioral changes in their occipital cortex are investigated using fMRI and occipital rTMS.

The study is not yet completed, but preliminary results can be reported. Subjects are right-handed, medication-free native English speakers, between the ages of 18 and 35, with 20/20 vision (either corrected or uncorrected). Subjects are randomized to being blindfolded or not. Exclusion criteria included any history of neurologic disorders, head trauma or prolonged loss of consciousness, learning disorders or dyslexia, central or peripheral disorder of somatic sensation, metal in the body, skin damage on the hands, any history of switching handedness, any smoking history (to prevent frequent departures from the GCRC), and any prior experience with Braille. Blindfolded subjects were fitted with a specially designed blindfold that completely prevented all light perception.

Blindfolded and nonblindfolded control subjects were blindfolded temporarily for serial MRI studies. Sets of functional MRI data were collected at baseline prior to the study, repeatedly during the blindfolding period, and on the sixth day, one day after removal of the blindfold. These serial fMRI studies showed increasing activation of the striate and peristriate cortex during tactile and auditory stimulation while the subjects remained blindfolded. On the first day of the blindfolding period comparison of tactile stimulation versus rest in both blindfolded and sighted subjects revealed activation in the contralateral somatosensory cortex, but none in the occipital cortex. On the fifth day of blindfolding, comparison of stimulation versus rest in blindfolded subjects showed additional BOLD activation in occipital, "visual," regions. Sighted subjects continued to show no significant activation in the occipital cortex. On the sixth day, approximately 12 hours following removal of the blindfold, comparison of stimulation to rest reveals no occipital activation in either sighted or blindfolded conditions. Similarly, activation of striate cortex during auditory stimulation is seen at the end of the blindfold period and was absent prior to the blindfolding or in the control subjects.

TMS can be used in this experiment to assess the role that the emerging activity in the striate cortex might have in tactile or auditory processing. A Braille character recognition task was given to the subjects (either blindfolded or sighted controls) on the fifth and sixth days of testing. The right index finger was tested using a Braille stimulator and software designed specifically for Braille discrimination tasks. The task consisted of 36 pairs of Braille characters presented in succession with a brief pause (1400 ms) between each pair. Subjects were instructed to identify whether the pair of characters presented had been the same Braille formation or two different Braille formations by simply saying "same" or "different." Subject responses were recorded. Subjects' testing fingers were immobilized using double-sided tape. Subjects were given a practice trial before an initial baseline performance was recorded. TMS was then delivered to the visual cortex. This was immediately followed by a second set of Braille stimuli. Subjects were tested a third and final time after a 10 minute rest period. The Braille character sets were randomized for each subject. All subjects were tested twice on the fifth and then again on the sixth day of the study. For the blindfolded subjects this meant that the first test was done after five days of blindfolding and the second test less than 24 hours after removal of the blindfold.

All stimulation was delivered using a Magstim 70 mm figure of eight coil with pulses generated by a Magstim Rapid Stimulator (Magstim Inc., Dyfed, UK). The stimulation coil was held tangentially, flat against the scalp at the Oz position of the 10–20 electrode system. This scalp position overlays the tip of the calcarine fissure in most subjects, and when TMS is applied to this scalp position sighted subjects experience phosphenes thought to originate in V1 (Kammer 1999). A single train of 300 pulses of 1 Hz TMS was delivered to the visual cortex at an intensity of 110% of each subjects' motor threshold. Motor threshold was determined following the recommendations of the International Federation of Clinical Neurophysiology. These TMS parameters are well within current safety guidelines (Wassermann 1998). A train of repetitive TMS of these characteristics to this scalp position in sighted subjects transiently disrupts visual perception and visual imagery (Kosslyn *et al.* 1999).

For each subject, the number of errors in each block of trials was expressed as a percentage difference from baseline performance. The specificity of the TMS effects was tested by assuming that TMS effects would be short-lived, and hence the effects should be maximal in the block of trials immediately following the TMS and should be resolved or significantly less in the follow-up test after the 10 minute pause. The results in the two tests (days 5 and 6) in the nonblindfolded subjects were compared using paired t-test and given the lack of significant effects, they were collapsed as a single data point. The results in the two tests (days 5 and 6) in the blindfolded subjects were termed blindfold ON (day 5) and blindfold OFF (day 6) and analyzed separately. An overall analysis of variance (ANOVA) for group (sighted, blindfold ON or blindfold OFF) and block of trials (immediately after TMS and following 10 min rest period) was conducted. The Blindfold ON and OFF variables were considered single-group, paired comparisons. Block of trials was also handled as a within subject repeated measures variable. *Post hoc* comparisons were completed using Fisher's PLSD test setting significance at $p<0.05$. The overall ANOVA revealed a strong trend towards significant interaction of group and block of trials ($F=0.12$; $df=2$; $p=0.06$). The blindfold ON group was significantly different than the sighted group ($p=0.01$) and than the blindfold OFF group ($p=0.01$). This is remarkable as it reveals that the TMS effects in the blindfolded subjects changed significantly following removal of the blindfold for less than 24 hours, such that occipital TMS had a marked effect on tactile discrimination when the blindfold was ON, but had no effect when the blindfold had been removed. Indeed, only in the blindfold ON group was there a significant effect of TMS on errors (post TMS versus baseline, $p<0.01$; Fig. 12.5). Furthermore, this effect was transient, consistent with the short-lived effects of TMS (post TMS versus post Rest, $p<0.01$). The results in the blindfold OFF and the sighted groups did not differ from each other.

These results suggest that the occipital cortex can be recruited for processing tactile and auditory information when it is deafferented of visual input, even in transiently blinded normal subjects. These findings have several implications. The speed of these functional changes seen in the occipital cortex is such that it is highly improbable that new cortical connections are being established. The findings, therefore, strongly suggest that tactile and auditory connections to the "visual cortex" are present in sighted as well as blind individuals and can be unmasked under behaviorally desirable conditions. Furthermore, the rapid recruitment of the occipital cortex also suggests that the changes that take place in the occipital cortex of blind and blindfolded individuals do not involve the dramatic morphologic reorganization that is implied by true cross-modal plasticity. Rather, the fact that occipital networks are able to respond to nonvisual information so readily suggests that the occipital cortex functions in a metamodal capacity, and that it is somehow able to process sensory information without strict regard for its modality of input.

Error [% from baseline]

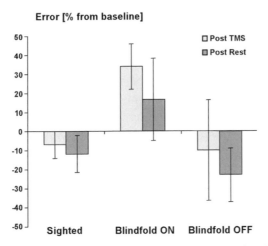

Fig. 12.5 Errors (expressed in percentage from baseline performance before (blue) and after (red) rTMS applied to the striate cortex. Data for the sighted subjects represents the average for two testing days in each subject given the lack of significant differences. Data in the blindfolded subjects are separated for the time point with the blindfold on (day 5) and the following day after removal of the blindfold (blindfold OFF). Bars represent mean for 5 subjects in each group ± standard error.

The rTMS results demonstrate that disruption of the occipital cortex significantly affects the performance of a tactile task in the blindfolded subjects. Nonblindfolded control subjects showed no significant effects from the stimulation. In our study, 1 Hz rTMS over the visual cortex led to increased errors in the blindfolded subjects. These findings confirm those found in the study with the early blind (Cohen *et al.* 1997), and are consistent with the findings that the occipital cortex contributes to tactile acuity in the blind (Kiriakopoulos *et al.* 1999; van Boven *et al.* 2000). The fact that no difference in tactile performance could be elicited by occipital rTMS after vision was restored to blindfolded subjects implies that overriding visual input masks tactile processing in the visual cortex revealed by temporary deafferentation. Although it is unclear why the blindfolded subjects' performance did not return to baseline following the 10 minute rest period, one likely explanation is that the effects of occipital rTMS persisted longer than the utilized rest period.

This study in visually deprived sighted individuals demonstrates that even transient loss of vision unmasks connections to the occipital cortex. The activity that subsequently arises in the occipital cortex in response to tactile and auditory stimuli over the course of only a few days suggests that the primary visual cortex is capable of particular kinds of functions rather than processing specific sensory modalities. If, however, one is to subscribe to a metamodal model of cortical function, the question remains: how is sensory specificity achieved in the brain? In brain of normal sighted individuals, the presentation of visual stimuli normally results in preferential activation of the occipital cortex, auditory information preferentially activates the auditory cortex, and so forth. If primary sensory modules function as metamodal operators, capable of performing sets of processes on data irrespective of their sensory modality of origin, what drives the tendency for information from one modality to be processed primarily in one cortical region and information from another modality to be processed primarily in another? In order to support both the metamodal hypothesis and the notion of functional specificity in the cortex, one needs a model that can account for both the multipotentiality of metamodal processing and the functional specificity commonly observed in the brain. Such a model exists in the field of computational neuroscience (Jacobs 1999), and can readily be applied to our findings with the blind and the blindfolded (Pascual-Leone and Hamilton 2001). Competition between expert operators can be used to explain how metamodal cortical networks that are predisposed to certain kinds of functions eventually become specialized to preferentially process information from a particular modality, and how this development is altered in the case of peripheral blindness or visual deprivation. Further studies employing "virtual lesion methodologies" will help experimentally test such ideas and hence provide novel insights into the organization of the central nervous system.

For example, an intriguing variation in the theme of metamodal activity in primary sensory networks is that it may be the connections that these networks share with conventional multimodal association areas rather than direct connections between primary unimodal networks that mediate behaviorally relevant processing. Most models of cortical organization incorporate neurons that send sensory information on one-way processing pathways from receptors to primary sensory cortices to higher order cortices and beyond. Primary sensory cortical areas like V1 are, however, richly and bi-directionally interconnected with higher order association areas, and it maybe the case that networks of feedback connections lead from multimodal areas back to primary sensory areas. Were this the case, one possible outcome would be that, in the absence of stimuli from one modality, stimuli from another modality would activate multimodal association areas that would then activate primary cortical areas via retrograde connections leading from multimodal to unimodal cortical areas.

It might even be the case that the activity of primary cortical areas seen in functional neuroimaging studies is of minor or negligible relevance to the adaptive perceptual changes noted in deafferented individuals. It may be that it is the activity of multimodal cortical areas and their networks of feedforward and -backward connections that lead to the improved acuity of compensatory senses. Thus, blind Braille readers may have increased tactile acuity because the heteromodal cortical areas that receive touch information have become more active and more richly connected to other cortical networks, including other primary cortical regions. Occipital cortical activity might simply be an epiphenomenal side effect of adaptive changes in multimodal cortical activity and connectivity. Unfortunately, none of the studies pursued to date have either established or refuted this transmodal model of intersensory primary cortical activity. Even the "virtual lesions" induced by TMS cannot, in the absence of converging evidence, unravel this problem. Although it might seem that occipital rTMS gives rise to deficits in tactile abilities in the blind, it could be that these behaviorally relevant lesions result from the spread of TMS activation via feedback connections to multimodal association areas, where the TMS is having its actual impact.

In order to distinguish between metamodal and transmodal processing in the occipital cortex of the blind, one needs to be able to observe patterns of brain activity with much finer temporal resolution than has been achieved with our current fMRI paradigms. Moreover, it would be difficult to investigate this issue using TMS without knowing how TMS applied to one location in the cortex is impacting regions to which the stimulated area is connected. To that end, using TMS in conjunction with fMRI or PET in order to investigate the impact of magnetic brain stimulation on the functional activity of interacting cortical networks in blind, sighted, and blindfolded individuals promises to shed critical insights.

Acknowledgments

Research supported in part by grants from the Spanish Ministerio de Educación y Ciencia (DGICYT), the Milton Fund, the National Eye Institute (RO1EY12091), the National Institute for Mental Health (RO1MH57980, RO1MH60734), the Harvard-Thorndike General Clinical Research Center (NCRR MO1 RR01032), the Spanish Organization for the Blind, and the National Medical Fellowships, Inc.

This chapter summarizes, in part, thesis work submitted by Roy H. Hamilton at Harvard Medical School in partial fulfillment of the requirements for the M.D. degree with honors in a special field (Thesis title: "Metamodal Cortical Processing Demonstrated in the Occipital Cortex of Blind and Sighted Subjects"; submitted February 2001).

References

Baron-Cohen, S. and Harrison, J. E. (eds) (1997) *Synaesthesia*. Blackwell Publishers, Oxford, UK.

Cheselden, W. (1728) An account of some observations made by a young gentleman, who was born blind, or lost his sight so early, that he had no remembrance of ever having seen, and was couch'd between 13 and 14 years of age. *Philosophical Transactions of the Royal Society of London*, **35**:447–50.

Cohen, L.G., Bandinelli, S., Sato, S. *et al.* (1991) Attenuation in detection of somatosensory stimuli by transcranial magnetic stimulation. *Electroencephalography and Clinical Neurophysiology*, **81**:366–76.

Cohen, L. G., Celnik, P., Pascual-Leone, A. *et al.* (1997) Functional relevance of cross-modal plasticity in blind humans. *Nature*, **389**:180–3.

Corbetta, M., Miezin, F. M., and Dobmeyer, S. (1990) Attentional modulation of neural processing of shape, color and velocity in humans. *Science*, **248**:1556–9.

Corbetta, M., Miezin, F.M., Dobmeyer, S. *et al.* (1991) Selective and divided attention during visual discriminations of shape, color, and speed: functional anatomy by positron emission tomography. *Journal of Neuroscience*, **11**:2383–402.

Cytowic, R.E. (1989) *Synaesthesia: A Union of the Senses*. Springer Verlag, New York.

Degenaar, M. (1996) *Molyneux's Problem: Three Centuries of Discussion on the Perception of Forms*. Kluwer Academic Publishers.

Deibert, E., Kraut, M., Kremen, S. *et al.* (1999) Neural pathways in tactile object recognition. *Neurology*, **52**:1413–7.

Descartes, R. (1972 [1662]) *Treatise on Man.* Harvard University Press, Cambridge, MA.

Gross, C. (1998) *Brain, Vision, Memory: Tales in the History of Neuroscience.* MIT Press, Cambridge, MA.

Hamilton, R., Keenan, J.P., Catala, M. D. *et al.* (2000a) Alexia for braille following bilateral occipital stroke in an early blind woman. *Neuroreport*, **11**:237–40.

Hamilton, R. H. and Pascual-Leone, A. (1998) Cortical plasticity associated with braille learning. *Trends in Cognitive Science*, **2**:168–74.

Hamilton, R. H., Pascual-Leone, A., Rodrigues, D. *et al.* (2000b) Increased prevalence of absolute pitch in blind musicians. *Society for Neuroscience Abstracts*, **26**:1977.

Haxby, J. V., Grady, C. L., Horwitz, B. *et al.* (1991) Dissociation of object and spatial visual processing pathways in human extrastriate cortex. *Proceedings of the National Academy of Sciences USA*, **88**:1621–5.

Howard, I. P. and Templeton, W. B. (1966) *Human spatial orientation.* Wiley, London.

Hull, J. M. (1992) *Touching the Rock: An Experience of Blindness.* Vintage Books, New York.

Hyvarinen, J., Carlson, Y., and Hyvarinen, L. (1981) Early visual deprivation alters modality of neuronal responses in area 19 of monkey cortex. *Neuroscience Letters*, **26**:239–43.

Jacobs, R. (1999) Computational studies of the development of functionally specialized neural modules. *Trends in Cognitive Science*, **3**:31–8.

Kammer, T. (1999) Phosphenes and transient scotomas induced by magnetic stimulation of the occipital lobe: their topographic relationship. *Neuropsychologia*, **37**:191–8.

Kiriakopoulos, E., Baker, J., Hamilton, R. *et al.* (1999) Relationship between tactile spatial acuity and brain activation on brain functional magnetic resonance imaging. *Neurology*, **52(Suppl. 2)**: A307.

Kosslyn, S. M. (1996) *Image and Brain: The Resolution of the Imagery Debate.* MIT Press, Cambridge, MA.

Kosslyn, S. M., Pascual-Leone, A., Felician, O. *et al.* (1999) The role of area 17 in visual imagery: convergent evidence from PET and rTMS. *Science*, **284**:167–70.

Macaluso, E., Frith, C. D. and Driver, J. (2000) Modulation of human visual cortex by crossmodal spatial attention. *Science*, **289**:1206–8.

Maccabee, P. J., Amassian, V. E., Cracco, R. Q. *et al.* (1991) Magnetic coil stimulation of human visual cortex: studies of perception. In W. J. Levy, R. Q. Cracco, A. T. Barker *et al.* (eds) *Magnetic Motor Stimulation: Basic Principles and Clinical Experience*, pp. 111–20. Elsevier, Amsterdam.

McGurk, H. and MacDonald, J. (1976) Hearing lips and seeing voices. *Nature*, **264**:746–8.

Melchner, L. V., Pallas, S. L., and Sur, M. (2000) Visual behaviour medicated by retinal projections directed to the auditory pathway. *Nature*, **404**:871–6.

Merzenich, M. (2000) Seeing in the sound zone. *Nature*, **404**: 820–1.

Mishkin, M., Ungerleider, L. G., and Macko, K. A. (1983) Object vision and spatial vision: Two cortical pathways. *Trends in Neurosciences*, **6**:414–7.

Morell, F. (1972) Visual system's view of acoustic space. *Nature*, **238**:44–6.

Morgan, M. J. (1977) *Molyneux's Question: Vision, Touch and the Philosophy of Perception.* Cambridge University Press, Cambridge.

Müller, J. M. (1965 [1838]) On the specific energies of nerves. In R. Herrnstein and E. Boring (eds) *Sourcebook of the History of Psychology.* Harvard University Press, Cambridge, MA.

Murata, K., Cramer, H., and Bach-y-Rita, P. (1965) Neuronal convergence of noxious, acoustic and visual stimuli in the visual cortex of the cat. *Journal of Neurophysiology*, **28**:1223–40.

Murray, E. and Mishkin, M. (1984) Relative contributions of SII and area 5 to tactile discrimination in monkeys. *Behavioural Brain Research*, **11**:67–83.

Pascual-Leone, A., Bartres-Faz, D. and Keenan, J. P. (1999) Transcranial magnetic stimulation: studying the brain-behaviour relationship by induction of "virtual lesions." *Philosophical Transactions of the Royal Society of London*, **354**:1229–38.

Pascual-Leone, A., Cohen, L. G., Brasil-Neto, J. P. *et al.* (1994) Differentiation of sensorimotor neuronal structures responsible for induction of motor evoked potentials, attenuation in detection of somatosensory stimuli, and induction of sensation of movement by mapping of optimal current directions. *Electroencephalography and Clinical Neurophysiology*, **93**:230–6.

Pascual-Leone, A. and Hamilton, R. H. (2001) The metamodal organization of the brain. *Progress in Brain Research* (in press).

Pascual-Leone, A. and Torres, F. (1993) Plasticity of the sensorimotor cortex representation of the reading finger in Braille readers. *Brain*, **116**:39–52.

Pascual-Leone, A., Walsh, V. and Rothwell, J. (2000) Transcranial magnetic stimulation in cognitive neuroscience—virtual lesion, chronometry, and functional connectivity. *Current Opinion in Neurobiology*, **10**:232–7.

Rauschecker, J. P. (1995) Compensatory plasticity and sensory substitution in the cerebral cortex. *Trends in Neuroscience*, **18**:36–43.

Sadato, N., Pascual-Leone, A., Grafman, J. *et al.* (1998) Neural networks for braille reading by the blind. *Brain*, **121**:1213–29.

Sadato, N., Pascual-Leone, A., Grafman, J. *et al.* (1996) Activation of the primary visual cortex by Braille reading in blind subjects. *Nature*, **380**:526–8.

Sathian, K., Zangaladze, A., Hoffman J. M. *et al.* (1997) Feeling with the mind's eye. *Neuroreport*, **8**:3877–81.

Sharma, J., Angelucci, A., and Sur, M. (2000) Induction of visual orientation modules in auditory cortex. *Nature*, **404**:841–7.

Shipp, S. and Zeki, S. (1989) The organization of connections between areas V5 and V1 in Macaque monkey visual cortex. *European Journal of Neuroscience*, **1**:309–32.

Stein, B. E., Meredith, M. A. (1993) *The Merging of the Senses*. MIT Press, Cambridge, Massachusetts.

Uhl, F., Franzen, P. and Lindinger, G. (1991) On the functionality of the visually deprived occipital cortex in early blind person. *Neuroscience Letters*, **124**:256–9.

Uhl, F., Franzen, P. and Podreka, I. (1993) Increased regional cerebral blood flow in inferior occipital cortex and the cerebellum of early blind humans. *Neuroscience Letters*, **150**:162–4.

Ungerleider, L. G. and Mishkin, M. (1982) Two cortical visual systems. In D. J. Ingle, M. A. Goodale, and R. J. W. Mansfield (eds) *Analysis of Visual BehaviorI*. MIT Press, Cambridge.

van Boven, R., Hamilton, R., Kaufman, T. *et al.* (2000) Tactile spatial resolution in blind Braille readers. *Neurology*, **54**:2230–6.

Walsh, V. and Cowey, A. (2000) Transcranial magnetic stimulation and cognitive neuroscience. *Nature Reviews Neuroscience*, **1**:73–9.

Walsh, V. and Rushworth, M. (1999) A primer of magnetic stimulation as a tool for neuropsychology. *Neuropsychologia*, **37**:125–35.

Wassermann, E. M. (1998) Risk and safety of repetitive transcranial magnetic stimulation: report and suggested guidelines from the International Workshop on the Safety of Repetitive Transcranial Magnetic Stimulation, June 5–7:1996. *Electroencephalography and Clinical Neurophysiology*, **108**:1–16.

Zangaladze, A., Epstein, C. M., Grafton, S. T. *et al.* (1999) Involvement of visual cortex in tactile discrimination of orientation. *Nature*, **401**:587–90.

Chapter 13

Excitability of Human Visual Cortex Examined with Transcranial Magnetic Stimulation

Babak Boroojerdi, Leonardo G. Cohen

Introduction

In the last 15 years, transcranial magnetic stimulation (TMS) has become a valuable method of study of the physiology and cognitive functions of the human brain. Using this technique, it is possible to stimulate the human cerebral cortex in a noninvasive and painless way (Barker *et al.* 1985). TMS elicits a magnetic field that passes virtually unaffected through the skin, skull and scalp (in simple terms, it elicits an electric field oriented perpendicular to the magnetic field). Induced currents in the tissue flow in a direction parallel to the coil (Maccabee *et al.* 1991b; Roth *et al.* 1991; Roth 1994). This method has an overall temporal resolution in the range of milliseconds, and a spatial resolution depending on the magnetic coils utilized, approximately down to a square centimeter. Examples of responses elicited by TMS include motor evoked potentials (MEP) elicited after stimulating the contralateral motor cortex. On the other hand, TMS can also cause a brief disruption of the cortical activity under the magnetic coil. For example, when TMS is applied over the visual cortex, it can block visual perception of letters briefly presented on a screen monitor (Amassian *et al.* 1989; Hotson *et al.* 1994; Ashbridge *et al.* 1997; Hotson and Anand 1999). If TMS is applied to the occipital cortex when the subject's eyes are closed, it can elicit positive perceptions (phosphenes, from the Greek *phos*, light, and *phainein*, to show), which are experienced as flashes/spots of light in the absence of visual stimuli (Marg 1991). At lower stimulation intensities, these phosphenes are usually perceived as white blobs. With increasing intensity, they may become more colorful (Boroojerdi *et al.* 2000a). Phosphene thresholds (PTs), configuration, color, and location in the visual field (Kammer 1999) have all been used as indirect functional measures to assess the topographic organization and excitability of the occipital cortex (Afra *et al.* 1998; Aurora *et al.* 1998; Aurora and Welch 1998). When applied to other cortical regions, TMS can also disrupt higher cognitive functions such as working memory (Grafman *et al.* 1994; Pascual-Leone and Hallett 1994) or memory-guided eye movements (Muri *et al.* 1996).

The purpose of this review is to discuss investigations of human visual cortex physiology using TMS.

Background

TMS-evoked phosphenes

Barker made the first report of TMS-elicited phosphenes in 1985 (Barker *et al.* 1985), using a large round coil of 14 cm outer diameter. Prior to that, Brindley and Lewin described phosphenes elicited using brief electrical pulses applied directly to the pia over the calcarine cortex of a blind subject (Brindley and Lewin 1968). Therefore, it was logical to expect that TMS could elicit similar phenomena. It was later understood that the phosphenes elicited by single-pulse TMS over the occipital cortex markedly differ from those obtained using electrical stimulation. The ability to elicit phosphenes varies depending on the magnetic coil configuration. Phosphenes are easily elicited by large circular coils, but harder to produce with small or figure-of-eight shaped coils (Amassian *et al.* 1989; Meyer *et al.* 1991). Phosphenes elicited by electrical stimulation through a 0.8 mm electrode were reported as small spots of white light. When using TMS, 10 of 15 subjects studied by Meyer *et al.* reported phosphenes that were white, cuneiform, and usually in the lower halves of the peripheral visual field (Meyer *et al.* 1991). When the TMS-induced currents flowed from right to left in the brain, phosphenes were predominantly elicited in the left visual field, suggesting a preferential activation of the right visual cortex (Meyer *et al.* 1991). It has also been reported that large magnetic coils can elicit phosphenes in peripheral regions of the visual field more often than small coils do; perhaps this is because the currents penetrate more deeply, where peripheral areas of the visual field are represented (Harrington 1976). However, this would not explain why the stronger, superficial electric field induced by a small diameter coil does not readily produce phosphenes at the fovea.

The minimum intensity of magnetic stimulation required to elicit phosphenes (phosphene threshold) is one of the most commonly used parameters of visual cortex excitability, which can be measured using TMS (Afra *et al.* 1998; Aurora *et al.* 1998; Boroojerdi *et al.* 2000a; Stewart *et al.* 2001). It has been shown that this parameter has low intrasubject and high intersubject variability (Stewart *et al.* 2001) and does not correlate with motor threshold, a common measure of motor cortex excitability (Boroojerdi *et al.* 2000c; Stewart *et al.* 2001).

TMS-evoked scotomas and their relationship to phosphenes

TMS can disrupt the activity of cortical regions located under the magnetic coil and therefore suppress or alter behavioral functions represented there (Amassian *et al.* 1989). By examining exactly when TMS causes functional suppression, it is possible to identify the timing of involvement of that cortical region in a given task or behavior. For example, Amassian and colleagues demonstrated suppressive effects on visual perception of a single TMS pulse delivered to the occipital cortex (Amassian *et al.* 1989). In their study, a trigram of randomly chosen alphabetical letters was presented and a TMS pulse was given over the occipital pole at different time intervals following letter presentation. The authors used a round Cadwell magnetic coil (Cadwell Laboratories, Kennewick, WA), placed with the inferior windings 2 cm above the inion. They showed that normal volunteers could not identify letters presented between 80 and 100 ms before a TMS stimulus. Given the latency, similar to the P_{100} component of the visual evoked potential, this suppression was interpreted as TMS interfering with the letter-processing neural activity in the underlying visual cortex (Beckers and Hömberg 1991; Masur *et al.* 1993; Epstein and Zangaladze 1996). Later studies revealed two additional periods of TMS-induced suppression: a very early dip occurring when the magnetic stimulus precedes the visual stimulus by 50–70 ms, and another one when the magnetic pulse follows the visual stimulus by 20–30 ms (Corthout *et al.* 1999, 2000). The first suppression has been described as a consequence of reflex eye closure and the second one as suppression of visual processing activity.

TMS delivered to occipital regions can suppress visual perception of motion. Beckers and coworkers (Beckers and Hömberg 1992; Beckers and Zeki 1995) demonstrated this phenomenon when TMS was delivered over region V5 20 ms before to 10 ms after the visual presentation. Additionally, these authors reported that TMS delivered over primary visual regions induced marginal changes in motion perception with a different timing following the onset of the visual stimulus (60–70 ms). They suggested that there are probably two physiologic pathways reaching V5 from the retina: a fast one, which bypasses V1, and a slow one through V1. Interestingly, Hoston and colleagues also reported suppression of visual motion perception delivered to the temporo–parietooccipital junction at later intervals of 100–175 ms following the onset of the visual stimulus (Hotson *et al.* 1994; Hotson and Anand 1999). Thus, bypassing of area V1 was not required to explain the results. Although TMS-induced disruption of motion perception seems to be a useful tool in studying human visual cortex, only further studies can shed light on the issue of the interrelation between different visual areas such as V1 and V5.

Few investigations have studied the relationship between TMS-evoked phosphenes and TMS-evoked visual suppression, which appear to be closely related phenomena. Kastner *et al.* (1998) demonstrated that TMS delivered through a round coil placed on the occipital pole can cause a transient scotoma in the lower visual field. Although subjects also reported perception of phosphenes, the authors did not feel that the phosphenes contributed to the phenomena of transient scotomas. Their argument was based on the fact that the intensity of magnetic stimulation required to elicit a phosphene was lower than that required to illicit suppression phenomena. At high stimulus intensities, their subjects could no longer see clear phosphenes. Another study pointed in a different direction. Kammer and associate (Kammer and Nusseck 1998; Kammer 1999) found that TMS-evoked phosphenes and transient scotomas overlapped within the same regions of the visual field. Therefore, the precise relationship between the two phenomena remains to be determined.

Stimulation with TMS predominantly activates superficial cortical regions. However, when delivered through large circular coils, it also activates subcortical structures.

It has been proposed that TMS-evoked suppression of visual perception is the consequence of transient disruption of activity in the primary visual cortex or the optic radiations (Amassian *et al.* 1989; Maccabee *et al.* 1991a; Meyer *et al.* 1991; Meyer and Diehl 1992; Masur *et al.* 1993). Beckers and Hömberg (1991) suggested an alternative site for this effect, associative regions, through disruption of a higher level "serial processor." Potts *et al.* (1998) coregistered the magnetic stimulation sites with MRI images and mapped these sites onto the surface of the occipital lobes to show the distribution of the visual suppression effect. Their results were consistent with disruption of secondary visual areas. Finally, it is possible that there are two processes operating at different time intervals and sites, one acting on deeper structures, requiring higher magnetic stimulation intensities and resulting in early inhibition, and one taking place at superficial cortical sites, requiring relatively low magnetic stimulus intensities and leading to late inhibition (Masur *et al.* 1993).

Unmasking of visual stimuli by TMS

Unmasking of visual stimuli by TMS is a related phenomenon described by Amassian and co-workers (Amassian *et al.* 1993). This phenomenon provided a positive index of the TMS effect on the visual cortex. A trigram of letters is flashed first (the target) with a low luminance, so when it is given alone, subjects make errors. This trigram is followed by a second trigram (the mask). At an interstimulus interval of about 100 ms, the mask can completely suppress the perception of the entire target trigram. When a TMS pulse follows the masking stimulus over calcarine cortex 60–160 ms later (peak at 100 ms), the target trigram is unmasked. Given the time delay needed for this unmasking, the authors suggested a site beyond calcarine cortex for this phenomenon.

Perception block of target disappearance

In this related paradigm, developed by Epstein and Zangaladze, the test pattern is composed of a grid of asterisks around a central fixation point (Epstein and Zangaladze 1996). Suddenly one of the asterisks disappears for a single frame of the video monitor. The subjects' instructions are to detect and report the disappearance of the asterisk (detecting the visual disappearance [DVD]), a task that under normal conditions can be accomplished by most individuals. TMS delivered 4 or 5 cm lateral to the occipital midline can abolish DVD in the contralateral hemifield. DVD in the inferior half-field could be abolished with stimulation delivered as much as 8 cm above the inion. These sites are considerably distant from the scalp position overlying the primary visual cortex, where the paracentral fields are represented.

These findings suggest that magnetic suppression occurs in the visual association cortex (Epstein *et al.* 1996). Marg and Rudiak (1994) have compared the depth of effective magnetic stimulation for motor and visual stimulation using two different size coils and plotting the threshold-induced electric fields for each coil vs. depth below the scalp surface (i.e., the perpendicular distance from the coil plane directly beneath the coil windings). The two field profiles cross at some distance below the scalp. Because the two fields are equivalent at this point, this is the presumed depth of stimulation (Epstein *et al.* 1990). They showed a deeper visual stimulation site (approx. 4 cm) than the site for motor stimulation (approx. 2 cm). Because both foveal and peripheral phosphenes had identical stimulation depths, the authors suggested a subcortical stimulation site, possibly in the optic radiation fibres adjacent to the posterior tip of the lateral ventricles. Although there is no direct evidence for the site of phosphene induction, given the results of the published studies, it is conceivable that phosphenes are generated near secondary visual areas. Future studies with coregistration of phosphene induction sites and brain anatomy (e.g., using neuronavigational MRI-based systems) could help clarify this issue.

Visual cortex excitability in migraine

Current knowledge about migraine pathogenesis is incomplete. Previous studies demonstrated increased amplitudes of visual evoked potentials (Gawel *et al.* 1983) in migraine patients. Based on this evidence, it was postulated that the visual cortex might be hyperexcitable in this condition, a hypothesis tested in three recent studies. Visual cortex excitability was assessed by measuring PTs to TMS in migraine patients with aura compared to normal volunteers without migraine. In the first study, TMS was delivered to occipital regions through a circular Cadwell coil (9.5 cm diameter, centered 7 cm above the inion; Aurora *et al.* 1998). The authors found a mean PT of $44.2 \pm 8.6\%$ (relative to the maximal output of the magnetic stimulator) in the patient group and $68.7 \pm 3.1\%$ in the control group ($p=0.0001$). Additionally, subjects with migraine were more likely to experience phosphenes with TMS than controls. These findings were interpreted to be indicative of hyperexcitability of occipital cortex in migraine patients compared with individuals from a normal population. A recent study by Mullener and co-workers examined the TMS-induced visual extinction phenomenon (see previous section) in seven migraine patients with visual aura compared to control subjects (Mullener *et al.* 2001). They found a significantly reduced amount of TMS-induced inhibition of visual perception in the patient population. This finding was interpreted as being indicative of deficient inhibitory mechanisms in the visual cortex of migraine patients.

Afra and associates compared PTs in migraine patients with and without aura between attacks and in healthy controls. In this study, TMS was delivered through a circular Magstim coil with 13 cm outer diameter (Magstim Co., Whitland, Dyfed, UK) applied to occipital regions (also centered 7 cm above the inion) (Afra *et al.* 1998). Endpoint measures were the prevalence of elicitation of phosphenes and PTs. The authors found comparable PTs in the three groups and a decreased prevalence for elicitation of phosphenes in migraine patients with aura. While differences in experimental settings or patient populations may account for the contradictory findings in these studies, the issue of the visual cortex excitability in migraine patients remains to be resolved.

Modulation of visual cortex excitability using low-frequency repetitive TMS (rTMS)

The development of noninvasive strategies able to reduce cortical excitability may be clinically beneficial in diseases associated with a hyperexcitable cortex. Examples of such conditions include photosensitive generalized epilepsy (Lee *et al.* 1980) and visual hallucinations associated with blindness (Charles Bonnet syndrome) (Ffytche *et al.* 1998). TMS has been used to induce lasting modulation of cortical excitability. For example, low-frequency (1 Hz) rTMS over the human motor cortex for a 15 minute period results in decreased motor cortex excitability (Chen *et al.* 1997; Wassermann *et al.* 1998). This rate of stimulation is similar to that utilized in paradigms geared to induce long-term depression (LTD)-like phenomena in animal models (Hess *et al.* 1996; Hess and Donoghue 1996; Kirkwood *et al.* 1993). A similar stimulation paradigm was also used to accomplish decreased excitability of the visual cortex (Boroojerdi *et al.* 2000c). In this study, visual cortex excitability was evaluated in eight normal volunteers by measuring PTs and the stimulus-response curves for the phosphene elicitation. TMS experiments were conducted in a dark room and the subjects were blindfolded during measurements. They wore a cotton swimmer's cap with a grid of 3×3 points (with each point 2 cm apart and centered over Oz, international 10–20 EEG electrodes positioning system). A Magstim Rapid magnetic stimulator equipped with a 9 cm figure-of-eight shaped coil was used to deliver magnetic stimuli. Because phosphenes could not be induced by single magnetic stimuli in some individuals, pairs of stimuli separated by a 50 ms interstimulus interval were used (Ray *et al.* 1998). The subjects were asked to describe its shape, color and brightness (in an arbitrary scale of 1–5, 5=the brightest phosphene). Using suprathreshold stimuli, the investigators first determined the optimal scalp position to evoke phosphenes. Magnetic stimulation was started over this point at 30% maximum stimulator output and the intensity was increased in 1% steps until phosphenes could be elicited in 3 out of 5 trials. This intensity was defined as the PT. Following phosphene determination, rTMS at 1 Hz was delivered for 15 minutes to the optimal scalp position for eliciting phosphenes and to a control site (on two different days in a random order). 1 Hz stimulation over the visual cortex resulted in a clear increase in PT (from 56.3±7.8% (S.D.) to 59.5±8.7% maximum stimulator output, $p=0.003$) while stimulation over the control position did not (57.0±7.8% and 55.7±6.8%, $p=0.17$) (Fig. 13.1).

1 Hz rTMS over the occipital cortex elicited no measurable changes in the excitability of other cortical areas such as the motor cortex. The motor thresholds were 51.2±9.5% and 51.5±8.99% before and after stimulation over the visual cortex ($p=0.59$) and 50.2±8.9% and 50.4±9.4% ($p=0.88$) before and following stimulation over the control position Cz. No correlation could be found between motor and phosphene thresholds (Spearman rank correlation coefficient $r=0.11$, $p=0.79$). The authors concluded that low-frequency TMS was a feasible noninvasive strategy to

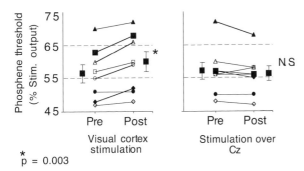

Fig. 13.1 Individual and mean phosphene thresholds (PT) before (Pre) and after (Post) 15 minutes of 1 Hz rTMS over the visual cortex and Cz. rTMS over the visual cortex led to a significant increase in PTs in all but one subject. From Boroojerdi *et al.* (2000c), with permission.

decrease visual cortex excitability. If so, it is conceivable that low-frequency TMS applied to a specific region could also induce a transient disruption of function of that region and therefore identify its functional role. Several studies have utilized rTMS to induce transient disruption of function of the occipital cortex during performance of different tasks.

Visual imagery and low-frequency rTMS

Visual imagery is often utilized in cognitive processes. Since the anatomic structures mediating visual imagery are incompletely understood, Kosslyn *et al.* (1999) studied the role of the primary visual cortex (specifically area 17) in this process. In their study, subjects' initial task was to memorize a visual display composed of four quadrants, each of which contained a set of stripes. They underwent a PET examination during visual imagination of the display. Subsequently they were asked to pay attention to two of the quadrants in reference to a specific dimension such as "Length." Subjects were instructed to determine whether the set of stripes in the first-named quadrant was greater along that dimension than the set of stripes in the second-named quadrant. The control condition displayed similar auditory stimulation but required no active imagination. The results demonstrated activation in area 17 associated with performance of the visual imagery task. This activation however, could theoretically be unrelated to the imagination task. To examine the functional relevance of this finding, the authors induced a short-lasting functional depression in activity of the occipital cortex by applying low-frequency TMS as described above. Using 1 Hz real or sham rTMS (Magstim Super rapid stimulator, double 70 mm figure-of-eight shaped coil, 90% of the subject's motor threshold), they stimulated the scalp overlying primary visual areas before performance of an imagery task or a control task similar to the one used in the PET study. TMS resulted in impaired performance in both the perceptual and the imagery tasks. The TMS data showed that the activation revealed by PET was functionally relevant to performance of the visual imagery task, a result consistent with the idea of an active involvement of the visual cortex in human visual imagery.

Functional role of the occipital cortex in blind individuals

Deafferentation in one sensory modality results in reorganizational changes in other sensory modalities (Rauschecker 1995). For example, the visual cortex of individuals who became blind at an early age is activated in association with tactile discrimination tasks such as Braille reading (see, for example Sadato *et al.* 1996 and Buchel *et al.* 1998). These findings suggest that the occipital cortex, our "visual brain," under certain conditions can operate as a "tactile brain." For this to be true, disruption of the function of the occipital cortex should theoretically result in, for example, accuracy errors in performance of tactile discrimination tasks in visually impaired individuals. Without this type of demonstration, it remains unclear if the occipital activation observed in neuroimaging studies plays an adaptive role in sensory compensation. To address this question, Cohen and co-workers studied the effect of disrupting the activity of the occipital cortex on Braille and Roman letter reading performance (Cohen *et al.* 1997). rTMS with a frequency of 10 Hz was applied to occipital regions while blind and sighted volunteers performed a tactile discrimination task (reading Braille and embossed Roman letters). A focal figure-of-eight shaped water-cooled Cadwell coil (7 cm outer diameter of each loop) was used. The stimulus intensity was 10% above the resting motor threshold for the first dorsal interosseus muscle. TMS was delivered randomly to different scalp locations (OZ, O1, O2, P3, P4, and Fz of the international 10–20 system of electrode placement and to the contralateral sensorimotor area). Subjects were asked to identify and read aloud letter-by-letter as fast and accurately as possible. In blind subjects, disruption of occipital activity with rTMS resulted in more accuracy errors than with stimulation of control sites. Additionally, rTMS elicited distorted somatosensory perceptions only in the blind group. Blind subjects reported missing dots, as well as phantom dots, and confusing sensations ("the dots don't make sense") associated with occipital stimulation. These results indicate that disruption of occipital activity substantially affected performance of tactile discrimination tasks in early blind individuals but not in sighted controls. A follow-up study was performed in individuals who became blind later in life. PET scanning during performance of the same tactile discrimination tasks in these subjects did not show occipital activation (Cohen *et al.* 1999). Accordingly, rTMS did not disrupt performance in this tactile discrimination task. Overall these studies suggest that the window of opportunity for the described form of functionally relevant cross-modal plasticity in blind humans is limited to childhood.

The results previously described do not preclude the possibility that the occipital cortex can play a role in tactile discrimination even in sighted individuals. A recent report by Zangaladze and associates demonstrated that TMS delivered to the occipital cortex of healthy volunteers could disrupt performance in a grating orientation discrimination task (Zangaladze *et al.* 1999). In their first experiment, the authors studied the ability of TMS to disrupt this task performed with the right index finger and eyes closed. At each stimulation site, TMS was applied 10–400 ms after the onset of grating presentation. The authors found that performance under the effects of stimulation at occipital sites was unaffected at 10 ms delay but was markedly impaired at 180 ms delay. In contrast, TMS delivered to control positions had no effect. Overall, these investigations underline the fact that the occipital cortex can contribute to the performance of tactile tasks in both blind and sighted individuals, perhaps to a different extent.

Experience-dependent changes in visual cortex excitability

Deafferentation results in cortical reorganization in motor (Donoghue and Sanes 1988; Sanes *et al.* 1990; Cohen *et al.* 1991; Brasil-Neto *et al.* 1992; Fuhr *et al.* 1992) and sensory (Wall *et al.* 1986; Allard *et al.* 1991; Merzenich and Jenkins 1993) systems. In the visual system, retinal lesions lead to rapid increases in the receptive fields of cortical cells near the edge of the deprived occipital cortex (Gilbert and Wiesel 1992; Pettet and Gilbert 1992). Visual deprivation leads to better consolidation of spatial memory in animals (Worsham and D'Amato 1973; Grimm and Samuel 1976) and results in lower visual recognition thresholds in normal humans (Suedfeld 1975). In the absence of vision, blind individuals may experience visual hallucinations (Charles Bonnet syndrome), interpreted as a release of cortical circuits that follows sensory input deprivation (Cogan 1973; Rosenbaum *et al.* 1987; Fernandez *et al.* 1997). Moreover, visual deprivation may induce substantial changes in information processing in other modalities. For example, the deprived visual cortex appears to be significantly involved in tactile (Cohen *et al.* 1997, 1999) and auditory (Kujala *et al.* 1995) discrimination tasks in blind individuals. Therefore, chronic visual deprivation leads to marked changes in excitability and function of the occipital cortex. Boroojerdi and coworkers addressed the question whether a short period of light deprivation (minutes to few hours) can elicit such changes in humans (Boroojerdi *et al.* 2000a). To assess changes in visual cortex excitability following light deprivation, the authors utilized two measures: TMS-induced phosphenes and blood oxygenation level dependent (BOLD) fMRI activation during photic stimulation (Ogawa *et al.* 1990). Sixteen healthy normal volunteers were investigated in TMS experiments, all of which were conducted in a dark room with just enough light for the investigator to perform the study. Additionally, nontransparent goggles were used to accomplish total darkness. In addition to occipital positions, TMS was delivered to parietal locations P3 and P4 and to the air (near the ear). Additionally, sham stimulation was delivered to occipital positions (involving tilted placement of the coil so that the sound, sensation and muscle twitch elicited by the coil at the back of the head was similar to occipital stimulation). A Cadwell high-speed magnetic stimulator, equipped with a water-cooled figure-of-eight shaped coil was used to deliver magnetic stimuli. Stimulus–response curves (phosphene intensity and prevalence as function of magnetic stimulus intensity) were also obtained to determine the number and intensity of the reported phosphenes.

PTs were determined at the onset of the light depri-vation period and 45, 90, 135 and 180 minutes later. Stimulus–response curves were determined at the onset of the experiment and after 180 min of light deprivation. In a different session, subjects underwent 90 min of light deprivation and were reexposed to room light (390 Lux) following this time period. PTs were tested after light deprivation repetitively for at least 120 min.

fMRI images were acquired in each subject before light deprivation, after 60 min of light deprivation, and after 30 min of reexposure to room light. Visual stimuli were presented binocularly via well-fitted lightproof goggles by flashing a matrix of 5×6 red LEDs at 2 Hz.

Of the 16 participants in the study, 9 (56%) reported visual sensations induced by TMS, similar to findings reported by other investigators (e.g., Meyer *et al.* 1991). All subjects showed a decreased PT over the course of the three hour period of light deprivation. During this time period, mean PT dropped from 63.0±8.3% to 48.0±7.6% maximum stimulator output ($p=0.0001$) (Fig. 13.2). PTs returned to normal values approximately 120 min following reexposure to light (Fig. 13.3). In the absence of light deprivation, PTs tested 45 min apart showed no significant changes (PT 53.0±9.7 and 52.0±8.4, $p=0.37$). Similarly, testing during sleep deprivation-induced drowsiness (to simulate drowsiness induced by light deprivation) did not result in PT changes in the absence of light deprivation (PT 53.0±9.7 and 54.0±12.0, $p=0.91$).

Stimulus–response curves for the number of elicited phosphenes 180 min after light deprivation onset were steeper than those obtained before light deprivation. These differences became significant at 50% and 60% maximum stimulator output ($p=0.02$). At higher stimulus intensities, a plateau level was reached (Fig. 13.4A). Although the average reported intensity of phosphenes had a higher value after 180 min compared to the onset of the experiment at intensities <70%, this difference was not significant (Fig. 13.4B). Before light deprivation, the visual cortex was significantly activated in

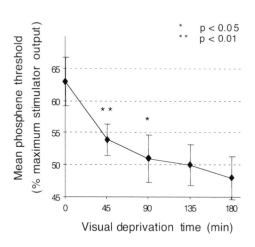

Fig. 13.2 Phosphene thresholds (PTs) over the time course of 180 minutes after onset of visual deprivation. Mean PT had a significant decrease after 45 and 90 minutes. Error bars indicate standard errors. From Boroojerdi *et al.* (2000a), with permission.

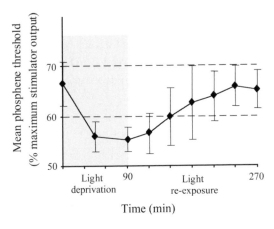

Fig. 13.3 Time course of the phosphene thresholds (PTs) following 90 minutes of visual deprivation and reexposure to room light. PTs returned to predeprivation values within approximately 120 minutes. From Boroojerdi et al. (2000a), with permission.

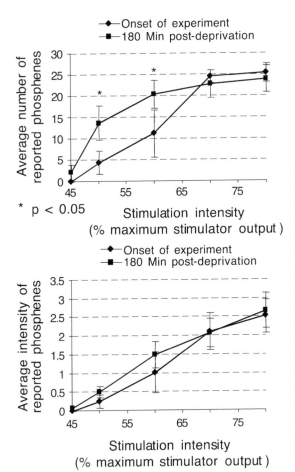

Fig. 13.4 (A) Average prevalence and (B) intensity of the elicited phosphenes as a function of stimulation intensity at the onset and after 180 minutes of light deprivation. A significantly higher number of phosphenes could be elicited at 50% and 60% stimulation intensity after 180 minutes. Similar plateau levels were reached with higher stimulation intensities. Although the reported intensity after 180 minutes of visual deprivation was higher, this difference was not statistically significant. From Boroojerdi et al. (2000a), with permission.

response to photic stimulation in all subjects. In all subjects, the number of activated voxels and mean change in signal intensity increased significantly following 60 min of light deprivation ($p=0.043$ for both parameters). This increase was maintained in all subjects 30 min after reexposure to light (Fig. 13.5A, B, and C). The authors concluded that light deprivation substantially increased visual cortical excitability.

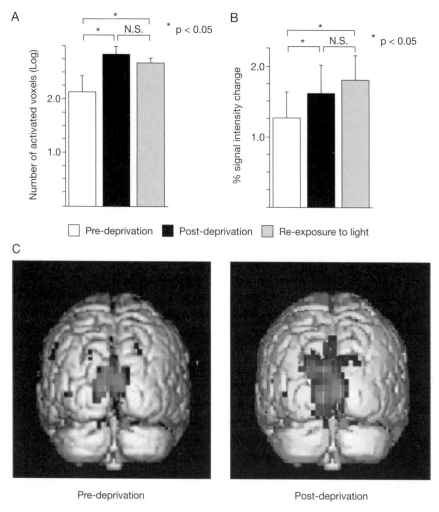

Fig. 13.5 (and color plate 22) (A) Number of activated voxels (log), and (B) mean MR signal intensity change of activated voxels in the occipital cortex to photic stimulation before, 60 minutes after the onset of visual deprivation, and 30 minutes following reexposure to light. A significant increase after 60 minutes of light deprivation was seen in both parameters and was maintained following 30 minutes of reexposure to light. Panel (C) is an example of visual cortex activation in one subject. Error bars indicate standard errors. Modified from Boroojerdi *et al.* (2000a), with permission.

To study the mechanisms underlying this phenomenon, Boroojerdi and associates, utilizing a pharmacologic approach, studied the effects of several CNS active drugs on light deprivation-induced visual cortex plasticity (Boroojerdi *et al.* 1999, 2000b, 2001). They used lorazepam (LZP), a short-acting benzodiazepine which acts as a positive allosteric modulator of $GABA_A$ receptors (McDonald 1995); dextrometorphan (DM), a drug that blocks NMDA receptors, required for LTP and experience-dependent plasticity (Artola and Singer 1987; Kirkwood *et al.* 1993; Bear 1996; Roberts *et al.* 1998); scopolamine (SCO), a muscarinic receptor antagonist (Frey *et al.* 1992; La Rovere and De Ferrari 1995); and lamotrigine (LTG), an antiepileptic drug which blocks voltage-gated Na^+ and Ca^{2+} channels (Leach and Brodie 1995; Wang *et al.* 1996). They found that LZP, DM, and SCO blocked rapid plastic changes associated with light deprivation. These findings suggested the involvement of GABAergic inhibition, NMDA receptor activation, and cholinergic transmission as mechanisms operating in rapid, experience-dependent plasticity in the human visual cortex. To further examine the involvement of GABAergic mechanisms in this process, magnetic resonance spectroscopy (MRS) was utilized to directly measure GABA in the visual cortex as a function of light deprivation time (Boroojerdi *et al.* 2000b). Serial edited GABA measurements of a 14 ml voxel centered in the visual cortex (including areas 17, 18, and 19 bilaterally) were performed before and during light deprivation. Light deprivation led to decreased visual cortex GABA concentration and GABA/creatine ratios. Thus, downregulation of cortical GABA was shown to be associated with this form of visual cortex plasticity.

Concluding remarks

An increasing number of studies have utilized TMS to investigate the human visual cortex. Based on the possibility of applying a short and localized stimulus over the human cortical surface noninvasively and virtually without pain, TMS has found a considerable use in studies of visual cortex excitability in association with different diseases such as migraine and environmental changes, in the studies of cross-modal plasticity following visual deafferentation and in physiologic studies of visual perception. Possible ways of modulation of visual cortex excitability using TMS are now being explored. They may lead to a completely different (therapeutical) use of this now mainly investigational tool.

Acknowledgment

The authors are grateful to D. Schoenberg for skillful editing of the chapter.

References

Afra, J., Mascia, A., Gerard, P. *et al.* (1998) Interictal cortical excitability in migraine: a study using transcranial magnetic stimulation of motor and visual cortices. *Annals of Neurology*, **44**:209–15.

Allard, T., Clark, S. A., Jenkins, W. M. *et al.* (1991) Reorganization of somatosensory area 3b representations in adult owl monkeys after digital syndactyly. *Journal of Neurophysiology*, **66**:1048–58.

Amassian, V. E., Cracco, R. Q., Maccabee, P. J. *et al.* (1989) Suppression of visual perception by magnetic coil stimulation of human occipital cortex. *Electroencephalography and Clinical Neurophysiology*, **74**:458–62.

Amassian, V. E., Cracco, R. Q., Maccabee, P. J. *et al.* (1993) Unmasking human visual perception with the magnetic coil and its relationship to hemispheric asymmetry. *Brain Research*, **605**:312–16.

Artola, A. and Singer, W. (1987) Long-term potentiation and NMDA receptors in rat visual cortex. *Nature*, **330**:649–52.

Ashbridge, E., Walsh, V. and Cowey, A. (1997) Temporal aspects of visual search studied by transcranial magnetic stimulation. *Neuropsychologia*, **35**:1121–31.

Aurora, S. K., Ahmad, B. K., Welch, K. M. *et al.* (1998) Transcranial magnetic stimulation confirms hyperexcitability of occipital cortex in migraine. *Neurology*, **50**:1111–14.

Aurora, S. K. and Welch, K. M. (1998) Brain excitability in migraine: evidence from transcranial magnetic stimulation studies. *Current Opinion in Neurobiology*, **11**:205–9.

Barker, A. T., Jalinous, R. and Freeston, I. L. (1985) Non-invasive magnetic stimulation of human motor cortex. *Lancet*, **1**:1106–7.

Bear, M. F. (1996) Progress in understanding NMDA-receptor-dependent synaptic plasticity in the visual cortex. *Journal of Physiology (Paris)*, **90**:223–7.

Beckers, G. and Hömberg, V. (1991) Impairment of visual perception and visual short term memory scanning by transcranial magnetic stimulation of occipital cortex. *Experimental Brain Research*, **87**:421–32.

Beckers, G. and Hömberg, V. (1992) Cerebral visual motion blindness: transitory akinetopsia induced by transcranial magnetic stimulation of human area V5. *Proceedings of the Royal Society of London*, **B249**:173–8.

Beckers, G. and Zeki, S. (1995) The consequences of inactivating areas V1 and V5 on visual motion perception. *Brain*, **118**:49–60.

Boroojerdi, B., Bushara, K. O., Corwell, B. *et al.* (2000a) Enhanced excitability of the human visual cortex induced by short-term light deprivation. *Cerebral Cortex*, **10**:529–34.

Boroojerdi, B., Cohen, L. G., Petroff, O. A. *et al.* (2000b) Mechanisms of light deprivation-induced enhancement of visual cortex excitability. *Society for Neuroscience Abstracts*, **26**:821.

Boroojerdi, B., Muellbacher, W., Grafman, J. *et al.* (1999) Cholinergic influences on visual deprivation-induced changes in occipital cortex excitability. *Society for Neuroscience Abstracts*, **25**:1315.

Boroojerdi, B., Prager, A., Muellbacher, W. *et al.* (2000c) Reduction of human visual cortex excitability using 1-Hz transcranial magnetic stimulation. *Neurology*, **54**:1529–31.

Boroojerdi, B., Battaglia, F., Muellbacher, W. *et al.* (2001) Mechanisms underlying rapid experience-dependent plasticity in the human visual cortex. *Proceedings of the National Academy of Sciences (USA)*, **98**:14698–701.

Brasil-Neto, J., Cohen, L. G., Pascual-Leone, A. *et al.* (1992) Rapid reversible modulation of human motor outputs after transient deafferentation of the forearm: a study with transcranial magnetic stimulation. *Neurology*, **42**:1302–6.

Brindley, G. S. and Lewin, W. S. (1968) The sensations produced by electrical stimulation of the visual cortex. *Journal of Physiology (London)*, **196**:479–93.

Buchel, C., Price, C., Frackowiak, R. S. *et al.* (1998) Different activation patterns in the visual cortex of late and congenitally blind subjects. *Brain*, **121**:409–19.

Chen, R., Classen, J., Gerloff, C. *et al.* (1997) Depression of motor cortex excitability by low-frequency transcranial magnetic stimulation. *Neurology*, **48**:1398–403.

Cogan, D. G. (1973) Visual hallucinations as release phenomena. *Albrecht Von Graefes Clinic Archives of Experimental Ophthalmology*, **188**:139–50.

Cohen, L. G., Bandinelli, S., Findley, T. W. *et al.* (1991) Motor reorganization after upper limb amputation in man. A study with focal magnetic stimulation. *Brain*, **114**:615–27.

Cohen, L. G., Celnik, P., Pascual-Leone, A. *et al.* (1997) Functional relevance of cross-modal plasticity in blind humans. *Nature*, **389**:180–3.

Cohen, L. G., Weeks, R. A., Sadato, N. *et al.* (1999) Period of susceptibility for cross-modal plasticity in the blind. *Annals of Neurology*, **45**:451–60.

Corthout, E., Uttl, B., Juan, C.-H. *et al.* (2000) Suppression of vision by transcranial magnetic stimulation: a third mechanism. *NeuroReport*, **11**:2345–9.

Corthout, E., Uttl, B., Ziemann, U. *et al.* (1999) Two periods of processing in the (circum)striate visual cortex as revealed by transcranial magnetic stimulation. *Neuropsychologia*, **37**:137–45.

Donoghue, J. P. and Sanes, J. N. (1988) Organization of adult motor cortex representation patterns following neonatal forelimb nerve injury in rats. *Journal of Neuroscience*, **8**:3221–32.

Epstein, C. M., Schwartzberg, D. G., Davey, K. R. *et al.* (1990) Localizing the site of magnetic brain stimulation in humans. *Neurology*, **40**:660–70.

Epstein, C. M., Verson, R. and Zangaladze, A. (1996) Magnetic coil suppression of visual perception at an extracalcarine site. *Journal of Clinical Neurophysiology*, **13**:247–52.

Epstein, C. M. and Zangaladze, A. (1996) Magnetic coil suppression of extrafoveal visual perception using disappearance targets. *Journal of Clinical Neurophysiology*, **13**:242–6.

Fernandez, A., Lichtshein, G. and Vieweg, W. V. (1997) The Charles Bonnet syndrome: a review. *Journal of Nervous and Mental Disorders*, **185**:195–200.

Ffytche, D. H., Howard, R. J., Brammer, M. J. *et al.* (1998) The anatomy of conscious vision: an fMRI study of visual hallucinations. *Nature Neuroscience*, **1**:738–42.

Frey, K. A., Koeppe, R. A., Mulholland, G. K. *et al.* (1992) *In vivo* muscarinic cholinergic receptor imaging in human brain with [11C]scopolamine and positron emission tomography. *Journal of Cerebral Blood Flow and Metabolism*, **12**:147–54.

Fuhr, P., Cohen, L. G., Dang, N. *et al.* (1992) Physiological analysis of motor reorganization following lower limb amputation. *Electroencephalography and Clinical Neurophysiology*, **85**:53–60.

Gawel, M., Connolly, J. F. and Rose, F. C. (1983) Migraine patients exhibit abnormalities in the visual evoked potential. *Headache*, **23**:49–52.

Gilbert, C. D. and Wiesel, T. N. (1992) Receptive field dynamics in adult primary visual cortex. *Nature*, **356**:150–2.

Grafman, J., Pascual-Leone, A., Alway, D. *et al.* (1994) Induction of a recall deficit by rapid-rate transcranial magnetic stimulation. *NeuroReport*, **5**:1157–60.

Grimm, V. E. and Samuel, D. (1976) The effects of dark isolation on the performance of a white-black discrimination task in the rat. *International Journal of Neuroscience*, **7**:1–7.

Harrington, D. O. (1976) *The Visual Fields: A Textbook and Atlas of Clinical Perimetry*, vol. 4. Mosby, St. Louis.

Hess, G., Aizenman, C. D. and Donoghue, J. P. (1996) Conditions for the induction of long-term potentiation in layer II/III horizontal connections of the rat motor cortex. *Journal of Neurophysiology*, **75**:1765–78.

Hess, G. and Donoghue, J. P. (1996) Long-term potentiation and long-term depression of horizontal connections in rat motor cortex. *Acta Experimental Neurobiology*, **56**:397–405.

Hotson, J., Braun, D., Herzberg, W. *et al.* (1994) Transcranial magnetic stimulation of extrastriate cortex degrades human motion direction discrimination. *Vision Research*, **34**:2115–23.

Hotson, J. R. and Anand, S. (1999) The selectivity and timing of motion processing in human temporo-parieto-occipital and occipital cortex: a transcranial magnetic stimulation study. *Neuropsychologia*, **37**:169–79.

Kammer, T. (1999) Phosphenes and transient scotomas induced by magnetic stimulation of the occipital lobe: their topographic relationship. *Neuropsychologia*, **37**:191–8.

Kammer, T. and Nusseck, H. G. (1998) Are recognition deficits following occipital lobe TMS explained by raised detection thresholds? *Neuropsychologia*, **36**:1161–6.

Kastner, S., Demmer, I. and Ziemann, U. (1998) Transient visual field defects induced by transcranial magnetic stimulation over human occipital pole. *Experimental Brain Research*, **118**:19–26.

Kirkwood, A., Dudek, S. M., Gold, J. T. *et al.* (1993) Common forms of synaptic plasticity in the hippocampus and neocortex *in vitro*. *Science*, **260**:1518–21.

Kosslyn, S. M., Pascual-Leone, A., Felician, O. *et al.* (1999) The role of area 17 in visual imagery: convergent evidence from PET and rTMS. *Science*, **284**:167–70.

Kujala, T., Huotilainen, M., Sinkkonen, J. *et al.* (1995) Visual cortex activation in blind humans during sound discrimination. *Neuroscience Letters*, **183**:143–6.

La Rovere, M. T. and De Ferrari, G. M. (1995) New potential uses for transdermal scopolamine (hyoscine). *Drugs*, **50**:769–76.

Leach, J. P. and Brodie, M. J. (1995) New antiepileptic drugs—an explosion of activity. *Seizure*, **4**:5–17.

Lee, S. I., Messenheimer, J. A., Wilkinson, E. C. *et al.* (1980) Visual evoked potentials to stimulus trains: normative data and application to photosensitive seizures. *Electroencephalography and Clinical Neurophysiology*, **48**:387–94.

Maccabee, P. J., Amassian, V. E., Cracco, R. Q. *et al.* (1991a) Stimulation of the human nervous system using the magnetic coil. *Journal of Clinical Neurophysiology*, **8**:38–55.

Maccabee, P. J., Amassian, V. E., Eberle, L. P. *et al.* (1991b) Measurement of the electric field induced into inhomogeneous volume conductors by magnetic coils: application to human spinal neuro-geometry. *Electroencephalography and Clinical Neurophysiology*, **81**:224–37.

Marg, E. (1991) Magnetostimulation of vision: direct noninvasive stimulation of the retina and the visual brain. *Optom Vis Sci*, **68**:427–40.

Marg, E. and Rudiak, D. (1994) Phosphenes induced by magnetic stimulation over the occipital brain: description and probable site of stimulation. *Optometry and Visual Science*, **71**:301–11.

Masur, H., Papke, K. and Oberwittler, C. (1993) Suppression of visual perception by transcranial magnetic stimulation—experimental findings in healthy subjects and patients with optic neuritis. *Electroencephalography and Clinical Neurophysiology*, **86**:259–67.

McDonald, R. L. (1995) *Benzodiazepines. Mechanisms of Action*. Raven, New York.

Merzenich, M. M. and Jenkins, W. M. (1993) Reorganization of cortical representations of the hand following alterations of skin inputs induced by nerve injury, skin island transfers, and experience. *Journal of Hand Therapy*, **6**:89–104.

Meyer, B. U., Diehl, R., Steinmetz, H. *et al.* (1991) Magnetic stimuli applied over motor and visual cortex: influence of coil position and field polarity on motor responses, phosphenes, and eye movements. *Electroencephalography and Clinical Neurophysiology supplement*, **43**:121–34.

Meyer, B. U. and Diehl, R. R. (1992) Examination of the visual system with transcranial magnetic stimulation. *Nervenarzt*, **63**:328–34.

Mullener, W. M., Chronicle, E. P., Palmer, J. E. *et al.* (2001) Suppression of perception in migraine-evidence for reduced inhibition in the visual cortex. *Neurology*, **56**:178–83.

Muri, R. M., Vermersch, A. I., Rivaud, S. *et al.* (1996) Effects of single-pulse transcranial magnetic stimulation over the prefrontal and posterior parietal cortices during memory-guided saccades in humans. *Journal of Neurophysiology*, **76**:2102–6.

Ogawa, S., Lee, T. M., Kay, A. R. *et al.* (1990) Brain magnetic resonance imaging with contrast dependent on blood oxygenation. *Proceedings of the National Academy of Sciences (USA)*, **87**:9868–72.

Pascual-Leone, A. and Hallett, M. (1994) Induction of errors in a delayed response task by repetitive transcranial magnetic stimulation of the dorsolateral prefrontal cortex. *NeuroReport*, **5**:2517–20.

Pettet, M. W. and Gilbert, C. D. (1992) Dynamic changes in receptive-field size in cat primary visual cortex. *Proceedings of the National Academy of Sciences USA*, **89**:8366–70.

Potts, G. F., Gugino, L. D., Leventon, M. E. *et al.* (1998) Visual hemifield mapping using transcranial magnetic stimulation coregistered with cortical surfaces derived from magnetic resonance images. *Journal of Clinical Neurophysiology*, **15**:344–50.

Rauschecker, J. P. (1995) Compensatory plasticity and sensory substitution in the cerebral cortex. *Trends in Neuroscience*, **18**:36–43.

Ray, P. G., Meador, K. J., Epstein, C. M. *et al.* (1998) Magnetic stimulation of visual cortex: factors influencing the perception of phosphenes. *Journal of Clinical Neurophysiology*, **15**:351–7.

Roberts, E. B., Meredith, M. A. and Ramoa, A. S. (1998) Suppression of NMDA receptor function using antisense DNA block ocular dominance plasticity while preserving visual responses. *Journal of Neurophysiology*, **80**:1021–32.

Rosenbaum, F., Harati, Y., Rolak, L. *et al.* (1987) Visual hallucinations in sane people: Charles Bonnet syndrome. *Journal of the American Geriatric Society*, **35**:66–8.

Roth, B. J. (1994) Mechanisms for electrical stimulation of excitable tissue. *Critical Review of Biomedical Engineering*, **22**:253–305.

Roth, B. J., Saypol, J. M., Hallett, M. *et al.* (1991) A theoretical calculation of the electric field induced in the cortex during magnetic stimulation. *Electroencephalography and Clinical Neurophysiology*, **81**:47–56.

Sadato, N., Pascual-Leone, A., Grafman, J. *et al.* (1996) Activation of the primary visual cortex by Braille reading in blind subjects. *Nature*, **380**:526–8.

Sanes, J. N., Suner, S. and Donoghue, J. P. (1990) Dynamic organization of primary motor cortex output to target muscles in adult rats. I. Long-term patterns of reorganization following motor or mixed peripheral nerve lesions. *Experimental Brain Research*, **79**:479–91.

Stewart, L. M., Walsh, V. and Rothwell, J. C. (2001) Motor and phosphene thresholds: a transcranial magnetic stimulation correlation study. *Neuropsychologia*, **39**:415–9.

Suedfeld, P. (1975) The benefits of boredom: sensory deprivation reconsidered. *American Scientist*, **63**:60–9.

Wall, J. T., Kaas, J. H., Sur, M. *et al.* (1986) Functional reorganization in somatosensory cortical areas 3b and 1 of adult monkeys after median nerve repair: possible relationships to sensory recovery in humans. *Journal of Neuroscience*, **6**:218–33.

Wang, S. J., Huang, C. C., Hsu, K. S. *et al.* (1996) Inhibition of *N*-type calcium currents by lamotrigine in rat amygdalar neurones. *NeuroReport*, **7**:3037–40.

Wassermann, E. M., Wedegaertner, F. R., Ziemann, U. *et al.* (1998) Crossed reduction of human motor cortex excitability by 1-Hz transcranial magnetic stimulation. *Neuroscience Letters*, **250**:141–4.

Worsham, R. W. and D'Amato, M. R. (1973) Ambient light, white noise, and monkey vocalization as sources of interference in visual short-term memory of monkeys. *Journal of Experimental Psychology*, **99**:99–105.

Zangaladze, A., Epstein, C. M., Grafton, S. T. *et al.* (1999) Involvement of visual cortex in tactile discrimination of orientation. *Nature*, **401**:587–90.

Chapter 14

Negative Phenomena Induced by TMS of Human Primary Motor Cortex

Ulf Ziemann

This chapter will focus on transient functional lesions that can be produced by transcranial magnetic stimulation (TMS) of human primary motor cortex. The text is divided into two main parts. The first part will deal with TMS-induced motor cortex inhibition. This is a purely physiologic and nonbehavioral approach. Motor cortex inhibition is defined here as a reduction in motor evoked potential (MEP) size. The second part will report on TMS-induced interference with motor performance. This is a behavioral approach. The two parts are tightly linked with each other: knowledge about the physiology of motor cortex inhibition may lead to a better understanding of negative modulation of motor cortex output on the behavioral level.

TMS-induced inhibition of motor cortex

Short-latency intracortical inhibition (SICI)

In the human and nonhuman primate neocortex, approximately 30% of the neuronal population contains gamma-amino butyric acid (GABA), the major inhibitory neurotransmitter (McCormick 1989; Jones 1993). In motor cortex, GABAergic neurons are of strategic importance as they control the balance between excitation and inhibition, and hence are crucial for the modulation of motor cortex output (e.g. Matsumura *et al.* 1991). Various forms of motor cortex inhibitory mechanisms can now be tested noninvasively in humans by TMS. If a low-intensity first (S1) and a higher-intensity second (S2) stimulus are delivered at short interstimulus intervals of 1–5 ms through the same stimulating coil over the motor cortex, S1 inhibits the S2-induced motor response (Fig. 14.1) (Rothwell *et al.* 1991; Claus *et al.* 1992; Kujirai *et al.* 1993; Ridding *et al.* 1995c; Rothwell 1996; Ziemann *et al.* 1996d). This is referred to as short-latency intracortical inhibition (SICI). The intensity of S2 is usually adjusted to produce a test motor evoked potential (MEP) of about 1 mV in peak-to-peak amplitude when given alone. The MEP is recorded by surface electromyography (EMG) from a voluntarily relaxed target muscle. The intensity of S1 is set clearly below MEP threshold (Kujirai *et al.* 1993; Ziemann *et al.* 1996d; Di Lazzaro *et al.* 1998b). In healthy subjects, maximum SICI is usually 10–30% of the test MEP and occurs at interstimulus intervals of 1–3 ms.

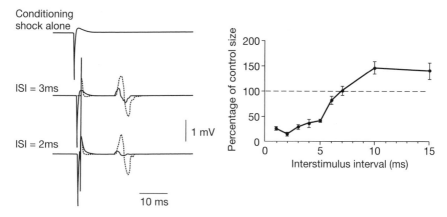

Fig. 14.1 Short-latency intracortical inhibition (SICI). MEPs by a suprathreshold magnetic cortical test stimulus in relaxed first dorsal interosseus muscle are inhibited by a prior, subthreshold conditioning stimulus at short interstimulus intervals of 1–5 ms. The left panel shows examples of EMG data from one healthy subject. The first trace shows absence of any MEP to the conditioning stimulus alone. The lower two records have two superimposed traces, the MEP to the test stimulus given alone, and the MEP to the test stimulus when given 3 (middle traces) or 2 ms (lower traces) after the conditioning stimulus. The larger MEP(dotted line) is the response to the test stimulus alone. It is dramatically suppressed at these two interstimulus intervals. Each trace is the average of 10 trials. The right panel shows the averaged group data of six subjects (means±SD). The conditioned MEP is given as a percentage of the test MEP (y-axis) and expressed as a function of the interstimulus interval (x-axis) (with permission, from Kujirai *et al.* 1993).

At longer interstimulus intervals (usually > 5 ms), the effect of S1 turns from inhibition to facilitation (Fig. 14.1, right panel) (Kujirai *et al.* 1993; Ziemann *et al.* 1996d; Ziemann 1999). Most studies have measured SICI in intrinsic hand muscles but similar SICI was found in a wide range of other muscles (Stokic *et al.* 1997; Chen *et al.* 1998; Hanajima *et al.* 1998b; Ziemann *et al.* 1998b). Therefore, it is likely that the inhibitory intracortical networks that regulate the excitability of motor cortex output are similar across the different motor representations.

One important question is where along the motor system the inhibitory effects of S1 on the test MEP occur: in the motor cortex, at subcortical or spinal level, or at a combination of these. The following evidence indicates that the effects of S1 are mainly or exclusively cortical. First, Hoffmann reflex experiments showed that S1 had no effects on the excitability of the spinal motor-neuron pool (Kujirai *et al.* 1993). Second, the subthreshold S1 did not produce a recognizable descending volley in epidural spinal recordings of conscious subjects, while an above threshold S2 evoked multiple descending waves (indirect or I-waves; Di Lazzaro *et al.* 1998b). At interstimulus intervals of 1–4 ms S1 induced a significant inhibition of the MEP and of all I-waves except the first one (Di Lazzaro *et al.* 1998b). Since the first I-wave is thought to be due to monosynaptic activation of the corticospinal neurons, these findings indicate that the SICI takes place in the motor cortex "upstream" from the corticospinal neuron. The resistance of the first I-wave against the modulatory effects of S1 has been confirmed by others (Hanajima *et al.* 1998a; Kobayashi *et al.* 1998). Finally, if the magnetic S2 was substituted by transcranial electrical stimulation (TES), the SICI disappeared (Kujirai *et al.* 1993). An important difference between TES and TMS is that TES (at just above MEP threshold intensity) activates the corticospinal system predominantly, by direct excitation of corticospinal axons, whereas TMS mainly activates transsynaptically by excitation of corticocortical neural elements that project onto the corticospinal neurons (Day *et al.* 1989a; Di Lazzaro *et al.* 1998a). Therefore, the failure of S1 to inhibit a test MEP elicited by TES further supports an inhibitory mechanism of the SICI "upstream" of the corticospinal neuron.

Another way to learn about the physiology of the SICI is to test its modulation by central nervous system active drugs (for review, Ziemann *et al.* 1998d; Ziemann 1999). All these studies were conducted in healthy subjects who took a single dose or up to three doses of the drug under study. Intracortical inhibition was measured before drug exposure, and then one or more times after drug intake. Agonists at the GABA-A receptor induced an enhancement of SICI (Ziemann *et al.* 1995, 1996b, 1996c; Di Lazzaro *et al.* 2000a). A similar enhancement of SICI was induced by *N*-methyl-D-aspartate (NMDA) receptor blockers, antagonists of glutamate, the major excitatory neurotransmitter in the mammalian central nervous system (Liepert *et al.* 1997; Ziemann *et al.* 1998a; Schwenkreis *et al.* 1999, 2000). Dopamine receptor agonists also increased SICI (Ziemann *et al.* 1996a, 1997b). In contrast, the dopamine D2 receptor antagonist haloperidol (Ziemann *et al.* 1997b) and the serotonin 1B/1D receptor agonist zolmitriptan (Werhahn *et al.* 1998) decreased SICI. Blockers of voltage-gated sodium and calcium channels, such as carbamazepine or phenytoin (Schulze-Bonhage *et al.* 1996; Ziemann *et al.* 1996c; Chen *et al.* 1997d), and muscarinic receptor blockers (Di Lazzaro *et al.* 2000b) had no consistent effect.

The physiologic and neuropharmacologic experiments reported here show that the SICI reflects the integrity and excitability of inhibitory neuronal circuits in the motor cortex upstream from the corticospinal neurons. The activity of these circuits is controlled mainly by agonists at the GABA-A receptor, glutamate, dopamine, and serotonin.

Modulation of SICI contributes to the control of motor cortex output both in health and disease. The SICI is reduced during slight tonic contraction of the target muscle (Ridding *et al.* 1995c). This suggests that voluntary drive reduces the excitability of inhibitory circuits in motor cortex. A reduction of SICI was also found starting some 100 ms before the onset of a voluntary movement. This reduction was specific for EMG agonists but did not occur in EMG antagonists (Reynolds and Ashby 1999). This supports the idea that a reduction in SICI may help to select the population of corticospinal neurons responsible for the forthcoming movement. Finally, a long-lasting (>60 min) reduction in SICI may be induced by repeated muscle contraction (Liepert *et al.* 1998; Ziemann *et al.* 2001) or repetitive TMS of the motor cortex (Ziemann *et al.* 1998b).

This activity-dependent reduction in SICI was prevented when subjects were pretreated with a GABA-A receptor agonist or an NMDA-receptor antagonist (Ziemann *et al.* 1998c, 2001). Activity-dependent changes in SICI may therefore reflect long-term potentiation (LTP)-like plasticity in human motor cortex.

In neurologic patients, measurement of SICI may detect abnormalities in motor cortex inhibition. A particularly instructive set of data was provided by a study of stiff-person syndrome, a disease that is characterized by continuous involuntary firing of motor units that is thought to be caused by an autoimmune mediated dysfunction of GABAergic neurons. This GABA dysfunction results in a pathologic decrease of SICI (Sandbrink *et al.* 2000). However, it appeared that a reduction of SICI seems to be a rather nonspecific abnormality that was found in a variety of epilepsies (Fong *et al.* 1993; Brown *et al.* 1996; Caramia *et al.* 1996; Hanajima *et al.* 1996; Inghilleri *et al.* 1998), movement disorders (Ridding *et al.* 1995a,b; Terao *et al.* 1995; Hanajima *et al.* 1996; Abbruzzese *et al.*, 1997), motor-neuron disease (Yokota *et al.* 1996; Ziemann *et al.* 1997d) and neuropsychiatric disorders, such as Tourette's disorder (Ziemann *et al.* 1997a) or obsessive-compulsive disorder (Greenberg *et al.* 1998, 2000).

Long-latency intracortical inhibition (LICI)

If two TMS pulses of above MEP threshold intensity are delivered at interstimulus intervals of approximately 50–200 ms, the conditioning first pulse (S1) inhibits the test MEP elicited by the second pulse (S2) (Fig. 14.2) (Claus *et al.* 1992; Valls-Sole *et al.* 1992; Roick *et al.* 1993; Triggs *et al.* 1993b; Claus and Brunhölzl 1994; Valzania *et al.* 1994). This form of inhibition is referred to as long-latency intracortical inhibition (LICI). LICI is inversely correlated with the intensity of S2. Strong inhibition was obtained with low intensities of S2 (Roick *et al.* 1993; Triggs *et al.* 1993b) while at high intensities of S2, LICI was either reduced (Roick *et al.* 1993), or even turned to facilitation (Triggs *et al.* 1993b).

Theoretically, LICI could take place at the motor cortical, subcortical, or spinal level. Intraoperative epidural recordings from the cervical spinal cord demonstrated that S1 inhibits the corticospinal volley produced by a magnetic S2 if the interstimulus interval was 100–200 ms (Chen *et al.* 1999; Nakamura *et al.* 1997). This inhibition operates predominantly on the late I-waves of the multiple descending volleys (see above), suggesting that LICI is primarily caused by inhibitory mechanisms in motor cortex "upstream" from the corticospinal neuron.

LICI was reduced in writer's cramp (Chen *et al.* 1997e), but increased (stronger and/or prolonged) in Parkinson's disease (Berardelli *et al.* 1996; Valzania *et al.* 1997), dystonia (Rona *et al.* 1998), Huntington's disease (Tegenthoff *et al.* 1996) and cerebellar ataxia (Wessel *et al.* 1996).

In summary, LICI reflects long-latency and long-lasting (up to several 100 ms) inhibition in human motor cortex. By analogy with intracellular recordings from pyramidal cells in slices of animal (Connors *et al.* 1988) and human neocortex (Avoli *et al.* 1997) it may be speculated that LICI is caused by GABA-B receptor mediated long-lasting

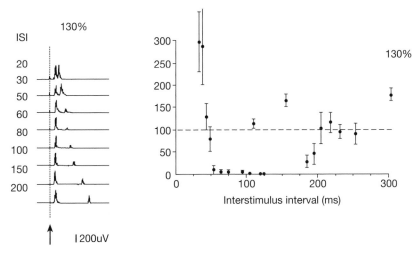

Fig. 14.2 Long-latency intracortical inhibition (LICI). The left panel shows rectified traces of MEPs elicited by paired TMS at increasing interstimulus intervals, recorded from the relaxed abductor pollicis brevis muscle of a healthy subject. The intensity of both pulses was 130% of motor threshold. Each trace is the average of ten trials. Note long-lasting inhibition of MEPs at intervals of 50–200 ms. The right panel shows the averaged group data of six subjects (means±SD). The test MEP is given as a percentage of the conditioning MEP (y-axis) and plotted as a function of the interstimulus interval (x-axis). Reprinted from Valls-Sole *et al.* *Electroencephalography and Clinical Neurophysiology* 1992;**85**:355–64.

inhibition. This is supported by pharmacologic experiments in humans that demonstrated an enhancement of LICI following treatment with the GABA reuptake inhibitor tiagabine (Werhahn *et al.* 1999).

Interaction between SICI and LICI

It is the current view that SICI and LICI are largely mediated through separate neural circuits in motor cortex: SICI is closely related to short-latency and short-lasting GABA-A receptor mediated inhibition while LICI reflects long-latency and long-lasting GABA-B receptor mediated inhibition. The separation into different neural circuits was supported by a dissociated behavior of SICI and LICI with increasing intensity of S2. SICI increases while LICI decreases, without any correlation between the degree of SICI and LICI (Sanger *et al.* 2001). Testing the interaction between SICI and LICI showed that SICI was reduced or eliminated in the presence of LICI (Fig. 14.3) (Sanger *et al.* 2001). Pharmacologic enhancement of LICI by a GABA reuptake inhibitor resulted in a concurrent reduction of SICI (Werhahn *et al.* 1999). These findings are consistent with the hypothesis that LICI inhibits SICI through presynaptic GABA-B receptors. This is paralleled by intracellular recordings from rat neo cor-tex which showed presynaptic GABA-B receptor mediated inhibition of GABA

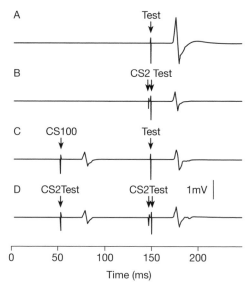

Fig. 14.3 Interaction between SICI and LICI. Traces show average MEPs from the first dorsal interosseus muscle of a single subject. The first conditioning stimulus (CS100) was adjusted to produce 1 mV MEPs, the second conditioning stimulus (CS2) was set to 80% of resting MEP threshold and the test stimulus (Test) was set to produce 1 mV MEPs in the presence of the CS100 stimulus. (A) MEP to the test stimulus alone; (B) CS2 (given 2 ms prior to the test stimulus) leads to clear inhibition of the test MEP (=SICI); (C) CS100 (given 100 ms prior to the test stimulus) also leads to inhibition of the test MEP (=LICI); (D) in the presence of the CS100 stimulus, the CS2 stimulus does not lead to a decrease in the test MEP compared to that shown in (C). With permission, from Sanger *et al.* (2001).

release and a marked decrease of the GABA-A receptor mediated inhibitory post-synaptic potential evoked by the second stimulus in a paired-pulse paradigm (Deisz 1999). This paired-pulse depression was maximal at interstimulus intervals between 100–200 ms and was inhibited by a GABA-B receptor antagonist (Deisz 1999).

In sum, paired TMS is capable of testing noninvasively a complex network of different inhibitory circuits and their interactions in human motor cortex.

Interhemispheric inhibition

In addition to testing inhibitory mechanisms within one motor representation of a given motor cortex (SICI, LICI), inhibitory afferent pathways to the motor cortex can also be tested. Two examples are given below. One relates to the connections between homologue representations of the motor cortexes of the two hemispheres, the other one to the cerebello–dentato–thalamo–motor cortex loop.

The hand areas of the two motor cortexes are connected, although sparsely, by callosal fibers (Gould *et al.* 1986; Rouiller *et al.* 1994). This transcallosal connection can be tested by a paired stimulation protocol (Ferbert *et al.* 1992; Ugawa *et al.* 1993; Netz *et al.* 1995; Salerno and Georgesco, 1996). A conditioning stimulus over one motor cortex (S1) is followed by a test stimulus (S2) over the other motor cortex. S1 inhibits the test MEP by on average 50% at interstimulus intervals of around 10 ms, if the intensities of both stimuli are clearly above MEP threshold (Fig. 14.4) (Ferbert *et al.* 1992; Netz *et al.* 1995; Salerno and Georgesco 1996). This inhibition is stronger from left to right motor cortex in right-handers, while mixed results were observed in left-handers (Netz *et al.* 1995). Epidural recordings from the cervical spinal cord demonstrated that S1 reduces the amplitude and number of late I waves produced by S2 (Di Lazzaro *et al.* 1999). This indicates that TMS over one motor cortex can

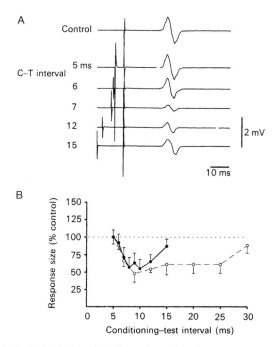

Fig. 14.4 Interhemispheric inhibition. (A) Effect of conditioning TMS delivered by a focal stimulating coil over the left motor cortex on test MEPs in the left first dorsal interosseus muscle produced by a test stimulus delivered through a second focal coil over the right motor cortex. The top trace shows the MEP to the test stimulus given alone. The lower five traces illustrate the effect of the conditioning stimulus given 5, 6, 7, 12 or 15 ms before the test stimulus (C–T interval). The traces are aligned to the onset of the test stimulus. Each trace is the average of ten single trials. (B) Mean±1 SEM time course of interhemispheric inhibition in six healthy subjects using two different intensities of the conditioning stimulus. MEPs were recorded in the relaxed first dorsal interosseus muscle, and the size of the conditioned MEP at each interstimulus interval is expressed as a percentage of the size of the test MEP (=100%). The conditioning stimulus was set to about 10% (filled circles) or 25% (open circles) above MEP threshold. With permission, from Ferbert *et al.* (1992).

inhibit the opposite motor cortex. However, there is no proof that this interhemispheric inhibition is mediated by transcallosal fibers exclusively, and some recent data point toward the participation of other pathways at a subcortical or even spinal level (Gerloff *et al.* 1998a).

Interhemispheric inhibition was abolished in patients with generalized cortical myoclonus (Brown *et al.* 1996), and in some patients with cortical–subcortical stroke (Boroojerdi *et al.* 1996). Also, in professional-level performing pianists, interhemispheric inhibition was found less effective than in nonmusician controls (Ridding *et al.* 2000).

It was proposed that interhemispheric inhibition may assist in the performance of symmetrical and asymmetrical bimanual movements, as well as suppressing unwanted movements of the opposite hand during unimanual tasks (Schnitzler *et al.* 1996). How much the reported abnormalities in patients and musicians reflect behavioral significance remains, however, to be determined.

Inhibition from cerebellum to contralateral motor cortex

The cerebellar hemispheres can be activated with transcutaneous electrical (Ugawa *et al.* 1991) or magnetic stimulation (Saito *et al.* 1995; Ugawa *et al.* 1995; Werhahn *et al.* 1996). On average, this leads to 50% inhibition of a test MEP elicited from the motor cortex contralateral to cerebellar stimulation at interstimulus intervals of 5–7 ms (Fig. 14.5) (Ugawa *et al.* 1995; Werhahn *et al.* 1996). It is thought that this inhibition results from activation of the cerebello–dentato–thalamocortical pathway. An inhibition starting at slightly longer interstimulus intervals of 7–8 ms is probably due to activation of peripheral nerve afferents at the level of the brachial plexus (Werhahn *et al.* 1996).

This inhibitory interaction between cerebellum and motor cortex is absent in patients with lesions along the cerebello–dentato–thalamocortical pathway (Di Lazzaro *et al.* 1994; Ugawa *et al.* 1994, 1997).

Long-lasting reduction of MEP size by repetitive TMS (rTMS)

Long-term depression (LTD) is a form of activity-dependent synaptic plasticity available in the adult mammalian neocortex (for review, see Linden 1994). In rat brain slices, LTD can be induced by low-rate (2 Hz) stimulation for 10 min along horizontal connection in motor cortex (Hess and Donoghue 1996). A similar phenomenon was observed when the human motor cortex was stimulated with low-rate rTMS. At a rate of 0.9–1 Hz and an intensity of 105–125% of MEP threshold (Wassermann *et al.* 1996; Chen *et al.* 1997a; Muellbacher *et al.* 2000) or 90% of MEP threshold (Maeda *et al.* 2000a,b), rTMS led to a progressive reduction in MEP size (Fig. 14.6), lasting for at least 1–30 min after the end of rTMS. This effect was specific for the motor representation stimulated with rTMS (e.g. the hand area) and did not occur in adjacent representations (e.g. the upper arm) (Muellbacher *et al.* 2000). A similar reduction in cortical excitability was also observed when 1 Hz rTMS was delivered over the human visual cortex. In this case, a significant increase in phosphene threshold, lasting for at least

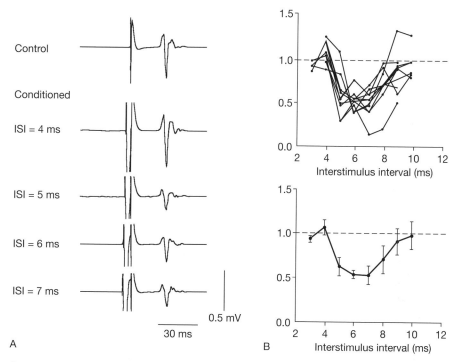

Figure 14.5 Inhibition from cerebellum to contralateral motor cortex. (A) Representative average MEP in one subject and (B) time courses of suppression in individual subjects (upper panel) and average time course (mean±SE) for all subjects (lower panel). (A) Suppression of MEP in the relaxed right first dorsal interosseous muscle after TMS of the left motor cortex induced by TMS with a double-cone coil placed over an appropriate position on the right side of the back of the head. The intensity of the conditioning stimulus was set at 5% less than the threshold for activation of the descending motor tracts at the inion. The test MEP was adjusted to about 0.7 mV. Conditioned MEP at interstimulus intervals (ISI) of 4, 5, 6, and 7 ms are shown; (B) Upper panel: the suppression begins at the interval of 5 ms in six subjects, and at 6 ms in the other two subjects. Lower panel: the average time course shows significant suppression at intervals of 5–8 ms. Reproduced from Ugawa *et al.*, Annals of Neurology, 1995;**37**:730–13, copyright 1995 John Wiley & Sons Inc. Reprinted by permission of Wiley-Liss, Inc., a subsidiary of John Wiley & Sons, Inc.

10 min after the end of rTMS, occurred (Boroojerdi *et al.* 2000). In summary, these studies demonstrate that low-rate rTMS may result in depression of the excitability of the stimulated cortex. Although the mechanisms underlying this effect are unclear, the similarity to the LTD experiments in animals suggest an LTD-like mechanism as the most likely candidate. If true, this will open up a completely new avenue of TMS research: TMS may be used not only to study the physiology of inhibition (see above) but to actively modulate excitability, for instance, by inducing long-lasting MEP depression. Potentially, this may be utilized for therapeutic purposes. Patients with

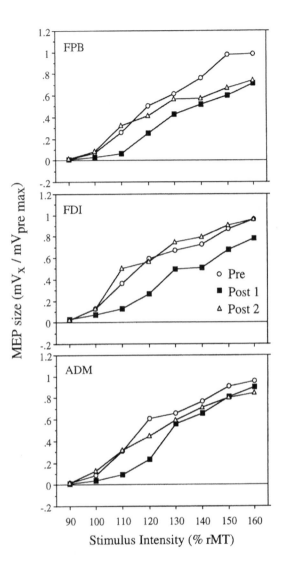

Fig. 14.6 Long-lasting reduction of MEP size by repetitive TMS (rTMS). MEP intensity curves of the left flexor pollicis brevis (FPB), first dorsal interosseus (FDI) and abductor digiti minimi (ADM) muscles before ("Pre," open circles), immediately after 15 min of low-rate rTMS (1 Hz, 115% of MEP threshold) applied to the right motor cortex ("Post 1," filled squares), and 30 min later ("Post 2," open triangles). Data are means of seven subjects, and are normalized to the individual maximum MEP obtained during "Pre." With permission, from Muellbacher *et al.* (2000).

writer's cramp, a special form of task-specific dystonia, exhibit a reduced or absent SICI (Ridding *et al.* 1995b). Subthreshold 1 Hz rTMS resulted in a normalization of the deficient SICI and a significant but transient reduction in writing pressure in some of these patients (Siebner *et al.* 1999).

TMS-induced functional lesion of motor cortex

Cortical silent period (CSP)

The CSP evoked by TMS refers to a complete or partial interruption of voluntary tonic activation of a target muscle, visible as a period of silence or decreased activity in the electromyogram (EMG) (Fig. 14.7). With surface EMG, the appearance of the CSP often shows maximal reduction early, followed by a period of partial return ("relative CSP"), before the voluntary EMG returns to the prestimulus level (Fuhr *et al.* 1991). Following the CSP there is often a short period of increased EMG activity ("rebound"). A CSP can be recorded in any target muscle but it is usually longest in the intrinsic hand muscles where it can reach a duration of 150–250 ms (Cantello *et al.* 1992). The duration of the CSP is an approximately linear function of the TMS intensity (Cantello *et al.* 1992; Haug *et al.* 1992; Inghilleri *et al.* 1993; Triggs *et al.* 1993a; Wilson *et al.* 1993). The level of muscle contraction either does not affect the duration of the CSP (Haug *et al.* 1992; Kukowski and Haug 1992; Triggs *et al.* 1992; Inghilleri *et al.* 1993; Roick *et al.* 1993) or leads to a slight shortening of up to 10 ms (Cantello *et al.* 1992; Wilson *et al.* 1993; Mathis *et al.* 1998). The duration of the CSP depends also on the "instruction set." It was shorter when the subjects were instructed to perform a rapid contraction in response to the TMS pulse and longer when they were instructed to relax (Mathis *et al.* 1998).

There is no doubt that the CSP is caused mainly or exclusively by cortical mechanisms. First, measurements of spinal motoneuron excitability, using F-waves or Hoffmann reflexes, showed a reduced spinal excitability during the early phase of the

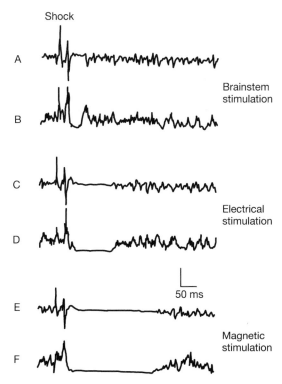

Fig. 14.7 Cortical silent period (CSP). (A, B) Silent period in the first dorsal interosseus muscle after brainstem, (C, D) transcranial electrical and (E, F) transcranial magnetic stimulation. Traces are averages of 10 single trials in one healthy subject. In A, C and E the EMG is unrectified and in B, D and F it is rectified. Vertical calibration is 3 mV in A, C and E and 400 μV in B, D and F. With permission, from Inghilleri *et al.* (1993).

CSP, but a fully recovered spinal excitability during the late phase (Fuhr *et al.* 1991; Cantello *et al.* 1992; Inghilleri *et al.* 1993; Roick *et al.* 1993; Triggs *et al.* 1993a; Ziemann *et al.* 1993). Second, the CSP after TMS is longer compared to the silent period after transcranial electrical stimulation (TES) of the motor cortex or electrical brainstem stimulation (Fig. 14.7) (Inghilleri *et al.* 1993). TMS activates the corticospinal system predominantly indirectly via corticocortical and thalamocortical fibers, in contrast to the mainly direct activation through excitation at the corticospinal axon by TES (Day *et al.* 1989a; Di Lazzaro *et al.* 1998a). Therefore, the longer silent period induced by TMS compared to TES points to an origin of the CSP "upstream" of the corticospinal neuron. Although the cortical nature of the late part of the CSP is beyond doubt, the exact mechanisms are presently not known. Many authors assume that the CSP is caused primarily by GABA-related inhibitory mechanisms (for review, Hallett 1995). However, recent neuropharmacologic studies in normal volunteers showed that single loading doses of GABAergic drugs do not always lengthen the CSP (Ziemann *et al.* 1996c; Mavroudakis *et al.* 1997). In some instances, GABAergic drugs even resulted in a shortening of the CSP (Inghilleri *et al.* 1996). However, enhanced neurotransmission through the GABA-B receptor, either by intrathecal application of the GABA-B receptor agonist baclofen in a patient with generalized dystonia (Siebner *et al.* 1998), or by increasing the GABA content in the synaptic cleft through the GABA reuptake inhibitor tiagabine in healthy subjects (Werhahn *et al.* 1999), resulted in a consistent prolongation of the CSP. Therefore, it may be suggested that the duration of the CSP is controlled by a GABA-B mediated cortical inhibitory mechanism. Alternatively to this physiologic interpretation, the duration of the CSP may also indicate the inaccessibility of the primary motor cortex by voluntary motor commands originating upstream from the motor cortex. This behavioral view is supported by an extremely prolonged CSP (lasting up to several seconds) in patients after ischemic stroke associated with a motor neglect syndrome (Classen *et al.* 1997), but extremely short or even lacking CSP in patients with Tourette's disorder associated with tics in the EMG target muscle (Ziemann *et al.* 1997a). In the stroke patients, the access of the voluntary command to primary motor cortex may be weak and easily disrupted, and once disrupted, difficult to reestablish. Conversely, in patients with Tourette's disorder, the access of the voluntary command to primary motor cortex may be rather direct and uncontrolled, and therefore difficult to disrupt. This behavioral view is supported by experiments in healthy subjects, which showed that the motor cortex never becomes inexcitable to a second TMS pulse during the CSP, while the voluntary motor drive, defined as the difference between rest and active MEP threshold, is abolished and does not recover until the end of the CSP (Tergau *et al.* 1999).

Ipsilateral silent period (ISP)

The ISP refers to a complete or partial interruption of voluntary tonic activation of a target muscle following focal TMS of the ipsilateral motor cortex (Ferbert *et al.* 1992).

It is assumed that the ISP is mediated through the corpus callosum by inhibitory inter-ference with the tonic activity in the opposite motor cortex. This view is supported by ISP studies in patients with partial or complete agenesis (Meyer *et al.* 1995) or surgical lesions of the corpus callosum (Meyer *et al.* 1998). In particular, those patients with an absent posterior trunk of the corpus callosum showed a deficient or absent ISP. The ISP is also absent in preschool children (Heinen *et al.* 1998). Children of this age still have physiologic mirror movements and it was inferred that the maturation of functionally competent callosal connections between the two motor cortexes occurs after the age of 5–6 years. Therefore, from the behavioral point of view, the ISP may reflect a measure of integrity of inhibitory interhemispheric interaction between the two motor cortexes, which is probably important in intended unimanual tasks to sup-press unwanted mirror activity in the opposite motor cortex. The ISP may be impaired in various other neurologic conditions. Of particular interest is the study of patients with early multiple sclerosis. Due to the preponderance of demyelinating lesions in the periventricular white matter, measurement of the ISP appears more sensitive than con-ventional electrophysiologic measures in detecting conduction abnormalities (Schmierer *et al.* 2000).

Delay of simple reaction time in the contralateral hand

Similar to the interruption of voluntary tonic activation (see above, CSP), TMS of motor cortex can also delay a movement of the contralateral hand to be performed in response to a go-signal for up to 150 ms (Fig. 14.8) (Day *et al.*, 1989b; Rothwell *et al.* 1989). The delay increased with increasing stimulus intensity and the closer the stimu-lus was applied to the expected time of the motor response (Day *et al.* 1989b; Rothwell *et al.* 1989; Ziemann *et al.* 1997c). The delay depended on effective stimulation of the motor representation of the task muscle, while stimulation outside this area had no effect (Taylor *et al.* 1995; Ziemann *et al.* 1997c). Despite the considerable delaying effect, TMS did not disrupt the usually triphasic agonist–antagonist–agonist EMG pat-tern of the motor response (Fig. 14.8) (Day *et al.* 1989b; Rothwell *et al.* 1989). The delay could not be explained by inexcitability of the motor cortex since a second brain stimulus, given in the middle of the delay period, was capable of producing a MEP (Day *et al.* 1989b; Rothwell *et al.* 1989). Furthermore, the premovement increase in excitability of the spinal motor neurons remained unaffected by the motor cortex stimul-us that delayed the simple reaction time (Ziemann *et al.* 1997c). Neither could the delay be explained by altering the time of the subject's intention to respond, since TMS delivered to one motor cortex before an attempted simultaneous bilateral wrist move-ment produced a far greater delay of the contralateral compared to the ipsilateral movement (Day *et al.* 1989b; Rothwell *et al.* 1989). In summary, these findings suggest that TMS of motor cortex inhibits a group of strategically important neurons, prob-ably in the motor cortex, that are then rendered unresponsive for a brief period to the command signals they receive to initiate the motor response. Since the delayed

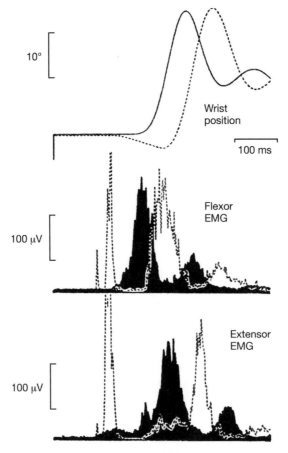

Fig. 14.8 Delay of simple reaction time in the contralateral hand. Rapid wrist flexion movements in a single healthy subject in response to an audio signal given at the start of the sweep, with (dotted lines) and without (solid traces) TMS delivered 100 ms after the start of the sweep. Shown are average wrist position (upper traces, flexion upwards), wrist and finger flexor (middle traces) and extensor (lower traces) rectified EMG activity. The control movement (average of 26 trials) is characterized by alternating bursts of activity in flexor and extensor muscles. In those trials in which TMS was given (average of 10 trials) the movement and associated pattern of muscle activities are the same but delayed by some 60 ms. Note the direct muscle responses in the flexor and extensor muscles occurring some 15 ms after the stimulus artifact producing, in this case, a small extension movement seen in the wrist position trace. Reproduced from Day *et al.* in Brain 1989;**112:** 649–63 with the permission of Oxford University Press.

movement was eventually executed in an intact form, the motor commands upstream from the inhibited site must have been held in some form of short-term memory for the duration of the delay. Finally, some form of internal monitoring system must exist to compensate for the fact that the execution of the intended movement had been disrupted. Most likely, this is realized by an internal reafference copy which would be capable of detecting even very small delays, in contrast to a feedback system that relies on long-loop peripheral afferent information, e.g. from muscle spindles.

Delay of simple reaction time in the ipsilateral hand

Similar to the interruption of tonic voluntary activation in the ipsilateral hand (see above, ISP) focal TMS of the motor cortex can also delay a movement of the ipsilateral hand to be performed in response to a go-signal for up to 40 ms (Meyer and Voss 2000). TMS delayed the execution of the ipsilateral finger movement when TMS preceded the onset of the intended movement by about 25–65 ms. Taking the corticomuscular conduction time of approximately 20 ms into account, TMS was effective ~ 5–45 ms before the motor command left the nonstimulated contralateral motor cortex. Such timing is compatible with an interhemispheric inhibition, most likely mediated via the corpus callosum, similar to the mechanisms responsible for the ISP described above. These findings support the idea that the neural structures mediating interhemispheric inhibition are important to suppress coactivation of the other hand during intended unilateral finger movements.

Interference of TMS with the motor response in a forced-choice task

In right-handers, nonfocal TMS over the vertex at an intensity below MEP threshold biases the subject hand to move in response to the TMS click (Ammon and Gandevia 1990). The subjects were instructed to randomly extend either their left or right index finger within 2–5 s after TMS. If the current in the round coil was directed anti-clockwise (as corrected according to the erratum by Day *et al.* 1990), i.e. the left motor cortex was stimulated preferentially, then the right hand was selected significantly more often than the left hand. Vice versa, with clockwise current direction, and thus preferential stimulation of the right motor cortex, the left hand was selected more often. When the coil was held over the occipital cortex, this response bias was not observed (Ammon and Gandevia 1990). The topographic specificity was studied more precisely in a second paper using a focal figure-of-eight coil (Brasil-Neto *et al.* 1992). In that study, the response bias for the contralateral hand was found only when the coil was placed over the motor cortex. Furthermore, only very fast responses with a response onset < 200 ms after the TMS click showed the bias (Brasil-Neto *et al.* 1992). Subjects were completely unaware of the induced response bias. This demonstrates that it is possible to influence movement preparation processes externally without disrupting the conscious perception of volition.

Interference of rTMS with movement sequences of the contralateral hand

It was a long held view that the primary motor cortex is an executive site for simple voluntary movements (for review, Porter and Lemon 1993). This concept has recently been challenged. Data from animal experiments and neuroimaging studies in humans suggested a participation of the primary motor cortex in the generation and processing of movements of greater complexity (e.g. Rao *et al.* 1993; Shibasaki *et al.* 1993; Georgopoulos 1994). To corroborate this novel concept further, the effects of rTMS over the primary motor cortex on the performance of finger sequences of the contralateral

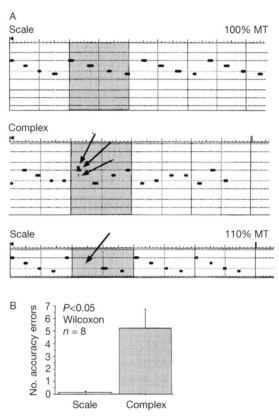

Fig. 14.9 Interference of rTMS with movement sequences of the contralateral hand. (A) Top: example of selective disturbance of the complex but not the simple sequence (scale) with TMS of primary motor cortex using exactly the same stimulus parameters (intensity=100% MEP threshold) for both sequences. Shaded areas indicate the periods of rTMS (5 Hz, train duration=2 s). The heavy black lines and dots indicate key presses on the piano. Their vertical position indicates which key was pressed (uppermost position=little finger, bottommost position=index finger). Interval between two vertical lines is 1 s. Total sequence length= 8 s=16 key presses at 2 Hz. Bottom: when the stimulus intensity was increased (110% MEP threshold), the scale sequence was also disrupted (missing sixth key press). Arrows indicate accuracy errors. (B) Difference in the number of accuracy errors between the scale and the complex sequence, with minimum stimulus intensity required to disturb the complex sequence. Error bars=1 SE. Reprinted from Gerloff *et al.*, *Brain*, 1998;**121**:1695–709, with permission of Oxford University Press.

hand were evaluated. It was found that rTMS intensities capable of disrupting the performance of an overlearned complex sequence did not affect simpler sequences (Fig. 14.9) (Gerloff *et al.* 1998b). To disrupt simple sequences, the rTMS intensity had to be increased. This effect was specific for rTMS of the contralateral primary motor cortex. These findings suggest that the primary motor cortex plays a greater role in the generation and processing of complex than simple finger movement sequences.

Interference of rTMS with movement sequences of the ipsilateral hand

Functional imaging and behavioral studies in stroke patients suggest that the primary motor cortex is involved in movement control of the ipsilateral hand (for review, Chen *et al.* 1997b). This was supported by an rTMS study that evaluated the effects of motor cortex stimulation on the performance of finger movement sequences conducted with the ipsilateral hand (Chen *et al.* 1997c). In right-handers, ipsilateral motor cortex rTMS induced timing errors in both a simple and a complex sequence, and with the complex sequence induced more errors when the left motor cortex rather than the right motor cortex was stimulated. Errors with right motor cortex stimulation occurred only during the rTMS period, but with left motor cortex stimulation also outlasted the rTMS period (Chen *et al.* 1997c). From these findings it was concluded that the motor cortex is involved in ipsilateral finger movement sequences and, in right-handers, the left motor cortex plays a greater role than the right motor cortex. This asymmetry of involvement of motor cortex in the control of the ipsilateral hand may be interpreted as indicating a novel aspect of motor dominance that, traditionally, has been restricted to the contralateral hand (e.g. Ziemann and Hallett 2001).

Interference of rTMS with motor learning

Recent neuroimaging (Karni *et al.* 1995; Honda *et al.* 1998) and TMS studies (Pascual-Leone *et al.* 1994, 1995) indicated that the human primary motor cortex is involved in motor learning and motor skill acquisition. One TMS study demonstrated that repeated ballistic pincer-grip movements result in a rapid increase in pincer-grip force and the maximum acceleration between thumb and index finger (Muellbacher *et al.* 2001). This behavioral improvement was paralleled by an increase in MEP size of hand muscles involved in the practice (Muellbacher *et al.* 2001). Low-rate (1 Hz) rTMS given immediately after a 5 min practice period resulted in a resetting of improved acceleration back to the baseline level (Muellbacher *et al.* in press). A second 5 min practice period replicated the improvement in acceleration from the first session, but this was again disrupted by rTMS given after the end of the second practice period. The disruptive rTMS effects were contingent upon stimulation of the primary motor cortex since rTMS delivered to the visual cortex did not interfere with improvement in motor behavior (Muellbacher *et al.* in press). These results indicate that the human primary motor cortex is involved in the early phase of motor learning (motor consolidation).

In summary, the interference of rTMS with behavioral aspects of motor control reported here provides broad evidence that the human primary motor cortex is more than an executive site for simple movements. It is involved in the processing and control of complex finger sequences and in motor learning.

References

Abbruzzese, G., Buccolieri, A., Marchese, R. *et al.* (1997) Intracortical inhibition and facilitation are abnormal in Huntington's disease: a paired magnetic stimulation study. *Neuroscience Letters,* **228:**87–90.

Ammon, K. and Gandevia, S. C. (1990) Transcranial magnetic stimulation can influence the selection of motor programmes. *Journal of Neurology, Neurosurgery and Psychiatry,* **53:**705–7.

Avoli, M., Hwa, G., Louvel, J. *et al.* (1997) Functional and pharmacological properties of GABA-mediated inhibition in the human neocortex. *Canadian Journal of Physiology and Pharmacology,* **75:**526–34.

Berardelli, A., Rona, S., Inghilleri, M. *et al.* (1996) Cortical inhibition in Parkinson's disease. A study with paired magnetic stimulation. *Brain,* **119:**71–7.

Boroojerdi, B., Diefenbach, K. and Ferbert A. (1996) Transcallosal inhibition in cortical and subcortical cerebral vascular lesions. *Journal of Neurological Science,* **144:**160–70.

Boroojerdi, B., Prager, A., Muellbacher, W. *et al.* (2000) Reduction of human visual cortex excitability using 1-Hz transcranial magnetic stimulation. *Neurology,* **54:**1529–31.

Brasil-Neto, J. P., Pascual-Leone, A., Valls-Sole, J. *et al.* (1992) Focal transcranial magnetic stimulation and response bias in a forced-choice task. *Journal of Neurology, Neurosurgery and Psychiatry,* **55:**964–6.

Brown, P., Ridding, M. C., Werhahn, K. J. *et al.* (1996) Abnormalities of the balance between inhibition and excitation in the motor cortex of patients with cortical myoclonus. *Brain,* **119:**309–17.

Cantello, R., Gianelli, M., Civardi, C. *et al.* (1992) Magnetic brain stimulation: the silent period after the motor evoked potential. *Neurology,* **42:**1951–9.

Caramia, M. D., Gigli, G., Iani, C. *et al.* (1996) Distinguishing forms of generalized epilepsy using magnetic brain stimulation. *Electroencephalography and Clinical Neurophysiology,* **98:**14–9.

Chen, R., Classen, J., Gerloff, C. *et al.* (1997a) Depression of motor cortex excitability by low-frequency transcranial magnetic stimulation. *Neurology,* **48:**1398–403.

Chen, R., Cohen, L. G. and Hallett, M. (1997b) Role of the ipsilateral motor cortex in voluntary movement. *Canadian Journal of the Neurological Sciences,* **24:**284–91.

Chen, R., Gerloff, C., Hallett, M. *et al.* (1997c) Involvement of the ipsilateral motor cortex in finger movements of different complexities. *Annals of Neurology,* **41:**247–54.

Chen, R., Lozano, A. M. and Ashby, P. (1999) Mechanism of the silent period following transcranial magnetic stimulation. *Experimental Brain Research,* **128:**539–42.

Chen, R., Samii, A., Canos, M. *et al.* (1997d) Effects of phenytoin on cortical excitability in humans. *Neurology,* **49:**881–3.

Chen, R., Tam, A., Butefisch, C. *et al.* (1998) Intracortical inhibition and facilitation in different representations of the human motor cortex. *Journal of Neurophysiology,* **80:**2870–81.

Chen, R., Wassermann, E. M., Canos, M. *et al.* (1997e) Impaired inhibition in writer's cramp during voluntary muscle activation. *Neurology,* **49:**1054–9.

Classen, J., Schnitzler, A., Binkofski, F. *et al.* (1997) The motor syndrome associated with exaggerated inhibition within the primary motor cortex of patients with hemiparetic stroke. *Brain*, 120:605–19.

Claus, D. and Brunhölzl, C. (1994) Facilitation and disfacilitation of muscle responses after repetitive transcranial cortical stimulation and electrical peripheral nerve stimulation. *Electroencephalography and Clinical Neurophysiology*, 93:417–20.

Claus, D., Weis, M., Jahnke, U. *et al.* (1992) Corticospinal conduction studied with magnetic double stimulation in the intact human. *Journal of Neurological Science*, 111:180–8.

Connors, B. W., Malenka, R. C. and Silva, L. R. (1988) Two inhibitory postsynaptic potentials, and GABAA and GABAB receptor-mediated responses in neocortex of rat and cat. *Journal of Physiology (London)*, 406:443–68.

Day, B. L., Dressler, D., Hess, C. W. *et al.* (1990) Direction of current in magnetic stimulating coils used for percutaneous activation of brain, spinal cord and peripheral nerve. *Journal of Physiology*, 430:617.

Day, B. L., Dressler, D., Maertens de Noordhout, A. *et al.* (1989a) Electric and magnetic stimulation of human motor cortex: surface EMG and single motor unit responses. *Journal of Physiology (London)*, 412:449–73.

Day, B. L., Rothwell, J. C., Thompson, P. D. *et al.* (1989b) Delay in the execution of voluntary movement by electrical or magnetic brain stimulation in intact man. Evidence for the storage of motor programs in the brain. *Brain*, 112:649–63.

Deisz, R. A. (1999) The GABA(B) receptor antagonist CGP 55845A reduces presynaptic GABA(B) actions in neocortical neurons of the rat *in vitro*. *Neuroscience*, 93:1241–9.

Di Lazzaro, V., Molinari, M., Restuccia, D. *et al.* (1994) Cerebro-cerebellar interactions in man: neurophysiological studies in patients with focal cerebellar lesions. *Electroencephalography and Clinical Neurophysiology*, 93:27–34.

Di Lazzaro, V., Oliviero, A., Meglio, M. *et al.* (2000a) Direct demonstration of the effect of lorazepam on the excitability of the human motor cortex. *Clinical Neurophysiology*, 111:794–9.

Di Lazzaro, V., Oliviero, A., Profice, P. *et al.* (1999) Direct demonstration of interhemispheric inhibition of the human motor cortex produced by transcranial magnetic stimulation. *Experimental Brain Research*, 124:520–4.

Di Lazzaro, V., Oliviero, A., Profice, P. *et al.* (2000b) Muscarinic receptor blockade has differential effects on the excitability of intracortical circuits in human motor cortex. *Experimental Brain Research*, 135:455–61.

Di Lazzaro, V., Oliviero, A., Profice, P. *et al.* (1998a) Comparison of descending volleys evoked by transcranial magnetic and electric stimulation in conscious humans. *Electroencephalography and Clinical Neurophysiology*, 109:397–401.

Di Lazzaro, V., Restuccia, D., Oliviero, A. *et al.* (1998b) Magnetic transcranial stimulation at intensities below active motor threshold activates intracortical inhibitory circuits. *Experimental Brain Research*, 119:265–8.

Ferbert, A., Priori, A., Rothwell, J. C. *et al.* (1992) Interhemispheric inhibition of the human motor cortex. *Journal of Physiology (London)*, 453:525–46.

Fong, J. K. Y., Werhahn, K. J., Rothwell, J. C. *et al.* (1993) Motor cortex excitability in focal and generalized epilepsy. *Journal of Physiology (London)*, 459:468P.

Fuhr, P., Agostino, R. and Hallett, M. (1991) Spinal motor neuron excitability during the silent period after cortical stimulation. *Electroencephalography and Clinical Neurophysiology*, 81:257–62.

Georgopoulos, A. P. (1994) New concepts in generation of movement. *Neuron*, **13**:257–68.

Gerloff, C., Cohen, L. G., Floeter, M. K. *et al.* (1998a) Inhibitory influence of the ipsilateral motor cortex on responses evoked by transcranial stimulation of the human cortex and pyramidal tract. *Journal of Physiology*, **510**:249–59.

Gerloff, C., Corwell, B., Chen, R. *et al.* (1998b) The role of the human motor cortex in the control of complex and simple finger movement sequences. *Brain,* **121**:1695–709.

Gould, H. J., Cusick, C. G., Pons, T. P. *et al.* (1986) The relationship of corpus callosum connections to electrical stimulation maps of motor, supplementary motor, and the frontal eye fields in owl monkeys. *Journal of Comparative Neurology*, **247**:297–325.

Greenberg, B. D., Ziemann, U., Cora-Locatelli, G. *et al.* (2000) Altered cortical excitability in obsessive-compulsive disorder. *Neurology*, **54**:142–7.

Greenberg, B. D., Ziemann, U., Harmon, A. *et al.* (1998) Decreased neuronal inhibition in cerebral cortex in obsessive-compulsive disorder on transcranial magnetic stimulation. *Lancet*, **352**:881–2.

Hallett, M. (1995) Transcranial magnetic stimulation: negative effects. *Advances in Neurology*, **67**:107–13.

Hanajima, R., Ugawa, Y., Terao, Y. *et al.* (1996) Ipsilateral cortico-cortical inhibition of the motor cortex in various neurological disorders. *Journal of Neurological Science*, **140**:109–16.

Hanajima, R., Ugawa, Y., Terao, Y. *et al.* (1998a) Paired-pulse magnetic stimulation of the human motor cortex: differences among I waves. *Journal of Physiology*, **509**:607–18.

Hanajima, R., Ugawa, Y., Terao, Y. *et al.* (1998b) Cortico-cortical inhibition of the motor cortical area projecting to sternocleidomastoid muscle in normals and patients with spasmodic torticollis or essential tremor. *Electroencephalography and Clinical Neurophysiology*, **109**:391–6.

Haug, B. A., Schonle, P. W., Knobloch, C. *et al.* (1992) Silent period measurement revives as a valuable diagnostic tool with transcranial magnetic stimulation. *Electroencephalography and Clinical Neurophysiology*, **85**:158–60.

Heinen, F., Glocker, F. X., Fietzek, U. *et al.* (1998) Absence of transcallosal inhibition following focal magnetic stimulation in preschool children. *Annals of Neurology*, **43**:608–12.

Hess, G. and Donoghue, J. P. (1996) Long-term depression of horizontal connections in rat motor cortex. *European Journal of Neuroscience*, **8**:658–65.

Honda, M., Deiber, M. P., Ibanez, V. *et al.* (1998) Dynamic cortical involvement in implicit and explicit motor sequence learning. A PET study. *Brain*, **121**:2159–73.

Inghilleri, M., Berardelli, A., Cruccu, G. *et al.* (1993) Silent period evoked by transcranial stimulation of the human cortex and cervicomedullary junction. *Journal of Physiology (London)*, **466**:521–34.

Inghilleri, M., Berardelli, A., Marchetti, P. *et al.* (1996) Effects of diazepam, baclofen and thiopental on the silent period evoked by transcranial magnetic stimulation in humans. *Experimental Brain Research*, **109**:467–72.

Inghilleri, M., Mattia, D., Berardelli, A. *et al.* (1998) Asymmetry of cortical excitability revealed by transcranial stimulation in a patient with focal motor epilepsy and cortical myoclonus. *Electroencephalography and Clinical Neurophysiology*, **109**:70–2.

Jones, E. G. (1993) GABAergic neurons and their role in cortical plasticity in primates. *Cerebral Cortex*, **3**:361–72.

Karni, A., Meyer, G., Jezzard, P. *et al.* (1995) Functional MRI evidence for adult motor cortex plasticity during motor skill learning. *Nature*, **377**:155–8.

Kobayashi, M., Hyodo, A., Kurokawa, T. *et al.* (1998) The first component of polyphasic motor evoked potentials is resistant to suppression by paired transcranial magnetic stimulation in humans. *Journal of Neurological Science*, **159**:166–9.

Kujirai, T., Caramia, M. D., Rothwell, J. C. *et al.* (1993) Corticocortical inhibition in human motor cortex. *Journal of Physiology (London)*, **471**:501–19.

Kukowski, B. and Haug, B. (1992) Quantitative evaluation of the silent period, evoked by transcranial magnetic stimulation during sustained muscle contraction, in normal man and in patients with stroke. *Electroencephalography and Clinical Neurophysiology*, **32**:373–8.

Liepert, J., Classen, J., Cohen, L. G. *et al.* (1998) Task-dependent changes of intracortical inhibition. *Experimental Brain Research*, **118**:421–6.

Liepert, J., Schwenkreis, P., Tegenthoff, M. *et al.* (1997) The glutamate antagonist Riluzole suppresses intracortical facilitation. *Journal of Neural Transmission*, **104**:1207–14.

Linden, D. J. (1994) Long-term synaptic depression in the mammalian brain. *Neuron*, **12**:457–72.

Maeda, F., Keenan, J. P., Tormos, J. M. *et al.* (2000a) Interindividual variability of the modulatory effects of repetitive transcranial magnetic stimulation on cortical excitability. *Experimental Brain Research*, **133**:425–30.

Maeda, F., Keenan, J. P., Tormos, J. M. *et al.* (2000b) Modulation of corticospinal excitability by repetitive transcranial magnetic stimulation. *Clinical Neurophysiology*, **111**:800–5.

Mathis, J., de Quervain, D. and Hess, C. W. (1998) Dependence of the transcranially induced silent "instruction set" and the individual reaction time. *Electroencephalography and Clinical Neurophysiology*, **109**:426–35.

Matsumura, M., Sawaguchi, T., Oishi, T. *et al.* (1991) Behavioral deficits induced by local injection of bicuculline and muscimol into the primate motor and premotor cortex. *Journal of Neurophysiology*, **65**:1542–53.

Mavroudakis, N., Caroyer, J. M., Brunko, E. *et al.* (1997) Effects of vigabatrin on motor potentials with magnetic stimulation. *Electroencephalography and Clinical Neurophysiology*, **105**:124–7.

McCormick, D. A. (1989) GABA as an inhibitory neurotransmitter in human cerebral cortex. *Journal of Neurophysiology*, **62**:1018–27.

Meyer, B. U., Röricht, S., Gräfin von Einsiedel, H. *et al.* (1995) Inhibitory and excitatory interhemispheric transfers between motor cortical areas in normal humans and patients with abnormalities of the corpus callosum. *Brain*, **118**:429–40.

Meyer, B. U. and Voss, M. (2000) Delay of the execution of rapid finger movement by magnetic stimulation of the ipsilateral hand-associated motor cortex. *Experimental Brain Research*, **134**:477–82.

Meyer, B.-U., Röricht, S. and Woiciechowsky, C. (1998) Topography of fibers in the human corpus callosum mediating interhemispheric inhibition between the motor cortices. *Annals of Neurology*, **43**:360–9.

Muellbacher, W., Ziemann, U., Boroojerdi, B. *et al.* (2001) Role of the human motor cortex in rapid motor learning. *Experimental Brain Research*, **136**:431–8.

Muellbacher, W., Ziemann, U., Boroojerdi, B. *et al.* (2000) Effects of low-frequency transcranial magnetic stimulation on motor excitability and basic motor behavior. *Clinical Neurophysiology*, **111**:1002–7.

Muellbacher, W., Ziemann, U., Wissel, J. *et al.* (2002) Early consolidation in human primary motor cortex. *Nature* (in press).

Nakamura, H., Kitagawa, H., Kawaguchi, Y. *et al.* (1997) Intracortical facilitation and inhibition after transcranial magnetic stimulation in conscious humans. *Journal of Physiology (London)*, **498**:817–823.

Netz, J., Ziemann, U. and Hömberg, V. (1995) Hemispheric asymmetry of transcallosal inhibition in man. *Experimental Brain Research*, **104**:527–33.

Pascual-Leone, A., Grafman, J. and Hallett, M. (1994) Modulation of cortical motor output maps during development of implicit and explicit knowledge. *Science*, **263**:1287–9.

Pascual-Leone, A., Nguyet, D., Cohen, L. G. *et al.* (1995) Modulation of muscle responses evoked by transcranial magnetic stimulation during the acquisition of new fine motor skills. *Journal of Neurophysiology*, **74**:1037–45.

Porter, R. and Lemon, R. (1993) *Corticospinal Function and Voluntary Movement*, vol 45. Clarendon Press, Oxford.

Rao, S. M., Binder, J. R., Bandettini, P. A. *et al.* (1993) Functional magnetic resonance imaging of complex human movements. *Neurology*, **43**:2311–18.

Reynolds, C. and Ashby, P. (1999) Inhibition in the human motor cortex is reduced just before a voluntary contraction. *Neurology*, **53**:730–5.

Ridding, M. C., Brouwer, B. and Nordstrom, M. A. (2000) Reduced interhemispheric inhibition in musicians. *Experimental Brain Research*, **133**:249–53.

Ridding, M. C., Inzelberg, R. and Rothwell, J. C. (1995a) Changes in excitability of motor cortical circuitry in patients with Parkinson's disease. *Annals of Neurology*, **37**:181–8.

Ridding, M. C., Sheean, G., Rothwell, J. C. *et al.* (1995b) Changes in the balance between motor cortical excitation and inhibition in focal, task specific dystonia. *Journal of Neurology, Neurosurgery and Psychiatry*, **59**:493–8.

Ridding, M. C., Taylor, J. L. and Rothwell, J. C. (1995c) The effect of voluntary contraction on cortico-cortical inhibition in human motor cortex. *Journal of Physiology (London)*, **487**:541–8.

Roick, H., von Giesen, H. J. and Benecke, R. (1993) On the origin of the postexcitatory inhibition seen after transcranial magnetic brain stimulation in awake human subjects. *Experimental Brain Research*, **94**:489–98.

Rona, S., Berardelli, A., Vacca, L. *et al.* (1998) Alterations of motor cortical inhibition in patients with dystonia. *Movement Disorders*, **13**:118–24.

Rothwell, J. C. (1996) The use of paired pulse stimulation to investigate the intrinsic circuitry of human motor cortex. In J. Nilsson, M. Panizza and F. Grandori (eds) *Advances in Magnetic Stimulation. Mathematical Modelling and Clinical Applications*, pp. 99–104. PI-ME Press, Pavia, Italy.

Rothwell, J. C., Day, B. L., Thompson, P. D. *et al.* (1989) Interruption of motor programmes by electrical or magnetic brain stimulation in man. *Progress in Brain Research*, **80**:467–72; discussion on 465–6.

Rothwell, J. C., Ferbert, A., Caramia, M. D. *et al.* (1991) Intracortical inhibitory circuits studied in humans [abstract]. *Neurology*, **41(Suppl 1)**: 192.

Rouiller, E. M., Babalian, A., Kazennikov, O. *et al.* (1994) Transcallosal connections of the distal forelimb representations of the primary and supplementary motor cortical areas in macaque monkeys. *Experimental Brain Research*, **102**:227–43.

Saito, Y., Yokota, T. and Yuasa, T. (1995) Suppression of motor cortical excitability by magnetic stimulation of the cerebellum. *Brain Research*, **694**:200–6.

Salerno, A. and Georgesco, M. (1996) Interhemispheric facilitation and inhibition studied in man with double magnetic stimulation. *Electroencephalography and Clinical Neurophysiology*, **101**:395–403.

Sandbrink, F., Syed, N. A., Fujii, M. D. *et al.* (2000) Motor cortex excitability in stiff-person syndrome. *Brain*, **123**:2231–9.

Sanger, T. D., Garg, R. R. and Chen, R. (2001) Interactions between two different inhibitory systems in the human motor cortex. *Journal of Physiology (London)*, **530**:307–17.

Schmierer, K., Niehaus, L., Roricht, S. *et al.* (2000) Conduction deficits of callosal fibres in early multiple sclerosis. *Journal of Neurology, Neurosurgery and Psychiatry*, **68**:633–8.

Schnitzler, A., Kessler, K. R. and Benecke, R. (1996) Transcallosally mediated inhibition of interneurons within human primary motor cortex. *Experimental Brain Research*, **112**:381–91.

Schulze-Bonhage, A., Knott, H. and Ferbert, A. (1996) Effects of carbamazepine on cortical excitatory and inhibitory phenomena: a study with paired transcranial magnetic stimulation. *Electroencephalography and Clinical Neurophysiology*, **99**:267–73.

Schwenkreis, P., Liepert, J., Witscher, K. *et al.* (2000) Riluzole suppresses motor cortex facilitation in correlation to its plasma level. *Experimental Brain Research*, **135**:293–299.

Schwenkreis, P., Witscher, K., Janssen, F. *et al.* (1999) Influence of the *N*-methyl-D-aspartate antagonist mementine on human motor cortex excitability. *Neuroscience Letters*, **270**:137–40.

Shibasaki, H., Sadato, N., Lyshkow, H. *et al.* (1993) Both primary motor cortex and supplementary motor area play an important role in complex finger movement. *Brain*, **116**:1387–98.

Siebner, H. R., Dressnandt, J., Auer, C. *et al.* (1998) Continuous intrathecal baclofen infusions induced a marked increase of the transcranially evoked silent period in a patient with generalized dystonia. *Muscle and Nerve*, **21**:1209–12.

Siebner, H. R., Tormos, J. M., Ceballos-Baumann, A. O. *et al.* (1999) Low-frequency repetitive transcranial magnetic stimulation of the motor cortex in writer's cramp. *Neurology*, **52**:529–37.

Stokic, D. S., McKay, W. B., Scott, L. *et al.* (1997) Intracortical inhibition of lower limb motor-evoked potentials after paired transcranial magnetic stimulation. *Experimental Brain Research*, **117**:437–43.

Taylor, J. L., Wagener, D. S. and Colebatch, J. G. (1995) Mapping of cortical sites where transcranial magnetic stimulation results in delay of voluntary movement. *Electroencephalography and Clinical Neurophysiology*, **97**:341–8.

Tegenthoff, M., Vorgerd, M., Juskowiak, F. *et al.* (1996) Postexcitatory inhibition after transcranial magnetic single and double brain stimulation in Huntington's disease. *Electroencephalography and Clinical Neurophysiology*, **101**:298–303.

Terao, Y., Hayashi, H., Shimizu, T. *et al.* (1995) Altered motor cortical excitability to magnetic stimulation in a patient with a lesion in globus pallidus. *Journal of Neurological Sciences*, **129**:175–8.

Tergau, F., Becher, V., Canelo, M. *et al.* (1999) Complete suppression of voluntary motor drive during the silent period after transcranial magnetic stimulation. *Experimental Brain Research*, **124**:447–54.

Triggs, W. J., Cros, D., Macdonell, R. A. *et al.* (1993a) Cortical and spinal motor excitability during the transcranial magnetic stimulation silent period in humans. *Brain Research*, **628**:39–48.

Triggs, W. J., Kiers, L., Cros, D. *et al.* (1993b) Facilitation of magnetic motor evoked potentials during the cortical stimulation silent period. *Neurology*, **43**:2615–20.

Triggs, W. J., Macdonell, R. A., Cros, D. *et al.* (1992) Motor inhibition and excitation are independent effects of magnetic cortical stimulation. *Annals of Neurology*, **32**:345–51.

Ugawa, Y., Day, B. L., Rothwell, J. C. *et al.* (1991) Modulation of motor cortical excitability by electrical stimulation over the cerebellum in man. *Journal of Physiology (London)*, **441**:57–72.

Ugawa, Y., Genba-Shimizu, K., Rothwell, J. C. *et al.* (1994) Suppression of motor cortical excitability by electrical stimulation over the cerebellum in ataxia. *Annals of Neurology*, **36**:90–6.

Ugawa, Y., Hanajima, R. and Kanazawa, I. (1993) Interhemispheric facilitation of the hand area of the human motor cortex. *Neuroscience Letters*, **160**:153–5.

Ugawa, Y., Terao, Y., Hanajima, R. *et al.* (1997) Magnetic stimulation over the cerebellum in patients with ataxia. *Electroencephalography and Clinical Neurophysiology*, **104**:453–8.

Ugawa, Y., Uesaka, Y., Terao, Y. *et al.* (1995) Magnetic stimulation over the cerebellum in humans. *Annals of Neurology*, **37**:703–13.

Valls-Sole, J., Pascual-Leone, A., Wassermann, E. M. *et al.* (1992) Human motor evoked responses to paired transcranial magnetic stimuli. *Electroencephalography and Clinical Neurophysiology*, **85**:355–64.

Valzania, F., Quatrale, R., Strafella, A. P. *et al.* (1994) Pattern of motor evoked response to repetitive transcranial magnetic stimulation. *Electroencephalography and Clinical Neurophysiology,* **93:**312–7.

Valzania, F., Strafella, A., Quatrale, R. *et al.* (1997) Motor evoked responses to paired cortical magnetic stimulation in Parkinson's disease. *Electroencephalography and Clinical Neurophysiology,* **105:**37–43.

Wassermann, E. M., Grafman, J., Berry, C. *et al.* (1996) Use and safety of a new repetitive transcranial magnetic stimulator. *Electroencephalography and Clinical Neurophysiology,* **101:**412–17.

Werhahn, K. J., Forderreuther, S. and Straube, A. (1998) Effects of the serotonin1B/1D receptor agonist zolmitriptan on motor cortical excitability in humans. *Neurology,* **51:**896–8.

Werhahn, K. J., Kunesch, E., Noachtar, S. *et al.* (1999) Differential effects on motorcortical inhibition induced by blockade of GABA uptake in humans. *Journal of Physiology (London),* **517:**591–7.

Werhahn, K. J., Taylor, J., Ridding, M. *et al.* (1996) Effect of transcranial magnetic stimulation over the cerebellum on the excitability of human motor cortex. *Electroencephalography and Clinical Neurophysiology,* **101:**58–66.

Wessel, K., Tegenthoff, M., Vorgerd, M. *et al.* (1996) Enhancement of inhibitory mechanisms in the motor cortex of patients with cerebellar degeneration: a study with transcranial magnetic brain stimulation. *Electroencephalography and Clinical Neurophysiology,* **101:**273–80.

Wilson, S. A., Lockwood, R. J., Thickbroom, G. W. *et al.* (1993) The muscle silent period following transcranial magnetic cortical stimulation. *Journal of Neurological Science,* **114:**216–22.

Yokota, T., Yoshino, A., Inaba, A. *et al.* (1996) Double cortical stimulation in amyotrophic lateral sclerosis. *Journal of Neurology, Neurosurgery and Psychiatry,* **61:**596–600.

Ziemann, U. (1999) Intracortical inhibition and facilitation in the conventional paired TMS paradigm. *Electroencephalography and Clinical Neurophysiology Supplement,* **51:**127–36.

Ziemann, U., Bruns, D. and Paulus, W. (1996a) Enhancement of human motor cortex inhibition by the dopamine receptor agonist pergolide: evidence from transcranial magnetic stimulation. *Neuroscience Letters,* **208:**187–90.

Ziemann, U., Chen, R., Cohen, L. G. *et al.* (1998a) Dextromethorphan decreases the excitability of the human motor cortex. *Neurology,* **51:**1320–4.

Ziemann, U., Corwell, B. and Cohen, L. G. (1998b) Modulation of plasticity in human motor cortex after forearm ischemic nerve block. *Journal of Neuroscience,* **18:**1115–23.

Ziemann, U. and Hallett, M. (2001) Hemispheric asymmetry of ipsilateral motor cortex activation during unimanual motor tasks: further evidence for motor dominance. *Clinical Neurophysiology,* **112:**107–13.

Ziemann, U., Hallett, M. and Cohen, L. G. (1998c) Mechanisms of deafferentation-induced plasticity in human motor cortex. *Journal of Neuroscience,* **18:**7000–7.

Ziemann, U., Lönnecker, S. and Paulus, W. (1995) Inhibition of human motor cortex by ethanol. A transcranial magnetic stimulation study. *Brain,* **118:**1437–46.

Ziemann, U., Lönnecker, S., Steinhoff, B. J. *et al.* (1996b) The effect of lorazepam on the motor cortical excitability in man. *Experimental Brain Research,* **109:**127–35.

Ziemann, U., Lönnecker, S., Steinhoff, B. J. *et al.* (1996c) Effects of antiepileptic drugs on motor cortex excitability in humans: a transcranial magnetic stimulation study. *Annals of Neurology,* **40:**367–78.

Ziemann, U., Muellbacher, W., Hallett, M. *et al.* (2001) Modulation of practice-dependent plasticity in human motor cortex. *Brain,* **124:**1171–81.

Ziemann, U., Netz, J., Szelenyi, A. *et al.* (1993) Spinal and supraspinal mechanisms contribute to the silent period in the contracting soleus muscle after transcranial magnetic stimulation of human motor cortex. *Neuroscience Letters*, **156**:167–71.

Ziemann, U., Paulus, W. and Rothenberger, A. (1997a) Decreased motor inhibition in Tourette disorder: Evidence from transcranial magnetic stimulation. *American Journal of Psychiatry*, **154**:1277–84.

Ziemann, U., Rothwell, J. C. and Ridding, M. C. (1996d) Interaction between intracortical inhibition and facilitation in human motor cortex. *Journal of Physiology (London)*, **496**:873–81.

Ziemann, U., Steinhoff, B. J., Tergau, F. *et al.* (1998d) Transcranial magnetic stimulation: its current role in epilepsy research. *Epilepsy Research*, **30**:11–30.

Ziemann, U., Tergau, F., Bruns, D. *et al.* (1997b) Changes in human motor cortex excitability induced by dopaminergic and anti-dopaminergic drugs. *Electroencephalography and Clinical Neurophysiology*, **105**:430–7.

Ziemann, U., Tergau, F., Netz, J. *et al.* (1997c) Delay in simple reaction time after focal transcranial magnetic stimulation of the human brain occurs at the final motor output stage. *Brain Research*, **744**:32–40.

Ziemann, U., Winter, M., Reimers, C. D. *et al.* (1997d) Impaired motor cortex inhibition in patients with amyotrophic lateral sclerosis. Evidence from paired transcranial magnetic stimulation. *Neurology*, **49**:1292–8.

Index